W9-BIV-156

LEARNING
ASSESSMENT
TECHNIQUES

LEARNING ASSESSMENT TECHNIQUES

A Handbook for College Faculty

Elizabeth F. Barkley and Claire Howell Major

JB JOSSEY-BASS™

A Wiley Brand

Copyright © 2016 by John Wiley & Sons, Inc. All rights reserved.

Published by Jossey-Bass
A Wiley Brand
One Montgomery Street, Suite 1000, San Francisco, CA 94104-4594—www.josseybass.com

No part of this publication may be reproduced, stored in a retrieval system, or transmitted in any form or by any means, electronic, mechanical, photocopying, recording, scanning, or otherwise, except as permitted under Section 107 or 108 of the 1976 United States Copyright Act, without either the prior written permission of the publisher, or authorization through payment of the appropriate per-copy fee to the Copyright Clearance Center, Inc., 222 Rosewood Drive, Danvers, MA 01923, 978-750-8400, fax 978-646-8600, or on the Web at www.copyright.com. Requests to the publisher for permission should be addressed to the Permissions Department, John Wiley & Sons, Inc., 111 River Street, Hoboken, NJ 07030, 201-748-6011, fax 201-748-6008, or online at www.wiley.com/go/permissions.

Limit of Liability/Disclaimer of Warranty: While the publisher and author have used their best efforts in preparing this book, they make no representations or warranties with respect to the accuracy or completeness of the contents of this book and specifically disclaim any implied warranties of merchantability or fitness for a particular purpose. No warranty may be created or extended by sales representatives or written sales materials. The advice and strategies contained herein may not be suitable for your situation. You should consult with a professional where appropriate. Neither the publisher nor author shall be liable for any loss of profit or any other commercial damages, including but not limited to special, incidental, consequential, or other damages. Readers should be aware that Internet Web sites offered as citations and/or sources for further information may have changed or disappeared between the time this was written and when it is read.

Jossey-Bass books and products are available through most bookstores. To contact Jossey-Bass directly call our Customer Care Department within the U.S. at 800-956-7739, outside the U.S. at 317-572-3986, or fax 317-572-4002.

Wiley publishes in a variety of print and electronic formats and by print-on-demand. Some material included with standard print versions of this book may not be included in e-books or in print-on-demand. If this book refers to media such as a CD or DVD that is not included in the version you purchased, you may download this material at http://booksupport.wiley.com. For more information about Wiley products, visit www.wiley.com.

Library of Congress Cataloging-in-Publication Data
Library of Congress Cataloging-in-Publication Data has been applied for and is on file with the Library of Congress.
ISBN 9781119050896 (paper); ISBN 9781119050926 (ebk.); ISBN 9781119050933 (ebk.)

Cover Design: Wiley
Cover Images: © Michael Krakoowiak/iStockphoto

Printed in the United States of America
FIRST EDITION
PB Printing   10   9   8   7   6   5   4   3   2   1

CONTENTS

PREFACE

Throughout most of America's history, few people questioned the value of a college education. Indeed, the premise that teachers were fulfilling higher education's promise of enabling learning went pretty much unchallenged until the mid-1980s, when intense reexamination of the quality of teaching and learning at all levels of education revealed that there were gaps—sometimes considerable ones—between what was thought to have been taught and what was actually learned. The decades that followed were rich with attempts to close that gap, as public and political entities demanded that colleges and universities increase and demonstrate their effectiveness. The proliferation of campus Teaching and Learning Centers, the increased focus on high-quality teaching in hiring, tenure, and promotion policies, the attention to monitoring learning through a "culture of evidence" coupled with the establishment and expansion of a new research discipline called the Scholarship of Teaching and Learning (SoTL) are some of the major indicators demonstrating the academy's push for improved teaching and learning.

Connecting Classroom Teaching and Assessment

K. Patricia Cross, Pat, was early to recognize the mounting pressures on institutions of higher education to provide evidence of student learning. In 1986, nearly 30 years ago now, she said:

> Student learning is a mission of every institution that teaches undergraduates. And it is quite fair to ask how well we do that job. For better or for worse—and much of it is "for the worse"—assessment is here, and everyone wants to know what students are learning in college. (p. 3)

While the assessment movement was largely being driven as a response to external demands (assessment as accountability), Pat saw its greater purpose as fostering an internal feedback loop to advance the quality of instruction and curriculum (assessment as improvement). As she put it:

> A concerted attack on the measurement of student learning will enable us to provide more adequate feedback to teachers, departments, and institutions (p. 3). Ultimately, the most sophisticated forms of assessment will be built into instruction and curriculum, providing continuous feedback on the processes of teaching and learning. (1986, p. 3)

Pat clearly thought that assessment should be built into the teaching and learning process, and that it should be teacher designed and teacher driven. She also knew, however, that most teachers weren't prepared for such work, in large part because graduate programs focused on helping students develop disciplinary content knowledge rather than pedagogical knowledge and educational research skills. Yet she urged teachers to ask questions about teaching and learning and to seek to answer them. These beliefs planted the seeds for her work in classroom assessment and research, and she argued that:

> If college teachers were to practice their profession at a more sophisticated level, they would discover that the classroom is, or should be, a challenging research laboratory, with questions to be pursued, data to be collected, analyses to be made, and improvement to be tried and evaluated. (1986, p. 6)

As Pat expanded on her ideas, she shared her vision for the role college teachers could play in improving student learning across the country:

> I believe that research on teaching and learning should be done in thousands of classrooms across this nation by classroom teachers themselves. What is needed if higher education is to move toward our goal of maximizing student learning is a new breed of college teacher that we shall call a Classroom Researcher. (1986, p. 13)

Thus Pat was in the vanguard of visionaries to see teaching as a valuable and scholarly activity that demanded inquiry and investigation.

Pat was able to put her ideas into action with support from three organizations that provided resources and staff time: The National Center for Research to Improve Postsecondary Teaching and Learning (NCRIPTAL) at the University of Michigan, the Harvard Seminar on Assessment, and the Harvard Graduate School of Education. Ultimately she established the Classroom Research Project at Harvard in 1988, which was funded by the Ford Foundation and the Pew Charitable Trusts. She also developed and refined her concept of a "Classroom Assessment Technique," an organized structure that guided teachers through the process and procedures to conduct formative assessment in their classrooms.

She and the project moved to the University of California, Berkeley, in the fall of 1988, when the first edition of *Classroom Assessment Techniques* was published by NCRIPTAL. This edition was the product of Pat Cross's work with her then graduate research assistant, Tom Angelo. The text introduced college faculty to the idea of classroom assessment, and it provided 30 Classroom Assessment Techniques (CATs) that instructors could use as the basis for collecting and analyzing information from their own courses. In 1993, the team of Cross and Angelo became Angelo and Cross with the publication by Jossey-Bass of the second edition of *Classroom Assessment Techniques: A Handbook for College Teachers*. The new book contained 50 CATs, with expanded advice and additional examples from practice.

Pat and Tom wanted to encourage college teachers to become more systematic and sensitive observers of learning as it takes place every day in their classrooms. If college teachers would use their classrooms as laboratories for the study of learning and make the results of their research public, they could advance the practice of teaching. Through Pat's writing and speeches, and Tom's conference and college workshops, CATs became known throughout higher education. *Classroom Assessment Techniques* became a best seller and remains a classic that provides college faculty with practical advice on how to assess the quality of teaching and learning in their own classrooms.

Classroom Assessment Reconsidered

It is now almost three decades since the publication of the first edition of *Classroom Assessment Techniques* (*CATs*) and over two since the edition published by Jossey-Bass. The higher education landscape has changed dramatically in the intervening years. When the book was written, instruction in higher education was typically taking place during a meeting between an instructor and a group of students at a shared location. This exchange occurred in a college classroom that was still relatively sequestered and private. Notions of higher education as an "ivory tower" reinforced the image that the academy operated in an elevated, rarified atmosphere that was above the practical concerns and probing eyes of everyday people. College courses today are no longer confined to a traditional classroom. Online learning, for example, is now mainstream. A survey of 2,800 institutions of higher education in 2011 indicated that as of Fall Semester, 6.7 million students, representing 32% of total enrollment, were taking courses online (Allen & Seaman, 2013). The growth in online education with the corollary development of MOOCs (Massive Open Online Courses) as well as flipped and blended classes challenge the basic concept of what a "classroom" is.

While there have been momentous changes in the instructional landscape, concern regarding the quality of undergraduate education and pressure on institutions to provide proof that they are worth the investment persists. The provocatively titled *Chucking College: Achieving Success without Corruption* (Ellison, 2012) advises young people "to design their own 21st-century higher education" because a college degree is no longer worth the cost. Ikenberry and Kuh (2015) observe that there is a "palpable sense of urgency to the need to document how college affects students" and advise "a clearer focus on the use of evidence of student learning in more productive and targeted ways" (p. ix, and pp. 1–2). Ensuring and demonstrating that a student's college experience is worthwhile seems to be the academy's best strategy for confronting these criticisms and changes.

As institutions attempt to meet multiple, competing demands for evidence of student learning, many prominent educational leaders propose that the most important and promising next step in assessment is to embed it in the classroom through the regular tasks and processes of teaching and learning. The 2014 survey conducted by the National Institute for Learning Outcomes Assessment (NILOA), for example, found that provosts believe that one of the most useful sources of evidence for improvement is the classroom (Jankowski, 2014). The Degree Qualifications Profile—a learner-centered framework for what college graduates should know and be able to do to earn a college degree—holds out a vision of powerful assessment as embedded in high-quality classroom assignments (Ewell, 2013). Richman and Ariovich (2013) describe the efforts of Prince George's Community College to develop a "revolutionary approach to assessing student learning" that they call the all-in-one assessment system in which grading, course, and general education outcomes assessment are combined through assignments designed by faculty and implemented in the classroom. It is against this backdrop that the idea for *Learning Assessment Techniques* was born, when our editor David Brightman asked us to write a new book on assessment for Jossey-Bass.

Learning Assessment Techniques

Learning Assessment Techniques: A Handbook for College Faculty reflects a new vision of course-based, teacher-driven, integrated learning assessment. It marks a fourth in the techniques series, which includes not only *Classroom Assessment Techniques: A Handbook for College Teachers* (Cross & Angelo, 1988; Angelo & Cross, 1993) but also *Collaborative Learning Techniques: A Handbook for College Faculty* (*CoLTs*; Barkley, Cross, & Major, 2005; Barkley, Major, & Cross, 2014) and *Student Engagement Techniques: A Handbook for College Faculty* (*SETs*; Barkley, 2010). Thus far, the books have focused on either teaching or assessment. In this book we have sought to erase this distinction and instead draw teaching and assessment together to create a seamless and unified process. To accomplish this, we selected what we feel are particularly effective ways for teaching and assessing students, regardless of the origins of the techniques. We have thus drawn upon techniques from the *CATs* book that are active learning techniques and techniques from the *CoLTs* and *SETs* books that produce assessable Learning Artifacts. We have also found new techniques by culling through countless books, websites, and blogs. Our goal was to present the techniques we felt accomplished both purposes the best.

Our LATs have two key characteristics. First, they are defined by their seamless integration of three components: (1) identification of a meaningful set of learning goals/outcomes, (2) an active learning instructional activity that requires students to create an assessable product providing direct evidence of their learning, and (3) guidance on how to analyze the artifact and report data to multiple stakeholders. LATs are not simply teaching or learning or assessment, but rather all three. Furthermore, they are designed to assess learning regardless of how the teacher will use the information. LATs guide teachers in the gathering of data that teachers can use for diagnostic, formative, or summative purposes (and often for all three), for grading or reporting to department chairs, or for quite different purposes such as classroom research and SoTL.

Since *Learning Assessment Techniques* builds upon the work of the three preceding techniques books (*Classroom Assessment Techniques, Collaborative Learning Techniques,* and

Student Engagement Techniques), there is naturally some overlap. For example Background Knowledge Probe is included in *CATs, SETs,* and *LATs.* Its distinction as a LAT is that we cast it as an integrated teaching-learning-assessment technique that gathers direct evidence of student learning and may be used for multiple assessment purposes. Finally, after careful consideration and in order to avoid confusion, we determined the following method for dealing with technique names: if we believed that our recasting of the technique resulted in an activity that was different in purpose or use from the original, we used a new name and then explained the difference in the technique and referenced the original. For example, our LAT 5 Quick Write is a broader, more flexible tool for which the popular CAT 6 Minute Paper and CAT 7 Muddiest Point are specific types. We have noted the origins of all techniques in the Key References and Resource section.

Overview of the Book

Through the guidance provided in this book, we hope to make it easier for faculty to carry out assessment as part and parcel of the teaching and learning process. We present this book in three parts. In Part 1, we provide an introduction that lays out the conceptual framework for LATs, describing why and how they support teaching to promote improved learning. In Part 2, we use the six steps of the LAT Cycle as an organizational framework to provide six chapters, one on each of the six steps of the assessment process. These chapters provide detailed guidance organized as a reference rather than in expository style. In Part 3, we provide six chapters correlated to the learning domains of the Significant Learning Taxonomy. We introduce each chapter with guidance on identifying relevant learning goals and outcomes, suggest ways in which outcomes can align with institutional learning goals and course competencies, and provide concrete, practical suggestions on how to assess achievement of learning goals related to that domain. We then follow this introduction with a collection of LATs carefully crafted to address teaching, learning, and assessment in that learning dimension.

Conclusion

This book was written to help college teachers efficiently and effectively identify what they believe is important for students to learn, implement appropriate activities to ensure that students learn it, and then document, interpret, and report student learning to a variety of stakeholders, including students themselves. We present these techniques to our fellow college teachers, therefore, as a collection of 50 carefully designed frameworks for accomplishing a conception of teaching, learning, and assessment as seamless and interrelated. Done well, our LATs involve both students and teachers in the continuous monitoring and improvement of students' learning. To conclude, we offer this book, with its guidance and its techniques, in the hopes of meeting the need for a new and different assessment text to meet the requirements of a changed world, a changed faculty, and a changed student body.

This book is dedicated to K. Patricia Cross and Thomas A. Angelo, whose seminal work with Classroom Assessment Techniques encouraged countless college teachers to use classroom research to improve student learning in their classrooms; to L. Dee Fink for his inspired vision and tireless dedication to helping teachers create significant learning experiences for students; and to David Brightman, our shared editor, for his brilliant leadership at Jossey-Bass and deep commitment to higher education.

ACKNOWLEDGMENTS

We are deeply grateful to K. Patricia Cross for her enthusiastic encouragement to write this new assessment book for college faculty. Thank you as well to Linda Bomstad, Amanda Brunson, L. Dee Fink, Pat Hutchings, Linda Suskie, and Maryellen Weimer for their manuscript reviews and their thoughtful, generous, and valuable feedback. Our appreciation also goes to Stacy Hughey-Surman for her help in creating the online version of the Learning Goals Inventory and to the University of Alabama for its willingness to house the survey's online version, as well as to Stacy, David Hardy, and Alan Webb for assistance with survey validation. Finally, we express our deep gratitude to the members of the Jossey-Bass team—especially Aneesa Davenport, Pete Gaughan, Cathy Mallon, and Shauna Robinson—for their commitment to maintaining the standards of excellence set by our former editor, David Brightman.

THE AUTHORS

Elizabeth F. Barkley is Professor of Music at Foothill College, Los Altos, California. With almost four decades as an innovative and reflective teacher, she has received numerous honors and awards, including being named California's Higher Education Professor of the Year by the Carnegie Foundation for the Advancement of Teaching, formally recognized by the California State Legislature for her contributions to undergraduate education, selected as "Innovator of the Year" in conjunction with the National League for Innovation, presented with the Hayward Award for Educational Excellence, and honored by the Center for Diversity in Teaching and Learning in Higher Education. In addition, her Musics of Multicultural America course was selected as "Best Online Course" by the California Virtual Campus. She was also named a Carnegie Scholar in the discipline of music by the Carnegie Foundation in conjunction with the Pew Charitable Trusts.

Beyond her academic discipline of music history, her interests include engaging students through active and collaborative learning; transforming F2F and online curriculum to meet the needs of diverse learners, especially those from new and emerging generations; contributing to the scholarship of teaching and learning; and connecting learning goals with outcomes and assessment. Barkley holds a B.A. and M.A. from the University of California, Riverside, and a Ph.D. from the University of California, Berkeley. She is co-author with Claire Howell Major and K. Patricia Cross of *Collaborative Learning Techniques: A Handbook for College Faculty* (Jossey-Bass, 2nd ed., 2014); author of *Student Engagement Techniques: A Handbook for College Faculty* (Jossey-Bass, 2010) and several music history textbooks, including *Crossroads: The Music of American Cultures* (Kendall Hunt, 2013), World Music: Roots to Contemporary Global Fusions (Kendall Hunt, 2012), *Crossroads: The Roots of America's Popular Music*

(Prentice Hall, 2nd ed., 2007); and co-author with Robert Hartwell of *Great Composers and Music Masterpieces of Western Civilization* (Kendall Hunt, 2014).

Claire Howell Major is Professor of Higher Education at the University of Alabama in Tuscaloosa, Alabama. She teaches courses on college teaching, technology in higher education, reading research in the field of higher education, and qualitative research methods. Her research interests are in the areas of faculty work, pedagogical approaches, technology for teaching, and online learning. She also focuses on issues of higher education in popular culture and higher education as a field of study. She typically draws upon qualitative methods to answer her research questions. Major holds a B.A. from the University of South Alabama, an M.A. from the University of Alabama at Birmingham, and a Ph.D. from the University of Georgia.

She has authored and co-authored several books, including *Teaching Online: A Guide to Theory, Research, and Practice* (Johns Hopkins University Press, 2015), *Collaborative Learning Techniques: A Handbook for College Faculty* with Elizabeth F. Barkley and K. Patricia Cross (Jossey-Bass, 2nd ed., 2014), *The Essential Guide to Qualitative Research: A Handbook of Theory and Practice* with Maggi Savin-Baden (Routledge, 2013), *An Introduction to Qualitative Research Synthesis: Managing the Information Explosion* with Maggi Savin-Baden (Routledge, 2011), and *Foundations of Problem-Based Learning* with Maggi Savin-Baden (Open University Press, 2004). Major also publishes her work in leading education journals and presents at both national and international conferences.

LEARNING ASSESSMENT TECHNIQUES

INTRODUCTION
Conceptual Framework

There are over seven thousand colleges and universities in the United States, each implicitly promising prospective students that they'll learn better there than they could on their own. We professors are the principal means by which colleges and universities aim to fulfill this promise of delivering effective education, yet although enabling learning is one of our primary jobs, few of us have had formal instruction on how to do it and do it well. Even fewer of us have had training on how to provide evidence of what students are learning in ways that are acceptable to external stakeholders. This book was written to support our fellow college professors who strive to be excellent teachers and who need strategies for reporting results of learning in their classrooms not only to students, but also to a variety of other interested parties ranging from hiring, tenure, and promotion committees to department chairs gathering data for institutional assessment initiatives. Since enabling learning is the raison d'être for both our profession as teachers and for our efforts in assessment, we start this book by establishing a conceptual framework that answers the following three questions:

How can we best teach to promote learning?
What is a Learning Assessment Technique (LAT)?
How do LATs support the kind of teaching that promotes significant learning?

How Can We Best Teach to Promote Learning?

The term *professor* refers to a person who "professes" their expert knowledge of a specific discipline. In higher education, a college teacher's possession of disciplinary content knowledge is presumably guaranteed through the academy's certification process. Modeled after the medieval guild system, the academy requires applicants to the teaching profession to be certified by a graduate degree that indicates that they possess advanced and increasingly

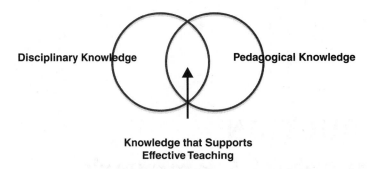

Figure I.1 Effective Teaching at the Intersection of Disciplinary and Pedagogical Knowledge

specialized knowledge in their subject area. Thus a required first step toward becoming a member of the professoriate today is to demonstrate one's credentials as an expert in the disciplinary content knowledge of one's particular field of study. Deep disciplinary expertise remains one of the critical factors that distinguish us from the many other sources students have for accessing knowledge today. While we still consider in-depth content knowledge essential, we propose that in order to effectively guide students in their own acquisition of knowledge, a college teacher also needs knowledge of pedagogy.

Pedagogy—the method and practice of teaching—helps teachers take an aspect of subject matter and, through careful and informed choices, enable students to learn it. In other words, the combination of disciplinary knowledge and pedagogical knowledge is an integrated amalgam that provides teachers with the most effective ways of presenting and formulating their subject so that they transform it into something that learners can comprehend. This concept of the interaction between disciplinary knowledge and peda-gogical knowledge suggests that the kind of college teaching that best promotes student learning is that which is informed by the knowledge represented within the space where the two overlap, as illustrated by Figure I.1. It also suggests that when there is insufficient disciplinary or pedagogical knowledge, the space for effective teaching shrinks, as indicated in Figure I.2.

We recognize that some teachers have acquired pedagogical knowledge without formal instruction and that they make effective teaching choices based simply on replicating or avoiding practices they observed as former students themselves. We also acknowledge that for centuries, students have been able to learn from professors who did not give a hoot about teaching but possessed deep knowledge of their discipline. (We suspect, however, that most of these students were either already capable learners or, caught in the crucible of the professor's indifference, quickly learned to become adept learners.) Accepting that there are exceptions, we propose that as a general rule, one needs both disciplinary and pedagogical knowledge to be an excellent and effective college professor today.

What Does Research Tell Us About Effective Pedagogy?

There is more research-based information about teaching and learning available to us today than ever before in history, and the amount of research continues to escalate. Between 1983 and

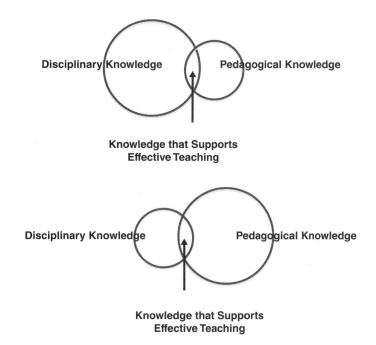

Figure I.2 Reduced Space for Effective Teaching Due to Imbalance of Knowledge

2012, the volume of the database maintained by the Educational Resource Information Center (ERIC) tripled, driving a major reorganization in 2014 to streamline the site that houses the 1.4+ million documents that now help us learn about teaching and learning (ERIC Retrospective, nd). Fortunately, we have several syntheses of the literature on what works in college-level teaching and learning that shed light on what effective teaching entails. We focus on three well-known and frequently cited syntheses: (1) Chickering and Gamson's (1987) "Seven Principles for Good Practice in Undergraduate Education," (2) Carnegie Mellon's Eberly Center for Teaching Excellence and Educational Innovation's current "Teaching Principles," and (3) Glassick et al. (1997), who expand on Boyer's (1987) proposal of the scholarship of teaching. Table I.1 identifies principles in these three important syntheses (ERIC Restrospective, nd).

As we look across these syntheses, we see several commonalities. All syntheses recommend that we establish and communicate clear learning goals (A6, B2, B3, B4, C1), that we design instructional activities that encourage active, engaged learning (A1, A2, A3, A5, A7, B6, C2, C3, C5), and that we provide feedback to students, as well as conduct our own reflective critique (A4, B1, B2, B3, B4, B5, B7, C1, C4, C6). In synthesizing the syntheses, then, we suggest that research on effective teaching at the college and university level emphasizes three interconnected and interrelated components:

1. Identifying and communicating clear learning goals and outcomes
2. Helping students achieve these goals through activities that promote active, engaged learning
3. Analyzing, reporting, and reflecting upon results in ways that lead to continued improvement

Table I.1 Principles of Good Teaching from Three Syntheses

Chickering and Gamson (1987), "Seven Principles of Good Practice in Undergraduate Education"	Carnegie Mellon Eberly Center for Teaching Excellence and Educational Innovation, "Teaching Principles" (http://bit.ly/1uZp3Pz)	Glassick et al. (1997), *Scholarship Assessed: Evaluation of the Professoriate*
A	B	C
The seven principles of good practice are: 1. Encourage contact between students and faculty 2. Develop reciprocity and cooperation among students 3. Encourage active learning 4. Give prompt feedback 5. Emphasize time on task 6. Communicate high expectations 7. Respect diverse talents and ways of learning.	Effective teaching involves: 1. Acquiring relevant knowledge about students and using that knowledge to inform our course design and classroom teaching 2. Aligning the three major components of instruction: learning objectives, assessments, and instructional activities 3. Articulating explicit expectations regarding learning objectives and policies 4. Prioritizing the knowledge and skills we choose to focus on 5. Recognizing and overcoming our expert blind spots 6. Adopting appropriate teaching roles to support our learning goals 7. Progressively refining our courses based on reflection and feedback	The characteristics of good scholarship of teaching include: 1. Clear goals 2. Adequate preparation 3. Appropriate methods 4. Significant results 5. Effective presentation 6. Reflective critique

What Is a Learning Assessment Technique (LAT)?

A LAT is a carefully designed three-part, interconnected structure that mirrors the phases and employs the elements of effective teaching by helping teachers to

1. **Identify Significant Learning Goals:** Through the Learning Goals Inventory (LGI), combined with guidance in Part 2 and the Part 3 chapter introductions, a LAT facilitates the identification of a set of significant learning goals.
2. **Implement Effective Learning Activities:** Each LAT provides a clearly defined instructional activity that promotes active, engaged learning and also requires students to produce a Learning Artifact that provides direct evidence of their progress toward the learning goals.
3. **Analyze and Report upon Outcomes:** A LAT offers guidance on how to assess the Learning Artifact at both the individual student and aggregated course level and how to share results with multiple stakeholders.

We use the trefoil knot in Figure I.3 to illustrate a LAT's nature, which is the intertwining of these elements of effective teaching. The three elements combine to make a unified whole; one cannot be separated from the other, and it is impossible to tell where one begins and the other ends.

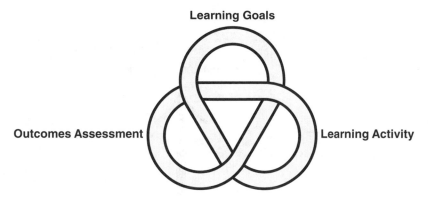

Figure I.3 A LAT's Interconnected Nature: Teaching, Learning, and Assessment

How Do LATs Support the Kind of Teaching that Promotes Significant Learning?

LATs support excellent teaching in today's complex and challenging educational environment by helping teachers identify significant learning goals, implement effective and pedagogically sound learning activities, and gather and report direct evidence of learning in ways acceptable to a variety of stakeholders—all with the ultimate goal of making changes that improve learning. We shall elaborate on each of these aspects.

Identifying Significant Learning Goals

As college professors, most of us flourish in the "thinking" world. When we consider college-level learning, we quickly understand and appreciate the acquisition, synthesis, and evaluation of knowledge that characterizes abstract thought. Bloom's *Taxonomy of the Cognitive Domain*, which classifies thinking into behaviors organized into a series of hierarchical levels, has guided countless teachers in the design and development of their courses for over half a century. It continues to be the most frequently referenced taxonomy for assessing learning. In 2001, a new group of cognitive psychologists led by L. W. Anderson (a former student of Bloom's) and D. R. Krathwohl (one of the members of the original team) published a revision because they believed that many of the ideas in the original taxonomy were still valuable, but they also wanted to incorporate new knowledge and thought into the framework (Anderson & Krathwohl, 2001, pp. xxi–xxii). A critical change in their revision of Bloom's taxonomy was a modification of the original taxonomic levels, as demonstrated in Table I.2.

A persistent problem with both Bloom's and Anderson and Krathwohl's taxonomies is that they focus only on the cognitive domain.[1] But learning involves more than rational thinking, and even the definition of cognition itself moves beyond pure intellectual reasoning to include processes such as intuition and perception. Furthermore, various models of

---

[1] Both have additional taxonomies that address other areas, but these other areas are treated as separate from the cognitive domain. Furthermore, these other taxonomies have not received the same attention as have the taxonomies of the cognitive domain.

Table I.2 A Comparison of Bloom's and Anderson and Krathwohl's Taxonomies

Bloom's Original Taxonomy (1953)	Anderson and Krathwohl's Revised Taxonomy (2001)	
Higher-Order Thinking Skills		
Evaluation		Creating
Synthesis		Evaluating
Analysis		Analyzing
Application		Applying
Comprehension		Understanding
Knowledge		Remembering
Lower-Order Thinking Skills		

"intelligence"—such as Gardner's "Multiple Intelligences" (which contains a bodily-kinesthetic component) and Goleman's "Emotional Intelligence" (which emphasizes the ability to monitor one's own and other's feelings)—challenge us to embrace a concept of learning that extends beyond logical thinking.

This broader, more inclusive perspective has substantial scientific support. Harvard clinical psychologist John Ratey observes that the brain and body systems are distributed over the whole person, and we cannot separate emotion, cognition, and the physical body. What is more, separating these functions "is rapidly coming to be seen as ridiculous" (Ratey, 2002, p. 223). Despite higher education's historical emphasis on the purely intellectual, therefore, many educators today recognize that the body, heart, and mind are all involved in learning.

Fink's Significant Learning Taxonomy

It is within this context that Fink proposed his taxonomy of significant learning. He believed that higher education was expressing a need for new kinds of learning—learning that went beyond just thinking and the acquisition of knowledge to learning that includes leadership and interpersonal skills, ethics, communication skills, character, tolerance, and the ability to adapt to change (2013, p. 33). Rather than just talking with professors as Bloom did, Fink spoke with students to determine what they believed were truly significant learning experiences that changed the way they lived their personal, social, civic, or professional lives. He tried to identify the features of learning that impacted students in ways that extended beyond a single course. The central idea in Fink's concept of significant learning is that teaching should result in something others can look at and say, "That learning experience resulted in something that is truly significant in terms of the students' lives" (2013, p. 7). He determined that significant learning experiences require both a process and an outcome dimension:

Process: Students need to be engaged in their learning and there needs to be a high energy level in the class.

Outcome: Students' participation in a course has to have a high potential for being of value in their individual, social, civic, and work lives and needs to result in lasting, significant change well beyond the end of the course.

Table I.3 Fink's Taxonomy of Significant Learning

Foundational Knowledge	Understanding and remembering the information, ideas, and perspectives that form the basis for other kinds of learning in the subject.
Application	Applying knowledge to real situations through critical and creative thinking, problem solving, performance, and skill so that foundational knowledge becomes useful.
Integration	Making connections between ideas, learning experiences, and different realms of life so that everything is put into context and learning is more powerful.
Human Dimension	Learning about the personal and social implications of what learners are learning, thus giving the learning significance as learners learn about themselves and others.
Caring	Developing new feelings, interests, and values that help learners care about what they are learning, which gives them the energy they need for learning more about it and making it part of their lives.
Learning How to Learn	Learning about the process of learning, including a particular kind of inquiry (such as the scientific method) as well as how to become a better, more self-directed learner, which enables learners to continue learning and do so with greater effectiveness.

Source: Fink (2013), pp. 35–37

From this belief system, Fink developed his Taxonomy of Significant Learning, described briefly in Table I.3. We explore each of the learning dimensions in this taxonomy in more detail in the introductions to each chapter on techniques, since the LATs in this book are organized into chapters that correspond with the domains in Fink's Taxonomy of Significant Learning.

To summarize, while there are many learning taxonomies, of which Bloom's and Krathwohl and Anderson's revision of Bloom's are the best known, we chose to correlate our techniques with Fink's Significant Learning Taxonomy because we believe his taxonomy best supports efforts to teach for the kind of learning students need to thrive in today's challenging world.

Implementing an Effective Learning Activity

Once a clear and significant learning goal has been identified, a teacher must implement an effective learning activity. For the purposes of enabling learning as well as efficient assessment, we propose that an effective learning activity promotes active, engaged learning and produces a Learning Artifact that can be analyzed for direct evidence of learning.

Promoting Active and Engaged Learning

Active learning is a term brought full force into the educational lexicon by Bonwell and Eison, who described it as "doing what we think and thinking about what we are doing" (1991). It has become an umbrella term for several pedagogical approaches, including cooperative and collaborative learning, discovery learning, experiential learning, problem-based learning, and inquiry-based learning. Active learning is based on the premise that learning is a dynamic process in which learners constantly make and change connections between what is new and what is already known, integrating new information into their existing personal knowledge and experience.

Although many of us (as well as our students) would like to think that we teachers can simply transfer knowledge into learners' brains, it is simply not possible. Students themselves need to do the work required to learn, but we can help them by reversing our typical roles in the classroom. Instead of working hard to present information as clearly as possible to students who are then expected to consume it passively, we can set up conditions that require them to be active participants in their own learning. Participating in active learning activities ultimately improves learning, and several recent studies, including a host of meta-analyses, support this assertion (see for example, Johnson, Johnson, & Smith, 2014).

Simply setting up conditions for active learning is not sufficient, however. College teachers today report to us how challenging it is to *engage* their students in the process of learning. *How* to promote student engagement has become an increasingly important topic in the national—even international—dialogue on effective teaching. In an effort to construct a conceptual framework and teaching-based model for promoting student engagement within the context of a college classroom, Barkley (2010) proposed that student engagement is a process and a product that is experienced on a continuum and results from the synergistic interaction between motivation and active learning. Thus engaging learning activities not only promote active learning, but also motivate students to spend the energy required to do the work of learning. Promoting active, engaged learning is fundamental to all of the LATs in this book.

Producing an Assessable Learning Artifact

An additional element of a LAT instructional activity is production of an assessable Learning Artifact. This shift from the intangible to the tangible is a defining characteristic that distinguishes each LAT from being simply an active learning technique. For example, a case study discussion is active learning, but until students write a case analysis that can be assessed, the discussion remains intangible without evidence that documents the learning in ways that can be communicated with others. Similarly, a role play is active learning, but until the role play is documented in a video or there are evaluation scores on a rubric that were entered while the role play was in progress, the role play also remains intangible without evidence that documents the learning in ways that can be shared with others. Thus it is at the point when the intangible active learning produces tangible evidence that the active learning technique becomes a Learning Assessment Technique (LAT). Viewed in this way, most, if not all, active learning techniques could become Learning Assessment Techniques. Surely that seamless integration of the teaching and learning process is what we should aim for in assessment. By making assessment an integral part of the teaching and learning process instead of an add-on, we hope to accomplish what should be the primary goal of assessment: to improve learning. To summarize, our LATs are designed to balance disciplinary content and sound pedagogy as they promote engaged, active learning that also produces an assessable Learning Artifact that can be evaluated for student achievement.

Analyzing and Reporting Learning Outcomes for Multiple Stakeholders

Our primary purpose as teachers is to facilitate learning, which is perhaps why the terms *teaching* and *learning* are so often paired. This persistent pairing can lull us into the erroneous assumption that one is the natural consequence of the other. But teaching does not automatically result in learning: those of us who have supposed our students had learned what we taught have frequently faced disappointing evidence to the contrary. Conversely, learning does not require having been taught. Indeed, asserting that one is "self-taught" is a badge of honor, and autodidacts who purportedly learned their discipline without the help of a teacher include such notables as George Bernard Shaw, Ernest Hemingway, Herman Melville, Frank Lloyd Wright, Karl Marx, and Buckminster Fuller.

Although it is possible and may even be a source of pride to learn without the help of a teacher, no self-respecting teacher could be satisfied—much less smug—if under their instruction, no student learned. Thus one can learn without the benefit of a teacher, but one cannot be considered an effective teacher in the absence of student learning. Since helping students learn is our primary purpose as teachers, how do we know students have learned? At what point can we congratulate ourselves for a job well done? How do we know when and how we need to improve? The answers to these questions lie in a third area: assessment. Assessment is the way that we teachers gauge for ourselves and for others whether and how well learning has happened.

While faculty are drawn to teaching for many different reasons, few of us are drawn to it because we love assessment; the mere mention of the term can cause some of us to question our choice of career. As college professors ourselves, we understand assessment aversion, but we also believe it does not need to be so onerous. A primary purpose for our writing this book was to help our colleagues assess more efficiently by offering a framework for making assessment part and parcel of the teaching and learning process. Our LATs present teaching, learning, and assessment as seamless and interrelated. Furthermore, LATs guide teachers' assessment efforts so that the data can be used for multiple purposes: providing learners with feedback, grading, reporting to department chairs and institutional assessment efforts, including in professional dossiers in hiring, promotion, and tenure, and contributing to the scholarship of teaching and learning (SoTL). Finally, LATs incorporate reflection and critique to identify the changes that can be made to "close the loop" and improve learning.

The LAT Cycle

We conceive of each LAT as being embedded within a larger framework we call the LAT Cycle, modeled after the Classroom Assessment Project Cycle (Angelo & Cross, 1993). The cycle includes three phases organized into six steps:

- Phase One: Plan
  - Step 1: Clarify what you want students to learn
  - Step 2: Determine why you are assessing their learning
- Phase Two: Implement
  - Step 3: Select a LAT
  - Step 4: Implement the LAT
- Phase Three: Respond
  - Step 5: Analyze and report results
  - Step 6: "Close the Loop" by identifying and making changes to improve learning

This cycle is represented in Figure I.4, with an actual LAT comprising Steps 4 and 5.

Each of the six chapters in Part 2 are correlated to these six steps and provide guidance organized in chunked, numbered components for easy reference.

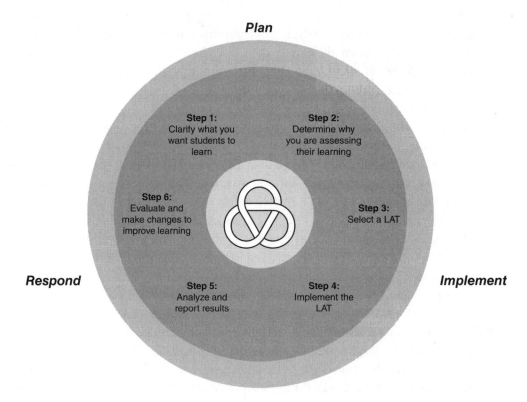

Figure I.4 The LAT Cycle

Conclusion

Today's college teachers are under increased pressure to teach effectively and to provide evidence of both what and how well students are learning. We propose that to teach effectively, college teachers need pedagogical knowledge as well as knowledge of their academic discipline. Several syntheses of pedagogical research propose that excellent college teaching includes (1) identifying and communicating clear learning goals and outcomes, (2) helping students achieve these goals through active, engaged learning, and (3) analyzing, reporting, and reflecting upon results in ways that lead to improvement. The 50 Learning Assessment Techniques (LATs) in this book mirror these three phases and elements of effective teaching. Each LAT, embedded within the larger LAT Cycle, provides faculty with feedback about their effectiveness as teachers, gives a variety of interested parties reliable measures of students' progress as learners, and involves both students and teachers in the continuous monitoring and improvement of students' learning.

PART ONE

THE LEARNING ASSESSMENT TECHNIQUES CYCLE

CHAPTER 1

Clarifying What You Want Students to Learn

If you don't know where you're going, how will you know when you get there? In this section we offer guidance on how to clarify what you want students to learn by providing information in the following areas:

1.1   Defining Learning
1.2   Aiming for Significant Learning
1.3   Using the Learning Goals Inventory (LGI) to Identify Significant Learning Goals
1.4   Expressing What You Want Students to Learn in Language that Is Helpful for Assessment
1.5   Identifying Course-Level Learning Goals
1.6   Considering the Challenges Related to Course Learning Objectives and Outcomes
1.7   Determining Course-Level Learning Objectives
1.9   Identifying Course-Level Student Learning Outcomes (SLOs)
1.9   Differentiating Between Learning Objectives and Learning Outcomes
1.10   Crafting a Course Learning Outcome Statement
1.11   Determining Performance Standards for Individuals and the Class as a Whole
1.12   Is All the Work Required Worth the Effort?

1.1   Defining Learning

The question of what constitutes learning has intrigued scholars for centuries, and today there is a wide variety of opinions about what learning is. These opinions are based in part upon differences in views about the nature of knowledge and how it is gained. Scholars also have different ideas about the catalysts for learning, the conditions that must be met in order for learning to occur, and the criteria by which we may judge that it has happened. Despite the variability on many aspects of learning, most scholars agree that learning involves acquiring new (or modifying existing) knowledge, behavior, skills, attitudes, or values. At its simplest, therefore, learning is change.

1.2   Aiming for Significant Learning

If we are going to spend time teaching, and our students are going to invest resources to attend class, it makes sense to try to achieve learning that is worthwhile. We chose to correlate this book with the Significant Learning Taxonomy (Fink, 2013) because we believe that this taxonomy supports learning that is meaningful and lasting, worthy of effort by both teachers and students. It moves beyond the cognitive domain to include dimensions that reflect a richer, more nuanced perspective on learning, and it is relational and interactive rather than hierarchical, thereby reflecting contemporary beliefs and values regarding learning.

1.3   Using the Learning Goals Inventory (LGI) to Identify Significant Learning Goals

The LGI was modeled after the Teaching Goals Inventory (TGI) developed by Angelo and Cross (1993) to help faculty identify what students should learn in their classrooms. The LGI lists 50 learning goals that are generally applicable to college-level teaching that are then clustered to correlate to the Significant Learning Taxonomy. The LGI is available either online or in Appendix B. Once you have completed the inventory and identified your goal profile, we recommend choosing your highest ranking goal (for example, Foundational Knowledge) and reading the introduction to the corresponding chapter in Part 2 (for example, Chapter 7: Teaching and Assessing for Foundational Knowledge). This will provide you with additional information on that learning dimension and examples in different disciplines for using these general learning goals to identify course-level learning goals.

1.4   Expressing What You Want Students to Learn in Language that Is Helpful for Assessment

Simply identifying course-level learning goals and then choosing a LAT from the corresponding chapter may be sufficient to implement LATs effectively. However, if you are planning to report your findings in more formal contexts, you will need to express what you want students to learn in the kind of precise language that allows you to measure, compare, and share results in ways that others will find acceptable as evidence. Doing this helps you proceed through the assessment process efficiently and effectively. Assessment language customarily moves from the general to the specific, using the terms *goals, objectives,* and *outcomes.* "Target Practice" is a popular and simple metaphor for understanding these three common terms, as displayed in Figure 1.1.

When we use this metaphor, we first describe what we intend for students to learn (goals), then identify the steps students need to take to reach the goal (objectives), and finally determine how closely students have achieved the goal based on actual evidence of their learning (outcomes). How this applies to an actual course is demonstrated in Table 1.1.

1.5   Identifying Course-Level Learning Goals

Most of us have a sense of what students should learn in a course. Indeed, the description published in an institution's course catalogue or schedule states learning goals in broad terms,

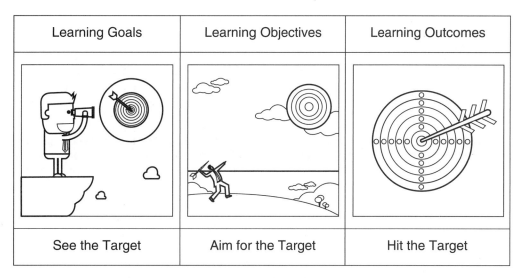

| Learning Goals | Learning Objectives | Learning Outcomes |
| See the Target | Aim for the Target | Hit the Target |

Figure 1.1 Differentiating Between Learning Goals, Objectives, and Outcomes

and many teachers quote or paraphrase this description at the top of their syllabi. Here is an example of a catalogue description for a course titled, "Principles of Cell Biology."

> An introduction to biological molecules, cellular structure and function, bioenergetics, the genetics of both prokaryotic and eukaryotic organisms, cell communication and signaling, the cell cycle, and elements of molecular biology.

Notice how the description conveys, albeit in general, discipline-based terms, what students should learn in the course. College courses today, though, are rarely stand-alone and instead are part of a larger context that you may want to consider as you identify your more specific course-level learning goals.

Considering Externally Mandated or Recommended Learning Goals

Externally recommended or mandated learning goals and competencies are those identified at the national, state, institution, college/school, program, and department level. Some goals, such as institutional core competencies and general education guidelines, focus on skills and abilities

Table 1.1 An Example of a Learning Goal, Objective, and Outcome

	Goal	Objective	Outcome
Survey of International Business	Students will acquire knowledge of international business terms and concepts.	Students will demonstrate understanding and appropriate use of international business terms and concepts.	In the oral presentation of their term project, successful learners will use and apply international business terms and concepts appropriately in their language and supporting material.

Table 1.2 Examples of Externally Recommended or Mandated Learning Goals

Context	Sample Goal
Institutional Core Competencies	A course that supports the communication core competency goal helps students develop analytical reading and writing skills, including evaluation, synthesis, and research; deliver focused and coherent presentations; and acquire active, discerning listening and speaking skills in lectures and discussions.
General Education: Humanities	A course meeting the Humanities General Education Area I Requirement must help students acquire knowledge and understanding of significant artistic, literary, and philosophical works and the historical and cultural context in which the works were created and interpreted.
College of Agriculture	Graduates of the College of Agriculture will be able to make sound, responsible judgments on the ethical policy issues involved in the production of food and fiber.
Program/Department Level	A course in the biology majors sequence must prepare students to use the scientific method to formulate questions, design experiments to test hypotheses, interpret experimental results to draw conclusions, communicate results both orally and in writing, and critically evaluate the use of the scientific method from published sources.

that transcend disciplinary boundaries. Others, such as professional accrediting agencies or department or program goals, are usually more discipline specific. Individual courses are the means by which larger stakeholders achieve their broad goals. Because college teachers are asked to demonstrate (and that means "assess") how well students in their courses are achieving these externally derived goals and competencies, you may want to adapt and rewrite them to apply to your specific course. Table 1.2 provides examples of these types of external goals, and Figure 1.2 displays how these goals drill down from the institution to the course level.

Institution:
Graduates of this institution will be able to analyze arguments, create and test models, solve problems, evaluate ideas, and verify the reasonableness of conclusions.

Department:
Upon completion of the core curriculum, students will be able to analyze current events and global issues in the context of historic patterns.

Course:
Upon completion of the course, students will be able to analyze the importance of urbanization, immigration, and the struggle for labor and women's rights as they pertain to the American historical experience.

Figure 1.2 Drilling Down from Institutional Core Competency to Course-Level Student Learning Outcome

Considering Students' Learning Goals

Empowering students as partners in the learning process is good for teachers, and it is good for students. Weimer (2002) identifies sharing power with students as the first key change required to shift to learner-centered teaching, but observes that for many of us, "[T]eacher authority is so taken for granted that most of us are no longer aware of the extent to which we direct student learning" (2002, p. 23). Empowering students to be active partners in their learning requires a subtle but thorough shift in focus away from what you are teaching to what and how students are learning, and taking their learning goals into consideration is an important initial step in adopting a more learner-centered teaching approach. Students' learning goals in a single course probably vary widely, and they may have difficulty articulating them. To assist you in guiding students to identify their learning goals, consider having students complete and self-score the LGI individually, and perhaps discuss their results in groups.

To conclude, identifying course learning goals—what you want students to gain from their experiences in your course—is a vital first step in the LAT Cycle. The LGI will help you identify goals correlated with Fink's Significant Learning Taxonomy. Integrating these general learning goals with course-specific learning goals, and possibly externally mandated or recommended goals along with student goals, will help you identify meaningful goals that engage students and are worthy of your teaching efforts.

1.6   Considering the Challenges Related to Course Learning Objectives and Outcomes

Most college teachers readily recognize the value of identifying learning goals, but they find taking the next steps—identifying objectives and outcomes—challenging both conceptually and practically.

1. Objectives and outcomes must describe an observable action, something that students *can do*. As teachers, we typically think in terms of what students should know; thinking in terms of student performance can represent a major conceptual shift.

2. Many of us believe that learning is and should be personal, value-laden, process driven, emergent, and nuanced. It can be fundamentally offensive to reduce the messy complexity of learning to a crisply defined, one-size-fits-all singular destination. In order to meet the need to identify something that is measurable and reportable (and thus satisfy the annoying assessment requirement), we may be tempted to sacrifice attempts to capture the intricacies of the deep learning we aspire to promote and instead opt for tidy, simplistic objectives and outcomes that often represent low-level cognitive skills. This not only trivializes the creativity and commitment we invest as teachers but it also fails to capture the depth and transformative nature of the learning we sense some of our students experience.

3. We know that some students will learn better than others. Conventional grading allows for evaluating achievement along an analog continuum in the gray areas between black and white. When we teach to objectives or outcomes, it "feels" binary: students either can do it or they can't.

4. We are apprehensive that as we are forced to report learning in outcomes referenced to measurable objectives, we will be pressured to "teach to the test." Some of us fear that this will limit the innovation and excitement of what we consider the best in college learning.

5. Objectives and outcomes are often written to satisfy external stakeholders and thus represent the hoped for learning of idealized, abstract students. These outcomes may therefore be occasionally—or perhaps consistently—out of alignment with the abilities, interest, and level of preparedness of the actual human beings who enrolled in our course.

6. If we are aiming for significant and enduring learning, our sights should be set far into the future—for learning that will remain long after the course is finished. Being forced to aim for and then document only what a student can do at the end of the academic term seems short-sighted.

7. Explicating course content into objectives and outcomes involves considerable effort, and the time it takes to do it could be spent on competing interests and responsibilities.

As college teachers ourselves, we share the above concerns; however, we believe that the objections and difficulties can be ameliorated. Examples of college teachers who have struggled with these challenges and successfully identified not only appropriate outcomes, but also strategies for measuring attainment of them, are plentiful. It is hard work and it is often work done best in collaboration with other faculty, but it is not impossible work. The guiding assumption is that if something can be learned, then there must be some way the learning can be demonstrated, and if the learning can be demonstrated, then there must be some way to measure it. Finally, it is simply a reality in today's higher education environment that more stakeholders are requiring teachers to identify learning outcomes, as well as provide acceptable evidence that students are achieving them. We are therefore offering you guidance on these additional steps so that your efforts can be less onerous, as well as more efficient and effective.

1.7   Determining Course-Level Learning Objectives

When we assess learning, we try to make the invisible learning inside a student's brain external and visible in a product or action that others can see. This represents an important conceptual shift of moving away from organizing instruction based on the content we want to cover to considering what students can do to demonstrate their learning. While course learning goal statements describe in general terms what we want students to learn, objectives provide the framework of steps students will take to achieve the goals in ways that make their learning visible.

For example, one of our goals might legitimately be that students "know" or "understand" or "appreciate" some aspect of foundational knowledge, but these words are open to many interpretations as well as potential misinterpretations. Translating goals into objectives that state something tangible that students do, such as "write" or "solve" or "identify," provides us with something observable that can be measured and compared. We find it helpful to write objectives as subcomponents that can represent both more detailed and comprehensive coverage and provide such a representation as an example below.

Goal: Students will acquire foundational knowledge of the multicultural music genres and styles of the United States.

Objective 1: Students will demonstrate detailed knowledge regarding the structural characteristics, stylistic categories, key musicians, and historical and social context of a variety of American music genres. This includes being able to

1A. Describe American music genres in terms of their structural characteristics, stylistic categories, and key musicians.

1B. Recall the key elements that shaped the historical and assimilation experience of five broad constituent groups: Native Americans, European Americans, African Americans, Hispanic/Latino Americans, and Asian Americans.

1C. Explain how American music genres reflect the "root" music traditions of the constituent group and the historical context in which the genre developed.

Table 1.3 Action Verbs Correlated to the Significant Learning Taxonomy

Foundational Knowledge	Application		Integration	Human Dimension	Caring	Learning How to Learn
Articulate	Act	Formulate	Arrange	Adapt	Appraise	Adapt
Assemble	Adapt	Generalize	Assemble	Analyze	Assess	Arrange
Choose	Administer	Generate	Break	Collaborate	Challenge	Assess
Cite	Analyze	Give	down	Communicate	Collaborate	Collaborate
Define	Apply	examples	Classify	Conclude	Communicate	Estimate
Describe	Appraise	Illustrate	Collaborate	Criticize	Conclude	Evaluate
Duplicate	Arrange	Implement	Combine	Estimate	Convince	Identify
Examine	Assess	Infer	Compare	Evaluate	Criticize	Illustrate
Explain	Calculate	Inspect	Consolidate	Help	Debate	Initiate
Identify	Categorize	Interpret	Contrast	Identify	Defend	Judge
Indicate	Change	Manage	Discuss	Illustrate	Dispute	Measure
Label	Collect	Manipulate	Distinguish	Infer	Estimate	Organize
List	Compose	Measure	Evaluate	Intervene	Evaluate	Question
Locate	Compute	Modify	Facilitate	Judge	Illustrate	Rate
Match	Construct	Operate	Incorporate	Justify	Intervene	Recognize
Name	Control	Organize	Infer	Manage	Judge	Reflect
Order	Convert	Perform	Integrate	Measure	Justify	Revise
Outline	Create	Plan	Judge	Praise	Measure	Summarize
Paraphrase	Debate	Practice	Measure	Propose	Modify	Synthesize
Quote	Deduce	Predict	Organize	Question	Propose	Systematize
Recall	Defend	Prepare	Question	Rate	Question	Tabulate
Recognize	Demonstrate	Present	Rate	Recognize	Rate	Test
Record	Derive	Produce	Recognize	Recommend	Recognize	Write
Relate	Design	Propose	Reconsider	Reconsider	Reconsider	
Rephrase	Detect	Provide	Relate	Reflect	Reflect	
Report	Develop	Question	Revise	Relate	Relate	
Reproduce	Diagram	Rate	Synthesize	Revise	Revise	
Restate	Differentiate	Regulate		Support		
Select	Discover	Revise		Test		
Show	Discriminate	Schedule		Validate		
State	Employ	Share				
Summarize	Establish	Show				
Tabulate	Estimate	Solve				
Tell	Evaluate	Synthesize				
	Extend	Use				
	Extrapolate	Verify				

It is useful to have a large repertoire of action verbs available as we convert goals to objectives, and you may find Table 1.3 helpful in this regard.

1.8   Identifying Course-Level Student Learning Outcomes (SLOs)

While course learning goal statements describe in general terms what we want students to learn, and objectives identify the steps students will take as they move toward those goals, SLOs state what achieving that goal would actually look like as an observable, measurable behavior. Like objectives, learning outcome statements are written in detailed operational terms, but in this case, the language must help us move from what we *hoped* would happen to *proof* of what happened derived from what actually *did* happen. SLOs, then, are explicit statements describing the knowledge, skills, abilities, and attitudes that we want a student to be able to demonstrate at the end (or as a result) of his or her experience in our course that shows us they have achieved our learning goals. Here is an example of an outcome:

> When given an aural exam consisting of listening examples of representative music that
> have not been studied, a successful learner will be able to identify genre and style.

1.9   Differentiating Between Learning Objectives and Learning Outcomes

Few words in the assessment lexicon are used in more confusing, contradictory ways than the terms *objectives* and *outcomes*. In section 1.4, we distinguished between the two terms in a way that is used in some assessment literature, but the two terms are also used interchangeably in other examples of assessment literature. Because this became so confusing to us, we offer the following to share how *we* came to terms with the terms.

In lay language, an objective is a target to aim for, while an outcome is the conclusion of an action. Thus learning objectives identify what we hope *will* happen, while learning outcomes reflect the reality of what actually *did* happen. Just as one cannot describe what happened until it has in fact happened, so one cannot determine a learning outcome until after the learner has done something to demonstrate their learning (or lack thereof). Thus we identify learning objectives before we teach, and we determine learning outcomes after we teach. Put another way, we teach through objectives, we assess for outcomes.

That said, we recognize that you can identify what you hope will be the outcome. Indeed, many accreditation and assessment programs ask faculty to identify learning outcomes in advance. To accomplish this, you may need to state the outcome in "future" terms—"a student will be able to"—or distinguish between *targeted outcome* and *actual outcome*. The targeted outcome is the predetermined achievement that we hope to see, a hypothesis about what learning will happen, while the actual outcome is the achievement we in fact saw. This satisfies external stakeholders who want to (1) know what we intend to accomplish in our teaching and (2) see evidence of what we actually accomplished in our teaching.

1.10 Crafting a Course Learning Outcome Statement

Learning outcome statements can be as simple as this:

> By the end of this course, a successful learner will be able to list the five major theories or perspectives in psychology.

It is this simpler form that we will use when we present learning outcomes in the LATs. In our own crafting of learning outcome statements for our courses, however, we find it helpful to identify two components: (1) the *conditions* (the product or performed action) that make the learning visible and (2) the *learning* represented in the action or product. In other words, say "when given x," or "in product x," "a learner will be able to do y." Table 1.4 illustrates.

The LATs in this book have been designed to provide you with an efficient way to establish both conditions and performance for assessing learning outcomes. For example, based on *LAT Best Summary*, your learning outcome statement might be: "In a *Best Summary* essay, successful learners will be able to accurately synthesize and explain in their own words core course concepts."

1.11 Determining Performance Standards for Individuals and the Class as a Whole

Assessing Achievement of Individual Students

We know that individual students in our class will achieve each learning outcome somewhere on a continuum between "didn't achieve it at all" to "mastered it." Thus once we establish what students should be able to do to demonstrate that they have achieved the outcome, it is helpful to identify the standard that represents the acceptable minimum. For example, you might state that on the postcourse exam of a *LAT 1 First Day Final*, a student must be able to answer at least 70% of the questions correctly in order to be deemed as having achieved the learning outcome.

Assessing Achievement at the Course Level

It is also appropriate to apply standards when you are analyzing and reporting aggregated data at the course level. Thus along with the learning outcome statement, you can specify the standard

Table 1.4 The Two Components of a Learning Outcome Statement

Conditions	Performance
When given x,	*a learner will be able to . . .*
When given an aural exam consisting of listening examples of representative music that have not been studied,	a successful learner will be able to identify the genre and style.
When given a case study,	a successful learner will be able to analyze and explain why a particular intervention was or was not effective.

that you believe is a fair overall minimum achievement level for the class as a whole. For example, you might feel that if 70% of the students in your class demonstrate achievement of the outcome, it is fair to say that the assignments and activities you have developed are helping students achieve the outcome. That performance standard is your target class outcome. If, after you have tabulated and analyzed the results, you find that 85% of the students achieved that standard, you may feel celebratory, just as if you find that only 60% of the students achieved it, you may feel disappointed. Examples of learning outcome statements with individual as well as aggregated performance standards are:

- When given an aural exam consisting of listening examples of representative music that have not been studied, a successful student will be able to identify the genre and style.
  Individual Minimum Performance Standard: 70% accuracy required for passing exam and to be deemed as meeting learning outcome.
  Target Class Performance Standard: 75% of students will receive a passing exam score, thereby demonstrating achievement of the learning outcome.
- When given a case study, a successful learner will be able to analyze and explain why a particular intervention was or was not effective.
  Individual Minimum Performance Standard: A minimum of Level 2 on each of the criteria in the assignment's assessment rubric is required to be considered as having achieved the learning outcome.
  Target Class Performance Standard: 60% of students will be able to demonstrate achievement of learning outcome by being ranked at a minimum of Level 2 on each of the criteria in the assignment's assessment rubric.

1.12 Is All the Work Required Worth the Effort?

Identifying your learning goals, determining learning objectives, and crafting learning outcome statements take time and effort. Given the many pressures we face as faculty, is it worth the effort? Truthfully, for some of us, it won't be. However, there are many benefits. Expressing what we want students to learn in assessment language promotes a core principle of a learner-centered course: responsibility for learning is shared between teachers and students because the emphasis is changed from what teachers must cover to what a student should be able to do as a consequence of instruction. This, in turn, benefits students on many levels. Often their anxiety is reduced because they are provided with clear direction, they know what the instructional priorities are, and they perceive that the grading is fair. Students also better understand how your course relates to other courses and to institutional learning goals. This, in turn, can help motivate them to put in the time and energy to learn well because they can more easily see the value in what you are teaching.

Carefully expressing what we want students to learn in assessment language also benefits multiple external stakeholders because course goals, content, and evaluation procedures are consistent, interrelated, and communicated clearly. Furthermore, effectiveness and efficiency are improved because all stakeholders are better able to determine which practices and materials are effective and which are not. In addition, departments and programs can better work together to create a more coordinated curriculum because the clear, logical instructional structure of each course provides the building blocks required for constructing larger, more complex systems.

Finally, the process of crafting good learning goals, objectives, and outcomes helps us as teachers. On a pragmatic basis, once the initial time and effort has been invested, it can save time and anxiety in grading. Indeed, we can encourage students to do more self-evaluation or peer evaluation because students know in clear, objective terms what is expected of them. Also, expressing what we want students to learn in assessment language helps us gather the information we need more efficiently to provide evidence to a variety of stakeholders on what and how well students in our courses are learning. We can then use this data for multiple purposes ranging from providing feedback to students to gathering information for our professional dossiers. Perhaps most satisfying, though, is the recognition that by participating in an evidence-based cycle of analysis and reflection designed to improve student learning, we are contributing in meaningful ways to the improvement of our profession and the betterment of the world.

CHAPTER 2

Determining Your Purpose for Assessing Student Learning

College teachers' lives are full of responsibilities, and we often find ourselves trying to be efficient in our efforts. The information we gather from students about their learning can serve myriad purposes, including to determine for ourselves how well students are learning, to provide learners with feedback on their progress, to improve our profession through the scholarship of teaching and learning (SoTL), and to provide information to institutional and external stakeholders. In this section, we provide information on the following areas:

2.1   Defining Assessment
2.2   How Learning Assessment Is Different from Grading
2.3   Types of Learning Assessment
2.4   Assessing Students to Determine for Ourselves How Well Students Are Learning
2.5   Assessing to Give Learners Feedback on Their Progress
2.6   Assessing to Improve Our Profession through the Scholarship of Teaching and Learning (SoTL)
2.7   Assessing to Provide Information to Institutional and External Stakeholders on How Well Students Are Learning
2.8   Crafting the Assessment Question

2.1   Defining Assessment

At its most fundamental level, assessment is the action of appraising the quality of something or someone. Within the context of education, the term *assessment* is used to describe appraisal of the knowledge, skills, attitudes, and beliefs that students have acquired, most often as the result of learning in their courses. Most definitions of assessment for educational purposes tend to stress that assessment is a process that involves goal setting and evidence gathering and this may occur at a number of levels: a system, an institution, a college, a department, or a program. In this book, when we use the term *learning assessment*, we are talking about assessment of student learning that happens *at the course level*. Thus when we say learning assessment, we mean the actions undertaken by teachers and by students to document student learning in a given course.

Table 2.1 Differences Between Grades and Assessment

Grades . . .	Assessment . . .
Focus on an individual student	Focuses on a cohort of students
Are letters that are indirect, symbolic representations of accomplishment	Attempts to pinpoint more precisely what was learned
May reflect class management goals related to student behavior that are separate from learning, such as attendance, participation, and on-time submission of assignments	Emphasizes only achievement of specified learning goals
May be the result of vague or inconsistent standards	Aims for exactness
Reflect student performance in individual courses or course assignments	May measure learning from ungraded co-curricular activities or look for skill development beyond course content, such as critical thinking

Source: Suskie (2009)

2.2 How Learning Assessment Is Different from Grading

College teachers have been providing feedback to students through graded assignments, activities, and tests for centuries. Is there a difference between graded assignments and assessment? For assessment specialists, there is. Essentially the grades we give are symbols of relative achievement in a class section. In an institution where twenty teachers may be teaching separate sections of English 1A, for example, each section will represent its own blend of a single teacher's pedagogy and that section's unique array of student abilities. Assessment specialists propose that the fundamental purpose of assessment is to determine how effective a course's assignments and tests are in fostering specific learning goals in order to understand and improve student learning. Additional differences between the two are identified in Table 2.1.

2.3 Types of Learning Assessment

There are many different types of learning assessment, and the result can be a bewildering terminology muddle. The different types may refer to the purpose of assessment, the timing of the collection of data, the type of measurement, or the form of appraisal. We believe that these distinctions are interesting in theory, but for most of us who are teaching, assessment is not typically an either/or practice. Thus our concept of *learning* assessment is not centered on any one of these types, but rather is a broad conceptualization of how to assess student learning outcomes (SLOs) at the course level. That said, we find three types of assessment particularly useful as concepts for understanding Learning Assessment Techniques (LATs):

1. ***Educative assessment*** is a term developed by Grant Wiggins to describe a process in which assessment is designed to help improve student performance rather than just "audit" it. While LATs can be used for both purposes, we strive to emphasize the educative aspect because our primary purpose in LATs is to improve learning.

2. *Embedded assessment* occurs within the class as an assignment linked to learning outcomes, thus achieving both grading and assessment purposes. All LATs are embedded assessments.

3. *Authentic assessment* simulates a real-world experience by evaluating ability to apply knowledge or perform tasks under conditions that approximate those found outside of the classroom. Wherever possible, we have attempted to create LATs that reflect the principles of authentic assessment.

2.4 Assessing Students to Determine for Ourselves How Well Students Are Learning

Many of us are interested in assessing students simply to determine for ourselves whether students are learning, for reasons that may include the following:

1. **To discover the current status of student knowledge and understanding:** Many teachers believe it is important to identify students' prior knowledge in order to determine appropriate starting points for instruction. In addition, an important principle in learning and motivation is to work at a level that is appropriately challenging: learning activities that are too easy are boring, while ones that are too hard are discouraging. Assessing where students are as the course progresses also helps teachers identify struggling students who need additional work, as well as those who may benefit from more challenging, advanced tasks. Certainly at the end of the course or a unit of study, we want to know if students have indeed learned what we attempted to teach them. Assessing students' current status of knowledge and understanding, therefore, provides us with important information at multiple points throughout the course.

2. **To solve a problem in our teaching:** At times we become aware of problems in our courses. Students may be paying too much attention to their phones, tablets, or laptops. They may not participate in discussions or do their homework. They may not demonstrate as much critical thinking as we would like. Conducting assessment can provide us with data about the reasons these problems are occurring, which in turn may point to potential solutions.

3. **To determine whether we need to change direction in our teaching:** Perhaps we have started down a path in teaching and are uncertain whether our approach is working. We may be lecturing and wondering whether students are understanding the information, or using collaborative groups and wondering if all students are participating. Conducting assessment can help us answer questions about whether our pedagogical choices are effective so that, if necessary, we can make changes in our approach.

4. **To find out how students are experiencing learning in our classrooms:** While many of us conduct assessment for the primary purpose of determining whether students are learning what they should and could, there are times that we want to know how students are experiencing the learning activities or classroom environment. Indeed, because course climate can influence learning itself (not to mention student evaluations), it can be quite useful to collect information about student experience as well as information on learning itself.

2.5   Assessing to Give Learners Feedback on Their Progress

Imagine trying to learn something with only a vague sense of what you are supposed to learn, and then not getting any feedback on how you are progressing. Your improvement would be haphazard, the process would be frustrating, and in the end you might even find you had learned nothing at all. Even worse, you might realize that what you *had* learned, you had learned wrong. To learn efficiently and effectively, learners need to know what they are supposed to learn as well as know what they need to be able to do to demonstrate that they have learned. They also need to receive rich, timely, individually relevant feedback throughout their learning efforts so that they can make necessary adjustments before it is too late. Thus an important use of assessment results is to provide constructive information to students.

2.6   Assessing Learning to Improve Our Profession through the Scholarship of Teaching and Learning (SoTL)

In 1990, Ernest Boyer, the president of the Carnegie Foundation for the Advancement of Teaching, made popular the term "the scholarship of teaching" in his now classic text *Scholarship Reconsidered*. This notion eventually was expanded to "the scholarship of teaching and learning." SoTL is scholarly inquiry into student learning. It aims to improve teaching and learning as it also addresses a vision for an appropriate balance between research and teaching and about how to evaluate and reward good teaching. As described by Huber and Hutchings, SoTL is "viewing the work of the classroom as a site for inquiry, asking and answering questions about students' learning in ways that can improve one's own classroom and also advance the larger profession of teaching" (2005, p. 1).

Today, a number of journals and conferences accept articles related to college teaching. At the International Society for the Scholarship of Teaching and Learning's 11th annual international conference in Quebec City, Canada, approximately 500 scholars of teaching and learning from around the world met to share their inquiries, perspectives, and research on issues related to "nurturing creativity and passion in teaching and learning" (https://www.issotl14.ulaval.ca, accessed 11–17–14). Those of us who pursue SoTL work can use assessment to provide the kind of evidence required to improve our profession through our individual contributions to the scholarship of teaching and learning.

2.7   Assessing to Provide Information to Institutional and External Stakeholders on How Well Students Are Learning

College teachers are being asked to provide evidence of what and how well students in their courses are learning to a variety of institutional and external stakeholders. We therefore can use results to provide evidence of the effectiveness of our teaching or the quality of student learning:

1. **As part of our professional dossiers:** Most of us have to provide evidence of our effectiveness as teachers, and this information is typically acquired through traditional student evaluations or ratings of courses. We want these student evaluations to be good, not

only to reassure ourselves that we are doing our jobs well, but because these evaluations have a high correlation to departmental chair evaluations, which in turn influence decisions that affect our professional careers. Student evaluations, however, do not always provide rich, substantive information. In addition, institutions are increasingly adopting electronic rating forms, which tend to have lower response rates. Department chairs and tenure evaluation committees have a difficult time conducting fair, thorough evaluations of teaching when there is low student response rates. Assessment can help us provide a more complete picture of our teaching effectiveness that we can use for our professional dossiers, whether for hiring, promotion, tenure, or merit review.

2. **For program reviews, whether internal or external:** Most programs must go through some sort of formal review, whether by an external disciplinary association such as Accreditation Board for Engineering and Technology (ABET) or National Council on Teacher Education (NCATE), or through an internal review process such as one that might be used for their institution's budget and resource allocation. A normal part of these reviews is the documentation that students have met predetermined learning outcomes.

3. **To institutional assessment efforts and accrediting agencies:** Pressures on institutions of higher education for assessment of learning continue to increase. Also, accreditation agencies are assuming more of the responsibility for stimulating and monitoring assessment. Thus we can use the data we gather to report on student learning both to our institutions and to accrediting agencies.

2.8 Crafting the Assessment Question

As you prepare to select and then implement a LAT, it is important to know, What is the question you are asking about student learning? Here are some examples of the kinds of questions you might consider.

1. **To what extent has the learning been successful?** That is, *how well* can students demonstrate accomplishment of the learning outcome? You typically can answer this question by looking at the final learning product, the assessable Learning Artifact. Based on your evaluation of this product, you should be able to determine achievement of the outcome for both individuals and the class as a whole.

2. **Has there has been cognitive or affective change in students over time?** This question may be answered by giving students a pretest, offering instruction, and then giving a posttest. The change that occurs between the pretest and posttest is considered to represent the change in learning over time. Many of the LATs we have described are useful as pretest and postassessment measures of change in learner knowledge and skills. Certainly the change that is documented may have occurred due to factors other than just the course activities; for example, students could gain knowledge on their own through informal learning. In higher education settings, however, it typically is not practical or possible to control for these external factors. Therefore, it often is sufficient to simply document that change has happened and thus not necessary to go into high-level research methods to prove that the improvement was a direct result of the course.

3. **How do these results compare with others**? It may be informative to analyze how the results compare to data gathered for other groups. Examples of these groups include students in the same course that you taught in other academic terms, students in the same or similar courses taught by other teachers, and subgroups of students differentiated by characteristics such as academic major, student level (such as freshman), prior background, and so forth.

CHAPTER 3

Selecting a Learning Assessment Technique

Learning Assessment Techniques (LATs) are unique teaching sructures that blend identification of learning goals, a learning activity that requires students to produce an assessable Learning Artifact, and guidance on how to analyze and display learning outcomes to share with multiple stakeholders. By so doing, the LATs mirror the elements of effective college teaching and provide college teachers with the tools they need to succeed and excel in today's increasingly complex teaching and learning environment. Following are some of the elements and considerations related to determining which LAT will best meet your needs:

3.1   Using the Learning Goals Inventory (LGI)
3.2   Considering Instructional Context When Choosing a LAT
3.3   Key Instructional Elements to Consider
3.4   Considering Clustering Multiple LATs Together

3.1 Using the Learning Goals Inventory (LGI)

The LGI is a survey available both online and as Appendix A that will guide you in identifying and prioritizing learning goals that are associated with the Significant Learning Taxonomy. The LATs in Part 2 of this book are organized to correlate with the taxonomy's six dimensions. Taking the inventory, determining your goal profile, and then looking at the chapter of LATs that corresponds to your highest ranking goal is the first step in deciding which LAT will best meet your needs. Within each chapter's set of LATs, the techniques are organized from our determination of simplest to most complex. At this basic level, which LAT you should choose depends on what you want students to learn, what you have determined is the best way to find out whether they have learned it, and to whom you want to report the results.

3.2 Considering Instructional Context When Choosing a LAT

Today's college teachers teach in a variety of educational activities and environments.

Traditional Classroom

Traditional classroom is a term used in various ways, ranging from class size (smaller classes of 50 or fewer students) to a specific instructional method (lecturing) to an institutional type (expressed in the image of brick and mortar, ivy-covered universities). In the context of the educational environment for assessment, we use the term *traditional classroom* as a proxy for the face-to-face or onsite classroom. All of the LATs in this book can be used effectively in a traditional classroom.

Online Classes

Online classes have become an increasingly prominent mode for offering instruction, and we have therefore given considered attention throughout this book to the use of LATs in the online environment. In each LAT we provide at least one example of how the LAT can be used in an online classroom. We acknowledge that there is no one way to teach online, and indeed, the variety of ways in which faculty teach online is constantly growing. One of the primary changes we have seen is in the timing of communication within online courses. In addition to asynchronous communication, more professors are using synchronous communication tools as well. We also recognize that the number of environments in which online courses occur is on the rise, as are the tools by which students access these environments. For example, many students are now accessing their course environments (and communicating with each other) through cellular phone apps or handheld devices. Most LATs can be used effectively in online and mobile learning environments, and in Table 3.1, we provide our top LAT online picks.

Collaborative Classrooms

Most of us tend to think of learning as something that happens in the mind of an individual. Moreover, when we assess learning, we typically begin with an individual Learning Artifact. However, there are now several scholars who conceive of learning as something beyond an individual act; learning is groups of individuals tapping into and building a networked intelligence (Major, 2015). Collaborative learning is an approach that fosters this view of learning, and it is a pedagogy that we advocate (see e.g. Barkley, Major, & Cross, 2014). Since learning can occur both individually and collaboratively, the basic question is, "Which learning activities are best done independently and which collaboratively?" LATs involve both individual and collaborative activities. If the literature from which we drew the activity most often described it as an individual one, we used that as our starting point, but then provide a variation that can allow for adapting an individual activity to a collaborative one. For those in which the original description was collaborative, we used that as our starting point. You can choose which to use based upon your needs and the needs of the students, and in Table 3.2 we offer our suggestions for the best LATs for collaborative learning.

Flipped Classroom

Flipped classroom is an instructional model in which the order of elements common in some courses is reversed. Rather than reading and completing activities outside of class and then

Table 3.1 Top 10 LAT Picks for Online Classes

	Taxonomy Dimension	LAT	Brief Description
1	Foundation	LAT 1 First Day Final	Students take a nongraded test the first day of the term that is similar to the Final Exam. They then self-rate their knowledge for the exam, and then identify the 3 questions they found easiest/most difficult. At the end of the term they take the real, graded Final Exam.
2	Application	LAT 14 Insights-Resources-Applications (IRAs)	In conjunction with an assigned reading, students complete a written assignment that includes three components: new perceptions or understandings (Insights), resources they have found that amplify the reading's themes or information (Resources), and an example from the students' personal experience that relates to the reading (Application).
3	Integration	LAT 23 Concept Maps	Students draw a diagram that conveys their ideas about or understanding of a complex concept, procedure, or process they have studied. The diagram is intended to suggest relationships between ideas, which it does in the form of a network in which boxes or circles represent ideas and in which the lines between the ideas represent connections.
4	Human Dimension	LAT 36 Digital Story	Digital storytelling at its most fundamental level is the practice of using computer-based tools, such as video, audio, graphics, and Web publishing, to tell stories. The stories may be personal or academic, but for either focus, students share relevant life experiences as they attempt to connect to an audience about a given issue.
5	Caring	LAT 39 Issue Awareness Ad	Students identify and analyze a problematic situation in the local community. They then write and deliver a speech that persuades others of the urgency of the problem and offers strategies for solving the problem.
6	Learning How to Learn	LAT 50 Personal Learning Environment	A Personal Learning Environment (PLE) is a set of people and digital resources an individual can access for the specific intent of learning. Students illustrate these potential connections through the creation of a visible network of the set. Nodes represent the resources, and ties suggest the relationship between the sources. A PLE then is a visual representation of a learner's informal learning processes and a concrete demonstration of an individual's capacity for future learning.
7	Application	LAT 15 Consider This	Students are given a theory or concept that they have been taught (for example, thesis statements, the scientific method, or push-pull factors) and are challenged to figure out a way to apply it in a new and different context.
8	Application	LAT 13 Quotation Commentaries	Students receive a handout with a set of quotations from a recent reading assignment and then comment on them, following a specific process: paraphrase, interpret, and comment.
9	Integration	LAT 26 Synthesis Paper	Instead of responding to or reviewing a single reading assignment, students consider several readings together, work to draw commonalities from them, and then write about readings in a formal paper.
10	Caring	LAT 41 Editorial	In this adaptation of the classic newspaper editorial essay, the instructor guides students through the process of writing an editorial on a topic that interests them.

Table 3.2 Top 10 LAT Picks for Collaborative Classrooms

	Taxonomy Dimension	LAT	Brief Description
1	Foundational Knowledge	LAT 7 Best Summary	Students individually prepare summaries of the main points at the end of a given unit of content, lecture, reading assignment, or other and then work in groups to compare, evaluate, and select the "best" summary.
2	Application	LAT 17 Think-Aloud Pair Problem-Solving Protocols	Student pairs receive a set of problems to solve as well as specific roles—problem solver and listener—that they switch as they move from problem to problem.
3	Integration	LAT 27 Case Study	Students receive a real-life scenario, or "case," related to course content. These cases usually present a brief history of how the situation developed and a dilemma that a key character within the scenario is facing, and students are charged with helping the character develop a solution to the problem.
4	Human Dimension	LAT 30 Free Discussion	Small groups of students are formed quickly and extemporaneously to respond to course-related questions. Their discussion is an informal exchange of ideas, but students are assessed on their ability to participate effectively.
5	Caring	LAT 42 Debate	In a debate, students research and analyze a controversial topic and then engage in a series of oral presentations of their arguments against an opposing team.
6	Learning How to Learn	LAT 44 Study Outlines	Study Outlines provide students with a structure to synthesize and organize course information in meaningful, useful ways so that they can prepare for tests.
7	Application	LAT 18 Peer Problem Review	In Peer Problem Review, students each receive a problem, try to solve it, and then pass the problem and solution to a nearby student. The student who receives the problem and response then analyzes and evaluates the solution.
8	Integration	LAT 25 Dyadic Essay	Students individually write an essay question and model answer on a reading assignment, lecture, or other. Pairs exchange questions, write responses to each other's questions, and then compare the model with their own. The students next discuss their responses and in a final step, complete a peer evaluation of each other's performance.
9	Human Dimension	LAT 34 Role Play	A Role Play is a created situation in which students deliberately act out or assume characters or identities they would not normally assume in order to accomplish learning goals. Students often research their roles through independent study, but instructors may also provide specific assignments, such as readings, to serve as source material for the play.

coming to class to hear a content-intensive lecture, students in flipped classes typically watch short video lectures or other content-rich preparatory work and then, during the onsite class session, participate in discussions, exercises, or projects. Our LATs can be used effectively in a flipped classroom, and in Table 3.3 we identify our top LAT flipped classroom picks.

Table 3.3 Top Ten LAT Picks for the Flipped Classroom

	Taxonomy Dimension	LAT	Brief Description
1	Foundational Knowledge	LAT 4 Guided Reading Notes	Students receive a copy of notes summarizing content from an upcoming assigned reading but that includes blanks. As students read, they provide the missing content and fill the blanks to create a complete set of notes that may be used as a study guide.
2	Application	LAT 12 Fact or Opinion	Students first read a text to identify and list facts. They then reread the text to look for where the author either overtly or covertly inserts opinion, and make a new list as they carefully consider the evidence and resist being taken in by the text's rhetorical force.
3	Integration	LAT 22 Sequence Chains	Students analyze and depict graphically a sequence of events, actions, roles, or decisions. Sequence Chains require students to create a visual map of the logic within a series.
4	Human Dimension	LAT 35 Ethical Dilemma	Students are presented with an ethics-based, discipline-related scenario in which someone must choose a course of action between two or more difficult alternatives. Students write an essay response to the case in which they proceed through a sequence of prescribed steps that conclude with their choice of the most ethical decision.
5	Caring	LAT 40 Proclamations	Students identify and analyze a problematic situation in the local community. They then write and deliver a speech that persuades others of the urgency of the problem and offers strategies for solving the problem.
6	Learning How to Learn	LAT 45 Student Generated Rubric	Teachers provide students with examples of outstanding disciplinary-based products such as an essay, research paper, musical composition, mathematical proof, or scientific lab report, which students analyze to determine the common characteristics and develop assessment rubrics. They then apply the rubric to test rubric viability.
7	Application	LAT 16 What's the Problem?	Students look at examples of common problem types in order to identify the particular type of problem each example represents.
8	Foundational Knowledge	LAT 9 Team-Tests	Students work in teams to prepare for instructor-created exams and then take the exams first individually and next as a group. This LAT thus proceeds in three steps: (1) group members study for a test together, (2) individuals take the test, and (3) the group takes the test.
9	Learning How to Learn	LAT 46 Invent the Quiz	Students write a limited number of test questions related to a recent learning module and then create an answer sheet, or alternately a model answer and scoring sheet, to accompany the test questions.
10	Learning How to Learn	LAT 49 Multiple-Task Mastery Checklist	Multiple-Task Mastery Checklist provides a structured format for carrying out a multistage formative assessment of a formal project. It involves identifying the sequence of steps or stages and ensuring that students master each one in sequence prior to moving forward to the next one.

Large Classes

Large classes have become a more common course structure. Taught frequently in auditoriums, these courses typically enroll several hundred students, and the lead instructor typically lectures. The challenge with such courses is managing students and keeping them engaged and involved in their own learning. Table 3.4 presents our recommendations for LATs that can be effective in this challenging course structure.

3.3   Key Instructional Elements to Consider

There are several key elements to consider as you choose a LAT, including

1. **How do you want students to access the content that initiates the learning process?** The LATs include a range of direct and indirect ways for students to access the information upon which the instructional activity is based. Some of the LATs are tied to a specific way to access content, such as an assigned reading or a lecture, while others are flexible or have multiple ways of conveying content. Select a LAT that provides you with a structure to share content in a way that makes sense for students in your course.

2. **What kind of product do you want students to produce?** Each of the LATs link the learning activity to the production of a Learning Artifact such as writing, presenting, or creating a product. The LAT you select should produce the form or product that you believe will best demonstrate student learning, as this is the product you will ultimately assess and likely grade.

3. **What is your purpose for assessing student learning?** It is also important to consider why and for whom you are collecting the data. For example, if you are conducting formative assessment to provide yourself and students with a sense of their progress, then you will want to choose a LAT designed for this purpose. Alternatively, if you are analyzing achievement of learning outcomes for your institution's assessment efforts, your institution may have specific kinds of data that they will determine as acceptable evidence and you will want your choice of a LAT to produce the kind of data best suited for that purpose.

4. **How complex of an activity to you want to implement?** The LATs vary from simple techniques that require minimum preparation and little effort to implement to complex techniques that involve considerable effort to employ effectively. To help you quickly determine the complexity of a technique, we provide at the top of each LAT our ratings of three elements: preparation, in-class implementation, and analysis. Table 3.5 provides information on the factors we considered as we made our determination.

3.4   Considering Clustering Multiple LATs Together

While any LAT may be used independently, they also work well when joined together in an instructional sequence. Acquiring foundational knowledge may be essential prior to application of knowledge, which may be important to prepare for integration of knowledge. Thus, you might link three LATs together, one from each category. For example, you could start with Guided Reading Notes for a single reading. Next you could move to an Insights-Resources-

Table 3.4 Top Ten LAT Picks for Large Classes

	Taxonomy Dimension	LAT	Brief Description
1	Foundational Knowledge	LAT 8 Snap Shots	The instructor presents questions during class along with several possible answers. Individual students choose which answer they think is correct, and the instructor makes a quick visual assessment of class results. Students then discuss answers with neighbor(s) and together choose an answer, after which the instructor makes another assessment and compares results.
2	Application	LAT 11 Prediction Guide	Students are presented with a series of questions that ask them to make predictions prior to a learning activity and then, after the learning activity, they revisit their predictions to evaluate accuracy and correct potential misconceptions.
3	Integration	LAT 24 Contemporary Issues Journal	Students look for recent events or developments in the real world that are related to their coursework readings and assignments, then analyze these current affairs to identify the connections to course material in entries that they write in a journal.
4	Human Dimension	LAT 30 Free Discussion	Small groups of students are formed quickly and extemporaneously to respond to course-related questions. Their discussion is an informal exchange of ideas, but students are assessed on their ability to participate effectively. *Depending upon class size, consider a variation in which students turn to a partner to talk instead of forming groups.*
5	Caring	LAT 37 Stand Where You Stand	Students read assignments with opposing opinions on a controversial issue. Then, after the teacher presents a statement that reflects one of the sides, students individually decide whether and how much they agree or disagree. They then go stand in front of one of four room-corner signs to signal their positions, take turns presenting their rationales, and move to another sign if the arguments they hear persuade them to change their minds. *Depending upon class size, consider using clickers or a show of hands to indicate position and do a quick count before or after a lecture.*
6	Caring	LAT 38 Three-Minute Message	Modeled on the Three-Minute Thesis (3MT) academic competition, students have three minutes to present a compelling argument and to support it with convincing details and examples. *Consider a twitter message variation in which students compose a 140 character message and tweet with the class hashtag (or alternately turn in index cards with the message in 140 characters). The purpose is similar to an elevator pitch, or handing someone a business card to quickly promote interest.*
7	Foundational Knowledge	LAT 3 Entry and Exit Tickets	Entry and exit tickets require students to reflect on a reading assignment, video, lecture, or other and then write a brief response to a question on an index card that is designed to gather information about their understanding of core facts, terms, concepts, and ideas.
8	Foundational Knowledge	LAT 5 Comprehensive Factors List	Students recall and list as many relevant factors as they can that are related to a topic that they have encountered through a reading assignment, lecture, illustration, performance, or other course experience.
9	Foundational Knowledge	LAT 6 Quick Write	A Quick Write is an activity in which learners write a response in a brief amount of time to an open-ended prompt posed by the teacher.
10	Integration	LAT 21 Knowledge Grid	Students demonstrate analytical and organizational skills by filling in the internal cells of a grid in which the first column and top row provide key categories.

Table 3.5 Key to Complexity Ratings for Each LAT

Preparation	
Rating	**Each Level Involves One or More of the Following Activities:**
Low	Choose the activity Write a single simple question/prompt
Moderate	Find readings/resources Develop a moderate-level question/prompt Create a rudimentary rubric or scoring system
High	Develop a complex assessment instrument Create a handout or document to introduce it Develop a thorough rubric
In-Class Implementation	
Low	Done as homework Few minutes in class
Moderate	Part of a class session (more than a minute or two)
High	A full class session Several class sessions
Analysis	
Low	Single question response (fill in the blank/multiple choice) with accurate or inaccurate determination Sentence or two written with simple scoring (e.g., relevant, not relevant)
Moderate	Extended response Rubric scoring
High	Long projects that require extensive reading and scoring

Application essay in which students make connections between the readings and their experiences. Finally, you could implement a microtheme in which the students synthesize readings and develop their own arguments about several works in a short writing sample. Thus LATs can work together and do not have to be a one-shot deal, as illustrated in Figure 3.1. In Table 3.6 we provide an overview of all 50 LATs with a brief description of each.

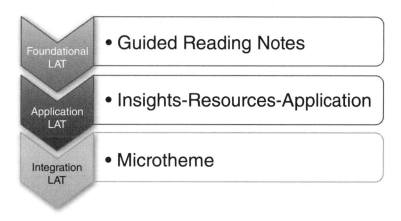

Figure 3.1 Clustering LATs in an Instructional Sequence

Table 3.6 LAT Quick Reference

Category	LAT	Technique	Brief Description
Foundational Knowledge	1	First Day Final	Students take a nongraded test the first day of the term that consists of questions that are similar to the Final Exam, and then identify the questions they found easiest and those they found most difficult. At the end of the term they take the real, graded Final Exam and the results are used as a reference point to demonstrate learning gains and achievement over time.
Foundational Knowledge	2	Background Knowledge Probe	Background Knowledge Probes are simple questionnaires that help you quickly take stock of the level of foundational knowledge and general preparedness that students have, along with their level of confidence in their responses, before beginning a content unit or learning module.
Foundational Knowledge	3	Entry and Exit Tickets	Entry and exit tickets require students to reflect on a reading assignment, video, lecture, or other and then write a brief response to a question on an index card that is designed to gather information about their understanding of core facts, terms, concepts, and ideas.
Foundational Knowledge	4	Guided Reading Notes	Students receive a copy of notes summarizing content from an upcoming assigned reading but that includes blanks. As students read, they provide the missing content and fill the blanks to create a complete set of notes that may be used as a study guide.
Foundational Knowledge	5	Comprehensive Factors List	Students recall and list as many relevant factors as they can relate to a topic that they have encountered through a reading assignment, lecture, illustration, performance, or other course experience.
Foundational Knowledge	6	Quick Write	A Quick Write is an activity in which learners write a response in a brief amount of time to an open-ended prompt posed by the teacher.
Foundational Knowledge	7	Best Summary	Students individually prepare summaries of the main points at the end of a given unit of content, lecture, reading assignment, or other, and then work in groups to compare, evaluate, and select the "best" summary.
Foundational Knowledge	8	Snap Shots	The instructor presents questions during class along with several possible answers. Individual students choose which answer they think is correct, and the instructor makes a quick visual assessment of class results. Students then discuss answers with neighbor(s), after which they together choose an answer again, and the instructor makes another assessment and compares results.
Foundational Knowledge	9	Team Tests	Students work in teams to prepare for instructor-created exams and then take the exams first individually and next as a group. The LAT thus proceeds in three steps: (1) group members study for a test together, (2) individuals take the test, and (3) the group takes the test.
Foundational Knowledge	10	Team Games Tournament	In this team games activity, home teams work together to learn content and then compete against tournament teams.
Application	11	Prediction Guide	Students are presented with a series of questions that ask them to make predictions prior to a learning activity and then, after the learning activity, they revisit their predictions to evaluate accuracy and correct potential misconceptions.

Table 3.6 (*Continued*)

Category	LAT	Technique	Brief Description
Application	12	Fact or Opinion	Students first read a text to identify and list facts. They then re-read the text to look for where the author either overtly or covertly inserts opinion, and make a new list as they carefully consider the evidence and resist being taken in by the text's rhetorical force.
Application	13	Quotation Commentaries	Students receive a handout with set of quotations from a recent reading assignment and then comment on them, following a specific process: paraphrase, interpret, and comment.
Application	14	Insights-Resources-Applications (IRAs)	In conjunction with an assigned reading, students complete a written assignment that includes three components: new perceptions or understandings (Insights), resources they have found that amplify the reading's themes or information (Resources), and an example from the students' personal experience that relates to the reading (Application).
Application	15	Consider This	Students are given a theory or concept that they have been taught (for example, thesis statements, the scientific method, or push-pull factors) and are challenged to figure out a way to apply it in a new and different context.
Application	16	What's the Problem?	Students look at examples of common problem types in order to identify the particular type of problem each example represents.
Application	17	Think-Aloud Problem-Solving Protocols	Student pairs receive a set of problems to solve as well as specific roles—problem solver and listener—that they switch as they move from problem to problem.
Application	18	Peer Problem Review	In Peer Problem Review, students each receive a problem, try to solve it, and then pass the problem and solution to a nearby student. The student who receives the problem and response then analyzes and evaluates the solution.
Application	19	Triple Jump	This three-step technique requires students to think through a real-world problem presented in a case-based scenario: (1) to articulate a plan for solving it, (2) to gather resources, and (3) to attempt to provide a viable solution to it.
Application	20	Digital Projects	Students create projects that enhance and document their learning of an important topic concept in the field. Digital Projects may include collages, photo albums, videos, infographics, web sites, blogs, podcasts, book trailers, or other.
Integration	21	Knowledge Grid	Students demonstrate analytical and organizational skills by filling in the internal cells of a grid in which the first column and top row provide key categories.
Integration	22	Sequence Chains	Students analyze and depict graphically a sequence of events, actions, roles, or decisions. Sequence Chains require students to create a visual map of the logic within a series.
Integration	23	Concept Maps	Students draw a diagram that conveys their ideas about or understanding of a complex concept, procedure, or process they have studied. The diagram is intended to suggest relationships between ideas, which it

(*continued*)

Table 3.6 (*Continued*)

Category	LAT	Technique	Brief Description
			does in the form of a network in which boxes or circles represent ideas and in which the lines between the ideas represent connections.
Integration	24	Contemporary Issues Journal	Students look for recent events or developments in the real world that are related to their coursework readings and assignments, then analyze these current affairs to identify the connections to course material in entries that they write in a journal.
Integration	25	Dyadic Essay	Students individually write an essay question and model answer on a reading assignment, lecture, or other. Pairs exchange questions, write responses to each other's questions, and then compare the model with their own. The students next discuss their responses and in a final step, complete a peer evaluation of each other's performance.
Integration	26	Synthesis Paper	Instead of responding to or reviewing a single reading assignment, students consider several readings together, work to draw commonalities from them, and then write about readings in a formal paper.
Integration	27	Case Study	Students receive a real-life scenario, or "case," related to course content. These cases usually present a brief history of how the situation developed and a dilemma that a key character within the scenario is facing, and students are charged with helping the character develop a solution to the problem.
Integration	28	Class Book	Individual students submit a scholarly essay or research paper that they believe represents their highest quality work from the course, and then all students' best papers are published together in a Class Book.
Integration	29	E-Portfolios	Students assemble examples of work that they have created throughout the semester during various assignments, and they supplement this digitized collection of examples with commentary about their significance.
Human Dimension	30	Free Discussion	Small groups of students are formed quickly and extemporaneously to respond to course-related questions. Their discussion is an informal exchange of ideas, but students are assessed on their ability to participate effectively.
Human Dimension	31	Nominations	Students learn about an important award relevant to the field of study, for example someone in economics might learn about the Nobel Memorial Prize in Economic Sciences, including what makes someone qualified for nomination. They then research outstanding individuals in the field, select one for nomination, and write a short profile page of the individual, indicating why he or she should be considered for the award.
Human Dimension	32	Editorial Review	Students assume roles as editors who must evaluate a set of works to select which ones to include in an upcoming publication, and then write to the authors with a decision and rationale about whether their work merits inclusion in the publication.
Human Dimension	33	Dramatic Dialogues	Students create a dialogue based on an imagined discussion of a problem or issue between two characters, imaginary or real, past or present.

Table 3.6 (*Continued*)

Category	LAT	Technique	Brief Description
Human Dimension	34	Role Play	A Role Play is a created situation in which students deliberately act out or assume characters or identities they would not normally assume in order to accomplish learning goals. Students often research their roles through independent study, but instructors may also provide specific assignments, such as readings, to serve as source material for the play.
Human Dimension	35	Ethical Dilemma	Students are presented with an ethics-based, discipline-related scenario in which someone must choose a course of action between two or more difficult alternatives. Students write an essay response to the case in which they proceed through a sequence of prescribed steps that conclude with their choice of the most ethical decision.
Human Dimension	36	Digital Story	Digital storytelling at its most fundamental level is the practice of using computer-based tools, such as video, audio, graphics, and Web publishing, to tell stories. The stories may be personal or academic, but for either focus, students share relevant life experiences as they attempt to connect to an audience about a given issue.
Caring	37	Stand Where You Stand	Students read assignments with opposing opinions on a controversial issue. Then, after the teacher presents a statement that reflects one of the sides, students individually decide whether and how much they agree or disagree. They then go stand in front of one of four room-corner signs to signal their positions, take turns presenting their rationales, and move to another sign if the arguments they hear persuade them to change their minds.
Caring	38	Three-Minute Message	Modeled on the Three-Minute Thesis (3MT) academic competition, students have three minutes to present a compelling argument and to support it with convincing details and examples.
Caring	39	Issue Awareness Ad	Students identify and analyze a problematic situation in the local community. They then write and deliver a speech that persuades others of the urgency of the problem and offers strategies for solving the problem.
Caring	40	Proclamations	Students identify and analyze a problematic situation in the local community. They then write and deliver a speech that persuades others of the urgency of the problem and offers strategies for solving the problem.
Caring	41	Editorial	In this adaptation of the classic newspaper editorial essay, the instructor guides students through the process of writing an editorial on a topic that interests them.
Caring	42	Debate	In a debate, students research and analyze a controversial topic and then engage in a series of oral presentations of their arguments against an opposing team.
Caring	43	Briefing Paper	Students select a current problem, and they research it through independent or group study. They next prepare a summary of the main issues involved and outline proposed solutions, which they then evaluate for strengths and weaknesses. In their papers, students often make a call to action.

(*continued*)

Table 3.6   (*Continued*)

Category	LAT	Technique	Brief Description
Learn How to Learn	44	Study Outlines	Study Outlines provide students with a structure to synthesize and organize course information in meaningful, useful ways so that they can prepare for tests.
Learn How to Learn	45	Student Generated Rubric	Teachers provide students with examples of outstanding disciplinary-based products such as an essay, research paper, musical composition, mathematical proof, or scientific lab report, which students analyze to determine the common characteristics and develop assessment rubrics. They then apply the rubric to test rubric viability.
Learn How to Learn	46	Invent the Quiz	Students write a limited number of test questions related to a recent learning module and then create an answer sheet, or alternately a model answer and scoring sheet, to accompany the test questions.
Learn How to Learn	47	Learning Goal Listing	Students generate and prioritize a list of their learning goals at the beginning of the academic term, a unit of study, or a specific learning activity. If time permits, students can estimate the relative difficulty of achieving these learning goals.
Learn How to Learn	48	What? So What? Now What? Journal	Students write journal entries to reflect on their recent course-related activities or experiences. The questions that comprise the name of this LAT provide students with a structure for critical analysis during these reflections, prompting students to respond to the main questions and relevant subquestions.
Learn How to Learn	49	Multiple-Task Mastery Checklist	Multiple-Task Mastery Checklist provides a structured format for carrying out a multistage formative assessment of a formal project. It involves identifying the sequence of project activities and ensuring that students master each one in the series prior to moving forward to the next one.
Learn How to Learn	50	Personal Learning Environment	A Personal Learning Environment (PLE) is a set of people and digital resources an individual can access for the specific intent of learning. Students illustrate these potential connections through the creation of a visible network of the set. Nodes represent the resources, and ties suggest the relationship between the sources. A PLE then is a visual representation of a learner's informal learning processes and a concrete demonstration of an individual's capacity for future learning.

CHAPTER 4

Implementing a Learning Assessment Technique

Each of the LATs originated as an instructional activity designed to promote active learning. In this section we offer guidance on topics related to the three phases of implementing a LAT: preparing, facilitating, and concluding the activity.

4.1 Creating Assessment Rubrics

In many LATs, we recommend using rubrics to help assess to what extent learning has occurred, and these are best created as part of the preparation phase. We support the use of rubrics for both assessment and instructional reasons. A rubric explicates a task into its component parts and then identifies a range of individual performance and achievement goals so that we can apply it to a piece of student work and determine which parts represent high-, medium, or low-quality work. Thus rubrics promote effective assessment because they establish clear, appropriate criteria and standards by which to measure student progress toward or achievement of learning goals. Rubrics also support assessment efforts because they help teachers of the same course, sequenced courses, or similar assignments within a department or program communicate with each other about departmental or institutional standards, criteria, and assessment.

Learning Assessment Techniques

Rubrics also support effective teaching because they clarify expectations for students and help students understand their specific strengths and weaknesses so that they can improve the quality of their effort incrementally.

Walvoord and Anderson (2010) identify two core elements of a rubric:

1. *Criteria*: these are the various "yardsticks" we use that indicate the different kinds of characteristics or features that are deemed important and worthy of measuring.
2. *Standards*: these are the "markers" on the yardsticks that indicate the level of quality we can identify, including which level is the minimum level for acceptable work.

We provide Table 4.1 to show a rubric for assessing creativity, an attribute historically difficult to assess. The first column identifies the criteria and the header row explicates the quality standards by which the criteria are evaluated.

We also provide several rubrics in the introductions to the chapters of LATs that were created by faculty working with the Association of American Colleges and Universities (AAC&U). Many examples of rubrics are available online that you can use as models to develop your own, assignment-specific rubric.

Table 4.1 Rubric for Assessing Creativity

	Imitative	Predictable/Routine	Creative	Very Creative
Variety of Ideas	Few ideas; ideas are very obvious	Ideas are predictable and/or from the same or similar contexts or disciplines	Ideas represent important and appropriate concepts from different contexts or disciplines	Large number of important and appropriate ideas that span multiple contexts or disciplines
Variety of Sources	Created product draws on few sources, or sources are inappropriate or untrustworthy	Created product draws on a limited set of sources but sources are appropriate and trustworthy	Created product draws on multiple sources, including different texts, media, resource persons, or personal experiences	Created product draws on a wide variety of sources, including different texts, media, resource persons, or personal experiences
Combination of Ideas	Ideas are copied or restated from sources	Ideas are combined in ways that are derived from the thinking of others (for example, of the authors in sources consulted)	Ideas are combined in original ways to solve a problem, address an issue, or make something new	Ideas are combined in markedly original and surprising ways to solve a problem, address an issue, or make something new
Overall Novelty and Value	Created product does not serve its intended purpose (for example, solving a problem or addressing an issue)	Created product serves its intended purpose (for example, solving a problem or addressing an issue)	Created product is interesting, new, or helpful, making an original contribution for its intended purpose (for example, solving a problem or addressing an issue)	Created product is exceptionally interesting, new, or helpful and makes an original contribution

Adapted from Brookhart (2013)

4.2   Creating Student Self-Evaluation Forms

Self-evaluation encourages students to take stock of their efforts and assess their progress or achievement of learning outcomes. Embedded within self-evaluation is the concept of "reflection." Reflection helps students be more self-aware as they discover their learning processes and develop patterns of self-directed learning. A simple means of guiding student self-evaluation is to ask one or more questions correlated with the learning activity, such as

- On the following 5–1 rating scale, rate how successfully you believe you accomplished the activity's goal of helping you to connect course concepts to your daily life.
- Which of the following common misconceptions in this subject are you still unclear about?
- What was your most/least successful or meaningful aspect of this assignment and why?
- How did this activity challenge your assumptions?

Self-assessment can also be accomplished in a more comprehensive assignment, such as the one described for evaluating achievement at the course level in Exhibit 4.1, "Sample Self-Evaluation Assignment."

4.3   Creating Peer Evaluation Forms

Peer evaluation can be an integral part of the assessment process. In collaborative learning activities, peers have a firsthand view of what is going on and are therefore well positioned to identify each other's levels and degrees of competence. In addition to asking students to evaluate peers in terms of process, teachers are increasingly using peer evaluation for content as well (such as in calibrated peer review). To ensure that peer evaluation is effective, work with students to develop a rubric that includes evaluation criteria and standards, devote time to instructing the students on how to apply the rubric to their peers' work, and then ask students to rate their peers according to those criteria. A simple sample peer evaluation form is provided as Exhibit 4.2, "Sample Peer Evaluation Form for Oral Presentation."

Exhibit 4.1 Sample Self-Evaluation Assignment

The assignment consists of two parts, which are the first and last pieces of work students complete in the course:

First Assignment: Personal Goals Statement
The purpose of this paper is to help you think through why you are taking this particular course and how it fits in with your overall learning goals. Prepare a paper (at least 750 words) that identifies your personal goals for this course in specific and detailed terms. Include a description of how you plan to meet your goals that is specified in a weekly time schedule corresponding to the academic term. If it helps, you are welcome to set weekly goals and a time schedule.

Last Assignment: What Have You Learned from the Class?
Write a self-evaluation paper (at least 750 words) in which you analyze how well you met your personal goals for the course. If your goals changed, discuss how, and if unforeseen goals emerged, describe what they were. Conclude the paper by assigning yourself an overall grade based on your performance in the course.

Adapted from The Teaching Professor Blog (Weimer, http://www.facultyfocus.com/articles/teaching-professor-blog/student-self-assessment-a-sample-assignment/#sthash.olcOM8VP.dpuf) (Accessed 4.1.15)

Exhibit 4.2 Sample Peer Evaluation Form for Oral Presentation

Title of Presentation _____

Name of Presenter _____

Name of Evaluator _____

Needs Improvement = 1; Adequate = 2; Outstanding = 3

Component	Rating
Organization: The presentation was well-organized, with a clear introduction and conclusion and easy-to-follow sequenced material in between.	
Delivery: The presenter's posture, gestures, eye contact, and vocal expressiveness made the speaker appear polished and confident.	
Supporting Material: The examples were appropriate and established the presenter's credibility and authority on the topic.	
Central Message: The central message was compelling, clear, consistent, and memorable.	
Total	

4.4   Introducing the Activity

Stimulate interest by developing a creative introduction to the topic that piques curiosity and encourages thinking. You might, for example, consider beginning with the following:

- Personal anecdote
- Narrative account (i.e., a story)
- Historical event
- Thought-provoking dilemma
- Real-world example
- Practical application
- Probing question

You could introduce these personally in a lecture or storytelling format, through a video, showing a picture, bringing in a news clipping, or other. The goal is to capture students' attention by making the topic interesting to them.

4.5   Providing Students with Information They Need About the Learning Assessment

Students have a right to be informed and should be willing participants in the process, so we generally advise that you provide them with information about the reasons that you are undertaking the activity, the learning goals of the activity, and what your plans are for the data. If you are using the findings for the purposes of the scholarship of teaching and learning (for example, you intend to present or publish your findings), you will most likely need to go through the Internal Review Board (IRB) process and gain permission to proceed. As a part of this process, you will need to show that students have given their informed consent to the process.

We also recommend sharing information about your findings with the students. Providing them with information about their individual results, aggregated results, and also about what you learned from the assessment can be a powerful tool for learning. The exception to this suggestion is when you believe for whatever reason that the results could have stifling effects on the learning of individuals or the group. Here is a checklist of suggestions for information to include when you introduce the activity to ensure that students understand the task clearly (Johnson, Johnson, & Smith, 1998; University of Waterloo, n.d.):

- *Explain the activity.* Provide students with a basic overview so that students see "the big picture."
- *Clarify the objectives.* Tell students the purpose of the activity so that they can see its benefit. For example, relate the task to larger class goals or prior knowledge or suggest new concepts that will be addressed.
- *Outline the procedures.* Describe exactly what students are going to do in a step-by-step format in order to minimize or eliminate confusion during the activity itself.
- *Present examples if needed.* Provide a concrete example that illustrates the process or shows a model final product so that students get a clearer idea of what they need to do.
- *Set time limits.* Establish a time limit so that students can pace themselves. If the estimate is on the low side, students may work quickly and efficiently, and the time limit can always be extended if needed.
- *Provide the prompt.* Most often, prompts will come in the form of questions or problems, but they may also include short topics or statements for exploration or debate. It may be appropriate to include the prompt with the activity introduction.
- *Provide necessary materials, including handouts.* When implementing a LAT, you may want to provide materials such as directions, prompts, evaluation rubrics, worksheets, and so forth in a written handout to be distributed or posted online. Thus, depending upon the LAT, you may want to create materials that are given to students prior to beginning the activity. In each LAT, we provide suggestions for the kinds of materials you will want to create ahead of time. These vary depending on the particular LAT you are employing. Materials may include information about the assignment, such as a handout with information about the length and time frame. They may also include work materials for students such as flip chart paper and markers. Successful implementation of a LAT depends upon advance planning and material gathering.
- *Query the students for understanding and let students ask questions.* Asking students whether they have questions before they begin the activity will provide an opportunity to clarify any aspects of the activity that may still be confusing.

4.6 Facilitating the Learning Assessment

One challenge for those of us accustomed to traditional lecturing is knowing what we should be doing while students are working. We recognize that our role has shifted from deliverer of content to a facilitator of learning activities, but it can still be unclear what strategies we can employ to help provide supportive rather than directive supervision. Following are suggestions drawn from Johnson and Johnson (1984) and Silberman (1996, pp. 24–26):

- *Be available to clarify instruction, review procedures, and answer questions about the assignment.* Students may believe they understand the assignments and instructions but encounter confusion or change their minds when they begin work. Clarifying these points for students early on saves students wasting time or struggling with the wrong assignment.
- *Paraphrase or ask a question to clarify what a student has said.* Students sometimes state ideas in a way that confuses you and potentially other students. Paraphrasing what the student has contributed provides an opportunity for clarification and can be reinforcing for the student by demonstrating that his or her idea has been transmitted and understood and helping make it clearer for other students.
- *Compliment the student on an interesting or insightful comment.* Students need reinforcement, and complimenting a student can be a powerful motivator.
- *Elaborate on a student's statement or suggest a new perspective.* Stopping to share with the group a new perspective on an idea can help the students delve into deeper levels of thinking about a topic.
- *Energize by using humor or by asking for additional contributions.* This approach can be particularly helpful when students are struggling with complex material and have become frustrated. It can help students put things into perspective, and make class fun. However, humor can be more challenging to convey through some mediums, such as in online courses.
- *Disagree with a student comment, but be gentle.* Instructors are sometimes hesitant to correct students for fear of stifling their creativity and causing students to be more reluctant to speak the next time, but if you overhear misinformation, it is important to correct it. If done gently and tactfully, students will appreciate that they got the correct response. It is also important for them to recognize that there is a difference of opinion or another side to the issue. Pointed questions are also a good way to redirect the conversation.
- *If appropriate, pull together ideas by pointing out relationships.* Students do not have the same familiarity with the course concepts that instructors do. If students are struggling with making connections between ideas and information, remind them how the task they're performing relates to something they studied previously or to something current in the news.

4.7   Concluding the Activity

Close the activity by calling time. You can then review with the students the goals of the activity. For example, you might

- State the main points yourself ("Today we talked about . . . ")
- Ask a student to summarize the main points
- Ask all students to state or write down what they believe were the main takeaways of the activity

You may also want to preview the sessions to come. How does the learning assessment activity relate to what they will be doing next? Such a preview can spur students' interests and help students to connect the ideas within a larger context.

4.8 Timing the Phases

One of the key questions of implementation is how to time the various phases. It is a difficult question to answer because it depends upon the LAT you have chosen and how much of it you will do in class, but trying to determine a realistic timeline will allow you the highest chances of success. Following are some strategies for creating a realistic timeline:

- Plan some time to introduce the activity. Students may have more questions than you anticipate, so be prepared to be flexible.
- Estimate how much time each of the phases will take, then plan some extra time for each.
- Plan a few minutes at the end of class to answer any remaining questions and to sum up key points.
- Plan an extra activity or discussion question in case some students finish working faster than others. This is called a sponge or extension activity (Barkley et al., 2014).

As you prepare to implement the LAT, you may also find that creating an instructional script is a useful activity. In such a script, you would indicate the phases you will want to complete. In general, you will follow three broad phases: beginning, during, and ending. Next to each phase, you would indicate how much time you expect it will take. We offer Exhibit 4.3 as a

---

Exhibit 4.3 Sample Instructional Script for an Online Class

Beginning to End (1 Week)

Beginning: Posted for Full Week
- Announce the activity through a post to the course site.
- Explain the objectives of the activity, telling students the following:
  - How the activity should promote their achievement of the learning objective
  - Why you want to assess their learning on that objective
  - How you intend to use the results
- Ask whether students have questions in a class discussion forum.

Middle (5 Full Days)
- Ask students to begin work.
- If work is open (such as in a Discussion Forum), observe student progress as they work.
- Answer student questions as appropriate.
- Consider prompting students when the end of the activity is approaching.

During the In-Class Activity (15 minutes)
- Ask students to begin work.
- Observe student progress as they work.
- Answer student questions as appropriate.
- Prompt students as appropriate (e.g., if there is a time limit, let them know when the end of the activity is approaching).
- If the activity takes students more than one class session to complete, check in with students on a regular basis.

Ending (2 Full Days)
- Call time (for example, by closing submission capability or locking the Discussion Forum), which is equivalent of collecting the Learning Artifact.
- If appropriate, facilitate a discussion of the activity.

sample instructional script for an online class, and the concept can be applied to other kinds of instructional formats such as traditional and flipped classes.

Of course effective instruction requires flexibility and adapting to the class's needs rather than rigidly remaining true to a script, but a script can be a helpful guideline when organizing the timing required for implementing a learning assessment technique.

4.9 Collecting the Learning Artifacts

When social science research first emerged as a field of inquiry, the researcher was viewed as separate and independent from the research. He or she maintained an objective distance from the researched. Over time that view of research has changed as people realized that the very act of conducting the research modified the outcomes of the research. Now much social research happens while the researcher is an active participant in the research. There are disadvantages to this, such as losing sight of the whole situation due to being too caught up the details. There are also advantages, in that those who are closely involved with what is being researched are best able to understand nuances in the data that an external observer might miss (Savin-Baden & Major, 2013). A teacher's collection of information for assessment purposes necessarily employs this latter model. That is, the teacher is an integral part of the research as well as the collector of evidence of whether students have learned.

When you gather evidence on student learning, it is most likely that you will be the primary person to collect the evidence. However, you may want to involve others in some part of the process as well. You may want individuals external to your class to review the results, such as other disciplinary experts or work force practitioners. You may have teaching assistants who can help provide the same function. These individuals can offer an outsider perspective to your insider view of the evidence, which may help you make better meaning of the data. You may also want students to participate in self-evaluation or in evaluating the work of their peers, which in turn can inform the teaching and learning phase of the activity, as it also helps them develop meta-learning skills. Who you select to collaborate in data collection will depend largely on your goals for the assessment as well as your own, unique professional circumstances.

4.10 Managing the Learning Artifacts

The next question you are faced with is what to *do* with the Learning Artifacts. This is an important question because

- Properly storing the Learning Artifacts is essential to safeguard the time and investment you have made in the assessment.
- You may need to go back to the data to provide evidence of your findings.
- Students may ultimately wish to claim their work.

Learning Artifacts, like any data, then, should be protected from physical damage or loss. The best way to accomplish this is to ensure that you are the primary person managing the source material and that you limit access to it. If you plan to publish or present findings from your assessment, you should take additional care to ensure student privacy and anonymity (unless you have designated otherwise in your research). Also, if you are planning to collect similar information from students over time, you should record the date, course, and section numbers on the artifacts. Consult your institution's policies for how long you need to keep the artifacts.

CHAPTER 5

Analyzing and Reporting What Students Have Learned

Most teachers have developed systems for communicating their evaluation of individual student work to their students, but few faculty have experience analyzing and sharing data about student learning in ways that are acceptable as evidence to external stakeholders. Finding out what students have learned and then sharing this information with others requires careful preparation and attention to details. There are many questions to consider, and the answers to the questions depend on your unique circumstances. In this section, we offer guidance on the following topics:

5.1   Identifying Whose Learning You Are Gauging
5.2   Considering Independent and Collaborative Data Analysis
5.3   Scoring Individual Learning Artifacts
5.4   Scoring Group Artifacts
5.5   Determining the Method of Data Analysis
5.6   Using Quantitative Data Analysis
5.7   Using Qualitative Data Analysis
5.8   Displaying Data and Findings
5.9   Interpreting Results
5.10   Writing Up the Results of the Assessment

5.1   Identifying Whose Learning You Are Gauging

We propose that course-level assessment begins with the individual student. When we assess an individual for formative reasons, we can use that information to refer students who need it to additional resources. We also can use the information to build homogenous or heterogeneous work groups. When we assess an individual for summative reasons, we can create progress reports and assign grades. While assessment typically begins with the individual, faculty and stakeholders usually want to know how well all the students within a particular course or class section are doing in meeting intended learning outcomes. This requires aggregating individual results. Such information can be used for a host of reasons, such as targeting instruction to the level of the whole class, reporting information about learning progress and learning outcomes to stakeholders, or engaging in the scholarship of teaching and learning.

5.2 Considering Independent and Collaborative Data Analysis

While many institutions accept an individual teacher's independent analysis of assessment data, others believe that external review is essential for ensuring validity or reliability. Thus you may want to consider collaborating with colleagues to analyze the data you collect. For example, you may ask faculty members in the same department or discipline along with teachers outside of the discipline to review a randomly selected sample of Learning Artifacts produced by students from one of the LATs you implemented in your course.

5.3 Scoring Individual Learning Artifacts

Most college teachers have spent considerable time scoring and analyzing student work, and are therefore experienced using one or more of the following systems:

1. **Accuracy Scoring**—Raw scores are provided that consist of determinations of correct and incorrect responses to questions; this is most often done with quantitative data.
2. **Narrative Scoring**—In this form of scoring, assessors provide written narrative that responds to specific facets of the work they are considering; this is most often done with qualitative data.
3. **Criterion/Rubric Scoring**—Rubric scores are templates that the assessor(s) use to score a student Learning Artifact, such as a paper or presentation, numerically based on how well it demonstrates certain attributes. Rubric scoring involves using a quantitative approach to assess qualitative data. Please see Chapter 4 for more discussion on rubrics and Table 4.1 for an example of a rubric developed to assess creativity.

These forms of scoring may be transformed into grades. Grades may involve comparison to other students, or they may involve comparison to an absolute standard. Please see Chapter 2, Section 2.2 for a discussion on how learning assessment is different from grading, but the essential distinction between grades and assessment is that grades are given for individual students and are internal to a specific class section, while assessment is focused on evaluating the achievement of all students enrolled in the course (and sometimes all sections of a course) and the data is intended to be shared primarily with external stakeholders. That said, there is considerable overlap and most teachers assess to accomplish both purposes.

5.4 Scoring Group Artifacts

While college teachers are familiar with grading individual Learning Artifacts, few of us have experience aggregating individual results in order to assess learning at the group level. To assess at the group level, a group develops an individual Learning Artifact. Thus the Learning Artifact is an individual unit for analysis, but it is produced by the group. Alternately, we can look at all of the individual scores together and search for patterns of information across them, in this way aggregating individual results to assess the performance of the group. Each LAT provides guidance on how to score and analyze both individual and aggregated data.

5.5   Determining the Method of Data Analysis

There are two broad categories of Learning Artifacts that we have classified according to the data they produce: quantitative and qualitative. Learning Artifacts that generate quantitative data are those that provide numeric information that may be counted. Tests, which may be graded for a numeric score such as an average, for example, are a form of quantitative assessment because the data they generate typically are described in quantities. Alternatively, the artifacts may comprise qualitative data, which is narrative or textual information. Qualitative information provides a rich, thick set of data that typically can be examined from multiple perspectives. Portfolios, for example, provide qualitative information that teachers can assess for the depth of student understanding of specific content or the development of specialized skills such as writing or presentation. Qualitative data can also be assessed using qualitative methods, in other words the data are described in terms of qualities. Both forms of data offer several possibilities for aggregating and analyzing data.

5.6   Using Quantitative Data Analysis

Data collected during assessment of student learning may be quantitative, which means that they come in the form of numbers. Test and quiz scores are a form of quantitative data, as are rubric evaluations, and thus quantitative analysis is the most appropriate form. The following are forms of quantitative data analysis.

Simple Counts and Tallies: Counts and tallies are the simple sums or totals of several numbers together. A faculty member, for example, might tally the number of students who turned in homework as follows:

35 (out of 40) students turned in homework.

Descriptive Statistics: The term *statistics* indicates a set of methods and rules for organizing and interpreting observations of quantitative data. The term *descriptive statistics* refers to what researchers use to describe sets of numbers, such as student test scores. For example, student quiz scores might include the following:

79, 93, 87, 72, 97, 81, 93, 80, 77, 72, 69, 67, 85, 91, 89, 80, 84, 87, 77, 72

Some statistical operations are common approaches for describing a data set:

Frequency—The number of times that the number/score appears. The frequency for scoring a 72 in the above list is 3.

Percentage—The proportion of students in the data set who received a given score. In the example, 15% of the students achieved a score of 72.

Mean—The sum of all the scores divided by the count, or the average score in a frequency distribution. In the example, 81.6 is the mean.

Median—The numeric score in the middle of frequency distribution that separates the higher half of the ordered data from the lower half. If the number of scores is even, the median is the average of the two center values. If it is odd, the center value is the median. In the example, the median score is 80.5.

Mode—The score that occurs most frequently in the data set. In the example, the mode is 72.

Range—The difference between the highest and lowest score in the data set. It is the maximum score – the minimum score. In the example, the range is 30.

Quartile—A division of the ordered data set into higher and lower halves. In the example above, the upper quartile is 88.5, the median is 80.5, and the lower is 73.25

Standard Deviation—The amount that scores vary from the mean. It is the square root of the variance. In the example, the standard deviation is 8.641, indicating that the difference between the scores and mean is approximately 9 points on average. Higher standard deviations indicate that the scores are more different from one another and from the mean than lower standard deviations.

The following URL links to a descriptive statistic calculator that automatically performs several statistical calculations of an entered data set, including frequency, mean, median, mode, quartiles, and standard deviation. http://www.calculatorsoup.com/calculators/statistics /descriptivestatistics.php

Inferential statistics are used to make inferences about a population of study participants based upon a sample of the participants. Inferential statistics are not used as frequently as descriptive statistics in course-level assessment, the latter of which typically is focused on describing the total population. At times, however, inferential statistics can have use in course-level assessment. The operation we see used most frequently in assessment efforts is correlation, which indicates the relationship between two or more variables (for example, the relationship between quiz scores and unit exams).

5.7 Using Qualitative Data Analysis

Data collected during assessment of student learning may be qualitative. These data tend to be associated with words or narrative, such as are present in student essays and papers as well as artistic representations, which also are a form of qualitative data. Key word and thematic assessment of student artifacts are a way to understand these data.

Key Word Analysis

The term *key word analysis* means what it sounds like it should mean. The analytic process involves examining words that have some sort of meaning in the larger context of the data. Key word analysis then is a way of summarizing a narrative data set, such as a set of essays.

Savin-Baden and Major (2013) and Bernard and Ryan (2010) suggest several ways to analyze key words, including the following:

1. *Frequent repetition of terms.* Noting words or synonyms that people frequently use.
2. *Unusual use of terms.* Noting use of words in an unusual way, which may reflect local usage. Patton (1990, p. 306, 393–400) calls these terms "indigenous categories" and contrasts them with "analyst-constructed typologies."
3. *Words used in context (key-words-in-context).* Noting key words and the words immediately surrounding it, then sorting phrases into groups with similar meaning.

We provide an example of key word analysis as follows:

Question:
In a single paragraph, describe the character Hamlet.

Student response:
Hamlet is the primary character in Shakespeare's play, *Hamlet*. Hamlet is young, smart, and full of promise. Hamlet's father has been murdered, and his Uncle has become King. Hamlet is faced with indecision and questions the unthinkable: whether his father has been murdered by his uncle. He is contemplating suicide. His angst is characterized in his famous soliloquy that begins with the line "To be, or not to be." He spends the entire play contemplating this question, and it nearly drives him mad.

While the sample text is small, it is still possible to see several key word patterns, as follows:

Frequent repetition: Hamlet, contemplating, father, murdered, play, uncle.
Unusual terms: angst, soliloquy.
Words in context: "drives him mad."

There are keyword density calculators, such as the following that can be helpful to a faculty who wants to assess for keywords http://darylkinsman.ca/tools/wordfreq.shtml

Thematic Analysis

Thematic analysis is a method of identifying, analyzing, and reporting patterns in the data (Braun & Clarke, 2006). Thematic analysis at a fundamental level is "the process of recovering the theme or themes that are embodied and dramatized in the evolving meanings and imagery of the work" (Van Manen, 1990, p. 78). This approach to analyzing a qualitative data set provides a general sense of the information through repeated reading and manipulation of the data. Braun and Clarke (2006) recommend doing the following when conducting thematic analysis:

1. Familiarize yourself with your data
2. Generate initial codes
3. Search for themes
4. Review themes
5. Define and name themes
6. Produce the report

Exhibit 5.1 Example of Thematically Coded Text

Hamlet is the primary character in Shakespeare's play, *Hamlet*. Hamlet is young, smart, and full of promise. Hamlet's father has been murdered, and his Uncle has become King. Hamlet is faced with **indecision** and **questions** the **unthinkable**: **whether** his father has been murdered by his uncle. He is **contemplating** suicide. His angst is characterized in his famous soliloquy that begins with the line **"To be, or not to be."** He spends the entire play **contemplating** this **question**, and it nearly drives him mad.

Analysis: The key phrases that seem to hold meaning indicate that the student understands at a basic level that Hamlet is thinking deeply, he questions his sanity, and he is indecisive.

It is through the process of immersion in data and looking at connections and interconnections between codes, concepts, and themes that an "aha" moment happens, and it happens at a somewhat intuitive level. Exhibit 5.1 shows an example of thematically coded text.

Cross-Case Comparisons

Once you have identified key words or themes, you can begin the process of making meaning across cases. By case, in this instance, we mean the case of the individual student product, whether a paper, video, performance, or other. Moving from understanding what is in one paper to identifying issues and themes across many papers is critical to understanding how the class performed as a whole. This level of understanding can be achieved through a cross case comparison. That is, once the individual case has been examined, the next step is to look across cases. Such analysis may be done by examining which words or themes are similar across cases, and thus grouping them together, or different across cases, and thus not grouping them. In our case of Hamlet, if several cases had "contemplating" or something similar (contemplative, contemplate, and so forth), then that would be considered a cross-case theme. If only one student identified "questioning," then that would be an outlier (which may still be worth reporting, but as an outlier, rather than a cross-case theme).

5.8 Displaying Data and Findings

There are many forms of quantitative and qualitative data display.

Quantitative Data Display

Quantitative data display is used to illustrate student achievement and performance at a glance. The key to effective quantitative data display is to keep it simple and present the information in the way that best represents student work.

Spreadsheet Sorted Display

A spreadsheet sorted display presents a full data set in spreadsheet format. To create a sorted display, you simply enter all the data values into a spreadsheet, such as Excel. This form of display typically is used to show data sorted by category of interest, such as tallies or total scores from quizzes over time, which you highlight by sorting the spreadsheet according to that column of data. A sorted display can be particularly useful for small classes, where data may be viewed at a glance.

Numeric Table

A numeric table is a display used to present summaries of data (Table 5.1). This kind of table is often issued to display information generated through descriptive statistical analysis, such as frequency, mean, median, and mode (Table 5.2). A numeric table, then, is good for demonstrating how students performed overall, for example on a given test or quiz. It is easy to create tables in most word processors, like Word or Pages.

Pie Chart

A pie chart is a graph in which a full circle is divided into sections (Figure 5.1). Pie charts typically are used to show the parts that make up a whole and may be used for comparing the

Table 5.1 Example of Frequency Table

Score	Frequency	Percentage
97	1	5
93	2	10
91	1	5
89	1	5
87	2	10
85	1	5
84	1	5
81	1	5
80	2	10
79	1	5
77	2	10
72	3	15
69	1	5
67	1	5
	20	100

Table 5.2 Table with Summary Data

Mean	71.95
Median	75
Mode	88, 75, 66
Range	63
Standard Deviation	16.42

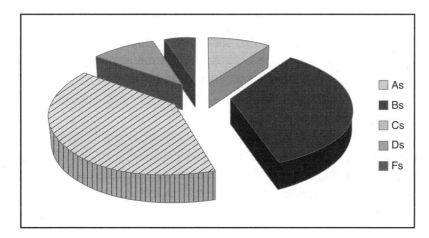

Figure 5.1 Example of Pie Chart

size of relative parts. They are useful for comparing groups of students to student performance as a whole. Most word processors have tools for creating quick graphs and charts.

Bar or Column Graph

A bar or column graph is a diagram using rectangular bars; with bar graphs, the bars are horizontal, but with column graphs, they are vertical (Figure 5.2). This form of data display is used to show numerical values of variables by the height or length of bars of equal width. It can

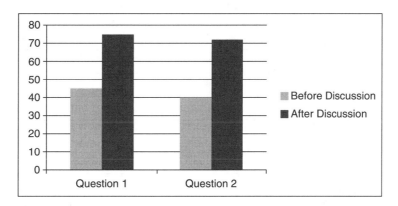

Figure 5.2 Example of Column Graph

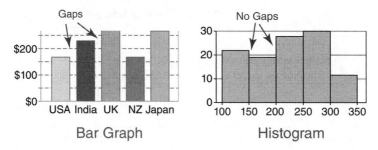

Figure 5.3 Example of Bar Graph and Histogram

be used to demonstrate descriptive statistics that benefit from comparison, for example the number of students receiving a particular grade on a given assignment or test. Most word processors have tools for creating bar graphs quickly.

Histogram

A histogram is a diagram consisting of bars that are grouped into ranges. This form of data display may be used to present ranges in a given value, such as percentiles (Figure 5.3). It may be used, for example, to display the number of students in each quartile.

Line Graph

A line graph shows discrete data points that are connected by lines (Figure 5.4). This form of data display is used to document differences between the different points. For example, it may be used to show changes between test scores over time.

Qualitative Data Display

Qualitative data display is used to summarize what can be voluminous information into a useable form for the intended audience. As with quantitative data display, the key to being effective is contingent on using the best format to get your message across in the most

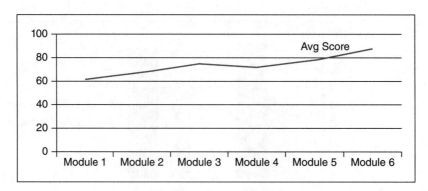

Figure 5.4 Example of Line Graph

parsimonious way. There are several different approaches that work well for qualitative data display.

Narrative Table

This form of data display is tabular. A table is used to summarize the qualitative information so that readers can understand it at a glance. This display approach typically is used to cross two or more dimensions, variables, or concepts of relevance to the topic of interest. Narrative tables may be used to display the results of key word analysis (Table 5.3), as from our earlier example.

A narrative table also might be used to display your direct observation of tasks that students completed during a specific activity, such as the observation of a problem-solving exercise shown in Table 5.4.

A table can be a useful way to record your scoring and sizing up of student achievements (Table 5.5).

Word Cloud

A word cloud is an image composed of words from a selection of text. It typically is used to visually display the frequency and distribution of words. A few free and useful tools exist for creating word clouds, including Wordle (www.wordle.com) and Tagxedo (www.tagxedo.com).

Table 5.3 Example of Table with Key Word Analysis

Key Word Analysis of Student Responses on *Hamlet* quiz:	
Frequent repetition:	Hamlet, contemplating, father, murdered, play, uncle
Unusual terms:	angst, soliloquy
Words in context:	"drives him mad"

Table 5.4 Example of Narrative Table

Phase	Observed Actions
1: Research design	Defined the case using a rupture or turning point Reviewed the literature to outline potential research directions

2: Data management	Gathered data from a variety of sources
	    Ordered data chronologically
	    Read over data for emergent themes and issues

3: Data analysis	Created structured questions Wrote the case study
4: Evaluation	Addressed theoretical conclusions of the case Developed practical implications and recommendations

Table 5.5 Table Summarizing Student Achievements

Noteworthy achievements	75% of students scored a B or higher on their final essay examination.
Unexpected findings	Students demonstrated noteworthy gains in their understanding of the significance of the field to society as a whole.
Meaningful differences	Students were able to answer the first and third questions handily. They struggled more with the second question.

Figure 5.5 Example of Word Cloud

Source: Image created at Wordle.com

This tool can be a useful way to display visual representations of student Learning Artifacts (for example, essays) or to highlight key words from your narrative scoring of student works (Figure 5.5).

Boxed Display

A boxed display presents a quotation from a selection of text that is set off in a boxed and possibly shaded area. This form of data display may be used to highlight a specific narrative that you found important and to frame it in a box. Doing so can help bolster the credibility of your scoring. For example, you might indicate in your assessment of student blogs about technology and students that students were able to determine that technology could be a distraction for them. You might use a quote like the following to support your claim.

Quotation from student paper

    Obviously technology can distract students from studying, but there have always •
been distractions. Freshmen are at the stage where they are becoming adults, and that
includes learning to take responsibility for their own actions. I think one of the
challenges for undergraduates is to figure out how to use technology to assist them in
learning rather than distract them. Actually, undergrads are probably not even thinking
about that, so perhaps I should say the challenge is for instructors to get students to use
technology productively.

Flow Chart

A flow chart is a diagram of a sequence of actions or events. It is used to illustrate directional flow
(Figure 5.6).

Modified Venn Diagram

A modified Venn diagram is used to display logical sets through overlapping circles (Figure 5.7).
It may be used to indicate shared or overlapping aspects of a concept, a category, or a process.

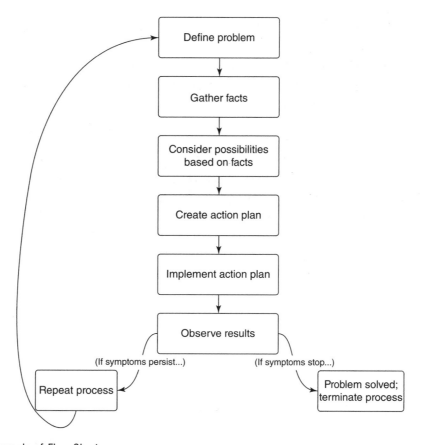

Figure 5.6 Example of Flow Chart

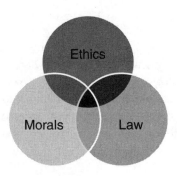

Figure 5.7 Example of Modified Venn Diagram

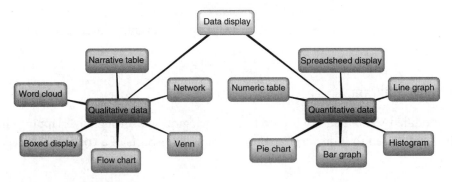

Figure 5.8 Example of Network Diagram

Instructors can use it for demonstrating key themes they identify through their assessments of student Learning Artifacts. They might also use a Venn to document student performance in different assessment measures.

Network

A network is an arrangement of intersecting horizontal and vertical lines (Figure 5.8). Nodes are connected by ties to illustrate connections between ideas or themes, such as may be generated through thematic analysis of student Learning Artifacts. This form of data display may be used to depict relationships between themes and subthemes or categories and subcategories. There are several online tools that can help instructors create such networks, including Popplet (www .popplet.com) and bubbl.us.

5.9   Interpreting Results

At this phase of the process, you are confronted with an unruly world of tallies and counts, frequencies and percentages, tables and graphs. It is your job to determine what everything *means.* This occurs through the process of interpretation. We recommend that you begin your interpretation by trying to get a sense of the big picture. Look at your questions: Has the learning outcome been met? To what extent has it been met? Has there been change over time? Do you see patterns of strength or weakness? Do the results match your expectations or were there surprises? Considering questions such as these will allow you to focus on the relevant information. The main issues to consider when interpreting information is what you want to know, what your efforts can tell you, and ultimately what they mean. The way you go about it depends on what you plan to do with the information and with whom you will share it.

5.10 Writing Up the Results of the Assessment

You may want to share your assessment efforts with others. This often means putting the results into written form and reporting them to invested stakeholders, whether students, department chairs, tenure review committees, assessment committees, or interested colleagues at other institutions. How you write about the results of the assessment depends largely upon the audience. There are some common elements, however, that cross the different audiences, and faculty who are writing about the results of their assessment efforts may wish to consider presenting the case and then constructing an overarching matrix that summarizes the plans for making use of the data.

Case Presentation

Recording and presenting information about the class itself is an important part of the process. This aspect of writing can help you ensure that data are not being decontextualized but rather are situated within the specific bounded case of a given classroom. The following elements can be useful to include in a discussion of the "case":

Description of the class: The course number and section, course description from the course catalog, information about the subject matter.

Statement of learning goals, outcomes, and objectives: Information about what students should know and be able to do by the end of the course.

Description of students: The level of students taking the course, the general demographic characteristics of the students, and any other noteworthy characteristics.

Description of perceived challenges for students meeting goals: What issues might present difficulty for students completing the course goals (e.g., motivation for taking a required course, older students who work full time, lack of preparation, level of difficulty of the course).

Description of LAT to help meet goals (along with why the LAT was chosen): A full description of the LAT, including the subject prompt, the learning activity, and the Learning Artifact, and a rationale for why you believe it can help students achieve the learning outcomes.

In the examples we present within the different LATs, we follow this general format.

The Learning Assessment Technique Matrix

Whether writing for yourself or others, it can be useful to grapple with the broad picture of the assessment you have undertaken. In particular, you may want to consider what you did, why you

Table 5.6 Example of Assessment Matrix

Assessment Matrix: Entry/Exit Tickets						
Student Learning Outcomes	**LAT**	**Subject/ Content Prompt**	**Intentional Active Learning Activity**	**Learning Artifact**	**Findings and Interpretations**	**Actions to Be Taken**
Students will be able to list the causes of the Cold War	Entry ticket	Read the specified assignment prior to coming to class	Answer a problem related to the assignment	The ticket students turn in at the start of class	Only 30% of tickets turned in were accurate causes of the Cold War; students are not reading or are not reading well	Implemented Guided Reading Notes (LATs) to help students improve their reading skills

did it, and what it all means. You may also want to consider what you plan to do about what you have learned. Finally, since the purpose of LATs is to improve student learning, we recommend that you "close the loop" by identifying what changes you intend to make based on assessment results. (We include guidance on this aspect in Chapter 6, Closing the Loop.) We suggest using something such as the following assessment matrix to summarize your processes and plans for improvement (Table 5.6).

Closing the Loop

The primary goal of learning assessment is to improve student learning, thus the last step in the LAT Cycle is designed to support your efforts to identify the changes you will make to accomplish that. If the data you gathered and analyzed indicate that the learning outcome has been met, celebrate. After you have reveled in the success of your teaching strategies and the learning accomplishments of the students, try to identify ways to improve. If the data you gather is more disappointing, don't be discouraged—just try to determine what you might change to improve results. In this section, we use the structure of the LAT Cycle as an organizing framework to guide you to reflect on the data to determine if adjustments could and should be made at different stages. Making the changes restarts the process that leads to continuous improvement.

6.1   Modifying Your Learning Goals, Objectives, and Outcomes
6.2   Adjusting Your Purpose for Assessing Learning
6.3   Selecting a Different LAT
6.4   Altering an Aspect of Implementation
6.5   Changing the Way You Analyze or Report Findings

6.1 Modifying Your Learning Goals, Objectives, and Outcomes

The LAT Assessment Cycle begins with clarifying what you want students to learn, so depending upon assessment results, you might consider any of the following:

Do you need to adjust the goal? If the targeted goal has been met, then you may want to turn your attention to focusing on a new goal. You might also consider expanding your goals to correlate better with externally mandated or recommended goals, such as departmental learning goals or institutional core competencies. Or you may want to consider implementing strategies that involve students in identifying learning goals.

Would it help to modify your objectives? Objectives translate goals into something tangible that students do, such as "write" or "solve" or "identify" in order to provide you with something observable that can be measured and compared. You may find that fine-tuning or changing your objectives can help improve either student learning or your assessment efforts.

Should your learning outcome statement be tightened or loosened? Your outcomes are the explicit statements that describe the knowledge, skills, abilities, and attitudes that you want students to be able to demonstrate at the end (or as a result) of his or her experience in your course that shows you that they have achieved your learning goals. Crafting a good outcome statement is difficult, and you may find that you need to amend the language so that it better points to something that is measurable. Alternately, you may find that in your attempts to craft a crisply defined outcome statement, you ended up focusing on low-level cognitive skills or less complex, nuanced learning and need to change the language in ways that can capture the depth and transformative nature of the learning you want your students to experience.

6.2 Adjusting Your Purpose for Assessing Learning

Would it be useful to modify or expand upon your purpose for assessing? If you have been assessing primarily for one purpose (such as to discover the current status of student knowledge and understanding in order to determine appropriate starting points), you may want to consider adopting another purpose (such as determining if there is change in knowledge or skills over time). Or if you are finding that the LAT you implemented made significant improvements in learning, you might want to consider writing up results to demonstrate effective teaching as part of your promotion dossier, or to share results in an article or conference presentation related to the Scholarship of Teaching and Learning.

Should you change your research question? For example, if your question focused on determining to what extent learning has been successful for that course, you may want to now start doing trend analysis by gathering results in subsequent academic terms, or compare results from your course to those from similar courses in the department.

6.3 Selecting a Different LAT

Would it be worthwhile to experiment with a new LAT? Or a different instructional context? Since each chapter contains multiple LATs correlated to that dimension of the Significant Learning Taxonomy, you may want to consider trying one of the other LATs to see if your results change. Or if you implemented the LAT in one instructional context (such as a traditional onsite class), you may want to see what would happen if you transferred the LAT to a new instructional context, such as a flipped or online class.

Have you considered making changes in various elements? For example, you may want to change products and have students make presentations rather than submit a written paper. Or you may want to choose a LAT that is better suited to collaborative learning. Alternately, you might consider clustering LATs together to create a sequence that aims for deeper, more comprehensive learning.

6.4 Altering an Aspect of Implementation

Could changes in preparatory materials help? Many of the LATs suggest or require creating preparatory materials such as hand-outs or rubrics. Perhaps changes can be made to make the materials more detailed, clearer, or simpler.

Might you introduce the activity in a way that is more engaging? Perhaps modifying your introduction to be more thought-provoking or to include a compelling, real-world example would better pique student interest.

Would it help to change any of the steps in the activity? Perhaps you need to make adjustments in the sequencing of the steps, or increase opportunities for time on task. If you have identified a frequent learning problem associated with one step, you might consider creating additional modules to target these learning obstacles.

Are there ways that you could make the timing of the phases more efficient? If the activity is taking up more class time than you prefer, are there ways to reduce the time by having students read hand-outs in preparation for class? Or do you need to set up more scaffolding for larger projects and establish a system for checking in on students on a more frequent basis?

6.5   Changing the Way You Analyze or Report Findings

Might you be more effective using a different type of data analysis? Consider reviewing the various data analysis methods described in Chapter 5 on analysis and reporting to see if changes in your approach might provide you with more relevant information. For example, if you have been using quantitative approaches, you may find that replacing these with a qualitative approach allows you to look at students' learning in more depth and detail. Conversely, if your approach was qualitative, you may want to consider adopting some quantitative methods to provide you with the kind of statistics many external stakeholders favor.

Could your results be displayed in a more compelling or advantageous manner? There are many ways to display data, and a review of Chapter 5 on analysis and reporting might suggest an alternative and more persuasive way to show results.

Would it be effective to involve students? Asking students to look at the results and suggest ways that they think would help them learn better might offer you some effective ideas for improvement. Or you might find that you want to involve students in doing peer evaluation or to take on a stronger role in self-evaluation.

PART TWO

LEARNING ASSESSMENT TECHNIQUES

CHAPTER 7

Teaching and Assessing for the Foundational Knowledge Domain

The techniques in this chapter focus on ways to teach and assess learning of the facts, principles, and ideas that comprise your course's foundational knowledge. This type of knowledge is called "foundational" because it provides the base layer of support for the other kinds of learning. One way to look at it is that it is the foundation upon which a building may be built; without it, the structure has no support and is likely to collapse. Another way is that like the clay a sculptor manipulates to construct a work of art, foundational knowledge is the information and ideas that a learner manipulates when solving problems or thinking critically. Although acquiring some basic foundational knowledge may be required to start the learning process, acquisition is never finished since foundational knowledge is continually refined, added to, and deepened as a learner progresses from novice to expert. Foundational knowledge, therefore, is an important component to teach and assess in advanced courses as well as introductory courses.

Clarifying Learning Goals Related to Foundational Knowledge

Most faculty believe that it is important to help students understand the basic facts, principles, and concepts of the discipline, but the challenge we face today is how much of it do students *really* need to remember? Given the abundance of information, the rapidity with which it changes, and the almost instant access to it through the Internet, retention of large amounts of information may be an impossible and perhaps unwise learning goal. Try to home in on what is really important for students to remember by identifying the essential, enduring understandings that you want to anchor the course. Fink offers two questions for formulating learning goals a related to foundational knowledge (2013, p. 83):

- What key information (facts, terms, concepts, relationships . . .) is important for students to understand and remember in the future?
- What key ideas or perspectives are important for students to understand in this course?

- What important "doing" outcomes do we want (such as those related to the Application domain), and then ask ourselves, "What would students need to *know* to do these tasks?"

Identifying Learning Outcomes for Foundational Knowledge

The two learner processes that underlie the acquisition and development of foundational knowledge are "remember" and "understand." Although most of us feel comfortable that we know what these two terms mean, it is helpful to define them in more specific language when we are crafting learning objectives and outcomes so that we are able to identify observable behavior that can be assessed. "Remembering" refers to a learner's ability to retrieve relevant knowledge from long-term memory, but it can be broken down into two assessable subprocesses: recognize and recall. Recognizing is easier than recall because the brain receives prompts that help in bringing it from memory to current consciousness. "Understand" refers to a learner's ability to grasp or construct meaning of something. In Table 7.1, we offer examples of learning processes and outcomes for Foundational Learning.

Table 7.1 Examples of Learning Processes and Outcomes for Foundational Knowledge

General Definition: The learner can retrieve relevant knowledge from long-term memory and construct meaning from instructional messages, including oral, written, and graphic communication.			
Learner Process	**Additional Terms**	**Definition**	**Sample Course Learning Outcome** *By the end of this course, a successful learner will be able to . . .*
Recognize	Identify	Locate relevant knowledge in long-term memory that is consistent with presented material.	. . . recognize typical forms of biases in a statistical analysis such as potential undercoverage, nonresponse, question wording, and response bias.
Recall	Retrieve	Retrieve relevant knowledge from long-term memory.	. . . recall the main stylistic categories (for example, prehistoric, medieval) of major works of art in world civilization.
Describe	List		. . . list the 5 major theories or perspectives in psychology.
Interpret	Clarify, paraphrase, represent, translate	Change from one form of representation to another (e.g., from verbal to numerical).	. . . paraphrase important speeches and documents from the Civil War period in U.S. history.
Exemplify	Illustrate, instantiate	Find a specific example or illustration of a concept or principle.	. . . identify the correct period of compositional style upon listening to a representative example of music not studied in class.
Summarize	Generalize	Abstract a general theme or major points.	. . . summarize the purposes of various subroutines in a specified computer program.
Infer	Conclude, extrapolate, interpolate, predict	Draw a logical conclusion from presented information.	. . . extrapolate the relationship expressed as an equation that represents several observations of values for two variables.
Explain	Describe, construct models	Construct a cause-and-effect model of a system.	. . . draw a diagram showing orders of magnitude, that is, what exists at different levels or scales, in relation to other objects.

Sources: Anderson and Krathwohl (2001), pp. 66–72; Fink (2013), pp. 85–86

Aligning Course Level Foundational Knowledge Learning Outcomes with Institutional Learning Goals

Today's campus assessment initiatives typically require faculty to align their course learning outcomes with broader institutional learning goals. Institutional learning goals related to foundational knowledge are usually stated in broad terms in documents such as guidelines for course inclusion in the General Education pattern or at the Department/Program level, as is shown in Table 7.2.

Assessing Achievement of Foundational Knowledge Learning Outcomes

Students must learn the facts, principles, and ideas that comprise our discipline's foundational knowledge *accurately* if they are going to be able to manipulate that knowledge effectively in higher-order tasks. One cannot think Bach lived after Mozart, velocity is another word for speed, or Shakespeare wrote *A Tale of Two Cities* and engage very meaningfully in higher-order tasks that apply this information. Ensuring students have a solid and accurate grasp of foundational knowledge that they can retrieve when needed is one of our fundamental responsibilities as teachers. Therefore, unlike the subjective, open-ended prompts that address higher-order tasks like application or integration, prompts to assess foundational knowledge are generally objective and closed-ended. Table 7.3 provides examples of assessment formats and sample prompts for the learner processes associated with the acquisition of foundational knowledge.

Table 7.2 Examples of Institution Level Learning Outcomes in Foundational Knowledge

General Education/Social Sciences Area Requirement	Courses meeting the GE requirement in Social and Behavior Sciences must ensure students can demonstrate knowledge and understanding of the interactions of people as members of societies, cultures, and social subgroups.
Biology Department	Upon completion of the core curriculum, students will be able to define and explain major concepts in the biological sciences.

Sources: Composite

Table 7.3 Formats and Sample Prompts for Assessing Foundational Knowledge

Learner Process	Assessment Formats	Format Description	Sample Assessment Prompts
Recognize	Verification	Learners decide whether information is correct or not.	Eukaryotic microorganisms lack membrane-bound organelles. True or False?
	Matching	Learners choose corresponding items from two lists.	Match the artist's name in Column A with the names of paintings in Column B.
	Forced Choice	Learners choose correct or best of several answers.	Which of the following colonial leaders was responsible for the call, "Join or Die?" John Adams, George Whitefield, or Benjamin Franklin?
Recall	Low Cue	No clues or related information provided.	What is the theory of phlogiston?
	High Cue	Clues and related information provided.	Ernest Rutherford at the University of Manchester discovered the internal structure of the _____ and the existence of the proton.

(*continued*)

Table 7.3   (*Continued*)

Learner Process	Assessment Formats	Format Description	Sample Assessment Prompts
Interpret	Constructed Response	Learners supply an answer.	Write an equation that corresponds to the following statement, using T for Total Cost and P for Pounds. "The total cost of mailing a package is $2.00 for the first pound plus $1.50 for each additional pound."
	Selected Response	Learners choose an answer.	Which of the following equations corresponds to the statement, where T stands for total cost and P for number of pounds? "The total cost of mailing a package is $2.00 for the first pound plus $1.50 for each additional pound." (a) $T = \$3.50 + P$ (b) $T = \$2.00 + \$1.50\,(P)$ (c) $T = \$2.00 + \$1.50\,(P - 1)$
Exemplify	Constructed Response	Learners supply an answer.	Locate an inorganic compound and tell why it is inorganic.
	Selected Response	Learners choose an answer.	Which of these is an inorganic compound? (a) carbon tetrachloride (b) germanium fluoride (c) silver oxalate
Infer	Completion Tasks	Learners are given a series of items and they determine what is next.	Describe the relationship as an equation involving x and y for situations in which if x is 1, then y is 0; if x is 2 then y is 3; if x is 3, then y is 8.
	Analogy Tasks	Learners complete an analogy: A is to B as C is to _____.	Bach and Handel are to Baroque music as _____ and _____ are to early 20th century music.
	Oddity Tasks	Learners determine which in a list doesn't fit.	Study the following three physics problems and determine which one involves a different principle from the other two.
Explain	Reasoning	Learners give a reason for a given event.	What causes clouds to form?
	Troubleshooting	Learners diagnose what could have gone wrong in a malfunctioning system.	Analyze this computer's crash dump to determine the cause
	Redesigning	Learners change a system to accomplish a goal.	Change the following harmonic progression to better meet 18th century common practice principles
	Predicting	Learners are asked how a change in one part of a system will create a change in another part.	What would happen if you changed the diameter of the cylinder in a bicycle pump?

Primary Source: Anderson and Krathwohl (2001), pp. 69–76

Conclusion

Foundational knowledge, as its name suggests, is fundamental to learning. Without it, students do not have the information and ideas they need to perform higher order thinking tasks. Because it is so basic, it is also essential that students learn foundational knowledge accurately and thoroughly because this lays the groundwork for future learning. In today's world, where information is virtually at our fingertips, we should make careful decisions about what students need to actually remember and what kinds of information we simply need to help them know how to locate. That said, as soon as students have even baseline knowledge, it is important to help them apply it so that it becomes personally meaningful.

For those of us who teach data-intensive courses, it is difficult to shift emphasis from requiring students to learn information to teaching them how to find and then use the information. Information recall is easier to teach and test, and many students find it a more comfortable and familiar way to learn. Nevertheless, changing a course's focus from "content coverage" (which is typically information-driven) to "uncovering the content" (which is process- and application-driven) is more appropriate and ultimately more valuable for students in the changed environment in which they must function both during and after college. We therefore turn our attention in the next chapter to offering ideas on how to teach and assess application learning.

LEARNING ASSESSMENT TECHNIQUE

Foundational Knowledge

1
First Day Final

Complexity involved in	
Preparation	HIGH
In-class implementation	HIGH
Analysis	MODERATE

Brief Description

Students take a nongraded test the first day of the term that consists of questions that are similar to the Final Exam, and then identify the questions they found easiest and those they found most difficult. At the end of the term they take the real, graded Final Exam and the results are used as a reference point to demonstrate learning gains and achievement over time.

Purpose and Use

A First Day Final activates prior knowledge and also provides students with a preview of what is to come, letting students know on the first day of class the kinds of things they are expected to learn in the course. Students can use the knowledge about their weaknesses and strengths that they gain from taking the first test to focus their study efforts. At the end of the term when students take the graded Final Exam, they can see the gains they made in acquiring and deepening foundational knowledge.

The Learning Artifacts are the completed Finals, both precourse and postcourse. The data you gather are useful for multiple purposes. In addition to its primary use as a pre- and postassessment to measure course learning outcomes, you can use the information to determine the most appropriate level at which to begin instruction. It can also help you identify those individuals who may need remediation, as well as those who are well prepared and who might benefit from more challenging assignments or be employed as tutors or team leaders. At the end of the term, you can use the pretest comparison to the posttest to measure learning that is a result of the course experience. This approach lets you observe change in student knowledge over time, which although an imperfect measure of the course's influence on learning (which could be due simply to maturation) is often the best measure teachers can get of change brought about by instruction.

Key Learning Goals

- Knowledge of central facts in this subject area
- Knowledge of key terms of this subject area
- Historical knowledge relevant to this subject area
- Knowledge of important theories in the subject area
- Knowledge of key individuals who have contributed to the field
- Clarity about common misconceptions in this subject area
- Knowledge about themselves as learners

Implementation

Preparation

- Create an exam that contains a representative sampling of questions that are equivalent in format and difficulty to those you intend to include on your Final Exam.
- Include questions about students' perceived difficulty of the exam questions, for example:
  - What three questions were the easiest?
  - What three questions were the most challenging?
- Write your First Day Final exam with instructions that provide assurances about your purposes as well as directions about what students should do, such as the following:
  - *Purposes:* This test is similar in format and difficulty to the Final Exam, but it will not be graded. Rather, the purposes of this exercise are to (1) help you recall any prior knowledge so that you can better connect this to what I will be teaching you, (2) help me determine the most appropriate level at which to begin instruction, (3) help you focus your study efforts throughout the course, and (4) provide a reference point for gauging how much you have learned by the end of the course when you take the graded exam.
  - *Directions:* Respond to the exam questions. After you have completed the exam but before you submit the exam to me, please rate the question difficulty by doing the following:
    1. Circle and put an "E" next to the three question numbers you found easiest.
    2. Circle and put a "D" next to the three question numbers you found most difficult.
- Decide how you intend to respond to students after you have evaluated the precourse exam. Will you return graded exams to individual students? Or provide them with only the total score of correct/incorrect responses? Will you share the aggregated results for the whole class?
- Create a Final Exam, using the pretest as a reference for both difficulty and format.
- At the end of the Final Exam add self-rating questions, such as the following:
  - After you have completed the exam but before you submit the exam to me, please
    1. Circle and put an "E" next to the three question numbers you found easiest.
    2. Circle and put a "D" next to the three question numbers you found most difficult.
- Decide how you intend to respond to students after you have evaluated the postcourse Final Exam. Consider providing individual students with both pre- and postcourse scores so that they can acknowledge and celebrate improvements.

Process

1. Announce the activity, explaining that the First Day Final precourse activity will not be graded, but rather that you plan to use the results to help you make more effective instructional decisions, help them focus their study efforts, and eventually measure learning outcomes. Consider also explaining to students that this activity will provide them with better understanding of your expectations for their learning and give them a preview of the format and difficulty level of the graded exam that they will receive at the end of the course.

2. Present students with the precourse exam and call time when you believe they have had sufficient time to complete it.

3. Collect the completed exam, which is the first of your two Learning Artifacts, and analyze results (see Analysis and Reporting information below).

4. Share the level of information regarding evaluated exams (individual or aggregate or both) you determined at the preparation stage, and consider using the results as the basis for a class discussion on your goals for student learning.

5. Teach the course.

6. Administer the postcourse exam (your Final Exam with the additional question rating items).

7. Collect the completed exam, which is the second of your two Learning Artifacts, and analyze results (see Analysis and Reporting).

8. Compare the precourse exam and the postcourse exam (See Analysis and Reporting).

Online

Create and administer both exams in your Learning Management System (LMS). Use your standard communication tool such as announcements, discussion forum, or email to share information about results from the first exam with students.

Analysis and Reporting

To examine individual responses, simply score the responses to exam questions and also note choices regarding easiest and most difficult questions. Create a table for tracking information such as shown in Table 7.4.

Table 7.4 Tracking Results of First Day Final

Student Name	Exam	Score	Q2 3 Easiest Questions	Q3 3 Most Difficult Questions
Student 1	First Day Final (Precourse)			
	Final Exam (Postcourse)			
Student 2	First Day Final (Precourse)			
	Final Exam (Postcourse)			

Table 7.5 Tally Sheet for Easiest/Most Difficult Questions

	Easiest	Most Difficult
Q1	///	
Q2	/	
Q3		//
Q4		////

The pretest phase of this activity should be ungraded, although you may consider awarding participation points. At the end of the term, follow the same process for the graded Final Exam.

To aggregate responses, consider the following:

- Evaluate correct and incorrect answers on individual precourse exams and calculate total/aggregated score for the group (either number correct or percentage).
- Examine each exam through an item-by-item process to determine which questions students performed uniformly well on and uniformly poorly on.
- Look at totals in responses to your question difficulty ratings (for example, Q2 and 3 on Table 7.4) on the precourse exam to determine if there are patterns in prior knowledge or in areas students deemed to be particularly challenging. Tally the easiest/most difficult ratings per question either on a master copy of the exam itself or by using a simple tally sheet such as the one excerpted as Table 7.5.
- Consider whether there is a relationship between the questions students answered correctly and those they found the easiest. Consider the relationship between incorrect answers and difficult questions. If there is not a relationship, consider why that might be the case.
- Next, examine and do the same analyses for the postcourse activity. Compare precourse and postcourse data.
- The displayed data may be used in your report to external shareholders. Simple tables or charts can be useful for reporting information. Consider a bar graph for reporting change between the first and final exam. Averages should be sufficient to document the change to knowledge or skills between the First Day Final and the actual, graded Final Exam administration.

Examples

Onsite: Introduction to Business Information Systems

This professor had a learning outcome that students will demonstrate an understanding and appropriate use of MS Office by creating reports, charts, graphics, slides, and files using personal productivity tools such as Word, Excel, Outlook, and PowerPoint. She decided to use First Day Final to help students focus their study efforts, as well as to measure their learning in ways that could be included in a report about her teaching in the teacher dossier she was preparing.

Table 7.6 Tracking Easiest/Most Difficult Question on the First Day (Precourse) Exam

Average Question Rating	Question No.	Category	Topic
Easiest 1	Q3	Word	Text, Lists, and Bullets
Easiest 2	Q7	Word	Tracking and Reviewing Changes
Easiest 3	Q14	Outlook	Contacts
Most Difficult 1	Q2	Excel	Managing Sheets and Workbooks
Most Difficult 2	Q6	Word	Automating Tasks
Most Difficult 3	Q20	Excel	Formulas

She began by administering a 12-question short exam that was similar in question format and difficulty to the Final Exam. The exam was organized into four parts correlated to the four tools (Word, Excel, Outlook, and PowerPoint), and within each part there were questions addressing use of those tools. She included questions that asked students to identify the 3 easiest and 3 most difficult questions. She displayed the results from the first exam in a table (see example in Table 7.6) that showed students' relative strengths and weaknesses on each tool coming into the course, thus providing guidance to her on how to target instruction and information to students on where to focus their study efforts.

At the end of the term, the professor administered the graded Final Exam. She found that the topics that students had determined were most difficult for them at the beginning of the term were now among the easiest and that they had improved their test scores by at least 30%. The professor shared the scores of the tests with the students, showing them the differences in their scores between the two tests. She also aggregated individual scores to create a bar graph that showed improvement by topic area, as displayed in Figure 7.1.

She included this graph as well as the tables along with a narrative report of her First Day Final activity in her dossier so that those colleagues reviewing it had solid information about the work she was doing.

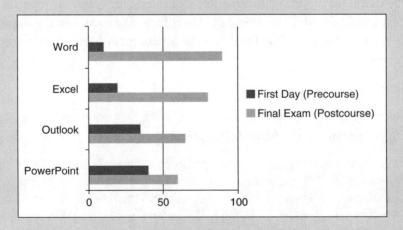

Figure 7.1 Introduction to Business Information Systems: Bar Graph Displaying Average Gains Between First Day Exam and Final Graded Exam on Four Productivity Tools

Online: English for Second Language Learners: Composition and Reading

The professor of this online course had the following learning outcome: students will be able to define and identify phrasal verbs. He decided to adapt First Day Final to serve as a pre- and posttest focused on this single student-learning outcome. Before students studied phrasal verbs, the professor provided students with a text and gave them an assignment in which they were instructed to find examples and describe their meaning. He scored the assignment and determined that while most students could find the verbs, only a few were able to describe their meaning. The professor developed a combination of video lectures, reading assignments, discussions, and short quizzes aimed at helping students learn the meanings. He then provided students with a text and assignment similar to the pretest to analyze as a posttest.

In a simple table, the professor recorded individual test scores as well as the change that took place between the pretest and posttest (Table 7.7). He provided students with information about their scores and the changes, and they were pleased to see their progress.

The teacher also developed aggregate scores, examining the tests by "item" (in this case the verbs) and looked at change over time. He identified several that were particularly challenging to a large number of students, both in the pretest and the posttest, and determined that he would focus more attention on helping students learn those difficult terms in future courses.

Table 7.7 English for Second Language Learners: Table Displaying Pre- and Posttest Scores on Identification and Understanding of Phrasal Verbs

Student Names	Pretest Score	Posttest Score	Change (%)
Josue	65	80	23
Ahmed	60	70	17
Elif	70	85	21
Mingda	65	85	31
Satsuki	70	90	29

Variations and Extensions

- Consider adding short answer questions to the first day exam (precourse) that ask students to self-assess various aspects that relate to their preparedness for the course, such as

    1. Given your experience as a student generally and in this subject matter specifically, what are the *strengths* you bring as a learner to this course? (For example, "I have done well in the courses that led up to this class." "I have good academic skills." "I learned about this information in a high school AP course.")

    2. Given your experience as a student generally and in this subject matter specifically, what are the *challenges* you bring as a learner to this course? (For example, "I have struggled with this subject matter in the past." "I am taking 22 units and working part-time, which is going to make it difficult for me to focus on this class.")

3. What learning/study strategies can you implement that will help you succeed in this class? (For example, "I can set up a schedule to help me manage my time." "I can seek tutorial services early before I get behind.")

4. What can your peers or I do to help you succeed in this class? (For example, "It would help me if you would look at my work before it is graded to see if I am on track." "I would like to form a study group with some of my peers.")

- The test might also be a performance-based assessment of student ability to apply content. Students could, for example, solve complex problems that demonstrate their application of knowledge, rather than focusing on foundational knowledge.

- After students have taken the first-day exam, consider asking them to share their perceptions of the exam with a partner or in small groups. Students may find that talking with their peers is reassuring and it also may give them an opportunity to forge friendships or study groups that can help promote success.

- Teams of students could work together on pretests and posttests, as in our LAT Team Tests.

- Instead of a comprehensive, course-level exam, use this as a basic pre- and posttest strategy on a content unit or module, as described in the previous online example.

- Although this LAT was intended for a single course, it would also be very effective to demonstrate learning gains over a sequence of courses.

Key References and Resources

Roediger III, H. L., & Butler, A. C. (2011). The critical role of retrieval practice in long-term retention. *Trends in Cognitive Sciences, 15*(1), 20–27. http://people.duke.edu/~ab259/pubs/Roediger&Butler%282010%29.pdf

Roediger III, H. L., & Karpicke, J. D. (2006). The power of testing memory: Basic research and implications for educational practice. *Psychological Science, 1*, 181–210.

LEARNING ASSESSMENT TECHNIQUE

Foundational Knowledge

2
Background Knowledge Probe

Complexity involved in	
Preparation	MODERATE
In-class implementation	LOW
Analysis	LOW

Brief Description

Background Knowledge Probes are simple questionnaires that help you quickly take stock of the level of foundational knowledge and general preparedness that students have along with their level of confidence in their responses before beginning a content unit or learning module.

Purpose and Use

This LAT prompts students to recall what they already know about an important topic before starting a new unit or lesson. Activating prior knowledge can help students better interpret and assign meaning to new information, thus encouraging them to construct bridges between what they already know and what you want them to learn. This extension of the traditional Background Knowledge Probe adds an indirect evidence component by asking students to articulate their level of confidence in where they are in that knowledge.

The Learning Artifact, which is the completed questionnaire, collects useful information on students' level of preparedness so that you can determine the most effective starting point for instruction. Additionally, the information can help you identify individuals who may need remediation or whose attitudes need to be addressed before they can engage effectively as learners. It can also uncover gaps or misconceptions in learning that need to be addressed so that students are able to make accurate connections to new material. Students' ratings of their level of confidence in the correctness of their responses provides you with additional insights regarding their readiness for new material. You may find, for example, that some students have the wrong idea about something and are convinced that they are right; this lets you know that you will have to work to overcome misconceptions. Alternately, you may find that they know the answer but are unsure; this lets you know that you need to build confidence for repeated success in answering the question correctly.

Key Learning Goals

- Knowledge of central facts in this subject area
- Knowledge of key terms of this subject area
- Historical knowledge relevant to this subject area
- Knowledge of important theories in the subject area
- Knowledge of key individuals who have contributed to the field
- Clarity about common misconceptions in this subject area
- Knowledge about themselves as learners

Implementation

Preparation

- Before starting a content unit or learning module, consider what foundational knowledge students may already possess. Although their knowledge may be minimal, try to determine at least one point most students are likely to know. With this as the starting place, identify additional, less familiar points. Use your list of points to prepare 5–10 objective or short-answer questions that will uncover students' existing knowledge or understanding and that can be evaluated quickly to determine whether the answer is correct or incorrect. Avoid specialized vocabulary that may be unfamiliar to students that may interfere with their recall.
- Add a question or two to have students self-assess their questionnaire readiness, for example:
  - Describe your confidence to answer each question correctly on a scale of 1 (lowest: "I am really unsure about the answer I chose") to 10 (highest: "I am certain that my answer is correct").
  - Describe your general level of confidence in completing the questionnaire on a scale of 1 (lowest: "Bombed it") to 10 (highest: "Aced it").
- Use your questions to create a questionnaire to distribute to students.
- Complete the questionnaire yourself to uncover any ambiguities or problems and to serve as an answer key.

Process

1. Announce the activity, explaining that the Background Knowledge Probe is not a test and will not be graded, but rather that you plan to use the results to help you make more effective instructional decisions.
2. Present students with the questionnaire, and call time when you believe they have had sufficient time to complete it.
3. Collect the completed questionnaire, which is your Learning Artifact.

Online

Create a quiz or survey in your LMS.

Analysis and Reporting

Evaluate correct and incorrect answers on individual responses using a simple system such as +/−. Look for patterns to determine if there are common misconceptions, errors, or gaps in knowledge. Sum up and average the confidence rating. Note if there are any incorrect answers that had a high rating of confidence on being correct, and alternately answers that were correct with low rating of confidence. This activity should be ungraded, although you may consider awarding participation points. To consolidate information to help inform teaching decisions, consider creating a table as shown in Table 7.8.

To aggregate findings across individual responses, conduct an informal assessment of the results by first summing up the individual correct responses for each question, and then determine a score of how students assessed each question. This approach will provide a count that tells you whether the class as a whole has more knowledge about some topics than about others and how accurate they are in their assessment of that knowledge. Also look at an average score of exams compared to an average self-rating score. Create a sorted spreadsheet or table to display results and consider sharing this with students. The displayed data may also be used in your report to external shareholders.

Table 7.8 Student Responses to Background Knowledge Probe

Student Name	Number Actual Correct	Average Confidence Rating of Correctness	Notable Incorrect Responses Rated with High Confidence of Correctness (7 or Higher)	Notable Correct Responses Rated with Low Confidence of Correctness (3 or Lower)
Atsina	3	5	2	1
Catherine	7	8	1	3
Jonathan	5	4	2	2
Gagandeep	8	10	0	1

Examples

Onsite: Introduction to Statistics

A teaching assistant was assigned to teach Introduction to Statistics in the Psychology Department. The course had an established learning goal that students will acquire basic statistical literacy. Unfamiliar with the level of foundational knowledge students were likely to bring with them, and wanting to engage students by teaching at a level that was neither boring nor too difficult, she decided to create a Background Knowledge Probe to take stock of students' incoming level of knowledge and confidence about their knowledge (Table 7.9). Here is an excerpt from the handout she provided students:

Table 7.9 Introduction to Statistics

This Background Knowledge Probe is intended to provide you with the opportunity to share what you know already about the topic of statistical testing that we will talk about this semester. I will not grade the inventory, but rather will use it to help me in planning our class sessions. Please try to answer the questions as accurately as possible by placing an x in the appropriate square beside it to demonstrate whether you believe each question is true or false, and then circle the number that best reflects your confidence in the correctness of your answer.

	Check Your Answer		Circle Your Level of Confidence in Your Answer (1 = Low; 10 = High)
	True	False	1 2 3 4 5 6 7 8 9 10
A survey question asks: How satisfied are you with the way the president is performing. It gives you options, ranking from very unsatisfied to very satisfied. The variable is at the ordinal level.			1 2 3 4 5 6 7 8 9 10
The only way to take a census from a population is to ensure that the data are collected from every individual in the population.			1 2 3 4 5 6 7 8 9 10
A survey question asks the following: What time did you wake up this morning? The variable is at the interval level.			1 2 3 4 5 6 7 8 9 10
A uniform distribution has a smaller standard deviation than a mound-shaped distribution.			1 2 3 4 5 6 7 8 9 10
A survey question asks the following: How many pairs of shoes do you own? The variable is at the nominal level.			1 2 3 4 5 6 7 8 9 10
Rate your overall level of confidence in completing this quiz			1 2 3 4 5 6 7 8 9 10

When she collected the responses, she did a quick tally of the number of correct responses to the content questions by item and determined an average, then noted the number of incidences in which students had marked an answer incorrectly but rated their confidence in its correctness highly, as well as incidences of correct answers that were rated with low confidence. She displayed these on a simple chart as demonstrated in Figure 7.2.

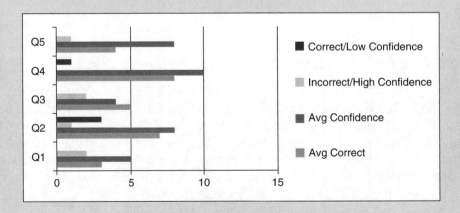

Figure 7.2 Sample Bar Chart

She used the results of the Background Knowledge Probe to (1) identify advanced students who needed more challenging work, (2) identify students with little or no background for whom she could recommend tutoring, (3) create a handout of basic terms with definitions, and (4) construct an additional online module to cover basic concepts. She also held a class lecture with a follow-up formative quiz to help reduce misunderstandings and to check progress.

 ### *Online: Technology and Higher Education*

As a part of their annual review process in the College of Education, faculty are required to document their efforts to assess student learning in a process that includes identifying a question, gathering data about it, examining the results, reporting results, and producing a plan for improvement. This education professor was teaching a new elective graduate-level online course on technology in higher education. She believed that to do well and understand the conversation, students needed a basic working knowledge of computer terms. She provided students with the inventory shown in Table 7.10.

She examined the results and scored the answers as either correct (+) or incorrect (−) and recorded the results in a simple table. She also scanned student ratings to determine which terms students had less confidence about in their knowledge. Based on her analysis, she determined that students knew more about more recent innovations (e.g. Web 2.0, social media, blogs) than about basic computer functions and decided to add a lecture about basic computer components and functions. In preparing her report for her annual review, she included the matrix shown in Table 7.11 to document her efforts.

Table 7.10 Basic Computer Terms

Please review the following terms and define them in the space provided.		
Terms	**Your Definition**	**Your Confidence in Your Definition**
1. Internet		1 2 3 4 5 6 7 8 9 10
2. Database		1 2 3 4 5 6 7 8 9 10
3. Search engine		1 2 3 4 5 6 7 8 9 10
4. Network		1 2 3 4 5 6 7 8 9 10
5. What is a firewall?		1 2 3 4 5 6 7 8 9 10
6. HTML		1 2 3 4 5 6 7 8 9 10
7. Web 2.0		1 2 3 4 5 6 7 8 9 10
8. Social media		1 2 3 4 5 6 7 8 9 10
9. Blog		1 2 3 4 5 6 7 8 9 10
10. Podcast		1 2 3 4 5 6 7 8 9 10

Table 7.11 Sample Assessment Matrix

Student Learning Outcomes	LAT	Learning Artifact	Findings and Interpretations	Actions to Be Taken
Students will recall basic facts about the Internet.	Background Knowledge Probe	Background Knowledge Probe "Basic Computer Term" Questionnaire	Students know more about more recent innovations (e.g. Web 2.0, social media, blogs) than about basic computer functions.	Added a lecture about basic computer components and functions.

Variations and Extensions

- After students have responded individually to the *Background Knowledge Probe*, but before giving students the correct answers, ask them to work in pairs or small groups to come up with mutually acceptable and correct answers. This provides an additional Learning Artifact.

Key References and Resources

Angelo, T. A., & Cross, P. K. (1993). CAT 1: Background knowledge probe. In *Classroom assessment techniques* (2nd ed.). San Francisco, CA: Jossey-Bass.

Barkley, E. F. (2010). Background knowledge probe. In *Student engagement techniques: A handbook for college faculty* (pp. 167–169). San Francisco, CA: Jossey-Bass.

Carnegie Mellon Eberly Center for Teaching Excellence and Educational Innovation. (nd). Prior Knowledge. http://www.cmu.edu/teaching/assessment/priorknowledge/index.html.

LEARNING ASSESSMENT TECHNIQUE

Foundational Knowledge

3
Entry and Exit Tickets

Complexity involved in	
Preparation	LOW
In-class implementation	LOW
Analysis	LOW

Brief Description

Entry and exit tickets require students to reflect on a reading assignment, video, lecture, or other and then write a brief response to a question on an index card that is designed to gather information about their understanding of core facts, terms, concepts, and ideas.

Purposes

This LAT prompts students to review material soon after they are exposed to it, an activity that is key for improving retention and recall. It also helps ensure that students come to class prepared (entry tickets) and that any misunderstandings are uncovered before proceeding to new material (exit tickets).

The Learning Artifact is the exit or entry ticket, and a quick review of responses allows you to efficiently assess student recall and understanding. Low in complexity, this technique provides a high return given the amount of time and energy you invest. You can use this formative assessment technique in several ways. For example, you can use insights gleaned to place students into working groups, recommend additional resources for further study, or guide teaching decisions based on uncovered misunderstandings or student questions.

Key Learning Goals

- Knowledge of central facts in this subject area
- Knowledge of key terms of this subject area
- Knowledge of important theories in the subject area
- Recognition of the difference between fact and opinion related to this subject area

Implementation

Preparation

*   Determine whether you want to use entry tickets (to help ensure that students have prepared for class and have understood the assigned material) or exit tickets (to gather information about whether students have understood in-class assignments and activities) or both.
*   Develop a prompt that requires a short response, such as a single question or a request to list 3–5 items. For example:
    *   Based on last night's reading assignment (or today's lecture), what causes x?
    *   List the top three concepts you learned from today's lecture (or this week's homework).
*   Determine how much time you will allot for student responses. Typically students should be able to respond to the prompt in 1–2 minutes.
*   Decide whether students should respond anonymously or include their names with their responses. (*Note:* Entry tickets can be used to track attendance.)
*   Decide how you will collect the responses. Index cards are useful, but you may also prepare a handout that has the question listed, or you may post it on a presentation slide and ask students to turn in their responses on their own paper.

Process

1. Present the content that students should master.
2. Announce the activity and the time frame for completing it.
3. Ask students to record their responses to your prompt.
4. Collect the cards/handouts from students.

Online

Have students post their responses to a question or two as a quiz or an assignment prior to or after a content module. If anonymous responses are desirable, have students respond to a survey (using for example Survey Monkey or Google Forms).

Analysis and Reporting

Score tickets using a simple system such as +/− to indicate correct/incorrect. You can also track individual responses over time to gauge improvement. Entry and exit tickets typically are ungraded, but they may be used in determining class participation points or, when tracked over time, they may be assigned a low stakes grade.

To aggregate responses, sort cards into two stacks (correct/incorrect) or keep a tally to determine the number and percentage of correct and incorrect responses. Bar graphs may be used to display correct and incorrect responses, which can help you to identify where widespread misunderstandings exist. Depending upon the question you asked, you may wish to do a qualitative analysis, for example a key word or content analysis of the cards to determine recurrent themes. When interpreting results, consider the following:

*   What percentage of students answered the question incorrectly, and is the percentage significant?

- What patterns did you see in the data? Were there any common mistakes?
- What changes in your teaching might you make to increase the percentage of correct responses?

Display results in a simple spreadsheet or table.

Examples

Onsite: History of Western Civilization to 800 AD

A history professor assigned out-of-class readings to help students prepare for lectures and class discussion and to help them achieve the goal of understanding of historical facts related in Western Civilization to 800 AD. He believed, however, that students were not always reading their homework assignments or processing the information appropriately, and so he decided to use entry tickets to help him solve both problems.

As students entered the classroom, they picked up an index card upon which they wrote their name as well as a response to a prompt that was projected on a presentation slide. The professor collected the cards, did a quick review of responses, and then used the information he gleaned to clear up misunderstandings before proceeding with his planned lecture and class discussion.

After class, he used the cards to both record attendance and keep an ongoing account of correct/incorrect responses, which he indicated with a +/− system based on accuracy. He assigned points at the end of the term based upon the total number of accurate responses (Table 7.12).

Table 7.12 History of Western Civilization to 800 AD: Table Displaying Tracking of Entry Ticket Participation

Students	Wk 1	Wk 2	Wk 3	Wk 4	Wk 5	Wk 6	Wk 7	Wk 8	Wk 9	Wk 10	Wk 11	Wk 12	Total +'s
Isaac	−	+		−	+	+	−	+	+	+	+	+	7
Seung-Woo	−	−		−	−			−	+	+	−	+	3
Maria	+	+	+	+	−	+	+	−	+	+	+	+	10
Yasmin	−		−	−	+	+	−	−	+	−	+	+	5
Landon	+	+	+	+		+	+	+	+	+	+	+	11
Bradley	−	+	−	−	+	−	−	−	−	+	−	+	4
Rosita	−	−	−	+	+	−	+	−	+	−	+	+	6
Wai Yin	+	+	+	−	+	+	+	−	+	+	+	+	10
Phil	−	−	+	−	−	+	−	−	+	−	−	+	4

Online: Calculus

An instructor had a course learning outcome that successful students would be able to choose the correct method for solving function problems of more than one variable. At the beginning of each module, the instructor would post an "entry ticket" assignment. For example, using a simple quiz format, he would present a problem and ask students to select from 3 choices the appropriate technique for solving the problem. Students next watched a video lecture in which the instructor demonstrated how he would solve the problem. He then used an "exit ticket" consisting of a similar problem for students to solve that demonstrated that they had understood the module.

The instructor kept a running record of individual student responses and also tracked aggregate responses. He used the individual responses to determine participation points and the aggregate responses to determine his next teaching strategy. For example, if most students answered incorrectly, he offered additional lectures or problem sets. At the end of the term, he compared individual scores with final test scores (Table 7.13) and found that most students had gains between the entry and exit tickets and that there was a correlation between entry tickets and test scores (0.94) and between exit tickets and test scores (0.97).

Table 7.13 Linear Algebra: Table Displaying Tracking of Correct Entry/Exit Ticket Answers with Test Score

Students	Correct Entry Ticket Answers (%)	Correct Exit Ticket Answers (%)	Test Score
Janice	85	90	91
Kwan	62	60	65
Ali	65	75	75
Faye	83	85	84
Omer	40	55	50
Yasmin	75	85	88
Phillip	90	95	92
Ashley	85	90	90
Jillian	70	80	85
Siyan	75	85	87

Variations and Extensions

- Exit tickets can be useful for gathering information about what students believe that they have and have not understood, which is a form of indirect assessment. To use them in this way, simply ask, "What unanswered questions do you have about today's lecture?" This is a form of "Muddiest Point" popularized by Angelo and Cross (1993).
- This technique is most often used to assess student understanding of foundational knowledge. It may also be used, however, to have students reflect on their own learning

strategies at a given moment in time (for example, at the end of a lecture, ask students to describe their own levels of attention or participation in class, or to indicate how hard they worked during a given class session or on preparing for class, much like in a Punctuated Lecture; Angelo and Cross, 1993).

• This technique may also be used to gather information about instructional strategies, for example: "How did the group work help you learn today? What might you like to see different about group work going forward?"

Key References and Resources

Angelo, T. A., & Cross, K. P. (1993). *Classroom assessment techniques: A handbook for college teachers* (2nd ed.). San Francisco, CA: Jossey-Bass.

Lemov, D. (2010). *Teach like a champion: 49 strategies that put students on the path to success*. San Francisco, CA: Jossey-Bass.

Marzano, R. J. (2012). Art and science of teaching: The many uses of exit slips. *Students Who Challenge Us, 70*(2), 80–81.

LEARNING ASSESSMENT TECHNIQUE

Foundational Knowledge

4
Guided Reading Notes

Complexity involved in	
Preparation	MODERATE
In-class implementation	LOW
Analysis	LOW

Brief Description

Students receive a copy of notes that summarize content from an upcoming assigned reading, but that includes blanks in place of key words. As students read, they supply the missing content into the blanks.

Purposes

Guided Reading Notes scaffold active learning by requiring students to read closely in order to locate the information needed to complete the guide. The technique helps them understand what is most important about the reading. It also allows students to create a complete set of notes that can serve as a study guide for an upcoming exam, paper, or project.

The Learning Artifact is the students' completed notes, which help you to determine whether students are (1) finishing the assigned readings and (2) understanding what it is that they have read. You can use information about student understanding of reading assignments to target instruction to correct misunderstandings and to fill knowledge gaps. This technique may also be used to gather baseline information early in the term to identify students who seem to have difficulties in understanding reading assignments. Such students may be referred for additional services, or you can use the information to assign ability stratified groups in order to provide the student with additional support.

Key Learning Goals

- Knowledge of important theories in the subject area
- Recognition of the difference between fact and opinion related to this subject area
- Clarity about common misconceptions in this subject area

- Implementation
- Preparation
- Selection of the reading assignment to be guided
- Creation of a handout that has a complete summary of the reading that you can use as a model for assessing student work
- Creation of an incomplete summary with critical information removed and blanks for students to fill in the content

Implementation

1. Present students with the Guided Reading Notes handout, and allow time for questions.
2. Ask students to complete the assigned reading and simultaneously complete the notes.
3. Collect the completed handouts.

Online

Have students complete the notes as part of an assignment in your LMS. If you have a small class, consider a folder program such as Box, Dropbox, or Goggle Docs for students' assignment submissions, including this one.

Analysis and Reporting

Score each Learning Artifact using a simple method such as counting the number of correctly filled-in blanks and marking incorrect or empty blanks. Return scored notes to students so that they know what they did incorrectly. Compare individual performance over time by using a spreadsheet that includes scores at each administration. Guided Reading Notes typically are not used for high-stakes grades, but rather as part of homework completion or participation.

To aggregate results, simply look for patterns of responses; for example, which blanks do students tend to fill incorrectly. If you have prior data on test performance of classes before implementing this LAT, consider before and after comparison on success. You may want to describe whether and to what extent the activity has improved student performance. You can display results in a simple spreadsheet or table.

Examples

Onsite: Evolution, Systematics, and Ecology

A biology professor must document that students are meeting learning outcomes identified by the departmental assessment committee, one of which is that students will be able to define the concept of evolution and describe the processes. The professor knew that some students struggled with the units on evolution because of the complexity of the concepts and others struggled due to religious beliefs. She therefore decided to assign guided reading notes. A sample excerpt of her handout is as follows:

Guided Reading Notes for Chapter 1: An Overview of Evolutionary Biology

1. Evolution is a _____ in the heritable characteristics of a population.
2. Fossils, selective breeding, and _____ have given scientists evidence that supports the theory of evolution.
3. Populations generally produce _____ offspring than the environment is able to support.

She told students that their responsibility was to summarize the chapter by filling in the blanks, and that they could use this as a study guide to prepare for an upcoming test.

She collected the handouts, scored each individual's work, and returned the notes to the students so that they could use them as study guides. After the test, she compared Guided Notes scores with test scores and was able to identify a large correlation (.957) between the notes and test performance (Table 7.14). She also was able to demonstrate that on the whole, students were achieving the stated learning outcomes.

Table 7.14 Evolution, Systematics, and Ecology: Table Displaying Comparison of Note Scores and Test Scores

Students	Note Scores	Test Scores
Gabriella	80	85
Josue	78	82
Omer	85	88
Scottie	70	75
Michaela	75	78
Andrea	85	90
Kennedy	70	72
Madison	80	80
Chance	75	78
Xueqing	80	82

Online: Introduction to Social Psychology

The professor of this online class wanted students to be able to describe different perspectives on sociological social psychology. Because it was an introductory class, he knew that many students had little background knowledge on the topic and had difficulty understanding the course readings. He decided to use Guided Reading Notes to help them stay engaged in the

Table 7.15 Introduction to Social Psychology: Guided Notes for Assigned Reading on "Three Faces of Psychology"

Key Points	Guided Reading Notes
Social structure and personality	All people occupy a position in the social system, and that position affects individuals through (1)._____, (2). _____, and (3). _____.
Group processes	There are general principles underlying groups across a variety of settings, and the interplay between the (4)._____ and (5). _____levels of analysis.
Symbolic interactionism	Human nature and (6)._____ are products of communication among people.

Source: House (1977)

reading and to let him know how well they understood what they were reading. Table 7.15 shows an excerpted example of the assignment he asked students to complete and post in the course's LMS.

The teacher implemented Guided Reading Notes for each module and was able to track an improvement in student performance on module scores over time (Figure 7.3). He decided to follow-up the next term and investigate increases in student ability to read independently.

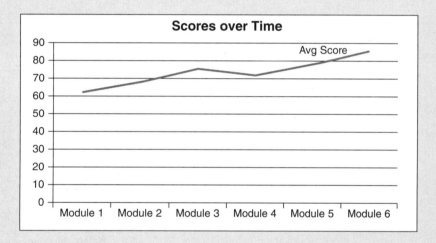

Figure 7.3 Introduction to Social Psychology: Changes in Average Scores on Modules Using Guided Notes

Variations and Extensions

- Guided Reading Notes may also be used during lectures or in conjunction with a video or podcast.
- While Guided Reading Notes typically are done to ensure students are developing foundational knowledge, they have also been used to help students develop and to assess higher-order thinking skills such as critical thinking. Instead of filling in blanks, have students take a more critical stance toward readings, asking them to organize information (for example, by creating a graphic organizer, such as a Venn diagram or a Tree Chart, or through evaluating and criticizing the information).

- For an indirect assessment, consider a Know-Want-Learn (KWL) chart, where students identify what they know, what they want to know, and what they still need to learn.
- Consider forming groups to complete the notes, or alternately to check their notes with each other to help improve accuracy.

Key References and Resources

Heward, W. L. (1996). Three low-tech strategies for increasing the frequency of active student response during group instruction. In R. Gardner III, D. M. Sainato, J. O. Cooper, T. E. Heron, W. L. Heward, J. W. Eshleman, & T. A. Grossi (Eds.), *Behavior analysis in education: Focus on measurably superior instruction* (pp. 283–320). Pacific Grove, CA: Brooks/Cole.

Heward, W. L. (2001). Guided notes: Improving the effectiveness of your lectures. Columbus, OH: The Ohio State University Partnership Grant for Improving the Quality of Education for Students with Disabilities. http://ada.osu.edu/resources/fastfacts/.

LEARNING ASSESSMENT TECHNIQUE

Foundational Knowledge

5
Comprehensive Factors List

Complexity involved in	
Preparation	LOW
In-class implementation	LOW
Analysis	LOW

Brief Description

Students recall and list as many relevant factors that they can that are related to a specific topic that they have encountered through a reading assignment, lecture, illustration, performance, or other course experience.

Purposes

Comprehensive Factors List is a form of brainstorming focused on the recall of information that is done in a list or bullet list format. It can help to improve student recall of information, and when students access their prior knowledge, they tend to be able to link new knowledge to it more ably. It also can be used to have students recall information, articulating it, which in turn can improve their retention of the information in their long-term memories.

The Learning Artifacts are the student generated lists of as many ideas, concepts, or terms that they can come up with. These can help you to help students activate prior knowledge while surfacing preexisting beliefs. This LAT provides insight into students' level of comprehension by illustrating whether students have understood and can remember the most important factors in a given lesson. Comprehensive Factors List may be used as a preassignment diagnostic assessment as well as a postassignment assessment of recall. It is also an effective pre- and postassessment tool for determining change over time.

Key Learning Goals

- Knowledge of central facts in this subject area
- Knowledge of key terms of this subject area
- The ability of students to translate key ideas from this subject area into their own words

- Clarity about common misconceptions in this subject area
- Knowledge of current issues related to the subject area

Implementation

Preparation

- Select a narrow topic or concept that will be useful for a brainstorming activity, in which students can generate many responses.
- Create the prompt for the assignment (e.g., "List all of the factors you can think of that are elated to X").
- Determine how students should record their responses; index cards can be useful and also can limit the volume of responses.
- Try out the prompt yourself to see how many factors you generate. This list can also be used for comparison when you review students' responses.
- Determine how much time to allocate to this activity. You will not need long; Comprehensive Factors List activities typically last approximately 3–5 minutes.

Process

1. Present the prompt, and tell students they will list all the factors they can think of related to the topic.
2. Announce the time limit for the activity, and ask students to begin.
3. Close the activity by telling students that the time has ended.
4. Collect the Learning Artifacts.
5. If desired, have student volunteers report some of their ideas.

Online

To preserve the "in the moment" nature, set up this LAT in a very limited timed "quiz" format or alternately have students do this activity in a synchronous chat session.

Analysis and Reporting

Collect responses and review the answers to determine how well students have recalled the main points. You may want to do a simple count of how many factors a student listed or use a simple scoring system to gauge quality, such as

1 Bull's-eye
0 On the board
−1 Missed the mark

Because this is a quick activity intended to gather formative data, you should not assign a high-stakes grade to it, although you may want to assign a participation grade. If you have students write their names on their responses, you may want to return their scored responses so that they have feedback on how well they did. If you decide to implement this LAT anonymously, you simply won't report individual results.

To aggregate data, determine an average number of items or do a simple tally of the percentage of scores in each of the quality indicators you created. Use a simple table to present your results; display percentages in a pie chart.

Examples

Onsite: Form and Function in Plants and Animals

A professor's learning goal was that upon completion of the course, students would know and understand Mendel's Laws of Inheritance. She crafted an outcome statement as follows, "In a Comprehensive Factors List activity given as a pop-quiz, students will be able to list and describe Mendel's three primary laws of inheritance." On the day of the activity, she passed out index cards and then presented the following prompt on a presentation slide: "Within a 5-minute time limit, list and describe Mendel's Laws of Inheritance." She called time, collected the cards, and scored the responses on a 3-point scale based on accuracy. She was pleased to see that most students could list the three laws, although some added additional erroneous laws and a significant percentage did not describe one or more law accurately.

The next session, she provided additional lecturing, focusing on the unique characteristics of each of the three laws and including multiple illustrations. At the end of class she used the Comprehensive Factors List again and was relieved to see that all students limited the number of laws to three and that the quality of their description had improved. She compared the quality of responses before and after her lecture, as shown in Figure 7.4.

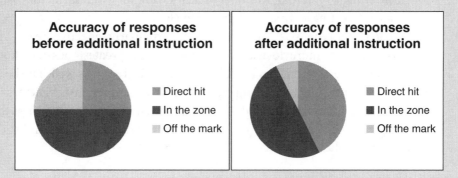

Figure 7.4 Comparison of Accuracy in Student Responses Pre- and Postlecture

Online: Social Work in the Schools

In this online course, the professor had a learning outcome that upon completion of the course, successful students would be able to quickly generate a list of the influence that bullies can have on their victims. She decided to use Comprehensive Factors List to help her assess achievement of the outcome and to use it in a pre/post administration to help her gauge how much student knowledge changed as a result of instruction.

Table 7.16 Results Table

	Average Number of Factors	Average Factors Score
Before Instruction	5	3.3
After Instruction	9	4.5

She created a prompt, "What are the main effects of bullying on the victims?" and then generated her own list of effects, which included feelings of worthlessness; triggers for use of tobacco, alcohol, or other drugs; and signals of increased mental health problems, such as depression and anxiety, absenteeism, and suicide. She posted the activity as a 5-minute timed quiz that students could take asynchronously. They then worked through the module asynchronously. When they completed it, they took the quiz again. She noted the results in Table 7.16.

She was pleased to see the improvement in student responses after instruction and reported the results to the students, who also seemed pleased with their progress.

Variations and Extensions

- Consider setting a limit to the number of factors, for an "essential factors list." This variation is desirable if you have a particularly large class.
- Individual Comprehensive Factors List is particularly effective (e.g., Miller, 2009), as students may stay more focused and generate the greatest possible numbers of ideas. Group Comprehensive Factors Lists, however, can be useful as well. The best approach may be to combine individual and group approaches to Comprehensive Factors List. One option is to have students brainstorm individually and then get into small groups to compare types of items generated. Groups may be asked to identify themes from their lists, which can help facilitate the analysis process.

Key References and Resources

Angelo, T. A., & Cross, K. P. (1993). Focused listing (pp. 126–131). *Classroom assessment techniques: A handbook for college teachers* (2nd ed.). San Francisco, CA: Jossey-Bass.

Fulks, J. (2006). Student learning outcomes assessment. http://www2.bakersfieldcollege.edu /courseassessment/Section_1_Introduction/Introduction1.htm.

Miller, J. (2009). Evidence-based instruction: A classroom experience comparing nominal and focused listing groups. *Organizational Management Journal, 6*(4), 229–238.

LEARNING ASSESSMENT TECHNIQUE

Foundational Knowledge

6
Quick Write

Complexity involved in	
Preparation	LOW
In-class implementation	LOW
Analysis	MODERATE

Brief Description

A Quick Write is an activity in which learners write a response in a brief amount of time to an open-ended prompt posed by the teacher.

Purposes

A Quick Write is a particularly flexible technique that can serve several purposes, as we describe in the Variations section of this technique. It requires students to direct and focus their attention on recalling what they know about a topic and to communicate that succinctly in a limited amount of time. Used with some regularity in onsite classes, it can encourage students to pay closer attention as they start to expect that they will be held accountable by having to recall and summarize the information later.

This LAT can help you gather information about students' foundational knowledge, since in it teachers pose prompts that require students to define a complex term, describe a difficult concept, delineate a complicated process, and so forth. The Learning Artifact is the Quick Write document. It provides you with a quick view of students' understand along with their ability to communicate that understanding. It has the advantage of a written assignment that can contain rich data, but it is brief, and thus is quickly administered and scored. A Quick Write can be useful as a diagnostic assessment by asking students what they know prior to a lesson, or used in process to determine student understanding, and it can also be used both pre- and postlesson to gauge a change in understanding.

Key Learning Goals

* Knowledge of central facts in this subject area
* Knowledge of key terms of this subject area

- Knowledge of important theories in the subject area
- Historical knowledge relevant to this subject area
- Knowledge of key individuals who have contributed to the field
- The ability to translate key ideas from this subject area into students' own words
- Clarity about common misconceptions in this subject area
- Knowledge of current issues related to the subject area

Implementation

Preparation

- Craft the prompt question and decide how you will present it (on the board, on a presentation slide, on a half-sheet handout, and so forth).
- Decide whether you want to have students include their names on their responses or submit their response anonymously.

Process

1. Announce the activity and explain the purpose of it.
2. Present the prompt, and tell students how to respond (e.g., complete sentences, word lists, or other writing form of your choice). Tell them how long they will have to respond.
3. Ask students to respond to the prompt.
4. Collect the Quick Write Learning Artifacts.
5. Tell students how you will report results (e.g., you may want to let them know that you will not respond to each individual Quick Write but will instead report full class results during the next session).

Online

The quick nature of this assignment can be accomplished online through synchronous chat rooms. If anonymous responses are desirable, you can assign the Quick Write as a quiz and limit student time to respond.

Analysis and Reporting

To examine individual artifacts, look at each item and give it a quick score, such as minus/check/plus for does not meet/meets/exceeds expectations. Alternately, if you are interested in the content students generate, you can analyze responses for key words. Assign a low-stakes grade or participation points.

To aggregate, tally responses and determine how many responses were in each scoring category you created (e.g. minus/check/plus). Note any outstanding responses or any common misunderstandings. Consider saving the Quick Writes from the beginning of the term and comparing them to those you collect at the end of the term to see if there are changes in terms of student knowledge and writing abilities. Report your results in a simple tally sheet or table. Bar graphs can be useful for displaying results that you collect over time.

Examples

Onsite: Introduction to Scientific Methods

In this introductory interdisciplinary course, in which both nonmajors and majors enroll, students use a scientific approach to learning about the physical universe and investigate topics in physics, chemistry, and biology. The instructor of this particular course finds that the students often approach science wanting to memorize basic facts, in part because that's what the departmental required examinations test students on, but she wants the students to move beyond rote memorizing into deeper levels of understanding of course content and critical concepts. She crafted a learning goal that stated that upon completion of the course, students will be able to make reasonable inferences about the principles that underlie common scientific facts. She decided to use Quick Writes to help promote deeper thinking and to help her assess student level of understanding before and after instruction.

The course met twice per week and they covered approximately one learning module per week. She used Quick Writes to introduce a new topic to the class to stimulate their interest in the concept and to get a "quick read" of where they were in their thinking. She used them again at the end of the week and compared responses from start to finish. She found a set of existing prompts online, which she adapted for her own use. A few sample questions are as follows:

- Hydrogen is the most abundant of the element in the universe. Why might this be the case?
- Telescopes have been called "time machines." What is a possible reason is for this?
- What could you personally do to have the biggest influence on reducing pollution? Why is this your choice?
- If you were a US farmer and could choose any one crop to grow, what would it be, from a scientific perspective, and why?

She wrote the prompt on the board and handed out index cards at the start of a class session. Students had 3 minutes to record their responses. She asked students to write their names on their cards, so she also had a useful way of keeping attendance in this relatively large class, and she used the cards as a factor in participation grades. She collected the responses immediately, doing so at the start and end of the lesson so that she had before-and-after responses.

- To analyze her results, she scored the cards quickly (Table 7.17), with a +/− to indicate whether the answer addressed the prompt question in a legitimate way (e.g., whether it was correct or incorrect, plausible or implausible, viable or nonviable).

She noticed that the pretest scores gradually improved over the term, and she believed that the activity helped students move beyond basic memorization to deeper levels of thinking about "why" and "how" things happen. She also noticed that the scores always improved after instruction and that there was a clear and steady gain in quality of post-instruction responses over the course of the semester.

Table 7.17 Results Table

Week	Pre-instruction + percentage	Pre-instruction − percentage	Post-instruction + percentage	Post-instruction − percentage
1	56%	45%	73%	26%
2	53%	47%	78%	22%
3	45%	55%	67%	33%
4	33%	77%	74%	26%
5	52%	48%	75%	25%
6	55%	45%	78%	22%
7	57%	43%	80%	20%
8	49%	51%	79%	21%
9	62%	38%	85%	15%
10	54%	66%	80%	20%
11	60%	40%	82%	18%
12	56%	44%	86%	14%
13	58%	42%	84%	16%
14	60%	40%	87%	13%
15	69%	31%	85%	15%
16	67%	33%	90%	10%

Online Course: Contemporary Mathematics

A professor of mathematics has to demonstrate teaching effectiveness for an upcoming promotion and tenure review. His student evaluations are generally high, but a new institutional mandate involving an upcoming accreditation visit has led to his college's requirement that professors demonstrate evidence of achieving student learning outcomes in addition to their regular student evaluation ratings.

This online course enrolls students from a wide range of backgrounds. Furthermore, many of the students suffer from "math anxiety" and don't believe that they will need to use math in their futures. One of the courses objectives is development of problem-solving skills through making connections between mathematics and modern society. He hopes that students will learn to value mathematics and see the importance of mathematical skills in their daily lives while learning core concepts.

The professor decided to use Quick Writes in the course, believing that the writing activity could help students deepen their thinking about critical math facts and recognize how they could use math in their lives or potential future careers. He also felt that it would be a good way to demonstrate student attainment of learning outcomes. He developed a list of prompt questions drawing from a variety of sources (including Cleland et al., nd). Some examples are as follows:

- Describe a practical career responsibility that might require you to measure an object's surface area, other than by a gift wrapper. Explain your rationale.
- Describe how those planning food preparation at a fast food restaurant might benefit from knowing the average amount of food eaten by males and females.
- Describe an algebraic technique that you could use to add and subtract positive and negative numbers. Identify one way that you might use the technique in the real world.

He posted one prompt at the start of each learning module and asked students to upload their responses to the questions as one of their assignments, completed at the end of the module.

The professor created a 4–1 rating scale for problem-solving with 4 representing the highest level of feasibility of the solution to 1 being the lowest. He had a couple of his colleagues also score the student cards to help ensure that his ratings were accurate. He took an average score from the three ratings he and his colleagues created and used a clustered bar graph (Figure 7.5) to illustrate the different scores in each week of the semester.

He could see that students had improved their written expression of problem-solving skills throughout the term and included the bar graph along with his description of the activity and his process of peer ratings in his promotion and tenure file.

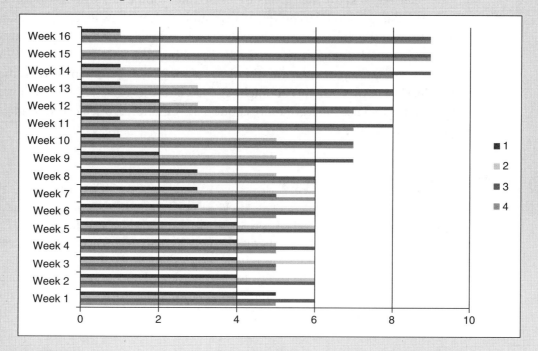

Figure 7.5 Results Bar Graph

Variations and Extensions

- If a class is particularly large, you might ask students to work in groups to summarize themes from individual cards and present you and perhaps the class with a summary of group responses.

- While Quick Writes are primarily used for gathering on-the-spot information about what a student knows about a given concept, term, issue, or other aspect of foundational knowledge, they also have multiple other applications, some of which can help you accomplish goals in other learning domains. We have adapted the following suggestions from several sources, including the *On Course e-Newsletter* (nd), "Six Ways to use Quick Writes to Promote Learning."

- To assess students' ability to apply knowledge they have learned, you might ask students to make a prediction about how the outcome of a case or experiment or other activity will turn out.

- To assess student ability to integrate information, you might ask them to find a statement in a reading or lecture with which they agree and then to describe the alternate points of view. Alternately, you might ask them to find the alternate points of view in other class readings.

- To assess learning in the human dimension, you might use a Quick Write to ask students to respond to a prompt, such as what was the most challenging or surprising fact about this course this first week, or how do you work best with others, and put students in groups so that they can get to know their peers by using the prompt as a discussion starter.

- A Quick Write is also a good technique to help students learn how to learn. For example, ask students to self-reflect and describe how they learn best or what learning dimensions they need to work on. Alternately you could ask something class specific, such as, "What is the most important thing you learned in the class session?" This variation is called the Minute Paper (Angelo & Cross, 1993). You might also ask students to describe something they are confused about and need to learn more about. This variation is often called Muddiest Point (Angelo & Cross, 1993).

Key References and Resources

Angelo, T. A., & Cross, K. P. (1993). CAT 7: Muddiest point. In *Classroom assessment techniques: A handbook for college teachers* (2nd ed., pp. 154–158). San Francisco, CA: Jossey-Bass.

Cleland, J., Rillero, P., & Zambo, R. (nd). Effective prompts for quick writes in science and mathematics. http://ejlts.ucdavis.edu/sites/ejlts.ucdavis.edu/files/articles/Jocleland.pdf.

On Course E-Newsletter. (nd). Six ways to use quick writes to promote learning. http://oncourseworkshop.com/life-long-learning/six-ways-use-quick-writes-promote-learning/.

LEARNING ASSESSMENT TECHNIQUE

Foundational Knowledge

7
Best Summary

Complexity involved in	
Preparation	LOW
In-class implementation	MODERATE
Analysis	MODERATE

Brief Description

Students individually prepare summaries of the main points at the end of a given unit of content, lecture, reading assignment, or other, and then work in groups to compare, evaluate, and select the "best" summary.

Purposes

Summarizing a reading assignment or lecture requires students to figure out what the main ideas are, what the crucial details that support those ideas are, and what information is extraneous so that they can communicate the gist of the material in ways that they can remember. Best Summary is a good technique for helping students develop this valuable ability and to recognize that some information is better than others, even if all information is factually correct.

The Learning Artifacts are the individual student summaries and the groups' indication of the best summary. These artifacts provide you with a way to determine how well students understand principles and concepts, as well as data about whether students can take a large concept and reduce it to its essentials. This technique is effective when used for improvement during a content module to spot-check student understanding. It is a technique that instructors can use to gauge where students are in their thinking in order to target their instruction to help students clarify or develop the knowledge they need to be successful.

Key Learning Goals

- The ability to translate key ideas from this subject area into own words
- Knowledge of important theories in the subject area
- Recognition of the difference between fact and opinion related to this subject area

---

Exhibit 7.1 Best Summary Sample Student Vote Count

Student Name:_____
Assignment:_____
Three most important points:

1.
2.
3.

This summary was/was not voted "best summary" (circle one)   Was   Was not
Rationale for selecting/not selecting this response as "best":
Team members' signatures:

_____

_____

Implementation

Preparation

- Select an assignment that students can summarize succinctly. Lectures, video documentaries, online lectures, and reading assignments are examples of appropriate assignments for Best Summary.
- Decide how you will collect information from students. A simple handout is ideal, and if the selection is particularly succinct, index cards will work as well.
- Determine the parameters of the assignment, particularly your expectations for the type and length of the response. For example, you might state that students should identify the three most important points in the lecture and restate them as simple sentences.
- Determine the criteria upon which you and the students will rate the summary (for example, you may choose to evaluate accuracy, importance, or usefulness) and how students will signal their choices. You might, for example, include a vote count on the handouts as demonstrated in Exhibit 7.1.

Process

1. Provide students with assignment instructions.
2. When students have completed the assignment, organize students into equal-sized teams and ask them to select and indicate the best summary from the members of their group.
3. Ask student teams to report out, reading the best summary and stating their reasons for naming it the best.
4. Collect the students' responses, keeping them organized by team.

Online

Assign students to groups and create separate discussion forums for the different groups. Post the assignment, ask students to prepare summaries of the main points, and then ask students to select the best summary to represent their group. Post the top summaries on the main course page or a whole class discussion forum.

Analysis and Reporting

Mark each summary on a simple scale that evaluates whatever assessment criteria you have selected, for example 4 = high importance to 1 = low importance. There are several ways to report results to students. This LAT has a built-in layer of peer evaluation—for example, as group members select the best summary—and that feedback is delivered at the time they make the decision. You may also want to respond to individuals by telling them your rating of their summaries. This technique is not typically graded; however, instructors may want to assign participation points, as this approach can provide students with incentive for attending class and paying close attention to the lecture. Consider giving an extra point to the "best summary" as extra credit.

You can use individual scores to assess student ability by aggregating the responses. You may look at all the scores, for example, to assess student ability to recognize and identify the most important information. You can also assess student ability to evaluate the quality of information (comparing group assessment of best summary with your own). You also may develop averages for each summary by adding the scores and dividing by the number of responses. For example, you might find that the average score on the summary is 3.6 (relatively high-importance). If you use this activity repeatedly, track student scores over time. You can develop a mean or median score of student responses over the term. You may also do a key word analysis of the summaries, for example a graphic display in a word cloud created at Wordle.com. To display your aggregated findings, develop a simple table showing average scores on the summaries. You may want to break out by demographic information (for example, first-year, second-year students or majors, nonmajors, and so forth if that is important to know).

Examples

Onsite: Introduction to Astronomy

How the seasons happen is a confusing concept for many students, and students often have preconceptions that are difficult to change. The professor of this course has a learning outcome that upon completion of the course, students will be able to describe what causes the seasons. To teach to this outcome, he has students read a textbook chapter that explains the seasons and then, when students come to class, he provides them with a handout in which he asks them to write a 4-point summary that explains what causes the seasons. After students have completed the assignment, he puts them into groups and asks them to select the most accurate summary provided by members of their group and then sign the handout to show their agreement that it is the best. He then asks each team to read their selected best summary aloud. The professor collects all of the handouts, keeping them organized by group, and then scores them for accuracy using a simple 4-point scoring system as shown in Table 7.18.

He often finds that even though some individuals in the group had inaccurate responses, together they were able to select the most factually accurate description. He makes notes of the misconceptions among the individuals and addresses these issues in lecture in the next class session.

Table 7.18 Best Summary Introduction to Astronomy Sample Scoring Table

Groups	Student Names	Professor's Rating (1–4)	Group's Vote for Best
Introduction to Astronomy **What Causes the Seasons "Best Summary"**			
1	Olivia	4	Micah
	Micah	3	
	Ching	4	
	Michaela	2	
2	Troy	3	Elena
	Jose	2	
	Elena	4	
	Treydon	3	
3	Joel	1	Heidi
	Heidi	4	
	Elle	2	
	David	4	

Online: Business Law I

The Business Department requires its instructors to include department-specified learning outcomes in their syllabi and to assess and report on them for inclusion in the departmental assessment report. One of these outcomes is that students will be able to define the key elements of a contract.

The instructor of this Business Law online course created a module that had several parts. For the first part, students were to review her video lecture on contracts. Next, they were instructed to post the four contract elements and a summary in their own words of each element. Students were then instructed to select the best summary from among the individuals in their group. The instructor reviewed each individual summary, rating them for completion (all four points) and accuracy (good description to poor description), as shown in Table 7.19.

The instructor posted the group-selected best summaries on the main course page, along with her notes about what was outstanding about them. She used this information as the basis for her report to the department's assessment committee.

Table 7.19 Best Summary Business Law I Sample Scoring Table

Business Law I Contract Elements Best Summary		
Student Names	Completion	Accuracy
Anna	4	3
Parker	2	1
Julian	4	4
Kimberly	3	2
Luke	3	3

Variations and Extensions

- Consider asking teams to trade and evaluate another team's summaries. This approach alleviates the pressure of having students make selections among students in their own groups, and thus may encourage them to speak up more candidly about what is good and bad about the various summaries.
- Consider having student groups rank order rather than selecting the best summary; doing so provides further information for assessment, as it provides additional details about their judgment of quality.

Key References and Resources

Nilsen, C., Odahlen, B., Geller, L., Hintz, K., & Borden-King, L. (2011, February). *Fifty ways to teach your students*. Presented at 30th Annual Conference on the First Year Experience. http://www.minotstateu.edu/cetl/pdf/50waystoteachyourstudents.pdf.

LEARNING ASSESSMENT TECHNIQUE

Foundational Knowledge

8
Snap Shots

Complexity involved in	
Preparation	LOW
In-class implementation	LOW
Analysis	LOW

Brief Description

The instructor presents questions during class along with several possible answers. Individual students choose which answer they think is correct and the instructor makes a quick visual assessment of class results. Students then discuss answers in small groups, after which they together choose an answer again and the instructor makes another assessment and compares results.

Purpose

When used frequently, this technique encourages students to stay focused and attentive during lectures or class activities. In addition, the act of taking the quiz provides both teachers and students with an opportunity to check understanding on the spot and make adjustments accordingly. This technique also presents an opportunity for peer coaching, as students participate in small group discussions in order to determine a consensus answer. Snap Shots is an effective technique in courses that require students to learn and retain substantial foundational knowledge.

The technique is called Snap Shots because it gives teachers a quick and observable record of a progress point. The record of responses is the assessable Learning Artifact, whether a show of hands or color-coded index cards (along with a quick tally of correct and incorrect responses) or the report generated by the automatic response system. This LAT is a simple way to collect data on how well students understand material that has just been presented, and it is particularly useful in large lecture classes, where it can be challenging to gauge student understanding in real time. Snap Shots can be used to assess students' prior knowledge when beginning a new module or unit of content. This usage will help you determine where to target instruction. The technique can also be used as a spot-check of understanding in the current module or unit. Used in this way, it helps teachers determine understanding or misunderstanding in-the-moment so that they can address misconceptions or make corrections in a timely manner.

Key Learning Goals

- Knowledge of central facts in this subject area
- Knowledge of key terms of this subject area
- Knowledge of important theories in the subject area
- Recognition of the difference between fact and opinion related to this subject area

Implementation

Preparation

- Develop a quiz that has a single question or just a few questions. The answers should be multiple choice (A, B, C, or D) or True (T) and False (F). The Carnegie Mellon Eberly Center for Teaching Excellence and Educational Innovation offers the following advice on creating questions (http://www.cmu.edu/teaching/assessment/assesslearning/concepTests .html):
  - Questions often describe a problem, event, or situation. Examples of appropriate types of questions:
    Asking students to predict the outcome of an event (e.g., What would happen in this experiment? How would changing one variable affect others?)
    Asking students to apply rules or principles to new situations (e.g., Which concept is relevant here? How would you apply it?)
    Asking students to solve a problem using a known equation or select a procedure to complete a new task (e.g., What procedure would be appropriate to solve this problem?)
  - Using prompts such as:
    Which of the following best describes . . .
    Which is the best method for . . .
    If the value of X was changed to . . .
    Which of the following is the best explanation for . . .
    Which of the following is another example of . . .
    What is the major problem with . . .
    What would happen if . . .
- Determine how you will display the quiz question(s). A slide projected on the screen is ideal, particularly for large classes, so that everyone can see the questions, but writing the question(s) on the board or on a flip board is also appropriate, particularly with smaller classes.
- Determine how students will make their responses visible. Consider the following options:
  - Students can indicate by a show of hands. This approach has the advantages of being easy and of showing you individual answers, but to have a Learning Artifact, you must take an extra step to preserve the data (e.g., tallying and recording in your notes or taking a smartphone photo).
  - You can create response cards, potentially color-coded (e.g., all Trues are blue and all Falses are green). This approach has the advantage of easy counting, but cards can be bulky and difficult to distribute and collect, particularly if you have a large number of students.
  - You can use an automated response system, such as clickers or a smartphone polling system. This approach has the advantage of being easy for data collection and

interesting for students. However, if using phones you will not know individual responses and you will exclude any students who do not own a smartphone.

- Determine how you will record scores. If you have asked for a show of hands, a quick photo (for example, by a smartphone camera) can serve as a useful record. If you have had students hold up cards, jot down the responses in your notes. If you have used a clicker system or phone polling system, simply save the results.

Process

1. Provide a brief lecture or demonstration of the concept(s) that lasts approximately 15 minutes.
2. Present a conceptual question, and ask students to answer the question individually and demonstrate their results. Give them 1 or 2 minutes to think and respond; record their scores.
3. Present the overall responses to the quiz questions with no discussion of the correct answer.
4. Ask students to work in small groups for 3–5 minutes to try to convince other group members as to the correctness of their answers.
5. Quiz the students again, and record their scores.
6. Go over the answer(s) to the question(s) and explain why answer is the more correct or the best choice.

Online

This LAT works well in synchronous Web conferencing sessions, with VoIP, which many LMSs offer. As you talk, post the question as well as one answer, and ask students to signal their agreement with the answer by "raising their hands." Then provide a different answer, and ask students who agree to "raise their hands." Continue until you have run out of potential answers. Ask students to discuss their responses in chat rooms. Re-administer the quiz after the appropriate time has lapsed. Alternatively, you can use discussion boards for students to discuss asynchronously.

Analysis and Reporting

Count the number of correct answers (displayed by a show of hands, cards or in clicker responses). This technique has a built-in layer of communicating the accuracy of their responses to students. When the correct answer is revealed, they know whether they have answered the question correctly or not. Snap Shots typically are ungraded or alternately counted as low-stakes grading measures, such as participation points.

You can quickly see the collected or average scores on the question(s), and it is possible for you to take a tally of correct and incorrect answers and record the scores. You can do a simple average of the information or, if you have used automated responses or polling software, you will also receive tables or graphs with the information readily analyzed. Simple tables or charts may be used to report aggregated information. A bar chart may be used to show average scores on the question(s) or to show correct answers before and after the group discussion. If you have the information, you can examine grades prior to implementing this activity and then afterward, with an eye toward illustrating the relationship between the activity and (hoped for) increased performance.

Examples

Onsite: Introduction to Geoscience

The professor of an introduction to geoscience course set a learning objective that by the end of the semester students would be able to answer questions about the basics of rocks and the rock cycle. To teach the concept, the professor used a 15-minute lecture introducing key concepts. He stopped and displayed the following questions in his presentation software (which he adapted from here: http://wps.prenhall.com/esm_tarbuck_earth_8/0,9073,1298259-,00.html):

What allows us to categorize rocks into three types: ingenuous, sedimentary, and metamorphic?
    Involvement of sediment
    Process of deformation
    Process of formation
    Magma or weathering
    Process of inflation
    Whether or not the rock melts
According to the rock cycle, which of the following is incorrect?
    Magma may crystallize to form ingenuous rocks
    Sedimentary rocks may weather to become ingenuous rocks
    Metamorphic rocks may melt to become magma
    Ingenuous rocks may metamorphose into metamorphic rocks

The professor asked the students for a show of hands. He noticed that most of the students had the wrong answer to both questions. He put students into working groups of four and asked the members to convince others of their responses. He polled them again after the group discussion and noticed that the number of correct responses improved dramatically (Figure 7.6).

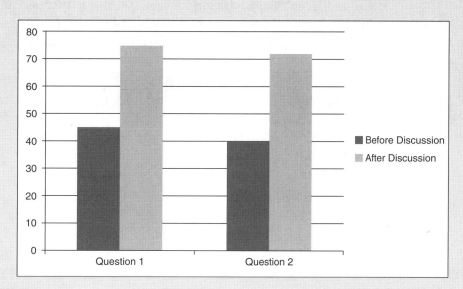

Figure 7.6 Introduction to Geoscience: Column Graph Displaying Pre/Post Correct Responses
Note: The heights of the columns show the percentage of correct responses.

He began to implement concept tests as a regular part of his instruction. Because he had information from tests before and after implementation of Snap Shots, he was able to compare test results. Student scores as well as attendance improved dramatically after his implementation of the quizzes.

Online: General Physics

The professor of an online course was teaching an introductory physics course. She had a learning outcome that students should be able to use simple algebra in the application of physics theories to make quantitative predictions. She also was preparing for a promotion and tenure review, for which she needed to provide evidence of teaching effectiveness.

She met with students synchronously once per week through a collaborative tool in her institution's LMS. This particular week, she gave a brief 10-minute lecture on the laws of motion. She posted a quiz question (related to a person in an elevator and the force of the elevator floor) and had students respond by using the "raise your hand" function in the system.

Because many of the students missed the question, she selected several students and asked them to form chat rooms for discussion. She gave the groups 5 minutes to discuss the question, then asked the students to come back to the main room, whereupon she asked the question again. Student scores improved in the second round. She explained the correct answer to the students, indicating why one answer was the better choice.

In developing her tenure portfolio, she provided a description of the lecture content and of the Snap Shots activity. She also provided the following chart, showing student scores before and after discussion, which she believed documented that the activity had been successful and also showed the value of her use of collaborative learning (Figure 7.7).

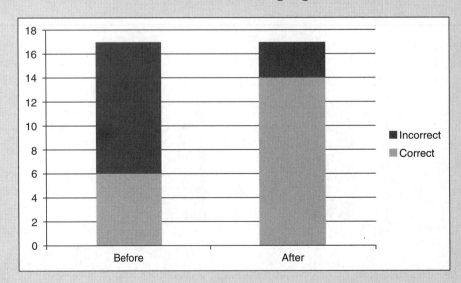

Figure 7.7 Introduction to Physics: Column Graph Displaying Pre/Post Correct Responses

Variations and Extensions

This LAT may be done with groups as well. Form students into teams and have the team members work together on answering the questions. Consider calling on groups to explain the rationale for their selections. This may provide you with insights into students' understandings and misunderstandings and possibly about the wording of the questions you are using.

Key References and Resources

Carnegie Mellon Eberly Center for Teaching Excellence and Educational Innovation. (n.d.). Using Concept Tests. http://www.cmu.edu/teaching/assessment/assesslearning/concepTests.html.

Cottell, P. G., & Millis, B. (2010). Cooperative learning in accounting. In B. Millis (Ed.), *Cooperative learning in higher education: Across the disciplines, across the academy* (pp. 11–33). Sterling, VA: Stylus Publishing.

Larsy, N. (nd). Peer instruction: Comparing clickers to flashcards. http://arxiv.org/pdf/physics/0702186.pdf.

Mazur, E. (1997). *Peer instruction: A user's manual.* Upper Saddle River, NJ: Prentice Hall.

McConnell, D. A., Steer, D. N., Owens, K. D., Knott, J. R., Van Horn, S., Borowski, W., . . . Heaney, P. J. (2006). Using concept tests to assess and improve student conceptual understanding in introductory geoscience courses. *Journal of Geoscience Education, 54*(1), 61.

LEARNING ASSESSMENT TECHNIQUE

Foundational Knowledge

9
Team Tests

Complexity involved in	
Preparation	HIGH
In-class implementation	HIGH
Analysis	MODERATE

Brief Description

Students work in teams to prepare for instructor-created exams and then take the exams first individually and next as a group. This LAT thus proceeds in three steps: (1) group members study for a test together, (2) individuals take the test, and (3) the group takes the test.

Purpose

By working together to prepare for the exam, students help each other deepen their understanding of the content. Because each student first takes the test independently, this technique emphasizes individual accountability. By retaking the test as a team, individual students benefit from the collective knowledge of the group. This technique, therefore, encourages both individual accountability and promotive interdependence among team members, accomplishing two key features of effective collaborative learning (Barkley et al., 2014). Since in this activity individual scores are often lower than group scores, it can help to underscore the power of collaboration.

This technique yields two different kinds of Learning Artifacts: individual test scores and group tests scores. The tests may be short quizzes on a single unit or substantial exams covering larger amounts of material. Test results may be used to gauge both individual and group understanding of foundational knowledge, and the collected data can also be aggregated at both levels. Instructors may use this technique during an instructional module or unit to assess student understanding of important course concepts in process. It can provide individuals, groups, and the teacher with information about whether students are making adequate progress toward their goals of developing foundational knowledge. Some instructors use this technique after a unit of content as a summative assessment of what students have learned. When they do so, however, they typically have it as an ongoing feature of the course, rather than a one-time assessment. This latter approach allows students to form strong bonds and to begin to feel responsible for each other's successes while allowing teachers to track information over time to document change and improvement.

Key Learning Goals

- Knowledge of central facts in this subject area
- Knowledge of key terms of this subject area
- Knowledge of important theories in the subject area
- The ability to translate key ideas from this subject area into own words

Implementation

Preparation

- Once you have determined the content that students should master and you have presented it in lecture, reading assignment, or other activity, the preparation for this technique is the same as preparing a good examination for individuals. Refer to a source such as Davis's *Tools for Teaching* (1993) chapter on testing and grading for tips on developing a good test.
- Also, consider creating a test study guide to provide students with a focused framework for preparing for the test. This can help alleviate student anxiety and provide them with scaffolding for learning success. Alternately, have them create their own study guides. See Study Outlines, LAT 44, for additional guidance.
- Create the test, which probably will involve a handout that students will complete in class.
- Determine a system for scoring. Most faculty who use this technique also use traditional grading methods, such as percentage of questions students answered correctly. Also determine how students will record their responses (bubble in on handout, scantron, or scratch cards?) and how you will let students know the correct responses (posting them or reviewing with the full class?).

Process

1. Form groups of 4–6. Consider a method for forming groups that ensure that each team contains members with comparable levels of ability (for example, ensure that each group has some high-achieving and low-achieving individuals).
2. Ask the groups to study together, allowing some instructional time for this step. Depending on the size and complexity of the material to be mastered, the groups may meet for 15 minutes, a full class period, or longer.
3. Administer the test for students to complete individually and to submit to the instructor for grading.
4. Before returning the graded individual tests, ask students to rejoin their groups to reach a consensus on the answer(s) and submit a group response to the test.
5. After groups have submitted their responses, entertain any urgent questions students might have. If they have had hot debate about answers, they will not want to wait until the following day to learn the answers. This is a teachable moment, and you can capitalize on it.

6. Let the groups know when you will report their individual and group scores, and if you plan further discussion based upon your analysis, let them know that as well.

Online

Use a discussion forum or Documents/Wiki. Organize students into groups of 5–6 and identify as Group A, Group B, and so forth, and create a forum for each group. Give groups time to work together to pool information, resources, and ideas to prepare for the test. Have students take the exam as individuals and then submit it to you for grading. Before you return the graded version back to them, ask all students to work together in their designated forum or document to create collaborative exam responses to submit. Assign (or have students select) a group leader who will submit the "group test" for the group.

Analysis and Reporting

Look at individual scores of the test, typically the percentage of answers each student answered correctly. (For example, you might note that student 1 got 80% correct, student 2 got 100%, and so forth.) Then examine each item of the test. Determine gaps in student knowledge by identifying where students consistently answered incorrectly (alternately consider whether the test question is poorly worded or is otherwise ambiguous and revise accordingly).

Examine individual tests according to the group. Do a simple statistical analysis of test scores to show differences between individual and group test scores. Use the averages of all individual and all group scores (for example, "the average individual scored x and the average team scored y").

Try to determine whether any groups are underperforming. (Consider recommending additional resources if you think necessary; also consider whether group membership needs to be reconstituted to ensure that groups are not perpetuating misinformation and thus misunderstanding among group members.)

Simple tables or charts can be useful for reporting information. Use a bar or column graph to display percentages correct or incorrect for both individual and then group performance. Consider also using a graph to display results based on item analysis.

Use a spreadsheet to track scores at each test administration and generate a line graph to track individual and group performance over time. In a narrative, consider the following:

Describe your interpretation of the differences between individual and group performance. Which is higher and why do you think so?

Describe your thoughts about changes in individual performance over time. It is likely that scores will increase as students become better test takers, but it is also possible that they will not improve. Consider what might be causing that; for example, consider whether the material has become more difficult.

If you have test performance data of classes before implementing Team Tests, consider a before and after comparison on success for both individuals and groups. You may want to describe whether the activity has, as might be anticipated, improved student performance.

Examples

Onsite: Music Composition and Theory

In order to transfer to a 4-year institution and be placed at the junior level, community college music majors needed to pass a comprehensive exam at the receiving institution assessing their knowledge of music theory. Despite what many faculty and students felt should be appropriate preparation, students were not doing well and were often required to repeat second-year theory at the transfer institution. This outcome was frustrating and discouraging, and the music theory faculty decided to work together to help students become more successful. They created an extensive bank of multiple-choice exam questions focusing on the kind of information they knew would be on the placement exam. They then worked with their college's Instructional Technology Department to set up a test bank that was self-grading and accessible online.

During the last course of sophomore music theory, the faculty had a stated learning objective that students would be able to score correctly a minimum of 70% on a comprehensive exam assessing understanding and recall of foundational knowledge in first- and second-year theory. At the beginning of the term, students were assigned to small groups. On a weekly basis, students went to the media center to take a practice quiz first individually and then retake it as a group. While taking the quizzes as a group, students helped each other review material, such as the steps they needed to take to identify intervals or the chords within a harmonic progression. The testing software maintained a record of both individual and group scores that faculty took into account for the course grades. They also tracked performance on each of the test items, as shown in Figure 7.8.

The following autumn, the community college theory faculty contacted faculty members at the local university to track placement of that year's transfer students. Scores and placement were so markedly improved that both institutions' faculty decided to work together to enhance the breadth and depth of questions in the test bank and to develop strategies for improving articulation in the music history and music performance courses.

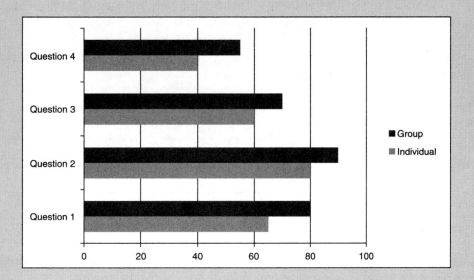

Figure 7.8 Music Composition and Theory: Bar Graph Displaying Individual and Group Scores on Test Items in the Practice Comprehensive Theory Exam

Online: English Poetry of the Romantic Period

In this graduate level course, the professor knew that students were anxious about the upcoming master's degree comprehensive examination. He believed that this anxiety was distracting them from focusing on what they needed to learn specifically in his course, which included a learning outcome of identifying the major Romantic Poets through a few lines of their writing. He decided to use Team Tests to address both issues: he used the content of his course to help prepare students for the type of questions they would be asked on the comprehensive exam.

The professor designed a sample test focusing on English Romantic poetry and explained to students that the test included identification and essay questions as well as quote identifications similar in style to the comprehensive exam. He then asked students to work in online groups to share study strategies as they reviewed the material and prepared to take the sample test.

He explained the testing strategy to the students. He asked them to sign an honor code stating that they would work independently on the first test and collaboratively on the second. He gave individual students the test first, through his institution's LMS. He asked each group to select a leader and re-administered the test to the group leaders who were told to work together with their groups to answer the questions. He set up a chat room for each group that the members could use to discuss their answers. By working in groups, students were able to fill in their knowledge gaps regarding his course while they learned additional passage identification techniques that prepared them for the comprehensive exam.

He analyzed the individual test results by item. He was able to report to individual students where they appeared to need the most additional work in preparation for the exam (for example, Fred had difficulty recognizing Keats and Byron, while Atseena had trouble identifying Shelley and Byron; Table 7.20).

He also analyzed the test the groups had completed. He noted that the groups on average scored higher than individuals (Figure 7.9).

He encouraged students to continue working together in preparation for the comprehensive exams, using the data he had collected to demonstrate to them that they learned more together than alone.

Table 7.20 English Poetry of the Romantic Period: Table Displaying Individual Scores on Test Items in the Practice Master's Comprehensive Exam

	Keats	Shelley	Blake	Browning	Byron
Fred	−	+	+	+	−
Atseena	+	−	+	+	−
Steven	−	+	+	−	+
Grace	−	−	−	+	+
Corban	+	+	−	−	−
Tasha	−	+	+	−	−

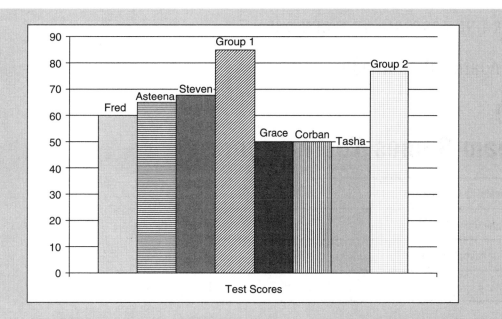

Figure 7.9 English Poetry of the Romantic Period: Column Graph Displaying and Comparing Individual and Group Scores on Practice Master's Comprehensive Exam

Variations and Extensions

- Ask groups to submit materials they create to prepare for the exam. For example, they can turn in a brief summary of each answer they formulated, a copy of the outline and material they used to organize their discussion, or a description of the procedures they adopted to prepare for the exam. Use this information for further analysis, for example of their study processes.

Key References and Resources

Barkley, E. F., Major, C. H., & Cross, K. P. (2014). CoLT 12: Test-taking teams. In *Collaborative learning techniques* (2nd ed., pp. 219–223). San Francisco, CA: Jossey-Bass.

Gooblar, D. (2014). Want to take group work to the next level? Give team tests. *ChronicleVitae*. https://chroniclevitae.com/news/656-want-to-take-group-work-to-the-next-level-give-teamtests?cid =at&utm_source=at&utm_medium=en#sthash.VGFdlvMm.dpuf.

Michaelsen, L. K., & Black, R. H. (1994). Building learning teams: The key to harnessing the power of small groups in higher education. In S. Kadel & J. Keehner (Eds.), *Collaborative learning: A sourcebook for higher education, 2* (pp. 65–81). State College, PA: National Center for Teaching, Learning and Assessment.

Michaelsen, L. K., Fink, L. D., & Knight, A. (1997). Designing effective group activities: Lessons for classroom teaching and faculty development. In D. DeZure (Ed.), *To improve the academy: Resources for faculty. Instructional and organizational development, 16* (pp. 373–397). Stillwater, OK: New Forums Press Co.

LEARNING ASSESSMENT TECHNIQUE

Foundational Knowledge

10
Team Games Tournament

Complexity involved in	
Preparation	HIGH
In-class implementation	HIGH
Analysis	HIGH

Brief Description

In this team games activity, home teams work together to learn content and then individuals representing the home team compete against students from other teams in a tournament.

Purposes

Team Games Tournament encourages students to help each other master course content and skills. While participating in their home teams (diverse achievement/ability teams) to prepare for the tournament, students coach each other in a form of peer teaching. They then strive to do their best while competing with students in newly formed tournament teams (similar achievement/ability). Both group structures have advantages, so this LAT provides a unique opportunity for students to both teach each other and learn from each other.

This technique is an unusual assessment technique in that it is in the form of a game, which many students find appealing. It also creates *Learning Artifacts* in the form of individual scores as well as group scores. These data provide a different perspective on student learning that in some ways is comparable to that created by tests. The benefit of this LAT as a form of assessment is that cooperative competition can motivate students to demonstrate their knowledge. Many times those with test anxiety may be more at ease in a game environment. Team Games Tournaments may be used during the instructional process to help you gauge students' knowledge and understanding of a unit or module of content, and then continued as a form of ongoing assessment of their progress. This LAT may also be used prior to a formal test or other assessment for students to review a unit of content. Used in this way, students may identify their own gaps in knowledge and thus self-assess and study accordingly. It is also possible to use Team Games Tournaments as a way of assessing knowledge after a given unit. That is, game scores may be used in lieu of more traditional assessments. This use does raise the stakes of the activity, however, which can increase competition, which some students will enjoy and others will not.

Key Learning Goals

- Knowledge of central facts in this subject area
- Knowledge of key terms of this subject area
- Knowledge of important theories in the subject area
- Recognition of the difference between fact and opinion related to this subject area

Implementation

Preparation

- Choose a method to organize students by achievement level. For example, create a list of students according to highest-to-lowest current class grade or recent quiz scores.
- Develop a list of home teams, generally comprising 4–6 members of differing achievement levels to ensure that each team has a mix of high-, average-, and low-achieving students. A stratified, diverse ability Home Team might include, for example:
  - **Home Team A:** Student 1A (high achieving), Student 2A (high average achieving), Student 3A (low average achieving), Student 4A (low achieving)
  - **Home Team B:** Student 1B (high achieving), Student 2B (high average achieving), Student 3B (low average achieving), Student 4B (low achieving)
  - **Home Team C:** Student 1C (high achieving), Student 2C (high average achieving), Student 3C (low average achieving), Student 4C (low achieving)
- Develop a list of Tournament Teams. Create Tournament teams by placing roughly equal-performing students from different Home Teams on a new Tournament Team that is stratified homogenously by similar level of academic achievement (i.e., high-achieving students compete against each other, average-achieving students compete against each other, low-achieving students compete against each other), for example:
  - **Tournament Team 1:** Student 1A, Student 1B, Student 1C
  - **Tournament Team 2:** Student 2A, Student 2B, Student 2C
  - **Tournament Team 3:** Student 3A; Student 3B; Student 3C
  - **Tournament Team 4:** Student 4A; Student 4B; Student 4C
- Create a set of fill-in-the-blank questions about a particular unit of content, with each question bearing a separate number. Ensure that you have developed a sufficient number of questions to fill the time so that student teams are not left with nothing to do. Make copies of the question sheet for each Tournament Team.
- Develop an answer sheet, and make copies for each team.
- Make decks of numbered cards that correspond to the number of Tournament Teams you will have (i.e., if you have 4 tournament teams, you will need 4 sets of cards). Each card

Table 7.21 Sample Tournament Team Score Sheet

Tournament Team Score Sheet for Team __					
Player's Name	Home Group Name	Score for Round 1	Score for Round 2	Score for Round 3	Total Points

should bear one number that corresponds to one of the questions on the list (e.g., if you have 50 questions, create 50 cards numbered 1–50).

- Prepare score sheets for each Tournament Team. (See Table 7.21.)
- Determine how you will score the answers. Some instructors choose to allocate a simple scoring system such as one point per question. Others choose to allocate based upon a hierarchical system, with the high scorer receiving six points, high middle receiving four points, low middle receiving two points, and low receiving one point.

Process
1. Form Home Teams, and ask these teams to review a unit of content.
2. Regroup students into Tournament Teams.
3. Announce a time limit for the game and ask a member of each team to pick up a set of numbered cards, a question sheet, an answer sheet, and a score sheet.
4. Each student in a team selects a card. The student with the highest number begins the game; the student with the next highest serves as Materials Manager.
5. The Materials Manager takes up the numbered cards and shuffles again.
6. The first student begins the game by picking a card from the top of the stack, turning it over on the table, reading the number.
7. The Materials Manager reads the corresponding question from the question list aloud.
8. The first student tries to answer the question as others listen.
9. Play goes in clockwise direction, at this point moving to student number three. Each successive student may elect to "pass" (without answering) or "challenge" (by providing a different answer from the Materials Manager/first player).
10. After the last person passes or challenges, the Materials Manager checks the answer on the answer sheet.
11. The first person to correctly answer the question (including the first student) keeps the card.
12. The game continues with the next play, as the student next in line selects a card and then answers the corresponding question.
13. When all the cards have been claimed, students count cards and record their scores in the score sheet.
14. Students compete in additional rounds until the time allotted has ended.

15. The Materials Manager returns the materials, including the tabulated score sheets to you; you then record total scores on the board for each Home Team and announce the winner (the Home Team with the highest score).

Online

This technique will likely be most effective in synchronous environments that simulate the onsite experience. Teachers using Web-Conferencing should form their Teams and assign them conference rooms. Students can work together in their Teams in conference rooms then answer questions in the Web-conference main room.

Analysis and Reporting

Review your Learning Artifacts, which are the student scorecards, and provide each one with a total score. Although you may use Tournament scores as part of the course grade, they are more typically ungraded, although participation points frequently are given. Consider awarding the highest scoring team bonus points.

To examine scores in the aggregate, identify the highest and lowest scores, and also determine a class average. Then look for any outlier home team scores to indicate which groups were most and least successful in preparation for the game, and then determine an average for all the home team scores. Display aggregated performance in bar charts or use line graphs to demonstrate aggregated performance of individuals or teams over time. If you wish to write a narrative for your report, describe the activity and the results, offering your interpretation of the reasons for high and low individual and team scores.

Examples

Onsite: Introduction to Genetics

The professor decided to use a Team Games Tournament to help students prepare for a major unit exam, which was tied to a learning goal of describing the process of natural selection. Prior to class she took her roster of 24 students and ranked them from highest achieving to lowest achieving based upon the results of their most recent quiz grades. The professor then organized this list into four quadrants, selecting one student from each quadrant to form six Home Teams. The professor then made another list in which the six students in each of the four quadrants were assigned to four Tournament Teams.

The professor also prepared by making a list of fill-in-the-blank questions related to evolution and natural selection such as: The person who wrote about the evolution of individuals was _____. The modern synthesis of evolution adds _____ to the Darwinian concept. An example of human polymorphisms is _____.

For the first 20 minutes of class, the professor asked students to work in their Home Teams to compile a summary of everything they knew about evolution to create a "Crib Sheet"

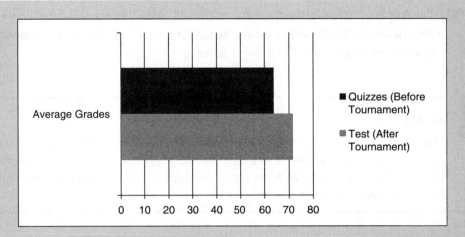

Figure 7.10 Introduction to Genetics: Bar Graph Displaying Prior Tournament Quiz Scores and Post Tournament Test Scores

that each Home Team Member could take with them when competing in the tournament. She then reformed the students into their Tournament Teams and gave each team a written list of instructions of the game. After reviewing the instructions and answering questions regarding the procedures, she told students to begin playing. After 30 minutes, the professor picked up the scored cards and announced the winning Home Team. Students competed in five tournament rounds.

Given that her concern was the quiz scores, she decided to look at average scores on the quizzes and average score on the test, which was based on questions similar to those in the quizzes. She saw an increase, and while she knew the measures, the quizzes and the test, were not exactly the same, she believed that the tournaments did help students prepare for the test by deepening their foundational knowledge (Figure 7.10).

Online: English Composition and Reading

An English instructor teaching a unit on Shakespeare decided to use Team Games Tournament to help students review and prepare for a multiple-choice examination. She created a list of students ranked by their scores on the previous exam. She then divided her list of 32 students into four quadrants, which would ultimately be the Tournament Teams. She next selected students from each of the four quadrants to constitute four heterogeneous Home Teams.

In a synchronous class session, she told students that they would play a Team Games Tournament to help them prepare for the next exam and that the winning team would receive a 5-point bonus on the exam. She then announced Home Teams and asked them to go to one of the four designated conference/chat rooms she had prepared in advance and spend 20 minutes reviewing the different Shakespeare plays they had studied. To guide their review, she had prepared a worksheet that asked students to list the date of the play, the main characters, the basic plot, and so forth.

Table 7.22 English Reading and Composition: Table Displaying Tournament Team Score Sheet

Tournament Team Score Sheet For Team 1					
Player's Name	Home Group Name	Score for Round 1	Score for Round 2	Score for Round 3	Total Points
Liam	Bears	4	4	6	12
Jesse	Lions	6	6	4	16
Lauren	Rattlers	2	2	1	5
Kelly	Leopards	1	1	2	4

When the class reconvened in the main chat room, she posted the list that organized students into Tournament Teams. Rather than using a deck of cards, however, the teacher simply read the question, and had students post their responses in Google Docs. The teacher later graded their responses, comparing scores of Tournament Teams and then selecting the winning Home Team. Table 7.22 shows a section of the scorecard she had for analysis.

She sent an announcement to the class informing them of the winning home team along with an attached answer sheet with the correct answers to the questions used in the tournament.

Variations and Extensions

• Pair this activity with another LAT, such as Best Summary, Guided Reading Notes, or Snap Shots, to help students prepare for the tournament.

Key References and Resources

Barkley, E., Major, C., & Cross, K. P. (2014). Team games tournaments. In *Collaborative learning techniques: A handbook for college faculty* (2nd ed., pp. 365–371). San Francisco, CA: Jossey-Bass.
Slavin, R. E. (1990). *Cooperative learning: Theory research and practice*. Boston, MA: Allyn and Bacon.

CHAPTER 8

Teaching and Assessing for the Application Learning Domain

Once students understand the basic facts, principles, and concepts that constitute a discipline's foundational knowledge, they need to *use* it in some manner. Indeed, given the split-second speed with which today's students access information combined with the breakneck rate at which it increases (a 2011 study suggests it more than doubles every two years [Gantz & Reinsel, 2011]), the real value of a college education may be in helping students learn how to effectively apply knowledge rather than simply acquire it. Because knowledge can be used in different ways, Fink subdivides the application dimension of significant learning into three categories: skills; learning how to manage complex projects; and developing the ability to engage in critical, creative, and practical thinking. The techniques in this chapter offer ideas for implementing and assessing structured activities that require students to use foundational knowledge in these three ways.

Clarifying Learning Goals Related to Application Learning

The category of application learning is the centerpiece of many college teachers' goals for learning in their courses. Nearly every professor we have met wants to move students beyond simply understanding and remembering information to working with that information in some manner of application. Fink (2013) organizes application learning into three categories: skills, managing complex projects, and thinking. Because the category of managing complex projects overlaps with research projects, which Fink squarely places in the Learning How to Learn domain, we treat this category in the Learning How to Learn chapter and focus here on Skills and Critical, Creative, and Practical Thinking.

Skills Goals

Many teachers want students to be able to apply foundational knowledge by engaging in a particular kind of action. This ability to do something is a skill, whether it is to write an essay, solve a problem, or retrieve information efficiently and appropriately from the Internet. These skills, as well as more physical skills such as those in sports, the arts, medicine, science, and engineering, are integral to the application category of the Significant Learning Taxonomy.

Critical, Creative, and Practical Thinking Goals

What constitutes "thinking" has been a topic that has fascinated philosophers throughout history. Instructing students on how to do it—and do it well—has challenged teachers for just as long. Fink's three categories of thinking, modeled after Sternberg's (1989) concept of the "triarchic mind," each possess unique characteristics, so we describe them separately.

Critical Thinking

Critical thinking is usually a central core competency that faculty as well as institutional leaders and administrators want teachers to help all students achieve by graduation. Defining "critical" thinking, however, is a conundrum that challenges even experts on the topic. A team of faculty experts working with AAC&U to craft a definition that could be generally applied across the country and in all academic disciplines defined critical thinking as "a habit of mind characterized by the comprehensive exploration of issues, ideas, artifacts, and events before accepting or formulating an opinion or conclusion." (See Exhibit 8.2.)

Creative Thinking

Once considered the domain of artists, inventors, and eccentrics, creativity today is recognized as an important, if not essential, skill for success in multiple arenas. Although most of us feel reasonably confident that we recognize creativity when we see it, actually pinning it down in a precise definition that applies across contexts has confounded scholars for decades. Consensus appears to be moving toward recognition of two core elements: production of something that is novel *and* valuable. Anderson and Krathwohl (2001, pp. 84–88) note that the novelty aspect is challenging for educators, and therefore shift the emphasis to synthesis. In their taxonomy, *create* requires students to construct an original product by drawing upon elements from many sources and then putting them together into a new structure. Faculty working on AAC&U's Creative Thinking VALUE Rubric also stress the importance of making connections and synthesizing. Thus in education, creative thinking is often a process by which students take preexisting ideas, influences, or objects and combine them in such a manner as to make a new and organized presentation that is more than what the student had at the beginning.

Practical Thinking

The third kind of thinking—practical thinking—means students "are learning how to answer questions, make decisions, and solve problems" (Fink, 2013, p. 48). To some extent, all three of these practical thinking tasks can be described as problem solving. Developing students' ability to solve problems efficiently and effectively is a goal most teachers share. Generally speaking, problems can be described as puzzles that require thinking to solve, but what constitutes a "problem" varies widely across the disciplines. When we think about a math problem, we typically think of a well-defined statement or proposition for which a correct or best answer can be determined using appropriate mathematical methods. When we think about a social problem, we think of a messy societal situation such as poverty, violence, or racism that is a composite of many factors and may actually not be solvable. Whether the problems we want students to grapple with are straightforward tasks designed to produce a specified result or complex quandaries that seem incapable of resolution, problem solving is fundamental to most disciplines. Helping students engage in effective problem solving is a practical application of thinking that will be valuable to them throughout their lives.

To identify learning goals related to application learning, Fink suggests asking ourselves questions that address how that learning is relevant in a particular course. Here are his examples of these questions (Fink, 2013, p. 83):

- What important skills do students need to learn?
- What kinds of thinking are important for students to learn? Critical thinking, in which students analyze and evaluate? Creative thinking, in which students imagine and create? Practical thinking, in which students solve problems and make decisions?

Identifying Learning Outcomes for Application Learning

The different categories of application learning involve multiple and diverse learning processes that also tend to be subject or discipline specific. Acknowledging the complexity, we offer the following examples of learning processes and outcomes for this dimension of the Significant Learning Taxonomy (Table 8.1).

Aligning Course Level Application Learning Outcomes with Institutional Learning Goals

In higher education today, almost all colleges and universities have mission statements that express their commitment to educating students in core competencies. Although the specific competencies and the language used to describe them vary from campus to campus, most share similar fundamentals and include learning outcomes that relate quite clearly to the application dimension of the learning taxonomy. Examples of these core competencies are critical thinking, inquiry and analysis, oral communication, problem solving, quantitative literacy, reading, and written communication. Sample language is provided in Table 8.2.

Assessing Achievement of Application Learning Outcomes

As learners move from novice to expert, their ability to apply foundational knowledge becomes increasingly accurate, efficient, and effective. Assessing achievement of application learning is therefore typically demonstrated and assessed along a continuum of criteria starting at novice-level performance and developing toward higher expert-level competence. These continuums of criteria are best represented and assessed through rubrics.

Table 8.1 Examples of Learning Processes and Outcomes for Application Learning

Skills (Procedures)
General Definition: The learner has procedural knowledge of subject-specific techniques and methods.

Learner Process	Additional Terms	Definition	Sample Course Learning Outcome *By the end of this course, a successful learner will be able to . . .*
Identify	Enumerate, name, describe	Demonstrate knowledge of the sequence of steps involved in a subject or discipline specific procedure.	. . . identify the steps in archeological seriation for determining the relative date of assemblages or artifacts.
Determine	Distinguish, differentiate	Demonstrate knowledge of the criteria used to determine *when* to use various procedures.	. . . differentiate between various criteria to choose an appropriate statistical procedure to use with data collected in a particular experiment.
Execute	Carry out, compute	Be able to carry out or do a specific procedure with a familiar task.	. . . play all 12 major diatonic scales with both hands simultaneously ascending and descending in 2 octaves.
Implement	Use, apply	Be able to carry out or do a specific procedure with an unfamiliar task.	. . . apply a social psychological theory of crowd behavior to crowd control.

Critical, Creative, and Practical Thinking
General Definition: The learner will be able to
Analyze (break material into its constituent parts and determine how the parts are related to one another and to an overall structure).
Conduct a comprehensive exploration of issues, ideas, artifacts, and events before accepting or formulating an opinion or conclusion.
Evaluate and make judgments based on criteria and standards related to quality, effectiveness, efficiency, and consistency.
Demonstrate creative thinking by putting elements together to form a novel, coherent, functional whole.

Learner Process	Additional Terms	Definition	Sample Course Learning Outcome
Investigate	Examine, explore, study, probe, scrutinize	The ability to seek, identify, and use relevant sources of information and extract key information and ideas to support a point of view or conclusion.	. . . carry out a systematic or formal inquiry to discover and examine appropriate facts.
Differentiate	Discriminate, select, distinguish, focus	The ability to distinguish the parts of a whole structure in terms of their relevance or importance, and then attend to the relevant or important information.	. . . distinguish between relevant and irrelevant numbers in a word problem.
Attribute	Deconstruct, ascertain	The ability to ascertain the point of view, biases, values, or intention underlying communications.	. . . ascertain the point of view of the author of an essay on a controversial topic in terms of his or her theoretical perspective.
Check	Test, detect, monitor, coordinate	The ability to test for internal inconsistencies or fallacies in an operation or product.	. . . detect inconsistencies in persuasive messages in a variety of media.
Critique	Judge, assess	The ability to judge the merits of a product or operation based on externally imposed criteria and standards.	. . . judge the merits of a particular land use proposal in terms of its likely impact on habitat fragmentation and destruction.
Generate	Originate	The ability to represent the problem and arrive at alternatives or hypotheses that meet certain criteria.	. . . generate multiple useful solutions for reducing the environmental effects of pesticide drift.

Sources: Composite

Table 8.2 Examples of Broader Institutional Learning Goals in the Application Learning Dimension

Institution Level Core Competency in Written Communication	This university ensures that all graduates are able to write with precision and clarity to express complex thought.
Institution Level Core Competency in Critical Thinking	Graduates of this institution will be able to analyze arguments, create and test models, solve problems, evaluate ideas, and verify the reasonableness of conclusions.

Sources: Composite

Assessing Skills Learning Outcomes

Many teachers want students to be able to apply foundational knowledge by engaging in a particular kind of action such as writing an essay or retrieving information efficiently and appropriately from the Internet. The skills are discipline and course specific, but the ability to increase proficiency applies to all. The challenge is to identify the stages in a continuum from novice to expert along with the specific behaviors or artifacts that demonstrate mastery of that stage. In Exhibit 8.1, we provide the rubric created by the Association of American Colleges and Universities (AAC&U) to assess the progression from novice to expert in acquiring the skill of writing.

Assessing Thinking Learning Outcomes

Critical Thinking

In AAC&U's work with hundreds of faculty experts to create definitions and rubrics for assessing many areas of learning, they include critical thinking. In their introduction to the rubric, they state that research suggests that success in all disciplines requires the capacity to think critically and that these habits of inquiry and analysis must be applied in various and changing situations throughout life. They therefore designed the rubric displayed as Exhibit 8.2, Assessing Critical Thinking Using the AAC&U Critical Thinking Value Rubric, to be trans-disciplinary and to be used with many different types of assignments. Thus, whether teachers are promoting critical thinking by requiring students to complete analyses of text, data, or issues, the rubric can be used as is or as the starting point for crafting a customized assignment rubric.

Creative Thinking

Several scholars have attempted to develop a means for assessing creativity, often focusing on "divergence." Divergent production, for example, is the ability to generate a diverse assortment of responses to a stimulus. Thus the *Torrance Tests of Creative Thinking* (Torrance, 1974, 1984) present the test taker with open-ended questions and then assess the diversity and quantity of responses. Another approach is represented by Gladwell's (2008) "divergence test," which prompts the test taker to use their mind to go in as many different directions as possible, in contrast to a "convergence test," in which a test taker sorts through possibilities to converge on the single correct or best answer. The responses are assessed based on quantity and uniqueness. If promoting and then assessing skill in creativity is important for your course goals, consider using or adapting the creativity rubric in Exhibit 8.3, the AAC&U Creative Thinking VALUE Rubric.

Practical Thinking

Practical thinking, whether it involves learning to answer questions, make decisions, or solve problems, is a process rather than a product. For this reason, efforts to assess practical thinking focus on a learner's ability to practice thinking through problems as he or she attempts to arrive at a solution. In the framing language of the AAC&U Problem Solving VALUE Rubric, the authors describe how the rubric attempts to distill the common elements of most problem-solving contexts and is designed to function across all disciplines. In addition, they explain how because the rubric is process- rather than product-focused, the work to be assessed needs to include some evidence of the student's thinking about a problem-solving task (e.g., reflections on the process from problem to proposed solution; steps in a problem-based learning assignment; record of think-aloud protocol while solving a problem). The rubric is provided as Exhibit 8.4, Assessing Practical Thinking Using the AAC&U Problem Solving VALUE Rubric.

Conclusion

For our purposes here, the application learning dimension involves students' using foundational knowledge in the development of skills or in the ability to engage in critical, creative, and practical thinking. Each of these areas involves multiple and diverse learning processes and tends to be subject or discipline specific. In this introduction we offered definitions, identified examples of learning outcomes, and provided rubrics that can be used as is or customized to assist in assessing student achievement in these areas. In the following chapter, we will help you guide students to make connections between ideas, learning experiences, and different realms of life so that everything is put into context and learning is more powerful.

Exhibit 8.1 Assessing Writing Skills Using the AAC&U Written Communication VALUE Rubric

Glossary

The definitions that follow were developed to clarify terms and concepts used in this rubric only.

- *Content development:* The ways in which the text explores and represents its topic in relation to its audience and purpose.

- *Context of and purpose for writing:* The context of writing is the situation surrounding a text: who is reading it? who is writing it? Under what circumstances will the text be shared or circulated? What social or political factors might affect how the text is composed or interpreted? The purpose for writing is the writer's intended effect on an audience. Writers might want to persuade or inform; they might want to report or summarize information; they might want to work through complexity or confusion; they might want to argue with other writers, or connect with other writers; they might want to convey urgency or amuse; they might write for themselves or for an assignment or to remember.

- *Disciplinary conventions:* Formal and informal rules that constitute what is seen generally as appropriate within different academic fields, e.g. introductory strategies, use of passive voice or first person point of view, expectations for thesis or hypothesis, expectations for kinds of evidence and support that are appropriate to the task at hand, use of primary and secondary sources to provide evidence and support arguments and to document critical perspectives on the topic. Writers will incorporate sources according to disciplinary and genre conventions, according to the writer's purpose for the text. Through increasingly sophisticated use of sources, writers develop an ability to differentiate between their own ideas and the ideas of others, credit and build upon work already accomplished in the field or issue they are addressing, and provide meaningful examples to readers.

- *Evidence:* Source material that is used to extend, in purposeful ways, writers' ideas in a text.

- *Genre conventions:* Formal and informal rules for particular kinds of texts and/or media that guide formatting, organization, and stylistic choices, e.g. lab reports, academic papers, poetry, web pages, or personal essays.

- *Sources:* Texts (written, oral, behavioral, visual, or other) that writers draw on as they work for a variety of purposes—to extend, argue with, develop, define, or shape their ideas, for example.

Evaluators are encouraged to assign a zero to any work sample or collection of work that does not meet benchmark (cell one) level performance.

Table 8.3 Assessing Writing Skills Rubric

| | Capstone | Milestone | | Benchmark |
	4	3	2	1
Context of and Purpose for Writing *Includes considerations of audience, purpose, and the circumstances surrounding the writing task(s).*	Demonstrates a thorough understanding of context, audience, and purpose that is responsive to the assigned task(s) and focuses all elements of the work.	Demonstrates adequate consideration of context, audience, and purpose and a clear focus on the assigned task(s) (e.g., the task aligns with audience, purpose, and context).	Demonstrates awareness of context, audience, purpose, and to the assigned task(s) (e.g., begins to show awareness of audience's perceptions and assumptions).	Demonstrates minimal attention to context, audience, purpose, and to the assigned task(s) (e.g., expectation of instructor or self as audience).
Content Development	Uses appropriate, relevant, and compelling content to illustrate mastery of the subject, conveying the writer's understanding, and shaping the whole work.	Uses appropriate, relevant, and compelling content to explore ideas within the context of the discipline and shape the whole work.	Uses appropriate and relevant content to develop and explore ideas through most of the work.	Uses appropriate and relevant content to develop simple ideas in some parts of the work.
Genre and Disciplinary Conventions *Formal and informal rules inherent in the expectations for writing in particular forms and/or academic fields (please see glossary).*	Demonstrates detailed attention to and successful execution of a wide range of conventions particular to a specific discipline and/or writing task(s), including organization, content, presentation, formatting, and stylistic choices.	Demonstrates consistent use of important conventions particular to a specific discipline and/or writing task(s), including organization, content, presentation, and stylistic choices.	Follows expectations appropriate to a specific discipline and/or writing task(s) for basic organization, content, and presentation.	Attempts to use a consistent system for basic organization and presentation.
Sources and Evidence	Demonstrates skillful use of high-quality, credible, relevant sources to develop ideas that are appropriate for the discipline and genre of the writing.	Demonstrates consistent use of credible, relevant sources to support ideas that are situated within the discipline and genre of the writing.	Demonstrates an attempt to use credible and/or relevant sources to support ideas that are appropriate for the discipline and genre of the writing.	Demonstrates an attempt to use sources to support ideas in the writing.
Control of Syntax and Mechanics	Uses graceful language that skillfully communicates meaning to readers with clarity and fluency, and is virtually error-free.	Uses straightforward language that generally conveys meaning to readers. The language in the portfolio has few errors.	Uses language that generally conveys meaning to readers with clarity, although writing may include some errors.	Uses language that sometimes impedes meaning because of errors in usage.

Reprinted with permission from VALUE: Valid Assessment of Learning in Undergraduate Education. Copyright 2015 by the Association of American Colleges and Universities. http://www.aacu.org/value/rubrics

Exhibit 8.2 Assessing Critical Thinking Using the AAC&U Critical Thinking VALUE Rubric

Glossary
The definitions that follow were developed to clarify terms and concepts used in this rubric only.

- *Ambiguity:* Information that may be interpreted in more than one way.
- *Assumptions:* Ideas, conditions, or beliefs (often implicit or unstated) that are "taken for granted or accepted as true without proof." (quoted from www.dictionary .reference.com/browse/assumptions)
- *Context:* The historical, ethical. political, cultural, environmental, or circumstantial settings or conditions that influence and complicate the consideration of any issues, ideas, artifacts, and events.
- *Literal meaning:* Interpretation of information exactly as stated. For example, "she was green with envy" would be interpreted to mean that her skin was green.
- *Metaphor:* Information that is (intended to be) interpreted in a nonliteral way. For example, "she was green with envy" is intended to convey an intensity of emotion, not a skin color.

Table 8.4 Assessing Critical Thinking Rubric

	Capstone 4	Milestone 3 2	Benchmark 1
Explanation of issues	Issue/problem to be considered critically is stated clearly and described comprehensively, delivering all relevant information necessary for full understanding.	Issue/problem to be considered critically is stated, described, and clarified so that understanding is not seriously impeded by omissions.	Issue/problem to be considered critically is stated but description leaves some terms undefined, ambiguities unexplored, boundaries undetermined, and/or backgrounds unknown.	Issue/problem to be considered critically is stated without clarification or description.
Evidence *Selecting and using information to investigate a point of view or conclusion*	Information is taken from source(s) with enough interpretation/ evaluation to develop a comprehensive analysis or synthesis. Viewpoints of experts are questioned thoroughly.	Information is taken from source(s) with enough interpretation/ evaluation to develop a coherent analysis or synthesis. Viewpoints of experts are subject to questioning.	Information is taken from source(s) with some interpretation/evaluation, but not enough to develop a coherent analysis or synthesis. Viewpoints of experts are taken as mostly fact, with little questioning.	Information is taken from source(s) without any interpretation/ evaluation. Viewpoints of experts are taken as fact, without question.

Influence of context and assumptions	Thoroughly (systematically and methodically) analyzes own and others' assumptions and carefully evaluates the relevance of contexts when presenting a position.	Identifies own and others' assumptions and several relevant contexts when presenting a position.	Questions some assumptions. Identifies several relevant contexts when presenting a position. May be more aware of others' assumptions than one's own (or vice versa).	Shows an emerging awareness of present assumptions (sometimes labels assertions as assumptions). Begins to identify some contexts when presenting a position.
Student's position (perspective, thesis/hypothesis)	Specific position (perspective, thesis/hypothesis) is imaginative, taking into account the complexities of an issue. Limits of position (perspective, thesis/hypothesis) are acknowledged. Others' points of view are synthesized within position (perspective, thesis/hypothesis).	Specific position (perspective, thesis/hypothesis) takes into account the complexities of an issue. Others' points of view are acknowledged within position (perspective, thesis/hypothesis).	Specific position (perspective, thesis/hypothesis) acknowledges different sides of an issue.	Specific position (perspective, thesis/hypothesis) is stated, but is simplistic and obvious.
Conclusions and Related Outcomes (Implications and Consequences)	Conclusions and related outcomes (consequences and implications) are logical and reflect student's informed evaluation and ability to place evidence and perspectives discussed in priority order.	Conclusion is logically tied to a range of information, including opposing viewpoints; related outcomes (consequences and implications) are identified clearly.	Conclusion is logically tied to information (because information is chosen to fit the desired conclusion); some related outcomes (consequences and implications) are identified clearly.	Conclusion is inconsistently tied to some of the information discussed; related outcomes (consequences and implications) are oversimplified.

Reprinted with permission from VALUE: Valid Assessment of Learning in Undergraduate Education. Copyright 2015 by the Association of American Colleges and Universities. http://www.aacu.org/value/rubrics

Exhibit 8.3 Assessing Creative Thinking Using the AAC&U Creative Thinking VALUE Rubric

Glossary
The definitions that follow were developed to clarify terms and concepts used in this rubric only.

- *Exemplar:* A model or pattern to be copied or imitated (quoted from www.dictionary.reference.com/browse/exemplar).
- *Domain:* Field of study or activity and a sphere of knowledge and influence.

Table 8.5 Assessing Creative Thinking Rubric

	Capstone 4	Milestone 3 2		Benchmark 1
Acquiring Competencies *This step refers to acquiring strategies and skills within a particular domain.*	Reflect: Evaluates creative process and product using domain-appropriate criteria.	Create: Creates an entirely new object, solution, or idea that is appropriate to the domain.	Adapt: Successfully adapts an appropriate exemplar to his/her own specifications.	Model: Successfully reproduces an appropriate exemplar.
Taking Risks *May include personal risk (fear of embarrassment or rejection) or risk of failure in successfully completing assignment, i.e., going beyond original parameters of assignment, introducing new materials and forms, tackling controversial topics, advocating unpopular ideas or solutions.*	Actively seeks out and follows through on untested and potentially risky directions or approaches to the assignment in the final product.	Incorporates new directions or approaches to the assignment in the final product.	Considers new directions or approaches without going beyond the guidelines of the assignment.	Stays strictly within the guidelines of the assignment.

	Capstone (4)	Milestone (3)	Milestone (2)	Benchmark (1)
Solving Problems	Not only develops a logical, consistent plan to solve problem, but recognizes consequences of solution and can articulate reason for choosing solution.	Having selected from among alternatives, develops a logical, consistent plan to solve the problem.	Considers and rejects less acceptable approaches to solving problem.	Only a single approach is considered and is used to solve the problem.
Embracing Contradictions	Integrates alternate, divergent, or contradictory perspectives or ideas fully.	Incorporates alternate, divergent, or contradictory perspectives or ideas in an exploratory way.	Includes (recognizes the value of) alternate, divergent, or contradictory perspectives or ideas in a small way.	Acknowledges (mentions in passing) alternate, divergent, or contradictory perspectives or ideas.
Innovative Thinking *Novelty or uniqueness (of idea, claim, question, form, etc.)*	Extends a novel or unique idea, question, format, or product to create new knowledge or knowledge that crosses boundaries.	Creates a novel or unique idea, question, format, or product.	Experiments with creating a novel or unique idea, question, format, or product.	Reformulates a collection of available ideas.
Connecting, Synthesizing, Transforming	Transforms ideas or solutions into entirely new forms.	Synthesizes ideas or solutions into a coherent whole.	Connects ideas or solutions in novel ways.	Reviews results superficially in terms of the problem defined with no consideration of need for further work.

Reprinted with permission from VALUE: Valid Assessment of Learning in Undergraduate Education. Copyright 2015 by the Association of American Colleges and Universities.
http://www.aacu.org/value/rubrics

Exhibit 8.4 Assessing Practical Thinking Using the AAC&U Problem Solving VALUE Rubric

Glossary
The definitions that follow were developed to clarify terms and concepts used in this rubric only.

- *Contextual Factors*: Constraints (such as limits on cost), resources, attitudes (such as biases) and desired additional knowledge which affect how the problem can be best solved in the real world or simulated setting.
- *Critique*: Involves analysis and synthesis of a full range of perspectives.
- *Feasible*: Workable, in consideration of time-frame, functionality, available resources, necessary buy-in, and limits of the assignment or task.
- "Off the shelf "solution: A simplistic option that is familiar from everyday experience but not tailored to the problem at hand (e.g. holding a bake sale to "save" an underfunded public library).
- *Solution*: An appropriate response to a challenge or a problem.
- *Strategy*: A plan of action or an approach designed to arrive at a solution. (If the problem is a river that needs to be crossed, there could be a construction-oriented, cooperative (build a bridge with your community) approach and a personally oriented, physical (swim across alone) approach. An approach that partially applies would be a personal, physical approach for someone who doesn't know how to swim.
- *Support*: Specific rationale, evidence, etc. for solution or selection of solution.

Table 8.6 Assessing Practical Thinking Rubric

	Capstone 4	Milestone 3	Milestone 2	Benchmark 1
Define Problem	Demonstrates the ability to construct a clear and insightful problem statement with evidence of all relevant contextual factors.	Demonstrates the ability to construct a problem statement with evidence of most relevant contextual factors, and problem statement is adequately detailed.	Begins to demonstrate the ability to construct a problem statement with evidence of most relevant contextual factors, but problem statement is superficial.	Demonstrates a limited ability in identifying a problem statement or related contextual factors.
Identify Strategies	Identifies multiple approaches for solving the problem that apply within a specific context.	Identifies multiple approaches for solving the problem, only some of which apply within a specific context.	Identifies only a single approach for solving the problem that does apply within a specific context.	Identifies one or more approaches for solving the problem that do not apply within a specific context.
Propose Solutions/ Hypotheses	Proposes one or more solutions or hypotheses that indicates a deep comprehension of the problem. Solution/hypotheses are sensitive to contextual factors as well as all of the following: ethical, logical, and cultural dimensions of the problem.	Proposes one or more solutions or hypotheses that indicates comprehension of the problem. Solutions/hypotheses are sensitive to contextual factors as well as the one of the following: ethical, logical, or cultural dimensions of the problem.	Proposes one solution or hypothesis that is "off the shelf" rather than individually designed to address the specific contextual factors of the problem.	Proposes a solution or hypothesis that is difficult to evaluate because it is vague or only indirectly addresses the problem statement.
Evaluate Potential Solutions	Evaluation of solutions is deep and elegant (for example, contains thorough and insightful explanation) and includes, deeply and thoroughly, all of the following: considers history of problem, reviews logic/reasoning, examines feasibility of solution, and weighs impacts of solution.	Evaluation of solutions is adequate (for example, contains thorough explanation) and includes the following: considers history of problem, reviews logic/reasoning, examines feasibility of solution, and weighs impacts of solution.	Evaluation of solutions is brief (for example, explanation lacks depth) and includes the following: considers history of problem, reviews logic/reasoning, examines feasibility of solution, and weighs impacts of solution.	Evaluation of solutions is superficial (for example, contains cursory, surface level explanation) and includes the following: considers history of problem, reviews logic/reasoning, examines feasibility of solution, and weighs impacts of solution.
Implement Solution	Implements the solution in a manner that addresses thoroughly and deeply multiple contextual factors of the problem.	Implements the solution in a manner that addresses multiple contextual factors of the problem in a surface manner.	Implements the solution in a manner that addresses the problem statement but ignores relevant contextual factors.	Implements the solution in a manner that does not directly address the problem statement.
Evaluate Outcomes	Reviews results relative to the problem defined with thorough, specific considerations of need for further work.	Reviews results relative to the problem defined with some consideration of need for further work.	Reviews results in terms of the problem defined with little, if any, consideration of need for further work.	Reviews results superficially in terms of the problem defined with no consideration of need for further work

Reprinted with permission from VALUE: Valid Assessment of Learning in Undergraduate Education. Copyright 2015 by the Association of American Colleges and Universities. http://www.aacu.org/value/rubrics

LEARNING ASSESSMENT TECHNIQUE

Application Learning

11
Prediction Guide

Complexity involved in	
Preparation	MODERATE
In-class implementation	MODERATE
Analysis	LOW

Brief Description

Students are presented with a series of questions that ask them to make predictions prior to a learning activity, and then, after the learning activity, they revisit their predictions to evaluate accuracy and correct potential misconceptions.

Purpose and Use

The process of the Prediction Guide helps students to activate prior knowledge as they think critically about a topic, identifying and challenging their preconceived ideas about key ideas, issues, or concepts. In addition to helping students connect new ideas and concepts to existing knowledge, this LAT has the benefit of increasing student curiosity about a topic. It also provides students with a purpose for engaging in the activity even if they are not intrinsically interested in the topic, as they will want to find out if their predictions were accurate. Finally, asking students to respond to questions prior to a content module scaffolds their learning by focusing their attention on significant concepts to come.

The Learning Artifacts are the completed guides, which reflect students' best guesses about what is going to happen in a reading, class activity, experiment, or other. Prediction Guides are an excellent method for assessing students' prior knowledge and uncovering misconceptions before starting a new unit of content. They are quick, efficient, and easy to score, so they provide a high value for the cost of time and energy it takes to implement. Prediction Guides often are done prior to a learning module, and you can use the information you gather from them to better target instruction. This LAT can also be successful as a pre-post assessment of student learning, as the technique demonstrates how well students have understood the content through their revised answers.

Key Learning Goals

- Analytical skills
- Critical thinking skills
- Decision-making skills
- Problem-solving skills

Implementation

Preparation

- Identify the major points that students should gain from the lesson.
- Consider what beliefs students are likely to have about the topic.
- Write 8–10 dichotomous statements (e.g. agree/disagree; yes/no; fact/opinion) that require students to make predictions about the material they are about to encounter.
- Create a handout of instructions for the activity and the questions.

Process

1. Announce the activity and the amount of time students will have to respond to the prompt.
2. Share the Prediction Guide with the class and ask the students to respond to each question.
3. Present the lesson, whether through lecture, demonstration, reading assignment, or other.
4. Ask students to reevaluate their answers in light of the new information from the lesson and to indicate whether they have changed their opinions. You may for example suggest that they write down on the handout where new content supports or refutes their beliefs.
5. Collect the Learning Artifacts.

Online

Present the Prediction Guide through a quiz format. Set a timer to curb students' looking up the answers as you are interested in their beliefs, not their research skills. Alternately have students post their Guides as an assignment in the LMS or submit them through a file sharing program such as Google Docs, Dropbox, Box, or other.

Analysis and Reporting

The Prediction Guide responses usually are scored simply as "correct" or "incorrect." Return the scored sheets to the individual students to let them know whether their predictions, and revised predictions, were correct. This activity is used as a diagnostic assessment, so it is typically ungraded, although you may consider assigning participation points. If you do a pretest and a posttest, you may choose to assign a grade to the posttest.

Tally the number of correct and incorrect responses for each item. Consider creating a bar graph or pie chart to visually display the results. If you choose to compare individual performance over time on multiple Prediction Guides, use a spreadsheet to track scores at each test administration.

Examples

Onsite: Introduction to Physics

The professor of this physics class has a course goal to help students use the basic concepts of physics to explore natural phenomena, including observation, hypothesis development, measurement and data collection, experimentation, and evaluation of evidence. He teaches a lesson on waves and oscillation, and he often gives demonstrations to spark student engagement. He and students enjoy these demonstrations, but he has wondered whether students are prepared for what they see. Knowing that prior knowledge can influence how students understand the demonstration and how well they will learn the material, he decides to use a Prediction Guide to help him assess the prior knowledge that they bring to the demonstration and to determine whether the demonstrations help them leave with better knowledge than that which they started. On the day of the experiment, he sets up a pendulum system in his lab. He explains that he will run several experiments with pendulums of different sizes and weights, and explains that students will predict the results. Reassuring students that they will not be graded based on their predictions, he encourages them to make the best guesses they can. He hands out the Prediction Guide and directs students to complete the hypothesis section only, marking a yes or no to indicate their best guesses (Table 8.7). He tells them they will complete the observed results section after the demonstrations.

He then carries out the demonstrations. At the conclusion, he asks students to record their observations and to compare what they hypothesized with what they observed. After the activity, the professor does a quick tally of correct and incorrect responses. He develops a clustered bar graph to illustrate the results. Figure 8.1 offers one example, from which he can plainly see that the demonstrations helped students and that generally they were able to understand what they were seeing and correct earlier misconceptions or knowledge gaps.

Table 8.7 Introduction to Physics: Pendulum Prediction Guide

Student Name:				
	Hypothesis		**Observed Result**	
Demonstration	Yes	No	Yes	No
1. I will release two pendulums simultaneously. The small pendulum has a length of 25 cm. The longer pendulum is 150 cm. The shorter pendulum will swing faster.				
2. A bowling ball is the bob for a pendulum. I will bring bowling ball back to my face and let it go. If I remain standing in the same spot, the bowling ball will hit me in the face in the return swing.				
3. I will release 4 pendulums of the same length and size but different masses. They will swing at different rates.				

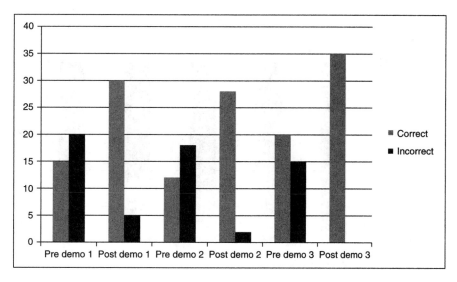

Figure 8.1 Pendulum Prediction Sample Clustered Bar Graph

 Online: Business Statistics

The professor of this online statistics course has a course objective that states that students will learn the foundations of statistical inference. Much of the course deals with probability, and the professor believes that students often bring misconceptions with them that interfere with their learning. In order to gauge prior knowledge and misconceptions so as to target her instruction, she decided to use a Prediction Guide. She has students make predictions about the learning module topic through a timed quiz, assuring students that the results will not factor into their grades and that they simply need to make the best predictions they can. Students then read a chapter and listen to video lectures about the topic. Table 8.8 is a sample prediction guide she uses in an introduction to probability unit, which she adapted from Lent (2012).

She tallied the correct and incorrect scores for each question and created a stacked column graph to display the results, which helped her quickly identify and make plans for targeting the areas in which students were weak (Figure 8.2).

Table 8.8 Business Statistics. Prediction Guide: Introduction to Probability

Read each statement. Click the button under "agree" if you agree with the statement or click the button under "disagree" if you disagree.		
	Agree	**Disagree**
1. The probability of zero means an event is impossible.	◉	◉
2. When studying probability you may be asked to play with dice.	◉	◉
3. The sum of the probabilities of all the possible outcomes equals one.	◉	◉
4. Two mutually exclusive events can happen at the same time.	◉	◉
5. You should understand fractions before beginning the study of probability.	◉	◉

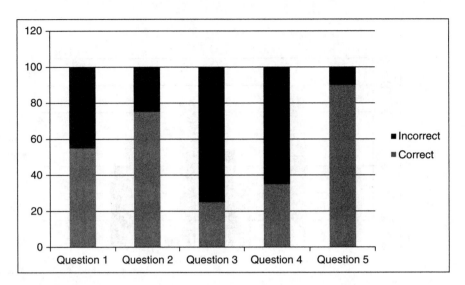

Figure 8.2 Student Scores

Variations and Extensions

- Have students respond to the Prediction Guides while working in pairs prior to the lesson. You may ask the pairs to come to consensus on their answers or allow them to submit separate ones.
- After implementing the assessment, hold a class discussion or a debate to allow students to express their opinions. Use the discussion as an additional data point to assess how well students have understood the concept. (See LAT 30, Free Discussion, for additional information about how to use discussion as an assessment technique.)

Key References and Resources

Duffelmeyer, F. (1994). Effective anticipation guide statements for learning from expository prose. *Journal of Reading, 37,* 452–455.

Lent, R. C. (2012). Overcoming textbook fatigue: 21st century tools to revitalize teaching and learning. http://www.ascd.org/publications/books/113005/chapters/Background-Knowledge@-The-Glue-That-Makes-Learning-Stick.aspx.

LEARNING ASSESSMENT TECHNIQUE

Application Learning

12
Fact or Opinion

Complexity involved in	
Preparation	MODERATE
In-class implementation	LOW-MODERATE
Analysis	LOW

Brief Description

Students first read a text to identify and list facts. They then reread the text to look for where the author either overtly or covertly inserts opinion and make a new list as they carefully consider the evidence and resist being taken in by the text's rhetorical force.

Purpose and Use

This technique helps students to become critical readers and to construct arguments when informed proponents of opposing points of view are not available. It aids students in seeing that scholarly articles and other assigned readings are voices in a conversation rather than something that is set in stone to be believed without question. Complex and challenging texts will begin to make sense when students see their responsibility to participate actively as they read and to evaluate an author's thesis, reasons, and evidence.

The lists that students create during the Fact or Opinion phases are the assessable Learning Artifacts. These can help teachers gauge to what extent students understand what is fact and what is not. Teachers may also consider using the artifacts for insights into where students are in their developmental processes by identifying which students see an issue from one side only or whether they are able to recognize that there can be different perspectives on a given issue. This LAT is best used during a lesson to spot check for student ability to understand the texts that they are reading. This usage can allow teachers to target their instruction. It may also be done at the end of a unit in order to assess how well they have mastered the content.

Key Learning Goals

- Reading skills
- Analytical skills
- Critical thinking skills

Implementation

Preparation

- Identify a topic in your discipline that relates to your learning outcome, and find an article, newspaper story, or excerpt from a larger text. The success of this LAT lies largely in finding a text that has a mixture of facts and opinions.
- Review the text, making a list of all the facts and all the opinions. This step will allow you to generate a list of statements.
- Duplicate the text, post it online, or place it on reserve in the library.
- Determine the parameters of the assignment, such as how long student responses should be, whether they should be bullet points or complete sentences, and how long they will have to develop them.
- Create a handout with your lists of statements, randomizing the list order so that fact and opinion statements are dispersed throughout the list.

Process

1. Explain to students that they are to read the text, making a sincere and conscious attempt to identify factual statements and those statements that are the author's opinions, feelings, or values.
2. Distribute the handout.
3. Provide students time to mark their responses.
4. Collect the Learning Artifacts.
5. Consider holding a class discussion.

Online

Simply post the assignment in an LMS or use a discussion forum. Alternately have students blog or Tweet their lists.

Analysis and Reporting

Mark each response on the Fact or Opinion list as either correct or incorrect. Tally the number of both. If you want to grade this activity, do it as a low stakes grade or as participation. Return the scored handouts to students so that they know which are correct or incorrect.

Look across the handouts to identify any patterns in statements that students misidentified. Examine average scores. Use a simple table, figure, or graph to display your results.

Examples

Onsite: General Biology

To help students learn to critically read texts addressing ethical issues in the discipline, the professor selected an article that argued that the creation, usage, and destruction of human embryonic stem cells is the first step toward reproductive cloning and that it fundamentally devalues the worth of a human being. She asked students to read the article quietly and independently in class, trying to understand the author's perspective and to distinguish fact from opinion, listing their insights on a 2-column fact/opinion handout. She collected the handouts and created a simple table (Table 8.9) to show the results, which she planned to share with students at the next session. She noticed that students were more likely to accurately identify facts than opinion, and determined to spend time on how to read critically since the ability to do so was a core course learning outcome.

Table 8.9 Fact or Opinion Results

Item	Correct Answer	Accurate	Inaccurate
1.	Fact	90%	10%
2.	Fact	85%	15%
3.	Opinion	65%	35%
4.	Fact	80%	20%
5.	Opinion	60%	40%

Online: Reading Educational Research

The overarching goal of the course is to help students become critical consumers of educational research and to help prepare them for doing their own research, specifically a thesis or dissertation. One specific learning outcome is that upon completion of the course, successful students will be able to critically evaluate educational research articles. In previous semesters, the professor had noticed that students were not always able to distinguish between the author's "findings" and the author's "opinions" and "conclusions." Moreover, the students seemed to give all information equal weight, regardless of the merit of the claim. These gaps in their understanding contributed to problems in their writing as well. For example, when writing literature reviews, students would use phrases like "the authors found" or "the authors discovered," when the authors had neither found nor discovered anything but instead were simply stating their hypotheses. The professor decided to use "Fact or Opinion?" to help students learn to distinguish the difference. She developed a handout with a list of statements that students were to identify as fact or opinion from the article (Table 8.10).

Table 8.10 Fact or Opinion?

Read the statement from the article by Mean et al. (2010) on online learning below. Indicate with a checkmark in one of the columns to the right whether you believe this statement is a fact or an opinion.

Statement	Fact	Opinion
1. Online learning has roots in the tradition of distance education, which goes back at least 100 years to the early correspondence courses.		
2. Online learning—for students and for teachers—is one of the fastest growing trends in educational uses of technology.		
3. With the advent of the Internet and the World Wide Web, the potential for reaching learners around the world increased greatly, and today's online learning offers rich educational resources in multiple media and the capability to support both real-time and asynchronous communication between instructors and learners as well as among different learners.		
4. Classes with online learning (whether taught completely online or blended) on average produce stronger student learning outcomes than do classes with solely face-to-face instruction.		
5. The field lacks a coherent body of linked studies that systematically test theory-based approaches in different contexts.		

She posted the article in her LMS and set the handout up as an untimed "quiz" that students completed. She analyzed the correct and incorrect responses and created a bar chart so that she could "see" the results (Figure 8.3). While most students answered the first few questions correctly, even four or five answering it incorrectly was not acceptable to her, as it was more than 10% of her small class. Moreover, about half of the students missed the last few. She knew she needed to target her teaching to help students improve their ability to read more critically.

She returned their scored papers, and put them into small groups to talk about their responses and to come to consensus on why the incorrect answers were incorrect. She also developed a handout of different parts of a traditional social science research paper, outlining which parts are typically arguments, which are presentations of findings, and which are conclusions. She handed out a list of verbs that social scientists tend to use to express opinion (I argue, assert, believe, etc.) and fact (I found, discovered, identified, etc.). Finally, she gave a brief lecture on fact and opinion in research.

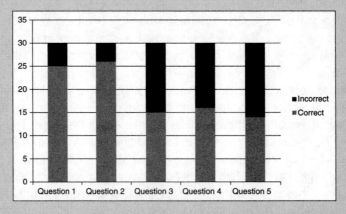

Figure 8.3 Correct and Incorrect Responses from Quiz

Variations and Extensions

- Have students submit their two lists individually along with a reflective essay on what they learned. This submission will provide an additional data point.

Key References and Resources

Barkley, E. (2010). Believing and doubting. In *Student engagement techniques: A handbook for college faculty* (pp. 195–198). San Francisco, CA: Jossey-Bass.

Bean, J. C. (2009). *Engaging ideas: The professor's guide to integrating writing, critical thinking, and active learning in the classroom* (2nd ed., pp. 142–143, 156–157). San Francisco, CA: Jossey-Bass.

LEARNING ASSESSMENT TECHNIQUE

Application Learning

13
Quotation Commentaries

Complexity involved in	
Planning	MODERATE
In-class implementation	LOW
Analysis	MODERATE

Brief Description

Students receive a handout with a set of quotations from a recent reading assignment and then comment on them, following a specific process: paraphrase, interpret, comment, and cite.

Purposes

This technique helps students learn how to use quoted material by interpreting, paraphrasing, synthesizing, and citing excerpts from assigned readings. It is a useful way to prepare students for more significant writing projects, as it teaches students how to use quoted material appropriately. The LAT also underscores the instructor's commitment to the value of the assigned reading, addressing a frequent student complaint that follow-up, in-class conversations do not draw explicitly enough on the text that students have been asked to spend time reading.

The Learning Artifacts are students' written analyses of quotations, and they are useful both for determining whether or not students have done preparatory assigned reading and to gain insights into how well they have processed and understood the reading. These artifacts also allow for investigating whether students know how to use quoted information appropriately. The LAT is most effective as a formative assessment of student understanding, and then using the results to target instruction. It may also be used to evaluate student performance, although this is most appropriate in courses where interpretation and citation of readings is an important learning outcome.

Key Learning Goals

- Reading skills
- Writing skills

- Analytical skills
- Research skills

Table 8.11 Scoring Responses

	Excellent	Good	Fair	Weak
Paraphrase				
Synthesis				
Cited excerpts				
Interpretation				

Implementation

Preparation

- Select the reading assignment for the activity. Any reading appropriate for the class can work, but scholarly articles work particularly well.
- Develop a system for scoring responses. It can be a simple 4-point scale rating the responses from "highly accurate" to "highly inaccurate" to something more complex, such as a rubric for evaluating each response according to specific criteria. See Table 8.11 for example.
- Create a handout that contains several brief passages from the text, followed by prompts such as the following along with space for responding to them.
  - *Paraphrase:* Rephrase the meaning of this passage in 3–5 sentences using your own words.
  - *Interpret:* Explain the meaning of this passage: Why is it significant?
  - *Comment:* Express your opinion of this passage: Do you agree/disagree? Find it valuable/not valuable?
  - *Cite:* Write out how you would cite the above using MLA format.

Process

1. Assign the reading and ask students to complete it.
2. Announce the Quotation Commentaries activity and distribute the handout with the quotations, answering any student questions.
3. Ask students to complete the handout.
4. Consider asking students to share their comments with the class, offering new insights or building upon or contradicting comments that have already been made.
5. Collect the handouts.

Online

Although this technique is particularly effective when students are able to interact "in the moment" as they respond to their quote and to the comments of others, you can modify it for an online course by selecting 4–5 quotations and creating a forum for each quote, asking students to post a response to each quote.

Analysis and Reporting

Use a scale or rubric to develop a score for each student's completed handout. To rate by scale, you can simply mark it with the score (and what the score means, for example 4 = highly accurate response to 1 = highly inaccurate response). Alternately use a rubric for analysis.

Examine individual performance over time by using a spreadsheet tracking scores at each test administration or by having students do it. Share scores with individual students. Consider scoring the longitudinal data (average over time or the improvement in scores). This activity is typically a low-stakes grade or used to determine participation points, although some instructors might weight it more depending upon course learning goals.

There are several different ways to analyze the data collected from individuals at an aggregate level.

- Average the individual scores to develop an aggregate (e.g. students averaged 80% correct scores).
- Examine each quotation for quality of responses, then note which quotation students scored the highest on, and note those that they scored the lowest on. Consider whether you need to provide additional instruction in areas of least understanding.
- Consider listing key words you would expect students to use in describing the quotations and then examining the key words they did use; compare your responses to theirs.

Quotation Commentaries, particularly if you use it over several administrations, can yield information that you can provide to stakeholders through simple tables or charts. For your item/quote analysis on individual artifacts, consider a bar graph or a table to illustrate percentages correct or incorrect. To interpret your findings, consider the following: Do students generally seem to understand the readings? Are they able to interpret the quotations when they appear out of context? Are they able to use their own words to express or rephrase the ideas? Are they able to cite it using the correct format?

Examples

Onsite: Introduction to Shakespeare

This professor uses a variation of Quotation Commentaries as a means to stimulate whole class discussion and detailed analysis of the dramatic works of Shakespeare. The learning outcome is to be able to identify the play from a quotation, to provide context and meaning, and to be able to explain the significance of the quotation to the play.

She selects a variety of quotations from the assigned plays, as they study them. Students use the quotations as the basis for their contribution to the discussion. The first student to talk about a specific quote must provide, at a minimum, basic information about the quote (identify who said it and describe the dramatic context). Other students build upon these comments adding insights regarding the quote's deeper meaning and relationship to the play's themes. She observes that the LAT helps to ensure students have done the reading and come to class prepared, that it gets discussion started quickly, and that the structure propels the discussion naturally as students must offer new and deeper insights as they build upon each other's contributions.

She also collects the handouts she uses for the activity at each administration. She is able to provide feedback to each student. When examining the information in aggregate, she can find the quotations where students are having the most difficulty and spend additional time unpacking those. In addition, for each quote, she develops a list of key words she would expect to see in descriptions of the quote. She then analyzes student responses for their use of key words. She compares her choices and their choices for an indication of differences.

For example, one quote is from Hamlet: "To be or not to be."

She creates a list of key words:

> Suicide
> Choices
> Decisions
> Consequences
> Dreams
> Fear
> Cruelty
> Pain
> Injustice

In examining student cards, she looks at the words students use most often in their summaries, comparing them to her own. She notices some similarities and some differences and uses these as a basis for class discussion.

 ### Online: Principles of Advertising

This professor is preparing for an annual merit review, for which he must show evidence of effective teaching. His chair wants teaching linked to specific learning outcomes, evidence of data collection, and plans for improvement. One learning outcome the professor has identified is that by the end of the term, students should be able to evaluate the effectiveness of advertisements. For the assignment, the teacher selects ads from a wide range of advertising campaigns spanning several decades and posts each one in a separate discussion thread. Students discuss the ads within the threads. To help focus the discussion, he includes a series of prompts asking students to determine the intended audience, identify the idea, product, or service the ad was designed to promote, and to analyze why, in their assessment, the ad was or was not persuasive.

Table 8.12 Principles of Advertising Qualitative Analysis

Student Names	Form	Visual	Language
Olesya	X		
Drew	X	X	
Natalia	X		
Joonseok	X	X	X
Scott		X	
Chang	X		
Myra		X	X
Bobby	X	X	
Samantha		X	
Austin	X	X	X

The professor conducts a qualitative analysis of the data students generate in their discussion posts, searching for when they describe something about form, when they describe something about images/visuals, and when they indicate language selection (Table 8.12).

He responds to each student with what they have done well, and then he looks across posts for what students have done well and what they can improve upon. For his report, he includes the information in Table 8.13.

Table 8.13 Principles of Advertising Learning Outcome Analysis

Learning Outcome	Data	Findings	Improvements Made
Students will be able to evaluate marketing slogans.	Student posts on a discussion thread in which they evaluate marketing data.	Students attend to form and visual information more often than to language, including grammar and diction.	Added a learning module on "language of advertising" that addresses language in slogans.

Variations and Extensions

- This LAT may be adapted to have students select the quotations themselves; this will provide additional information about how well they can assess what is important and what is not. Quotations that they select may be those that they especially liked or disliked, ones that they found to best illustrate the major thesis, ones that they found most difficult to understand, and so forth. Students say where their quoted passage is in the text (e.g., "page 3 paragraph 5"), and then read their quotation as all class members follow along on the specific page and passage with them (Brookfield & Preskill, 2005, pp. 72–73).

- If you use collaborative learning, have students work in groups to complete their commentaries. This provides a group-level artifact rather than an individual one.

Key References and Resources

Barkley, E. F. (2010). Quotes. In *Student engagement techniques: A handbook for college faculty* (pp. 167–169). San Francisco, CA: Jossey-Bass.

Brookfield, S. D., & Preskill, S. (2005). *Discussion as a way of teaching: Tools and techniques for democratic classrooms.* San Francisco, CA: Jossey-Bass.

LEARNING ASSESSMENT TECHNIQUE

Application Learning

14
Insights-Resources-Application (IRA)

Complexity involved in	
Preparation	MODERATE
In-class implementation	LOW
Analysis	LOW

Brief Description

In conjunction with an assigned reading, students complete a written assignment that includes three components: new perceptions or understandings (Insights), resources they have found that amplify the reading's themes or information (Resources), and an example from the students' personal experience that relates to the reading (Application).

Purpose

This LAT challenges students to (1) reflect upon and identify what they have learned, (2) connect what they have learned to their personal experience, and (3) search out additional sources that deepen their knowledge or understanding of the reading's themes or information. All of these activities are deep learning strategies that help students not only to deepen their knowledge of the reading provided but also to improve their meta-learning skills.

IRAs create a written record of student ability to make application of recently received material to new situations. This technique provides faculty with a document that they can scan relatively quickly in an attempt to determine how well students have internalized and can extend their learning. It is an alternative to longer and more extensive written responses to gathering information about student ability to apply knowledge to new situations. This technique is perhaps best used during a unit of instruction to help faculty ensure that students are understanding course readings so that faculty can target their instructional activities to the student level of need. Alternately, it can be effective at the end of a unit to document that students have understood the information and can apply it to new and different situations.

Key Learning Goals

- Analytical skills
- Creative thinking skills
- Critical thinking skills
- Decision-making skills
- Research skills

Implementation

Preparation

- Identify a reading that invites deep thinking, further research, and application to a reader's personal life.
- Create assignment instructions, perhaps on a handout or a presentation slide, that ask students to write a brief assignment that specifies the three components: Insights (I), Resources (R), Application (A).
- Determine the level of responses you want, whether a single bullet point or sentence or a fuller paragraph. Consider the following example:
  - Insight (I): One-sentence bullet points that represent new understandings about the meaning or nature of the reading's topic.
  - Resource (R): One additional resource such as a book, article, Web site, film, or news item that has similar thoughts, ideas, or themes that amplify the reading.
  - Application (A): A sentence that relates the reading to an example from the student's current or past experience.
- Create a system for scoring the postings, such as a simple tally (+/−) or a rubric. If the latter, you should choose what you want to assess the results for, whether quality of response, completeness of response, accuracy of response, or other. You might use a rating scale (e.g., 4 = very high; 3 = high; 2 = low; 1 = very low) to assess categories such as the following:
  - Insights: **Clarity** of the perception or understanding
  - Resources: **Quality** of the resource (academic vs. popular source)
  - Application: **Appropriate Fit** of the reading to the experience

Process

1. Present the assignment, and provide students with time to work.
2. Consider providing time for students to report out so that they can learn from each other's ideas.
3. Collect the written records of student responses for analysis.

Online

Ask students to submit their work in whatever format you prefer, whether as an LMS assignment, a blog post, an email to you, a Box or Dropbox submission, or other.

Analysis and Reporting

This LAT is a flexible one, and your analysis can be more or less in-depth, depending upon your goals. Use the rating system you have developed to score individual responses, whether by a +/− system or a more extensive rubric. If you have required more extensive responses from students (paragraphs instead of a single bullet point or sentence), you can provide additional narrative to explain your rating.

To examine aggregated information, simply look across responses for each item (I, R, and A), and average the scores. Determine whether there are any noticeable trends, for example that students perform better or worse in one of the areas than others. If you used a simple yes/no scoring system, consider a bar graph to report the results for each category.

If you used a rubric assessment, consider a numeric table to report your averages across categories.

Examples

Onsite: Public Health Nursing

The professor of this course was concerned that students were only memorizing information for quizzes and tests rather than learning at a deeper level to apply in their future careers. The professor developed a learning goal that students would be able to apply basic theories and principles used in nursing administration to new situations. The professor decided to implement IRAs to help students achieve this goal and to help her assess how well they had achieved it.

The professor assigned an article about Lewin's Force Field Analysis. In brief, Lewin suggests that to understand what is needed for change, you examine the current state of affairs, the positive forces for change (driving forces), and the obstacles to change (restraining forces). She then lectured about non-compliance in reporting diseases. She talked about the two kinds of forces that influenced agencies' reporting, leading students through a force-field analysis of the situation. She presented a handout that outlined the specifics of the IRA assignment, suggesting that they provide one sentence for each of the following:

- New perceptions or understandings (Insights)
- A resource they have found that amplifies the reading's themes or information (Resources)
- An example from the student's personal experience that relates to the reading (Application)

She allowed students to complete their responses as homework. When they came to class the next day, she took up the responses and scored them. She provided individuals with scores, but she also aggregated information across categories, as shown in Figure 8.4.

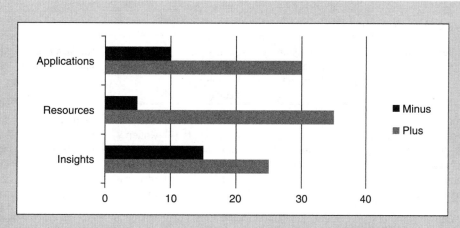

Figure 8.4 Aggregated Scores

When looking across categories, she found that most students were able to link the concept to additional articles. She found that some had trouble with application, but that most students had trouble with insights. She talked with the class about why this might be, and through discussion determined that students needed additional work on deep reading of materials. She planned future instructional activities that helped them focus on critical reading of texts.

 ## Online: Survey of International Business

This professor wanted to create a matrix that documented student achievement of learning outcomes for her fourth year review for promotion and tenure. One of her learning goals was that students will be able to connect theory and practice in their study of the global commercial community. She decided to use IRAs in conjunction with a set of reading assignments on international marketing functions, creating a discussion forum for students to post both their own essays and to comment upon the essays of their peers.

After students completed their posts, she responded to each of them individually, telling them what they did well and what they could improve upon. She next reviewed her own comments to look for themes across the classroom, and noted that students were strongest at sharing their insights and at making applications from the readings to their own lives. She believed that the activity helped students deepen their understanding of key topics because it encouraged them to find personal relevance as they connected what they were learning to their own experiences. Students were weakest at suggesting additional scholarly resources, most often recommending popular rather than academic sources. She determined that they needed additional instruction in what counts as an academic source and how to go about locating the same.

Table 8.14 [need caption]

Student Learning Outcomes	LAT	Subject/ Content Prompt	Intentional Active Learning Activity	Learning Artifact	Findings and Interpretations	Actions to Be Taken
Students will be able to connect theory and practice in their study of the global commercial community.	IRA	Read the specified assignment prior to coming to class.	Respond to the prompts for Insights, Resources, and Applications.	The written record of the response to IRA	Students most often suggest popular rather than academic articles.	Teach students how to locate scholarly articles in the field.

She developed a report of her findings, first presenting information about the class, the students, her instructional methods, and so forth. She described IRAs and how she implemented them and also included the matrix in Table 8.14 to summarize what she had done and submitted this in her fourth year dossier.

Variations and Extensions

- Instead of using this LAT in conjunction with a reading, use it for other kinds of learning activities such as discussion follow-up or video viewing.
- To make the learning activity a collaborative one, ask students to exchange their responses with a partner. After they have had a few minutes to read the shared work, ask them to compare and contrast their ideas and then to record their discussions as "further thoughts." This variation provides you with additional data into how well they can communicate their ideas and integrate ideas of others into their own work.
- To do the collaborative activity online, create a threaded discussion forum for the IRAs, and ask students to post theirs and then read and comment on at least two other students' IRAs by a deadline. Encourage students to make substantive comments by suggesting that they identify similarities and differences between various students' posting, connect ideas to previous readings, and/or provide additional insights or resources. This variation too will provide additional information, in particular through peer-responses to each other's comments.

Key References and Resources

Barkley, E. F. (2010). SET 32: Insights-resources-application. In *Student engagement techniques: A handbook for college faculty* (pp. 287–288). San Francisco, CA: Jossey-Bass.

Conrad, R., & Donaldson, J. A. (2011). *Engaging the online learner* (p. 80). San Francisco, CA: Jossey-Bass.

LEARNING ASSESSMENT TECHNIQUE

Application Learning

15
Consider This

Complexity involved in	
Preparation	LOW
In-class implementation	LOW-MODERATE
Analysis	HIGH

Brief Description

Students are given a theory or concept that they have been taught (for example, thesis statements, the scientific method, or push-pull factors) and are challenged to figure out a way to apply it in a new and different context.

Purpose

This technique's value as an instructional activity lies in the way it challenges students to move beyond surface-level thinking. Students have to relate previous knowledge to new situations. They have to look for meaning, and search for a solution to a problem (how to use the knowledge). The LAT requires thought, and it requires students to actively grapple with the information.

This LAT provides a written Learning Artifact that may be used to assess students' deep understanding of a topic as well as their ability for divergent thinking, since they are required to identify the topic's underlying qualities and then to generate a novel and reasonable application. Requiring students to suggest ways to apply something they have learned to new situations, provides you with information that can help you to determine how well students have internalized a concept to which they have been exposed. Consider This is typically used as a formative assessment, meaning that it is done to improve learning. It is typically done at the end of a learning module, since its primary purpose is to gauge the depth of student understanding.

Key Learning Goals

- Analytical skills
- Creative thinking skills

- Critical thinking skills
- Decision-making skills
- Problem-solving skills

Implementation

Preparation

- Choose a concept that is important to your course or academic discipline that students have studied in some depth.
- Reflect on the topic and try to think of ways yourself that the underlying concepts could be applied in a new context. This process will help you to ensure that the topic is sufficiently generative and to determine how much time to allocate for the assignment.
- Create a handout with a prompt question that outlines the activity, and provide a space for a response, as we illustrate in the following:

  > Consider This
  > We have studied the Scientific Method this semester and have used it as our model for creating and conducting several experiments. For this activity, you will consider the concept of the Scientific Method and suggest a novel application for it. Please use the space provided below for your response.

- Try to identify one or two examples that you can use as models to provide to students. Use an example from the list you developed, or when you repeat this assignment in a subsequent class, consider using student examples as models. You might for example provide a model like the following one:

  > Here is one example students generated last academic term: "In the scientific process, scientists formulate a question, develop a hypothesis, predict a logical consequence of the hypothesis, then test their conjecture and draw conclusions that they share with others. This same process could be used by detectives who are investigating a crime, and the information they gather along with their findings could be judged in a court of law."

- Establish the parameters of the assignment, such as the approximate length of responses, the number of responses, the level of plausibility of the response, etc. Consider how restrictive you want to be, focusing on what you want to limit through your parameters (for example, you may prefer to be more open ended to allow for maximum creativity, or you may want to bound the activity to accomplish a specific goal).
- Create an assessment rubric that includes elements such as quantity, novelty, and appropriateness.

Process

1. Announce the Consider This activity as well as the time frame.
2. Present students with the handout and a sample response, as suggested above.
3. Ask students to complete the handout.
4. Collect the handout at the end of the allotted time.

Online

Present the central concept, a sample response, and instructions about the parameters of the assignment (such as length of response, number of responses, etc.) in your LMS's assignments area, and ask students to respond by a specific date and time. Alternately have them email their assignments to you, or submit them through a more central system like Dropbox.

Analysis and Reporting

Review your Learning Artifact, which is the Consider This handout that students complete and return to you. Use the rubric you created to analyze each artifact for elements such as originality and appropriateness. Comment on any handout where information the student has provided does not fit within the rubric (e.g. a particularly novel response, or alternately a completely unworkable one). Provide individuals with their rubric scores (if you return the originals to them, make copies for yourself for further analysis), along with any written comments and suggestions for improvement. Consider whether you would prefer a more thematic or holistic analysis. This assessment is well-suited to grading, particularly if you have given students sufficient time to demonstrate their best work. Because it requires them to apply knowledge in new ways, however, it can cause students anxiety. For this reason, it may be best to assign a small percentage of the grade to it, or alternately, particularly if you do the assignment completely in class, to include it in a "participation" grading category.

Aggregate the individual scores on the rubric, tallying the number of responses in each cell. Develop a median or average score for each category and also consider looking at the mode to determine whether there are significant differences between those two scores. Consider counting the number of responses, providing a high number, a low number, and an average number (e.g. the top number of responses generated was 7, the lowest number was 2, and the average was 4). If you have chosen a thematic or holistic analysis, examine the assignments for central themes or concepts that cross individual papers. Put the aggregated scores into a paragraph, a bar graph, or a table, whatever makes the most sense for your discipline.

Examples

Onsite: Geography and Globalization

A professor was concerned that her students were too western centered in their thinking, which she hoped to help them get beyond in her course on geography and globalization. She wanted information about whether her perception was correct, and decided to find out in her current class section. The course had a learning outcome stating that by the end of the course, successful students would be able to demonstrate understanding of the push-pull factor in relation to human migration. The students first read assignments related to push and pull factors present in America today for immigrants, and then she implemented Consider This.

Table 8.15 Geography and Globalization: Scoring Table on Consider This

Category	Responses
Average number of examples	5
Average score on quality	High Average
Continents included in analysis	North America, Western Europe
Continents not included	Eastern Europe, Asia, Australia, Africa, South America, Antarctica

She gave students the topic, and asked them to generate as many examples as they could of how the underlying principles of push and pull had worked in other contexts, and requested that students submit their responses to her in writing.

The professor scored the responses based upon both the quantity of responses generated (using a simple tally) and quality of responses (using a simple scoring scheme of excellent, average, or poor). She graded the assignments through a combination of the quantity/quality scoring systems (see Table 8.15). The professor noted that students were able on average to generate five additional situations that illustrated push and pull factors and that the mean was between average and excellent. She noted, however, that they tended to stay in western hemisphere countries and to go back through time, rather than branching to other parts of the world and staying in the present. She had evidence of the area that she needed to work on to improve student learning, and in a subsequent round of Consider This, she limited students to continents not included in the first round. She found their range had greatly improved.

Online: Music History: 18th Century Classicism

This professor's department regularly collected information from professors on student performance in meeting learning outcomes, requiring all instructors to submit evidence that they were collecting information from students and using what they were learning to make improvements.

A core concept in this course is sonata-allegro form, as this form is the basis for first movement formal organization in classical symphonies, concertos, string quartets, piano sonatas, and so forth. Thus understanding sonata-allegro form was a key course-learning outcome. To ensure students fully internalized the structure of the form, this professor assigned Consider This to the base groups she had established at the beginning of the term, presenting it as the prompt for each group's private discussion area and instructing groups to create three applications to novel contexts. At the deadline, they posted their responses on the course discussion forum.

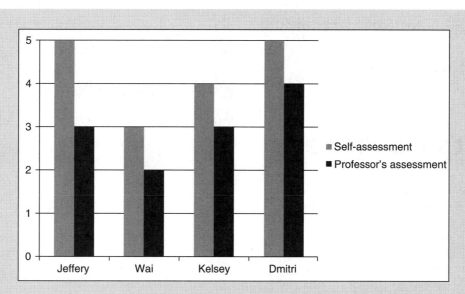

Figure 8.5 Excerpt from Comparison of Self- and Professor Assessment on Scores for the Novel Category

The professor rated the responses by a rubric, and she also asked students to self-assess their responses. She used both her scores and the self-assessment scores in reporting results to students, and noted that students scored themselves consistently higher (80% or above, or higher than 4 out of 5, on all categories) than she assessed them (60%, or 3 out of 5, on the same categories). In her semester report to the department assessment committee, she included both the student ratings and her rating, and she indicated that she planned to ensure that her expectations for performance were clear in the future by providing an extensive handout detailing expectations (Figure 8.5).

Variations and Extensions

- Although many students will find this technique challenging and fun, those students who do not understand the underlying topic sufficiently or cannot generate an application in a novel context may find it too difficult and get frustrated. Working in small groups will help support such students, but if the assignment is graded, ensure that your assignment process and evaluation rubric address individual accountability and that you report your results to any external stakeholders as group work.
- To make it an online group assignment, consider forming students into groups and assign each group its own private threaded discussion area so that members can communicate their ideas. At the deadline, have groups communicate their ideas to the whole class discussion thread.

Key Reference and Resource

Ten assessments you can perform in 90 seconds. TeachThought.com. (http://www.teachthought.com /teaching/10-assessments-you-can-perform-in-90-seconds/).

LEARNING ASSESSMENT TECHNIQUE

Application Learning

16
What's the Problem?

Complexity involved in	
Preparation	MODERATE-HIGH
In-class implementation	MODERATE
Analysis	LOW

Brief Description

Students look at examples of common problem types and seek to name the particular type of problem each example represents.

Purpose

One of the first steps in good problem solving is being able to correctly identify what kind of problem one is dealing with in order to determine the appropriate principles and techniques needed to solve it. To do this, students must be able to look beyond surface differences among problems and perceive underlying similarities. Students practice this important skill in this technique, which is an adaptation of *Problem Recognition Tasks* (Angelo & Cross, 1993, pp. 214–217) and *What's the Problem?* (Barkley, 2010, pp. 252–253). By participating in this LAT, students can increase their efficiency and effectiveness in problem solving by learning to generalize problem types instead of seeing problems as isolated exemplars.

The assessable Learning Artifact from this LAT is the students' record of their responses to the problems, which may take the form of a completed handout, a paper and pencil quiz, or an online submitted assignment. An initial determination of problem-solving skills can help you identify which students are strongest/weakest in problem solving and give you the information you need to form groups, whether choosing homogenous ones or heterogeneous ones based upon ability, or to recommend additional support for students who are struggling. This technique is well suited to assessing students' readiness for specific problem-solving assignments or to identify gaps in the collective knowledge in order to know where to target teaching, so it often occurs before or early into a learning module or unit. This technique also makes a useful pre-post assessment, which allows you to determine whether students have improved their problem-solving ability as a result of having participated in the class.

Key Learning Goals

- Reading skills
- Analytical skills
- Critical thinking skills
- Decision-making skills
- Problem-solving skills

Implementation

Preparation

- Identify two or more types of problems in your content area that students find difficult to distinguish between. (*Note:* This technique naturally lends itself to disciplines that contain well-defined problems with correct answers. But there are also disciplines or types of problems within disciplines that are messier and more complex, that include a large array of relevant variables both known and unknown, and that may not have a single correct solution. If using these kinds of problems, plan to inform students that there may be multiple solutions and to choose one, justifying their responses with reference to the evidence provided in the example.)
- Choose or craft several examples of each problem type.
- Depending upon your teaching goals and the skill level of your students, determine the appropriate level of complexity of the task. (Consider the following questions: Will you provide students with information about the types of problems and ask them simply to match type with example? Will you provide them only with the examples and ask them to name the problem type?)
- Create a handout containing the problem examples.
- Determine who will be involved in the assessment. Self- and peer assessment can be useful to this technique.

Process

1. Provide students with a handout and explain the directions, allowing time for questions.
2. Ask students to work through the examples, identifying the type of problem each example represents.
3. Consider asking students to report out their responses orally.
4. Collect written student responses.

Online

Post the problems as an assignment or quiz in your LMS. If you have a small class, students could email you their responses or alternately submit them through a file sharing service like Dropbox, Box, or Google Docs.

Analysis and Reporting

Examine individual submissions, marking the number of correct and incorrect responses. Record individual data in a table or spreadsheet, noting correct (+) and incorrect (–) responses. Look at overall scores to see how well individuals and the class did. Look for information that can benefit individual students (e.g., Jane needs to work on problem type 2, John on problem types 2 and 4, and so forth). Let students know their overall scores, and if you have identified any problems specific to individuals, let them know that as well. A simple tally sheet for each student in which you list the overall scores and record the correct and incorrect items should be sufficient. When used as a post-instruction activity, What's the Problem may be graded. If used as a pre-instructional assessment or as a quick check during instruction to determine whether students are understanding the concepts, it is best not to grade. To determine a grade, simply identify the percentage of correct and incorrect scores and grade accordingly.

When reporting the results of your assessment to others, you will probably want to aggregate individual results to note overall trends. You can record aggregate data as a simple tally of information, noting the number of correct and incorrect responses. Note any patterns in the data (questions that most students got correct, questions that most got incorrect). You might also consider showing differences among problem types, as in

- All four students answered problem 1 correctly.
- Three out of four students missed problem 2.

A narrative in which you explain your interpretation of the scores and what you plan to do about them can be useful.

Examples

Onsite: Critical Reading

A professor wanted to know that students had developed skills in identifying fallacies in arguments. She decided that by the end of the course, she wanted them to be able to recognize quickly a minimum of 20 fallacy types, and she listed this information in the objectives section of her syllabus. To teach students about fallacies, she started with five common types (e.g., Confusing Cause and Effect, Red Herring, Straw Man, Ad Hominum, and Post Hoc) and created a presentation slide with a series of short paragraphs such as the following:

> Presidential Candidate X claims that the federal government should not fund the acquisition and construction of the Seawolf Class Attack Submarines. Presidential Candidate Y says he deeply opposes this position, saying it will leave the country defenseless.

> To assess student learning after explaining the fallacies to students in a presentation, she presented the slide and asked students to number a sheet of paper and list the appropriate

fallacy by the appropriate number. She collected these Learning Artifacts from the students and marked them accordingly, and then tallied the correct and incorrect responses, as follows:

Exhibit 8.5 What's the Problem? Assignment

Total scoring:

- # of correct responses: 12
- # of incorrect responses: 3

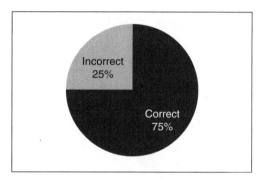

Figure 8.6 Pie Chart

She next looked at the information on a "by problem" basis. That is, she analyzed the groups' responses to problem 1, to problem 2, and so forth and determined the number of correct and incorrect responses on each (see Table 8.16).

Table 8.16 Correct and Incorrect Responses

	Problem 1	Problem 2	Problem 3	Problem 4	Total
Seung-Woo	+	−	+	+	75%
Christina	+	−	+	−	50%
Rosita	+	+	+	+	100%
Jason	+	−	+	+	75%

In the following session, she shared individual scores with each student, as well as aggregated scores, so that students could compare their individual results with the full-class results. She was also able to use this information in a report she wrote for her merit promotion to document her teaching effectiveness.

Online: Music Theory and Composition

The fundamental learning goal of this course was for students to learn, understand, and apply the voice leading rules known as 18th Century Common Practice Technique (e.g., avoid parallel fifths and octaves; leading tones must resolve to the tonic; never make a melodic movement of an augmented interval; and so forth). The professor was frustrated that although students appeared to "know" the rules, they often did not recognize when they violated them in their harmonization assignments. For the instructions, he created a numbered list of the basic rules. For the assignment, he provided 4-measure harmonic progressions, with each progression containing 2–3 errors. He asked students to go through the examples, find and circle the errors, and enter the number of the rule the harmonization had violated.

He asked students to post their responses. These served as his Learning Artifacts. He assessed the individual student scores first, providing a separate report for each student on which questions they answered correctly and which they answered incorrectly. He next looked for patterns in the data, searching for the ones that the most students marked inappropriately the most number of times. This provided him with information he could use to identify where the problems were in student thinking about the rules. He reported the aggregate scores to the group as well (Figure 8.7).

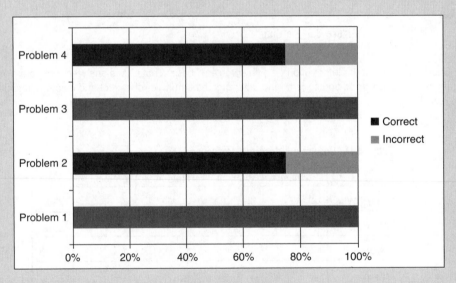

Figure 8.7 Aggregated Scores

Variations and Extensions

- This LAT can be a useful individual assessment, but it can also be done with student pairs or small groups. Simply ask students to work together to identify the type of problem and give the groups rather than individuals feedback.

Key References and Resources

Angelo, T. A. & Cross, K. P. (1993). CAT 19: Problem recognition tasks. In *Classroom assessment techniques* (2nd ed., pp. 214–217). San Francisco, CA: Jossey-Bass.

Barkley, E. (2010). What's the problem? In *Student engagement techniques* (pp. 252–253). San Francisco, CA: Jossey-Bass.

LEARNING ASSESSMENT TECHNIQUE

Application Learning

17
Think-Aloud Problem-Solving Protocols (TAPPs)

Complexity involved in	
Preparation	MODERATE-HIGH
In-class implementation	MODERATE
Analysis	HIGH

Brief Description

Student pairs receive a set of problems to solve as well as specific roles, problem solver and listener. The problem solver "thinks aloud," talking through the steps of solving a problem. The partner listens to the problem solver, following the steps, attempting to understand the reasoning behind the steps, and recording the problem-solving process as he or she hears it. The pair alternate roles as they work through the problems in the set.

Purpose

This technique has several potential benefits to students. Articulating one's own problem-solving process and listening carefully to another's process helps students practice what they have read about or heard in a lecture. This LAT places the emphasis on the problem-solving process rather than the product, helping students diagnose errors in logic. Depending upon the problems used, this LAT can also help increase student awareness of the range of possible successful (and unsuccessful) approaches to problem solving. This technique improves analytical skills by helping students formulate ideas, rehearse concepts, understand the sequence of steps underlying their thinking, and identify errors in someone else's reasoning. Since it requires students to relate information to existing conceptual frameworks and apply existing information to new situations, it can also promote deeper understanding. Every student is active at once, half the room with solving problems and the other half with trying to record the information accurately.

The assessable Learning Artifact from this technique is the partner student's record of the problem-solving student's steps and missteps. The partner may also be asked to make an evaluation of how accurate or effective the process was, which adds an additional layer of assessment of evidence of learning. This technique is often used during a learning module or unit to determine how well students are understanding the problem-solving process so that teachers can target instruction to help clear up any potential misunderstandings. It can be used at the end of a unit to help students prepare for an upcoming examination.

Key Learning Goals

- Analytical skills
- Critical thinking skills
- Problem-solving skills

Implementation

Preparation

- To prepare for this LAT, spend sufficient time developing an appropriate set of field-related problems that students can solve within a limited time frame. The problems should engage students in basic problem-solving skills such as identifying the nature of the problem, analyzing the knowledge and skills required to reach a solution, identifying potential solutions, choosing the best solution, and evaluating potential outcomes. To be most effective, the problems should challenge students, requiring them to concentrate and focus their attention, whether they are solvers or listeners.
- Develop a handout that contains the problem set (Table 8.17). The handout may be divided into two, with problems on the left hand side and a blank area on the right hand side for recording the responses.
- Solve the problems yourself, specifically noting what steps you have to follow to solve the problem.
- Consider whether students need practice solving problems, or working through the various steps of problem solving, prior to using this activity. Since the focus of this LAT is their

Table 8.17 Problems and Processes

Problems	Processes
Which of the following describe 5? (select all that apply) 1. whole number 2. irrational number 3. integer 4. real number	Amy says that 5 is a whole number, because it . . . She says it is not an irrational number, because it . . . She say it is an integer, because it . . . She says it is a real number, because it . . .
Is 5/7 an integer?	Fred says it is an integer because . . .
Which of the following are rational numbers:? 6 5/7 0 1 1/8	Amy says they are all rational numbers because . . .

meta-cognitive processing, they need a general understanding of problem solving in order to be able to articulate their steps.

- Create an extra problem or two (an "extension" or "sponge"). Students will solve problems at different speeds, so the additional problems are for students who complete the problems quickly so that they do not sit around bored waiting for the other students to finish. Consider crafting a particularly challenging "bonus" question for extra credit.

Process

1. Ask students to form pairs and explain to students the roles of problem solver and listener. The role of the problem solver is to read the problem aloud and talk through the reasoning process in attempting to solve the problem. The role of the listener is to encourage the problem solver to think aloud, describing the steps to solve the problem. The listener should record the process as accurately and fully as possible.
2. Ask students to solve a set of problems, alternating roles with each new problem.
3. Call completion when students have solved all problems.
4. Come to closure. If all pairs have worked on the same problem set, select pairs at random to report out their solution or "take a vote" on the most challenging problems and share and examine solutions along with tips for improvement as a class.
5. To create a useful Learning Artifact, have both students review the other's records of their processes and their answers. Have students sign their name to each other's forms to signal their agreement to the accuracy of the record.
6. Take up the signed student recordings and explanations of their peer's problem-solving processes.

Online

Using this LAT online provides students with the opportunity to share their thinking processes and to have comments on these, which sometimes go undiscussed and unrecognized in an online environment. This LAT is best done synchronously, for example through Web conferencing with VoIP. It can also be done asynchronously if a student posts a video of himself or herself solving a problem which another student then watches and records the process, ultimately submitting their videos (or links) and reports to the teacher.

Analysis and Reporting

To examine individual Learning Artifacts, review first the individual's response to the problem, marking this as accurate or inaccurate. Next, review the individual's problem-solving process, which his or her peer has recorded. Mark accurate steps with a +1 and inaccurate steps with –1. Tally the responses, and return them to the students so that they know whether their answers were correct and where they fell short in the problem-solving process. You probably will not want to grade this assignment, since students are working on different problems, but a participation grade can help students to understand that it is an important activity.

To aggregate the responses across the classroom, simply note the number of accurate and inaccurate answers, and then the number of accurate and inaccurate steps in the problem-solving process. You may want to compare their steps to the set of steps you developed when preparing for this LAT. Note patterns in responses, such as whether a majority of the students had difficulty at a given step.

Examples

Onsite: Programming in BIOPERL

The purpose of this course was to teach students to create utility software programs using a specific scientific programming language. To achieve this goal, students needed to become competent in a complex problem-solving process of retrieving, manipulating, and analyzing sequences from a variety of databases. The instructor noticed that some of his students were able to go through the steps relatively easily, while others tended to make process mistakes that resulted in programming errors that were time-consuming and frustrating to find later. Historically, these struggling students simply dropped the course at this point, so the instructor was searching for ways to reduce attrition and alleviate student anxiety.

He decided to use TAPPS to structure practicing the problem-solving process with a peer, and to use recent quiz scores to partner a student who was having difficulties with a student who was doing well. He assigned a complex problem that had a fairly structured solution. He asked students to complete the problem, and then he recorded their results in a spreadsheet display, a sample of which is shown in Table 8.18.

Table 8.18 Problem Results

	Peijun	Landay	Xiang	John	Ginny	Jason
Answer	Correct	Correct	Incorrect	Incorrect	Correct	Correct
Step 1	+	Omitted	+	+	+	+
Step 2	+	+	+	+	+	+
Step 3	+	+	−	−	+	+
Step 4	+	+	+	+	+	+
Step 5	+	+	+	+	+	+

From this, he could see exactly where the breakdown was happening, and he targeted his instruction to provide additional information to students, and he used peer teaching to have those students who were regularly answering the problems correctly help teach those who were struggling how to solve the problem.

The result was not only that students gained competence sooner than in the previous semester when they had worked independently, but also student retention significantly improved.

Online: Elementary Algebra

In this course, the instructor asked students in the online section to use TAPPS to solve a series of problems to prepare for an upcoming test, which would require them to respond to word problems based upon the principles they had been studying in class. He recommended that students use VoIP, such as Skype, so that they could see each other as they worked through their problems together; he suggested using the telephone if they lacked VoIP technology.

Students submitted their problems and recorded problem-solving processes to him through his LMS assignment. He created a table to display his results (Table 8.19), which he included in his teaching dossier as evidence that he was engaging in effective teaching practices, through collecting evidence of student learning from students and using it to make change.

Table 8.19 Table of Results

Description	Percentage
Accuracy of responses	83%
Average # of successful steps (out of 4)	75%
Average # of missteps	18%

Through examining the steps that typically resulted in missteps, he was able to target his teaching and provided an additional video lecture showing how to work through the difficult area.

Variations and Extensions

- While students work in pairs in the main approach to this technique, their activity is to listen and record and not to truly collaborate. This activity, however, can be a more collaborative activity, as evidenced in Barkley et al. (2014) and Barkley (2010), with TAPPS. In this variation, students not only listen and record but also help each other through the problem-solving process by offering guidance and encouragement, stopping short of actually solving the problem. This variation can be beneficial to student learning, but it is important to remember during analysis that you are capturing the problem-solving abilities of pairs rather than individuals.

Key References and Resources

Lochhead, J., & Whimby, A. (1987). Teaching analytical reasoning through thinking-aloud pair problem solving. In J. E. Stice (Ed.), *Developing critical thinking and problem solving abilities* (pp. 72–93). New Directions for Teaching and Learning, No. 30. San Francisco, CA: Jossey-Bass.

MacGregor, J. (1990). Collaborative learning: Shared inquiry as a process of reform. In M. D. Svinicki (Ed.), *The changing face of college teaching* (pp. 19–30). New Directions for Teaching and Learning, No. 42. San Francisco, CA: Jossey-Bass.

Millis, B. J., & Cottell, P. G. (1998). *Cooperative learning for higher education faculty* (p. 114). Phoenix, AZ: Oryx Press.

LEARNING ASSESSMENT TECHNIQUE

Application Learning

18
Peer Problem Review

Complexity involved in	
Preparation	MODERATE
In-class implementation	MODERATE
Analysis	HIGH

Brief Description

In Peer Problem Review, students each receive a problem, try to solve it, and then pass the problem and solution to a nearby student. The student who receives the problem and response then analyzes and evaluates the solution.

Purpose

Peer Problem Review involves two activity stages: solving problems and evaluating solutions. The purpose of the first stage is to provide students with an opportunity to practice effective problem solving. The purpose of the second stage is to help students learn to evaluate potential solutions. Peer Problem Review can replace traditional drill-and-practice exercises by adding in higher-order thinking skills during the second, "solution evaluation" stage.

The Learning Artifacts are the solved problems and the evaluation of solutions. Peer Problem Review is an effective technique for gathering information that can help you target your teaching to the group's level of knowledge and ability. It can help you identify what students know and what they don't know about solving relevant problems, which can help you determine working groups, recommend additional resources or assistance to students who need it, and so forth. Peer Problem Review can allow you to spot check for student understanding in the middle of an instructional unit. Peer Problem Review also works as a pre-post assessment, as you receive information about their starting place and ending place and thus can evaluate change over time. When used as a postmodule assessment, Peer Problem Review can also help you determine whether students have understood what you have taught them about different kinds of problems in your field.

Key Learning Goals

- Analytical skills
- Critical thinking skills
- Decision-making skills
- Problem-solving skills

Implementation

Preparation

- Determine how many problems you will need. You will need at least two (one for each student in the pair) plus some extra problems as "extensions" for students who work quickly and finish before everyone else. You may also develop a problem set, which consists of 3–5 problems for students to work on prior to exchanging them.
- Draft the problems, making sure to write ones that are important in your field but that can be solved/responded to in a relatively short period (e.g., 5–15 minutes). Be sure to select problems that are roughly equal in complexity and that take approximately the same amount of time to solve. Work through the solutions yourself so that you can determine the amount of time it will take students to solve the problems. Depending on the complexity of the problem, you will need to estimate how long each stage of this activity will take so that you allow enough time for thinking and reflection.
- Develop the assessment instrument. You may, for example, create a handout with the problem, a space for solving the problem, and a place for evaluating the solution.
- Think through the instructions you will give to students regarding time limits and the length of the responses.
- This LAT has the added benefit of peer evaluation, which can be helpful to the speed, accuracy, and efficiency of your review.

Process

1. Announce the activity and tell students the parameters, including the amount of time they will have to work on the problem and how much time they will have to evaluate the solution. (*Note:* Be prepared to extend the time limit if the majority of the students seem to still be on task or to call time sooner than you anticipated if the majority of the students seem to be wrapping up.)
2. Form pairs, and distribute a different problem to each student in the pair, asking each student to generate a possible solution and record it.
3. Ask students to swap problems with the other member of their pair.
4. Each student reviews and evaluates the response to the problem he or she holds after the exchange. Students may also add any additional information. The student evaluates the solution, the rationale for the evaluation, and signs his or her name.
5. The activity concludes after the problem evaluation. You may consider asking students to report out on their evaluations orally in class.

Online

Adapt this for the online environment by assigning pairs, assigning problems, and asking the pairs to exchange by email (or other method of their choosing) and then submit the problems and solutions to you through email or the LMS.

Analysis and Reporting

Create a list of student names. By each name, use a simple tally system for assessing the students' contributions and their accuracy; use a system such as +/−. Next examine their evaluations for accuracy. Record your responses. See Table 8.20 for an example.

Table 8.20 Example of a Tally Sheet

	Problem 1	Problem 2	Evaluation Problem 1	Evaluation Problem 2
Shienni	+			+
Pui-Ching		+	+	
Susan	+			+
Michael		−	+	
Janet	+			−
Ribhi		−	−	

Because students may be working on different problems, grading can cause students anxiety and worry that they are being judged against different criteria than their peers and we therefore recommend against grading this assessment. However, if you do choose to grade, you may assign percentages to the answers, for example, 50% for each correct response and 50% for the evaluation. Either way, provide students with a response regarding their performances.

This technique may also be effective for reporting information to students and to external constituents. You can consider the following:

- Correct responses. For example, out of 6 question attempts, 4 were answered correctly.
- Evaluations: For example, out of 6 evaluations, 4 students identified correct responses.
- Problems with the problems: For example, Problem 1 received more correct responses than Problem 2, indicating that students may need additional work on the content of Problem 2.
- Use a simple table to report numeric findings. Consider writing them up in a report with narrative explaining your views of the responses and how you plan to respond to them.

Examples

Onsite: Urban Planning

This assistant professor was planning for a promotion and tenure review in which she had to demonstrate evidence of teaching effectiveness. Due to a recent accreditation review, faculty in her department had become more aware of the need to document learning outcomes and were asking tenure candidates to demonstrate that they were helping students achieve these learning outcomes. This professor decided to use Peer Problem Review to demonstrate that students could evaluate a residential rezoning problem. She planned to include the activity in her teaching dossier.

To conduct the activity, in class, she formed pairs, and gave each student in a pair a handout with a problem (pairs received different problems). She asked students to review the problem and determine a solution, write the solution on the handout, and pass the handout to their partners. The next student evaluated the solution and recorded the evaluation on the handout. The assistant professor asked these students to report on which solution they felt was best and to describe why.

She next collected the responses and developed a report of the results of the activity. She noted the number of correct and incorrect responses, and also noted her ratings of their evaluations of the collected solutions. She indicated which problems students struggled with the most, and which the least, and she indicated how she helped to address the deficiencies in student knowledge after the exercise. She submitted the activity and the results with her teaching dossier as evidence of teaching effectiveness (Table 8.21).

Table 8.21 Example Matrix

Student Learning Outcomes	LAT	Learning Artifact	Findings and Interpretations	Actions Taken
Students will be able to evaluate a rezoning problem.	Peer Problem Review	Problems and solutions from each student	Students struggled with the concept of use (both nonconforming and conditional use) but showed more facility with zoning and variances.	Added a lecture about use. Brought in expert to answer questions about use in the real world.

Online: Advanced Pathophysiology and Patient Management

The instructor of this course had a learning outcome that students would be able to identify a limited set of diseases from their most common symptoms. During a unit introducing the diseases, this professor used Peer Problem Review to assess student understanding. He developed two patient descriptions, in which he outlined their general demographics and listed their symptoms.

Problem 1: An 8-year-old boy has presented to the pediatrician with high fever, cough, chills, fatigue, aches, pains, loss of appetite. His parents say it came on suddenly. What illness that we have studied this term might he have?

Name of problem solver: _____
Solution (state your rationale):
Name of evaluator: _____
Evaluation of solution (circle your response):
   Accurate diagnosis
   Inaccurate diagnosis
Explain your rationale:

Problem 2: A 6-year-old girl has presented to the pediatrician with vomiting, diarrhea, abdominal pain, fever, chills, achiness. What illness that we have studied this term might she have?

Name of problem solver: _____
Solution (state your rationale):
Name of evaluator: _____
Evaluation of solution (circle your response):
   Accurate diagnosis
   Inaccurate diagnosis
Explain your rationale:

The professor's LMS has a peer review option, so he used this tool and assigned peer reviewers manually to create peer review pairs. He also created the rubric in the LMS for reviewers to indicate whether they thought the solution was accurate or inaccurate, including space for the rationale. Students completed their assignments and their peer reviews. He assessed them as shown in Tables 8.22 and 8.23.

Table 8.22 Scores

Problem 1: Answers	Problem 1: Evaluation	Problem 2: Answers	Problem 2: Evaluation
75%	90%	88%	95%

Table 8.23 Instructor Interpretation of Student Rationale

Problem 1: Answers	Problem 1: Evaluation	Problem 2: Answers	Problem 2: Evaluation
Students who answered the question incorrectly did not note the high fever.	Most students were able to evaluate the response correctly, potentially by examining the original student logic.	This question has a clearer response, but students who missed it did not note the fever, which likely contributed to inaccuracy of response.	Most students were able to evaluate the response correctly, potentially by examining the original student logic.

The following week, the professor sent each student feedback about their solutions and their evaluations. He also told the class which problem appeared to be most difficult given the number of incorrect responses, and he suggested that they review these symptoms prior to the next exam, which he informed them would be case-based, much like the Peer Problem Review activity.

Variations and Extensions

- This technique works well as a group activity. Simply place students in teams and have teams develop solutions, pass the problem to a nearby group, and then work on the next problem. When time is up, student teams evaluate the solutions to the problem they are holding and report to the full class. When you analyze the information, you are looking at a composite of the group knowledge, rather than individual knowledge. You may still look across the groups' responses to analyze and report data at the aggregate level.

Key References and Resources

Barkley, E. (2010). SET 27: Send-a-problem. In *Student engagement techniques: A handbook for college faculty* (pp. 267–271). San Francisco, CA: Jossey-Bass.

Barkley, E., Major, C. H., & Cross, K. P. (2014). CoLT 14: Send-a-problem. In *Collaborative learning techniques: A handbook for college faculty* (2nd ed., pp. 232–237). San Francisco, CA: Jossey-Bass.

Kagan, S. (1992). *Cooperative learning* (2nd ed., pp. 10–11). San Juan Capistrano, CA: Resources for Teachers.

Millis, B. J., & Cottell, P. G., Jr. (1998). *Cooperative learning for higher education faculty* (pp. 103–105). Phoenix, AZ: Oryx Press.

LEARNING ASSESSMENT TECHNIQUE

Application Learning

19
Triple Jump

Complexity involved in	
Preparation	HIGH
In-class implementation	HIGH
Analysis	HIGH

Description

This three-step technique requires students to think through a real-world problem presented in a case-based scenario to (1) articulate a plan for solving it, (2) gather resources, and (3) attempt to provide a viable solution to it.

Purpose

The Triple Jump Problem-Solving Demonstration is particularly effective in courses that are practical in nature and are well-suited to real-world or clinical problems. While students work through it, they learn directly about course content through gathering and applying resources. Students gain experience at solving real-world problems that are messy and may have multiple correct answers or multiple ways to arrive at an answer.

The technique is an effective assessment of a student's ability to plan and work through the problem-solving process, as it aims to document their processes in real time, including reasoning and decision making, self-directing learning, and self-assessment skills. The Learning Artifacts for this assessment technique are the tangible product from initial problem-solving planning, the record of resources consulted, and the final analysis and solution. They can also include your own notes (and potentially the notes of external assessors if you have involved others in this assessment activity). Thus this LAT provides evidence of both problem-solving ability and self-regulation. The LAT is an extensive assessment of student problem-solving ability. As such, it is time intensive. It is typically done after a learning module and can take several class periods to accomplish or be done out of class time.

Key Learning Goals

- Analytical skills
- Creative thinking skills
- Critical thinking skills
- Decision-making skills
- Problem-solving skills
- Research skills

Implementation

Preparation

- Seek out current resources and cases to develop a real world scenario that involves a compelling problem. The problem should be well-designed but open ended so that it allows students to demonstrate thinking outside the box.
- Think through the timing and the resources you will need. Since it requires students to demonstrate problem-solving ability in real time, this LAT is time and resource intensive. You will need a sufficient time span to conduct the activity that involves research on the students' part, usually about 3 hours. You will also need to decide how students will think through the problem (verbally or in writing) and how they will report out (presentation to the full class or video-taped responses). Consider especially how you will deal with all of the students finishing their work simultaneously (in which case videotaping can be a useful option).
- The best method for analyzing and scoring student results on the Triple Jump is to use a rubric for evaluating the performance. Consider the following criteria as you create one:
  - Define problem
  - Identify necessary resources
  - Identify potential strategies for solving it
  - Propose solutions
  - Evaluate potential solutions
- Consider whether you will include other faculty as assessors (doing so can make the assessment feel more authentic but can create a problem of variation in scoring and data analysis). Also consider the potential for using peer review as a part of this assessment.

Process

1. Give students a complex real-world problem.
2. The student reads through the case and presents an oral or written review of the case, including
   - Interpretation of the evidence presented in the problem
   - Initial exploration of critical elements of the problem
   - Generation of potential solutions
3. The student conducts an information search independently.
4. Each student uses the information that he or she has gathered to find a problem resolution and prepare a presentation of the findings. The student presents the resolution of the

problem. This phase is time intensive, and asking students to video their responses can help alleviate the time sensitivity of having several students presenting at the same time.

5. The student also presents a self-assessment of performance.
6. Next, you collect the written or video assignments and self-assessments.

Online

Present the problem in a centralized course environment. Set the window of time for students to complete the work. If doing it synchronously, plan for about 3 hours. If asynchronously, allow students from 3 days to a week to complete the work. Collect data as follows:

- Ask students to video themselves working through the problem and submit to you.
- Ask them to complete their research online and submit a list of sources they used to you.
- Ask students to submit their final solutions in video format.

Analysis and Reporting

Report the results of your rubric scoring to students in writing. If it is possible given the timeframe and number of students you have, providing oral feedback to students can be useful. This activity is best-suited to a high-stakes graded activity. If it is not graded, students will not take it as seriously and thus may not exert the necessary effort.

Because of the rich data it generates and the potential for intensive assessment of the various phases, information viewed in aggregate can provide valuable information.

- Looking at data from an aggregate level, you can review the Learning Artifacts you have collected and analyze them for themes. You might recognize consistent themes; for example, you may note that students typically identify the central problem correctly. Alternately you might note that students struggle to quickly select the most useful resources for solving the problem.
- Consider using a table to record the aggregated results of student performance on this assessment. Look for trends in the different areas, such as consistently high or low scores.
- Use a narrative format to report overarching themes you see in the students' performance.

Examples

Onsite: Psychology: Psychometrics

This instructor had a learning goal stating that students will be able to recognize clinical signs of depression. A second outcome stated that students will be able to identify a way to diagnose depression. The instructor decided to use Triple Jump to teach and assess these skills. She presented students with a real-world scenario of a high school senior who was showing signs of depression. In the scenario, the parents were asking for a psychological evaluation, and students were to assume the position of the consulted psychometrist. Students completed the

Triple Jump: they reasoned through the problem in writing (30 minutes). They left their written responses with the professor, as they consulted the school library and Internet for additional information (2 hours). Finally, they recorded their responses to the problem; some used their tablets or smartphones, while others used library equipment that the professor had reserved ahead of time. He used peer evaluation as a way to gather additional data, having students review each other's responses.

The instructor collected and averaged peer review scores to return to students. He also rated the students' written work and videotapes himself using a problem-solving rubric that included space for extensive comments to students.

The instructor examined the data at an aggregate level as well. He looked across categories to develop a composite of the class's performance. He also examined his own comments to the students, looking for common themes across them. He wrote a narrative, outlining both the aggregate scores and the common themes he had identified. He included the Figure 8.8 in which he analyzed their processes and how well they performed, as a class, at each level.

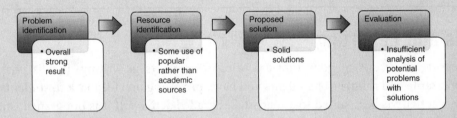

Figure 8.8 Analysis of Responses

Online: Nursing Care for Older Adults

The instructor of this online nursing course had a learning outcome stating that students will be able to develop an appropriate protocol for working with difficult patients. This learning outcome corresponded with one in the college of nursing's curriculum map, and as such, it was one that instructors had to embed in each course. Instructors also had to document student achievement in this area for the School of Nursing's assessment committee.

The instructor developed a problem about a developmentally disabled 19-year-old who is 30 weeks pregnant. The problem indicates that the patient is difficult and argumentative and has been physically abusive to past health care workers. She presented the problem in the course LMS. Students had to develop a protocol for how they would interact with the patient. As their first assignment, they submitted their initial analysis of the problem. Over the next two days, they conducted research and then had one additional day to post their video solutions to the problem.

The instructor had recruited two of her colleagues to help assess the student results. Each instructor rated the initial analysis and the final analysis according to a rubric. They then averaged the scores on each item to give to each student. The instructors aggregated the individual results to determine an overall picture of student problem-solving skills. They were able to report the results to their college's assessment committee, which they did by way of a written description of the course and the activity and the Table 8.24.

Table 8.24 Aggregated Problem-Solving Scores

Category	Aggregated Scores
Define problem	3.75
Identify necessary resources	2.75
Identify potential strategies for solving it	3.20
Propose solutions	3.41
Evaluate potential solutions	2.98

Variations and Extensions

- Make this a collaborative assignment by asking students to work in groups to work on the problem. You will then evaluate each group's solution as the individual unit.

Key References and Resources

Feleti, G., & Ryan, G. (1994). The triple jump exercise in inquiry-based learning: A case study. *Assessment & Evaluation in Higher Education, 19*(3), 225–234.

LEARNING ASSESSMENT TECHNIQUE

Application Learning

20
Digital Projects

Complexity involved in	
Preparation	MODERATE
In-class implementation	MODERATE
Analysis	HIGH

Brief Description

Students create projects that enhance and document their learning of an important topic or concept in the field. Digital Projects may include collages, photo albums, videos, infographics, websites, blogs, podcasts, book trailers, or other.

Purpose

This LAT challenges students to summarize and synthesize their course learning and to deepen that learning through the act of creation. It provides students with an opportunity to "make" something relevant to the subject area, and this allows them to construct their own knowledge as they construct the project. This LAT also helps students develop skills in digital literacy, such as locating, evaluating and integrating images, videos, and links.

Digital Projects provide teachers and students with an alternative to conventional written reports, and they give teachers the opportunity to assess student knowledge and understanding as well as student ability to creatively document and display that understanding. This technique also provides an opportunity to assess student communication skills. Because of the intensive amount of time that students spend in creation of digital products, they tend to be best used as a summative assessment of student achievement and performance. Elements of the learning activity and Learning Artifact may be reported to internal and external stakeholders.

Key Learning Goals

- Technological skills
- Creative thinking skills

- Decision-making skills
- Problem-solving skills

Implementation

Preparation

- Determine topic, content, and design parameters.
- Try to create a digital product yourself, particularly if you have never done so before. This will provide you with an idea about how much time and effort will be involved.
- If projects are to be complex, consider working backward to schedule "check points" or "milestones," such as submitting a topic, creating an outline, developing a storyboard, completing a draft, gaining feedback, or other. This approach can help keep students on track and making good progress. See Multiple-Task Mastery Checklist (LAT 49) for suggestions.
- Determine the tools students will need to use. You may predetermine the tools, or you may allow students freedom of choice, depending upon your goals for the activity.
- Determine whether the projects ultimately will be private or public. There are advantages to each. With private projects, students may feel more comfortable and protected, while with public ones, they will communicate with a broader audience. If you want the projects to be public, you should consider issues of copyright as well as student privacy (you may want to advise students to use pseudonyms for example if posting work in a public online space).
- Create a rubric for assessing the project for whatever criteria you determine, including creativity. You might include the following for example:
  - Variety of ideas
  - Variety of sources
  - Communication of something new
- Create a handout with parameters and with the evaluation rubric to guide students in their thinking and provide them with a schedule for completion of the task.
- Determine who will be involved in the assessment. Peer evaluations or external "expert" assessors can add to the perceived value of the assignment and can provide you with additional data.

Process

1. Present the handout to the students and answer any questions about the activity.
2. Provide students with time to complete the work and monitor student progress as needed.
3. Close the activity by having students present or share their Learning Artifacts.

Online

The type of project will determine how this LAT may best be implemented online. A range of programs exist for creating collages, photo albums, videos, blogs, and other potential artifacts. You will simply need to determine whether to require a certain technology so that results are similar across artifacts, or whether to provide students with the option of choosing the program they believe best-suited for the work.

Analysis and Reporting

Use the completed rubric you created to evaluate projects for elements such as originality and appropriateness. Consider a holistic analysis of the project, analyzing for specific content. Provide additional narrative that describes anything unique about their projects.

To aggregate results, use one of the rubrics and tally the number of responses in each cell. Look across the projects themselves to determine the key themes and issues that cross them. Conduct a thematic analysis in which you look across projects to determine similarities and differences. Use a numeric or narrative table to describe the results of the rubric review, and also consider using a Network to display the key themes and subthemes you noticed in the data.

Examples

Onsite: Recording Studio Production Techniques

The professor of this course wanted to participate in the scholarship of teaching and learning. She planned to develop a research report that she could use to present at a teaching and learning conference, and she hoped ultimately to write an article about her work. She articulated her learning outcome as follows: students will learn to use various tools required for mixing music to create a new product. The question she wanted to answer related to her teaching was how to engage students in a learning activity to help them use the tools they needed to master.

The professor had been lecturing about tools for mixing music for some time, but she decided to use a project-based learning approach instead. She hoped that the more authentic assignment would help inspire students to learn more tools. The professor assigned a midterm "Mashup" in which each student was required to seamlessly blend a minimum of three prerecorded songs into a single song. Among the elements that were evaluated was how well the combination transformed the original content into a recording that might be considered new and hence comply with "fair use" copyright law.

The professor provided students with guidelines for the project. She used a portion of class time each week as "studio time" but also required them to complete some of the work as homework. When students completed the assignment, they presented their mashups to the class.

Students evaluated each other's work and voted on the top three. The professor reviewed them with a rubric to assess their creativity in completing the assignment. She also developed a network to show the main tools that students used on their assignments. Figures 8.9a and 8.9b showed how her new project-based method stimulated student creative thinking about the tools that they might use.

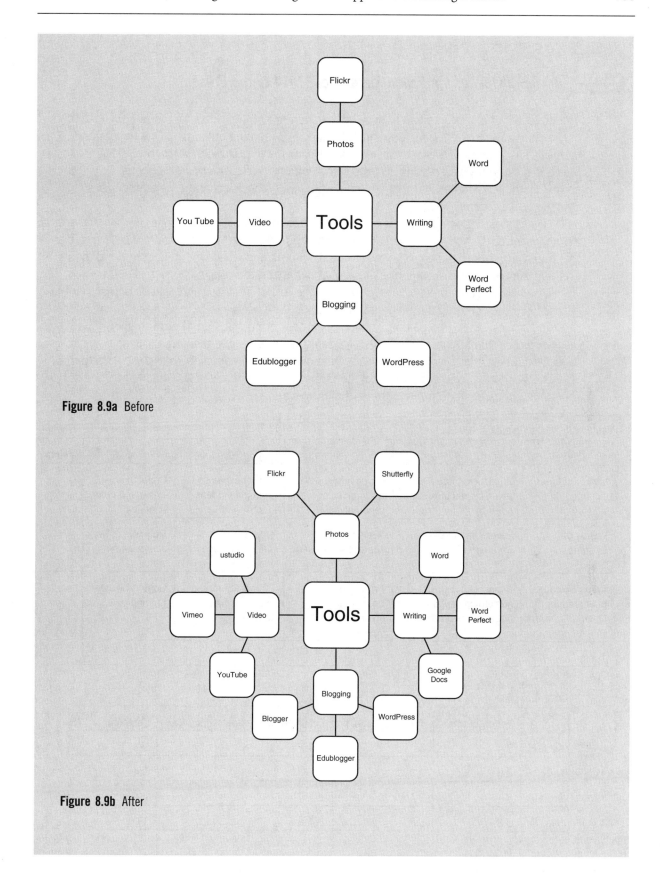

Figure 8.9a Before

Figure 8.9b After

Online: History of the United States from 1914 to the Present

The professor of this course had to develop a written report that documented how well students in her course were meeting the department's specified learning outcomes. One of the core themes in this survey of the political, economic, social, and cultural development of the United States is the country's increasing struggle with economic security for all Americans. One of the course learning outcomes was that students would be able to describe American citizens' struggle with economic security.

The professor decided to offer students the option of substituting a musical montage set to images for one of the required course essays. Students were instructed to find several songs that had lyrics addressing an issue related to this theme and weave them together, and then to find appropriate images to set to the music that enhanced the song's message.

She had students present their projects to the rest of the class and asked each student to assess each project using a pre-agreed-upon rubric. She completed the same rubric and provided scores based upon a combination of student evaluations and her evaluation. She discovered that the assignment engaged students and challenged their creativity as they strove to make the best image/lyric juxtapositions. She created a numerical table (Tables 8.25 and 8.26) showing the rubric evaluations for student scores in each category, which she used in her report to document students' achievement of the learning goal.

Table 8.25 Rubric Evaluations

	4	3	2	1	Points
Variety of Ideas	Project expressed several ideas of various types	Project expressed a few ideas of various types	Project expressed a couple of ideas	Project expressed only one idea	
Variety of Sources	Several sources were used	A few different sources were used	A couple of different sources were used	Only one or two sources were used	
Communication of Something New	Project communicated something new and original excellently	Projected communicated something new very well	Project attempted to communicate something new	Communicated nothing new	
Total					

Table 8.26 Average of the Professor's and Peers' Scores

	Variety of Ideas	Variety of Sources	Communication of Something New	Total (out of 12)
Ashley	3.4	3	3.4	9.8
Isaac	2.6	2.8	3	8.4
Shon	3	3.4	3	9.4
Sammy	3.8	3.8	3.4	11
Juan	2.8	3	2.6	8.4

Variations and Extensions

- Digital Projects may be done as a group effort. Students can learn deeply when working together, not only content but also in learning how to complete projects together, which can be beneficial in their future careers. Group projects can be more difficult to assess, however, particularly for individual effort and performance. Use group projects if gaining discrete individual data is not important to your assessment efforts.

Key References and Resources

Groom, J. (nd). How to write up assignments like a blogging champ. http://ds106.us/handbook/success-the-ds106-way/writing-up-assignments/.

Pennsylvania State University. (nd). Instructor's guide to media activities. http://mediacommons.psu.edu/faculty/.

University of Wisconsin Madison. (2012). Teaching with digital media assignments? http://www.engage.wisc.edu/dma/.

CHAPTER 9

Teaching and Assessing for the Integration Domain

Almost all college professors understand the value of teaching students foundational knowledge and how to apply this knowledge through critical, creative, and practical thinking. These kinds of learning resonate with traditional models of what knowledge is, how it is acquired, and how it is passed on to subsequent generations. The third realm of significant learning—integration—builds upon these established and familiar learning domains and involves helping students understand and make connections among different things.

Clarifying Learning Goals Related to the Integration Domain

Fink describes the realm of integrative learning as "when students learn how to connect and relate various things together" (2013, p. 48). He notes that when students are able to see and understand the connections between different things, they acquire a new form of power, especially intellectual power (p. 36). At its most fundamental level, learning in the Integration domain involves the integration of ideas. Fink notes that sometimes students make connections between specific ideas and sometimes between whole realms of ideas. In explicating the integrated learning domain, Fink notes three key kinds of connections today's educators are emphasizing: interdisciplinary learning, learning communities, and connecting academic work with other areas of life. Because learning communities typically extend beyond the course level, we do not address them in this chapter.

Interdisciplinary Learning

Because many of today's real-world problems are larger and more complex than any single discipline can solve, higher education needs to help learners look at problems from multiple disciplinary perspectives. This can be achieved in a variety of ways. For example interdisciplinary curriculum—courses that are collaboratively designed around a central theme or important issue—can be taught through two or more coordinated courses or team teaching of a single course. However interdisciplinary learning is promoted, Fink observes that the common element is "the goal of helping students learn how to connect and integrate different kinds of information, perspectives, and methods of inquiry and analysis—all in order to develop a more holistic understanding of a problem or issue" (2013, p. 49).

Connecting Academic Work with Other Areas of Life

Many teachers today try to help students find value in their classes creating experiences that connect in-class work to areas outside of the classroom. Service learning, for example, combines instruction with community service to encourage a heightened sense of community and civic engagement. As another example, some professors assign autobiographical essays or interviews with family members that aim to help the student connect the academic topics of the course to more personal experience. Field education and internships provide yet another avenue that supports connections between formal academic study and the "real world."

To identify learning objectives and outcomes related to integration learning, Fink suggests asking ourselves questions such as the following (Fink, 2013, p. 83):

- What connections (similarities and interactions) should students recognize and make in this course . . .
  - . . . among the information, ideas, and perspectives in the course and in other courses or areas?
  - . . . between material in this course and the students' own personal, social, and work lives?

Identifying Learning Outcomes for Integration Learning

In Table 9.1 we focus on procedural processes and offer suggestions for both learning subprocesses and sample learning outcomes.

Table 9.1 Examples of Learning Processes and Outcomes for Integration Learning

General Definition: The learner will be able to combine various parts and see how they relate to one another or to a unified whole.			
Learner Process	**Additional Terms**	**Definition**	**Sample Course Learning Outcome** By the end of this course, a successful learner will be able to . . .
Incorporate	Unite, combine, coordinate, blend	Combine elements to form a unified whole.	. . . identify the interactions between geography and other realms of knowledge such as history, politics, economics, social structure, and so on.
Organize	Find coherence, integrate, outline, parse, structure	Determine how elements fit or function within a structure.	. . . determine which of several types of essays (e.g., expository, persuasive, analytical, argumentative) are appropriate in a given situation.
Assimilate	Differentiate, discriminate	Recognize the components or parts of a larger structure.	. . . differentiate between various components of a complex problem in order to develop a more inclusive solution.
Reorganize	Assemble, create	Reorganize elements into a new pattern or structure.	. . . identify relationships or interactions about the ideas in the readings.

Sources: Multiple, including Anderson and Krathwohl (2001) and Fink (2013)

Aligning Course Level Integrative Learning Outcomes with Broader Institutional Learning Goals

Institutional learning goals related to learning in the integration dimension may be stated in a variety of locations. Some institutions state integrative learning as one of their core goals. Many institutions have departments and programs that focus on integrative learning, and these will have mission statements that address learning outcomes related to this dimension. Examples of these kinds of statements are provided in Table 9.2.

Assessing Achievement of Learning in the Integration Domain

Because of Fink's wide conceptualization of this category, assessment can be a challenge. We have chosen to focus primarily on his notion of integration of ideas in this section. Thus the LGI and the LATs we have selected for inclusion reflect aspects of classification, categorization, and comparison of ideas. They include items and activities that allow students to synthesize information into an integrated whole. They also allow students to make connections between their learning in their course and other disciplines and fields as well as with their daily lives. Assessing such learning is not always easy, but we hope that our suggestions will give teachers sound advice for going about this complex task. Exhibit 9.1 offers definitions and framing language as well as a rubric for assessing the specific components and benchmarks related to this dimension of the Significant Learning Taxonomy.

Conclusion

The Integration domain of the Significant Learning Taxonomy takes a step beyond the doors of the traditional classroom. This departure reflects what Fink perceives as three kinds of connections today's educators are emphasizing in learning: interdisciplinary learning, learning communities, and connecting academic work with other areas of life. Each of these areas provide students with knowledge, skills, and understanding that enrich and deepen their learning on multiple levels. In this chapter, we provide techniques that focus on both teaching and assessing learning in the Integration domain.

Table 9.2 Examples of Institution Level Learning Goals in the Integration Domain

	Learning Goals
Institution	A core mission of this institution is to provide students with opportunities to integrate their learning across general education, majors, and the co-curriculum, as well as prior professional, academic, and life experiences inside and outside the classroom.
Program	This program focuses on enabling individuals to find a higher purpose in their life through curriculum that connects multiple aspects of their life, equipping them to make life decisions based on this higher purpose and empowering them to develop this purpose into effective, transformative leadership.
General Studies	A core learning goal of the General Studies Curriculum is to prepare students for successful learning in a complex world, where traditional academic disciplines are merging and overlapping. Courses in the General Studies Curriculum foster integrative learning by challenging students to grapple with complex problems that mirror those in our complex world.

Sources: Composite

Exhibit 9.1 Assessing the Integrative Learning Dimension Using the AAC&U Integrative Learning VALUE Rubric

Definition

Integrative learning is an understanding and a disposition that a student builds across the curriculum and co-curriculum, from making simple connections among ideas and experiences to synthesizing and transferring learning to new, complex situations within and beyond the campus.

Framing Language

Fostering students' abilities to integrate learning—across courses, over time, and between campus and community life—is one of the most important goals and challenges for higher education. Initially, students connect previous learning to new classroom learning. Later, significant knowledge within individual disciplines serves as the foundation, but integrative learning goes beyond academic boundaries. Indeed, integrative experiences often occur as learners address real-world problems, unscripted and sufficiently broad to require multiple areas of knowledge and multiple modes of inquiry, offering multiple solutions and benefiting from multiple perspectives. Integrative learning also involves internal changes in the learner. These internal changes, which indicate growth as a confident, lifelong learner, include the ability to adapt one's intellectual skills, to contribute in a wide variety of situations, and to understand and develop individual purpose, values, and ethics. Developing students' capacities for integrative learning is central to personal success, social responsibility, and civic engagement in today's global society. Students face a rapidly changing and increasingly connected world where integrative learning becomes not just a benefit . . . but a necessity.

Because integrative learning is about making connections, this learning may not be as evident in traditional academic artifacts such as research papers and academic projects unless the student, for example, is prompted to draw implications for practice. These connections often surface, however, in reflective work, self-assessment, or creative endeavors of all kinds. Integrative assignments foster learning between courses or by connecting courses to experientially based work. Work samples or collections of work that include such artifacts give evidence of integrative learning. Faculty are encouraged to look for evidence that the student connects the learning gained in classroom study to learning gained in real-life situations that are related to other learning experiences, extracurricular activities, or work. Through integrative learning, students pull together their entire experience inside and outside of the formal classroom; thus, artificial barriers between formal study and informal or tacit learning become permeable. Integrative learning, whatever the context or source, builds upon connecting both theory and practice toward a deepened understanding. Assignments to foster such connections and understanding could include, for example, composition papers that focus on topics from biology, economics, or history; mathematics assignments that apply mathematical tools to important issues and require written analysis to explain the implications and limitations of the mathematical treatment; or art history presentations that demonstrate aesthetic connections between selected paintings and novels. In this regard, some majors (e.g., interdisciplinary majors or problem-based field studies) seem to inherently evoke characteristics of integrative learning and result in work samples or collections of work that significantly demonstrate this outcome. However, fields of study that require accumulation of extensive and high-consensus content knowledge (such as accounting, engineering, or chemistry) also involve the kinds of complex and integrative constructions (e.g., ethical dilemmas and social consciousness) that seem to be highlighted so extensively in self-reflection in arts and humanities, but they may be embedded in individual performances and less evident. The key in the development of such work samples or collections of work will be in designing structures that include artifacts and reflective writing or feedback that support students' examination of their learning and give evidence that, as graduates, they will extend their integrative abilities into the challenges of personal, professional, and civic life.

Glossary

The definitions that follow were developed to clarify terms and concepts used in this rubric only.

Academic knowledge: Disciplinary learning; learning from academic study, texts, etc.

Content: The information conveyed in the work samples or collections of work.

Contexts: Actual or simulated situations in which a student demonstrates learning outcomes. New and challenging contexts encourage students to stretch beyond their current frames of reference.

Co-curriculum: A parallel component of the academic curriculum that is in addition to formal classroom (student government, community service, residence hall activities, student organizations, etc.).

Experience: Learning that takes place in a setting outside of the formal classroom, such as workplace, service learning site, internship site, or another.
Form: The external frameworks in which information and evidence are presented, ranging from choices for particular work sample or collection of works (such as a research paper, PowerPoint, video recording, etc.) to choices in make-up of the e-portfolio.
Performance: A dynamic and sustained act that brings together knowing and doing (creating a painting, solving an experimental design problem, developing a public relations strategy for a business, etc.); performance makes learning observable.
Reflection: A meta-cognitive act of examining a performance in order to explore its significance and consequences.
Self-assessment: Describing, interpreting, and judging a performance based on stated or implied expectations followed by planning for further learning.

Table 9.3 Integrative Learning VALUE Rubric

	Capstone 4	Milestone 3	Milestone 2	Benchmark 1
Connections to Experience *Connects relevant experience and academic knowledge*	Meaningfully synthesizes connections among experiences outside of the formal classroom (including life experiences and academic experiences such as internships and travel abroad) to deepen understanding of fields of study and to broaden own points of view.	Effectively selects and develops examples of life experiences, drawn from a variety of contexts (e.g., family life, artistic participation, civic involvement, work experience), to illuminate concepts/theories/frameworks of fields of study.	Compares life experiences and academic knowledge to infer differences, as well as similarities, and acknowledge perspectives other than own.	Identifies connections between life experiences and those academic texts and ideas perceived as similar and related to own interests.
Connections to Discipline *Sees (makes) connections across disciplines, perspectives*	Independently creates wholes out of multiple parts (synthesizes) or draws conclusions by combining examples, facts, or theories from more than one field of study or perspective.	Independently connects examples, facts, or theories from more than one field of study or perspective.	When prompted, connects examples, facts, or theories from more than one field of study or perspective.	When prompted, presents examples, facts, or theories from more than one field of study or perspective.
Transfer *Adapts and applies skills, abilities, theories, or methodologies gained in one situation to new situations*	Adapts and applies, independently, skills, abilities, theories, or methodologies gained in one situation to new situations to solve difficult problems or explore complex issues in original ways.	Adapts and applies skills, abilities, theories, or methodologies gained in one situation to new situations to solve problems or explore issues.	Uses skills, abilities, theories, or methodologies gained in one situation to contribute to understanding of problems or issues.	Uses, in a basic way, skills, abilities, theories, or methodologies gained in one situation in a new situation.

| Integrated Communication | Fulfills the assignment(s) by choosing a format, language, or graph (or other visual representation) in ways that enhance meaning, making clear the interdependence of language and meaning, thought, and expression. | Fulfills the assignment(s) by choosing a format, language, or graph (or other visual representation) to explicitly connect content and form, demonstrating awareness of purpose and audience. | Fulfills the assignment(s) by choosing a format, language, or graph (or other visual representation) that connects in a basic way what is being communicated (content) with how it is said (form). | Fulfills the assignment(s) (i.e. to produce an essay, a poster, a video, a PowerPoint presentation, etc.) in an appropriate form. |

Reprinted with permission from VALUE: Valid Assessment of Learning in Undergraduate Education. Copyright 2015 by the Association of American Colleges and Universities. http://www.aacu.org/value/rubrics

LEARNING ASSESSMENT TECHNIQUE

Integration

21
Knowledge Grid

Complexity involved in	
Preparation	MODERATE
In-class implementation	LOW
Analysis	LOW

Brief Description

Students demonstrate analytical and organizational skills by filling in the internal cells of a grid in which the first column and top row provide key categories.

Purpose

This technique helps students develop a clear understanding of the similarities and differences among related ideas. As students complete the grid, their choices make their organizing explicit and produce a visible form of comparison and contrast of associated information. This helps students gain more control over what they remember, how they remember it, and how well they can recall it when they need it. Students may find the visual display of information a clear, gratifying representation of their learning.

The Learning Artifacts are the completed Knowledge Grid Handouts. These Grids provide teachers with information about students' sense of the intersection of different concepts within a learning module. They are visible representations of how students understand relationships between important and related concepts.

Used at the beginning of a module as a pretest, it can help teachers identify how much information students are beginning with, which can guide instructional decisions such as how to form groups or where to target a lecture. Additionally, the open-ended nature of the grid helps capture a wider range of knowledge as well as identify specific student's special expertise. Comparing pre- and post-grids provides teachers and students with information on how much students have learned over the module or course.

Table 9.4 Sample Grid

	Subpoint 1	Subpoint 2	Subpoint 3	Subpoint 4	Subpoint 5
Item 1					
Item 2					
Item 3					
Item 4					
Item 5					

Key Learning Goals

- The ability to differentiate closely related concepts in the subject area
- The ability to compare different aspects of a topic
- The ability to classify information in the subject area
- The ability to connect a concept to other concepts within this course

Implementation

Preparation

- Select a topic and two or three categories to be used for organizing the information.
- Determine whether you will give students items to sort into the grid or whether they will generate their own. If the former, make a list of several good examples of items in each category, making sure that all items clearly belong only to one category.
- Set the parameters (such as length, time for doing, and so forth).
- Make a grid by drawing a large rectangle and dividing it into as many rectangles of equal size as you have categories, and label it accordingly, for example, Table 9.4.
- Create a handout of the grid.

Process

1. Present students with the handout, and allow time for questions.
2. Have students work independently to fill the grid.
3. Close the activity and collect the Learning Artifacts.

Online

This activity may be created in a word process program and then posted and returned in a LMS.

Analysis and Reporting

Check each grid to determine whether students have accurately filled in the grid, scoring their answers with a simple +/– and tallying the number of each. Report scores to individuals by handing back their scored grids so that they can see how many of their responses were accurate. This activity may be assigned a low stakes grade or a participation grade.

Look across all grids to see if there are patterns in the incorrect or incomplete responses that can help you see which categories are most difficult for students to understand. Use a simple table, figure, or chart to display results.

Examples

Onsite: Romantic Poets

In a Romantic Poets class, the professor developed a learning outcome that stated that students will be able to compare and contrast the works of different Romantic-era poets. The professor found that students could identify key themes treated by the different poets, but they did not always make finer distinctions between the ways in which the poets treated these themes.

He decided to use a Knowledge Grid to help him promote and assess student ability to make such distinctions. He created a grid with the primary Romantic poets on the left and with key themes across the top of the grid, as shown in Table 9.5.

He completed the grid himself and came up with 3–5 points per cell.

During the next class session, he handed a blank grid to students and asked them to complete it during class, instructing them to include one main point per cell that showed how the poets portrayed each of the themes. He collected the Learning Artifacts and scored them. He checked the responses against his own answers and simply put a check (✓) when an answer was accurate and an x (✗) when the answer was inaccurate or incomplete. He kept track of all responses on a separate grid as he worked, as shown in Table 9.6.

Table 9.5 Knowledge Grid on Main Themes in Romantic Poets

	Nature	Technology	The Individual	The Supernatural
Blake				
Wordsworth				
Coleridge				
Byron				
Shelley				
Keats				

Table 9.6 Knowledge Grid on Main Themes in Romantic Poets Responses

	Nature	Technology	The Individual	The Supernatural
Blake	✓✓✓✓✓ ✓✓✓✓✓ ✓✓✓✓✓ ✗✗✗✗✗	✓✓✓✓✓ ✓✓✓✓✓ ✓✓✓✗✗ ✗✗✗✗✗	✓✓✓✓✓ ✓✓✓✓✓ ✗✗✗✗✗ ✗✗✗✗✗	✓✓✓✓✓ ✓✓✓✓✓ ✓✓✗✗✗ ✗✗✗✗✗
Wordsworth	✓✓✓✓✓ ✓✓✓✓✓ ✓✓✓✓✓ ✗✗✗✗✗	✓✓✓✓✓ ✓✓✓✓✓ ✗✗✗✗✗ ✗✗✗✗✗	✓✓✓✓✓ ✓✓✓✓✗ ✗✗✗✗✗ ✗✗✗✗✗	✓✓✓✓✓ ✓✓✓✓✓ ✓✓✗✗✗ ✗✗✗✗✗
Coleridge	✓✓✓✓✓ ✓✓✓✓✓ ✓✓✓✗✗ ✗✗✗✗✗	✓✓✓✓✓ ✓✓✓✓✓ ✗✗✗✗✗ ✗✗✗✗✗	✓✓✓✓✓ ✓✓✓✓✓ ✓✗✗✗✗ ✗✗✗✗✗	✓✓✓✓✓ ✓✓✓✓✗ ✗✗✗✗✗ ✗✗✗✗✗
Byron	✓✓✓✓✓ ✓✓✓✓✓ ✓✓✓✓✓ ✓✗✗✗✗	✓✓✓✓✓ ✓✓✓✓✓ ✓✓✓✓✗ ✗✗✗✗✗	✓✓✓✓✓ ✓✓✓✓✓ ✓✓✓✓✓ ✓✓✗✗✗	✓✓✓✓✓ ✓✓✓✓✓ ✓✓✓✓✓ ✓✗✗✗✗
Shelley	✓✓✓✓✓ ✓✓✓✓✓ ✓✓✓✓✓ ✗✗✗✗✗	✓✓✓✓✓ ✓✓✓✓✓ ✓✓✓✓✓ ✓✓✓✓✗	✓✓✓✓✓ ✓✓✓✓✓ ✓✓✓✓✓ ✓✗✗✗✗	✓✓✓✓✓ ✓✓✓✓✓ ✓✓✓✓✓ ✗✗✗✗✗
Keats	✓✓✓✓✓ ✓✓✓✓✓ ✓✓✓✓✓ ✗✗✗✗✗	✓✓✓✓✓ ✓✓✓✓✓ ✓✓✓✓✓ ✗✗✗✗✗	✓✓✓✓✓ ✓✓✓✓✓ ✓✓✓✗✗ ✗✗✗✗✗	✓✓✓✓✓ ✓✓✓✓✓ ✓✓✓✓✗ ✗✗✗✗✗

From his scorecard, he created a table to demonstrate the percentage of accurate responses in each cell so he would know how well the group did as a whole (Table 9.7).

Table 9.7 Percentage of Accurate Responses

	Nature	Technology	The Individual	The Supernatural
Blake	75%	65%	50%	60%
Wordsworth	75%	50%	45%	60%
Coleridge	65%	50%	55%	45%
Byron	80%	70%	85%	80%
Shelley	75%	95%	80%	85%
Keats	75%	75%	65%	70%

Online: Music of Multicultural America

This professor uses a Knowledge Grid as both a pre- and postassessment tool. As a pretest, she finds that the open-ended nature of the prompt helps capture a wide range of student knowledge and that the "authentic" nature of the task appeals to students. In addition to helping her assess students' overall starting points, the grids help her identify students with special expertise that she can consider inviting to give an in-class presentation. At the end of the term, she distributes the grid again to assess how well students have achieved the course's learning outcomes. Afterward, she shares their earlier grids, and students compare the two, and often report how gratifying it is to see how much they have learned. She quickly evaluates the grids by assigning one point for each accurate substantive information item and a one point penalty for each inaccurate information item.

Music of Multicultural America

Knowledge Recall Grid
Name_____
Directions: You are hosting a visitor from another country who asks you about American music. Use single words/short phrases to indicate the information and ideas you would share with your visitor (Table 9.8).

Table 9.8 American Music

	The Social/Historical Context	Key Representative Artists	Structural Characteristics
Native American Music			
Gospel			
Blues			
Jazz			
Country			
Urban Folk Revival			
Rock 'n' Roll			
Tejano, Banda			
Salsa, Reggae			
Hip-Hop, Rap			

Table 9.9 is a segment of the table she creates, demonstrating pretest and posttest total scores.

Table 9.9 Pretest and Posttest Scores

	Pretest Total Score	**Posttest Total Score**
Sarah	9	29
Yington	10	25
Grecia	5	20
Hannah	11	29
Soham	15	30

Variations and Extensions

- Ask students to explain briefly why the items they have placed in a given category belong together. Doing so provides an additional data point.
- Assign students to work in groups to complete the grid. This provides a different data point, representing the consensus of the group rather than the work of the individuals.
- Consider using the grid as a matrix. This "Defining Features Matrix" requires students to categorize concepts according to the presence (+) or absence (−) of important defining features (Angelo & Cross, 1993).

Key References and Resources

Angelo, T. A., & Cross, K. P. (1993). CAT 9: Defining features matrix. In *Classroom assessment techniques* (2nd ed., pp. 164–167). San Francisco, CA: Jossey-Bass.

Tague, N. R. (2004). Decision matrix. In *The quality toolbox* (2nd ed., pp. 219–223). Milwaukee, WI: ASQ Quality Press.

LEARNING ASSESSMENT TECHNIQUE

Integration

22
Sequence Chains

Complexity involved in	
Preparation	LOW
In-class implementation	LOW
Analysis	LOW

Description

Students analyze and depict graphically a sequence of events, actions, roles, or decisions. Sequence Chains require students to create a visual map of the logic within a series.

Purpose

Students identify specific points in a series and then apply knowledge and reasoning to arrange these points in an orderly, coherent progression. Thus, Sequence Chains may help and promote logical, sequential thinking. The activity also produces a graphic that can be useful for remembering as well as for planning.

The Learning Artifacts are the Sequence Chains that students create. Sequence Chains are perhaps best used in courses that require students to organize information to emphasize continuity or connections. They are particularly useful as formative assessments that can indicate whether students are understanding chains of events or activities so that they can improve their performance. They may also be used as a summative assessment at the end of a learning module or unit to determine whether students have understood.

Related Learning Goals

*   The ability to differentiate closely related concepts in the subject area
*   The ability to compare different aspects of a topic
*   The ability to think holistically: to see the whole as well as the parts
*   The ability to synthesize disparate but related information into a whole
*   The ability to connect a concept to other concepts within this course

Table 9.10 Sample Rubric

Category	Exemplary	Average	Poor
Order of Events	All events appear in a logical and correct order.	Some of the events are in the correct logical sequence.	Organizational logic was not evident; events presented in incorrect order.
Quantity of Events	An ample number of events represent the phenomenon.	A sufficient number of events represent the phenomenon.	An insufficient number of events represent the phenomenon.
Graphics	The sequence is illustrated in a meaningful way.	Illustrations appear in the sequence chain.	There are no illustrations to represent.

Implementation

Preparation

- Choose what students should organize into a sequence or series. Decide whether or not students will generate the items to be organized, or whether you will provide them with a scrambled list of items.
- If allowing students to generate the list of items they are going to organize, know—and communicate to students—the level of information upon which they should focus. Will they supply and organize main topics? Subtopics? Supporting details? Also let students know how the items should be labeled. Should they use words? Phrases? Full sentences?
- Decide as well whether or not students will do any additional work with the sequence such as explain the connection between the items in the series.
- Create a sample Sequence Chain to uncover potential problems and to have a model against which to compare student work.
- You may want to use a simple scoring system, such as +1 for each correct event listed in order, and –1 for any errors in the events listed or in the ordering of events.
- If you plan to use one, create a rubric for assessing the chains according to whatever criteria you wish to assess. See Table 9.10 for an example.

Process

1. Announce the activity, set a time limit, and either provide students with a scrambled list of items, or have them generate their own list of items.
2. Ask students to arrange the items into a sequence. If students will do an additional activity with the sequence (such as explaining the relationship between items), give them directions and clarify your expectations. They may complete this work in or out of class.
3. Have students document their work, whether turning in a handwritten or typed chain or by drawing their sequences on flip-chart paper.
4. Collect the Learning Artifacts.

Online

Many tools available today allow for the creation of visually appealing and interactive timelines, giving sequence chains created online an extra dimension. To implement this technique online, use one of the collaborative *mind mapping* tools; the timeline tools in particular will be effective for this approach. Ask students to each take a section of the sequence and complete their portions of the timelines to develop a full sequence chain. Alternately, many synchronous tools such as video conferencing or chat sessions that also have *whiteboard* tools offer one possibility for adaptation.

Examples

Onsite: History of Western Civilization—Ancient Through the Middle Ages

The professor had a goal that students would be able to outline the chronology of important historical events they would cover in the course. Rather than having students simply memorize dates—which tends to strengthen students' perception of history as a collection of isolated pieces of data—the professor wanted students to understand how historical events unfolded as a complex series of cause and effect.

He used Sequence Chains toward the end of each learning module. For example, he created an activity on the unit "The Fall of the Western Roman Empire." To start, he asked students to generate a list of as many events as they could remember that were related to the topic. He then gave them a handout that asked them to present the order of events in chronological order. He held a class discussion on the topic, encouraging them to take notes from the discussion, and at the end took up their lists (he told them ahead that he would not be grading them).

He reviewed their lists and gave them a baseline score for the number of activities they remembered. He also gave them additional bonus points for catching new information in class discussion (Table 9.11).

He used the Sequence Chains to determine what he needed to review with students prior to the tests. And he gave them back their scored sheets so they would have them as study guides.

Table 9.11 Analysis of Sequence Chain Reponses

Chronological Order of Events	Changes Based on Class Discussion
Marcus Aurelius ascended to the throne.	
Dozens of emperors were put into power by the army.	28
Civil war began.	General Diocletian took the position of emperor.
Constantine took over.	

Online: Human Physiology

The professor of this online course decided to use Sequence Chains to help students develop an understanding of genetic copying from DNA in the nucleus to new protein in the cytoplasm via mRNA. She asked students to create chains of the order of events. She asked them to not only show the order but also to describe and illustrate them. She reviewed her findings in Table 9.12.

She could see from the results that students were better at the more surface level understandings of what the events where and were less able at providing sound descriptions of what happened at each phase. Some did the bare minimum for the assignment and did not even describe or supply graphics. She decided to target her teaching to helping students move beyond listing to truly understanding of what happens at each phase prior to the exam on the topic.

Table 9.12 Sequence Chain Analysis

Category	Exemplary	Average	Poor
Order of Events	100	0	0
Quantity of Events	77	25	0
Description of Events	25	50	25
Graphics	50	25	25

Variations and Extensions

- Organize the sequence according to specific parameters. For example, an *Events Sequence Chain* helps students organize a series of episodes or occurrences; a *Human Interaction Sequence Chain* helps students organize mutual or reciprocal actions; and a *Cause and Effect Sequence Chain* helps students organize information into antecedent and consequence.
- Consider multiple, parallel graphics for more comprehensive or complex series. For example, Sequence A could contain a list of events, Sequence B the location of the event, and Sequence C the people involved in the event.
- Ask students to work in groups to complete their Sequence Chains.

Key References and Resources

Barkley, E. F., Major, C. H., & Cross, K. P. (2014). Sequence chains. In *Collaborative learning techniques: A handbook for college faculty* (2nd ed.). San Francisco, CA: Jossey-Bass.

Hall, T. & Strangman, N. (1999–2004). Graphic organizers. http://www.cast.org/ncac/Graphic Organizers3015.cfm.

Kagan, S. (1990). The structural approach to cooperative learning. *Educational Leadership, 47*(4), 12–15.

Kagan, S. (1996). *Cooperative learning.* San Clemente, CA: Kagan Cooperative Learning.

Moore, D. W., & Readence, J. E. (1984). A quantitative and qualitative review of graphic organizer research. *Journal of Educational Research, 78*(1), 11–17.

LEARNING ASSESSMENT TECHNIQUE

Integration

23
Concept Maps

Complexity involved in	
Preparation	LOW
In-class implementation	MODERATE
Analysis	HIGH

Brief Description

Students draw a diagram that conveys their ideas about or understanding of a complex concept, procedure, or process they have studied. The diagram is intended to suggest relationships between ideas, which it does in the form of a network in which boxes or circles represent ideas and in which the lines between the ideas represent connections.

Purpose

Concept Maps engage students by challenging them to synthesize and be creative as they organize their hierarchy of associations of concepts they have learned (or will learn) about during a course, whether through readings, lectures, or other into a meaningful graphic. This type of a graphic organizer is called different names (such as Word Web or Mind Map). We use the term Concept Map because this is how the activity is referred to in most of the assessment literature. Figure 9.1 from Novak and Cañas (2008) is a concept map of features of some concept maps.

A Concept Map requires students to illustrate their own ideas and concepts and show connections between them. By documenting the connections they make between concepts, students deepen their understanding of them. They learn how ideas are connected, and they begin to get a feel for the distance between ideas, including developing an understanding of which ideas are more central and which are more peripheral. Students can purposefully manipulate their understandings, changing their mental structures as they go, correcting misconceptions as needed. This technique then also helps students to recognize that the connections they make between concepts are changeable (Angelo & Cross, 1993).

The Learning Artifacts, which are the physical Concept Maps that represents student thinking, allow instructors to see how students organize details. The Maps also document connections students make among theories and concepts. The Learning Artifact, then, illustrates students' conceptual schemata in a demonstrable and assessable record.

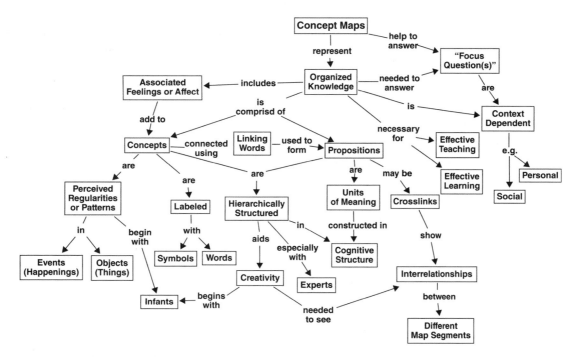

Figure 9.1 Concept Map

Concept Maps are a flexible technique. Instructors can use Concept Maps for assessing prior knowledge to help individuals who need additional resources and to help instructors target instruction to the class's needs. In addition, instructors can use Concept Maps to gauge students' achievement and growth in conceptual understandings, which they can in turn use for grading and reporting purposes.

Key Learning Goals

- The ability to differentiate closely related concepts in the subject area
- The ability to compare different aspects of a topic
- The ability to think holistically: to see the whole as well as the parts
- The ability to synthesize disparate but related information into a whole
- The ability to connect a concept to other concepts within this course

Implementation

Preparation

- Choose a concept, procedure, or process that you want students to map that is important to your course and that is rich in associations and connections.
- Brainstorm for a few minutes, writing down terms and short phrases that represent the most important components of the concept.
- Map the concept yourself so that you can uncover potential problems. Your own diagram can also serve as a model against which to assess student work.
- Map a parallel concept to provide an example of the process to students, who may be unfamiliar with the notion of a concept map.

- Decide what materials you want students to use (e.g., flip charts, large format paper, colored markers, or crayons) and assemble the materials. Pay particular attention to how much space they might need to represent distances between concepts; they might need large paper, for example, for exceedingly complex topics.
- Create a system for scoring the maps. Novak and Gowin (1984) suggest awarding points for the following:
  Valid Propositions (1 point each)
  Levels of Hierarchy (5 points for each level)
  Number of Branchings (1 point for each branch)
  Crosslinks (10 points for each valid cross-link)
  Specific Examples (1 point for each example)
  They base their recommendations on the notions that the number of hierarchical levels suggests the degree of "subsumption," the number of branches suggests level of differentiation, and the number of cross-links suggests the extent to which the knowledge has been integrated.
- You might instead use a rubric such as shown in Table 9.13.

Process

1. Announce the activity and set the time frame for completing it.
2. Describe and demonstrate the process to students.
3. Have students sketch out a diagram starting with the central idea and adding additional words, phrases, or images along with lines or arrows to show the connections.
4. Collect the maps when students have completed them.

Online

Several tools can allow for the creation of Concept Maps online. For example, Popplet (www .popplet.com) or Bubbl.us (www.bubbl.us) can allow for the creation of maps that students can download as PDFs and submit as assignments. If this LAT will be an ongoing activity in your course, consider purchasing a software package that assists in the development of Concept Maps, such as *Inspiration* (http://www.engagingminds.com/inspiration/descript.html). Students can also use presentation or word processing software that includes drawing, although these might not be as easy to use as tools that are specifically purposed to the creation of maps and networks.

Analysis and Reporting

Analysis of Concept Maps can be challenging at first because instructors do not typically have practice in assessing relations between concepts. This is why developing a rubric can be useful. Use your scoring system or rubric to assess individual maps. Consider also a holistic assessment of the completeness and quality of the map. Report the results of your scoring to students. A tallied score will be helpful, and a comment from you about the quality of the effort can also be useful for students. Concept Maps can be graded informally through a simple participation grade, or more formally with a grade assigned based upon the number and quality of the responses.

Table 9.13 Sample Concept Map Evaluation Rubric

Concept Map Element	Very Good (4)	Good (3)	Poor (2)	Very Poor (1)
Breadth of Net	Map includes the important concepts and describes domain on multiple levels	Map includes most important concepts; describes domain on limited number of levels	Important concepts missing and/or describes domain on only one level	Map includes a minimum of concepts with many important concepts missing
Embeddedness and Interconnectedness	All concepts interlinked with several other concepts	Most concepts interlinked with other concepts	Several concepts linked to other concepts	Few concepts linked to other concepts
Use of Descriptive Links	Links succinctly and accurately describe all relationships	Links are descriptive and valid for most relationships	Some links unclear or vague; some invalid or unclear	Links are vague; show inconsistent relationships
Efficient Links	Each link type is distinct from all others, clearly describes relationship; used consistently	Most links are distinct from others; discriminate concepts; present variety of relationships; used fairly consistently	Several links are synonymous; don't discriminate concepts well; don't show a variety of relationships; used inconsistently	Most links synonymous or vaguely describe relationships and aren't distinct from other links
Layout	Map is contained in a single page, has multiple clear hierarchies, is well laid out, and provides a sufficient number of relevant examples with links	Map is contained in a single page, has several clear hierarchies, is fairly well laid out, and provides a sufficient number of fairly relevant examples with links	Map is not contained in a single page, has unclear hierarchies, is poorly laid out, and provides some fairly relevant examples with links	Map is not contained in a single page, is confusing to read with no hierarchical organization
Development Over Time *(This is for Concept Maps where a "base map" is constructed at the beginning of the course and a corresponding "final map" at the end of the course)*	Final map shows considerable cognitive progression from base map and a significantly greater depth of understanding of the domain	Final map shows some cognitive progression from base map and a somewhat greater depth of understanding of the domain	Final map shows minimal cognitive progression from base map and a slightly greater depth of understanding of the domain	Final map shows no significant cognitive progression from base map and no increase in the understanding of the domain

The rubric is from the following URL: https://uwaterloo.ca/centre-for-teaching-excellence/teaching-resources/teaching-tips/assessing-student-work/grading-and-feedback/rubric-assessing-concept-maps

To examine aggregated data, look at the different concepts generated, and do a simple tally of how many students came up with which results. Compare categories on your scoring matrix, and tally and average the results for each category. To report aggregated information, create a narrative table to describe the tally of concepts. Consider whether it works to use one of the maps, the one that is the most extensive in number of concepts and links, as a starter and list the number of times each concept was listed by a student. Create a numeric table to display the results of your assessment rubric.

Examples

Onsite: Physics

The professor of this course was coming up for a promotion and tenure review. He had decent but not outstanding student evaluations. He believed they were not as high as they might be because he had many nonmajors in his course who found the topics unengaging. He wanted to augment his evaluations with evidence of student learning to document the good work he believed he was doing in teaching.

One of the course's learning goals was that students would demonstrate increased understanding of key principles of the field as well as the relationships between the principles. He taught a short lesson on electric currents as a part of the course, and one of the outcomes was that students would be able to describe current flow, conductivity, resistivity, resistance, and capacitance and its relationship to time. He decided to use Concept Maps to document and demonstrate improvements in student learning as a result of the course.

Prior to the lesson, he explained Concept Maps and provided students with an example of one on a related topic, an electric field. He announced the topic: electric currents. He then asked students to begin by brainstorming as many topics as possible and to then draw them, illustrating the connections. He was astounded by how few concepts students could actually name. He next assigned readings, and then he re-administered the Concept Map activity. He noted that they were able to list many concepts, but the connections between ideas were still unclear. He then lectured on the topic, trying to focus on demonstrating connections between ideas. He employed note-taking teams to have students work together to fill in any gaps they might have had in their lecture notes (See "Word Webs" in Barkley et al., 2014, for additional information about this collaborative learning activity). At the end of the unit, he re-administered the Concept Map activity again and was very happy to see that students could name more concepts, as well as better demonstrate the relationships between and among ideas.

He wrote up the results of his work, first by presenting a case. He next presented his data in a numeric table (Table 9.14), documenting mean scores for each administration.

Table 9.14 Mean Scores

Concept Map Element	1st Administration (before instruction)	2nd Administration (during instruction)	3rd Administration (after instruction)
Number of Concepts	1.8	2.26	3.2
Breadth of Net	1.46	2.06	3.13
Embeddedness and Interconnectedness	1.66	2.33	3.33
Use of Descriptive Links	1.73	2.27	3
Efficient Links	1.86	2.47	3.27
Layout	1.8	2.33	3.33

Online: Application of Learning Theories to Instruction

The Education Technology Program was undergoing a program review. As a part of this, all instructors had to document that they have collected data about student achievement of learning goals and outcomes and how they planned to make instructional changes as a result. This professor had a stated learning goal that students would understand the various theories from a range of disciplines that inform educators' understanding of the ways in which students learn. Her outcome was that successful students would be able to create a Concept Map that documented their understanding of this information.

Throughout the term, the instructor introduced various conceptions of learning through readings, video lectures, and independent work. She then posted the announcement of the Concept Map activity. She told students they should list as many theories as they can and then show relationships between them, and to construct their diagrams using free software such as Popplet, Prezi, or bubbl.us.

Students completed their maps, and they were able to generate a number of theories of how people learn, including some of the primary ones such as behaviorism, constructivism, and cognitivism. Students also listed, however, some general ideas about learning that she would not necessarily consider to be theories, such as "instructivism" and "multiple intelligences." She realized that they were not completely understanding the difference between primary theories and secondary concepts. She determined they needed further information about the differences, and that they needed to understand which theories are widely accepted as central and which were good ideas or concepts, but did not necessarily have the same level of acceptance and validity. She reported her assessment in the matrix shown in Table 9.15.

Table 9.15 Sample Matrix

Student Learning Outcomes:	LAT	Subject/ Content Prompt	Intentional Active Learning Activity	Learning Artifact	Findings and Interpretations	Actions to Be Taken
Demonstrate the various theories from a range of disciplines that inform educators' understanding of the ways in which student learn.	Concept Maps	Reading assignments, video lectures, etc.	Create concept maps	The maps	The students were able to generate a large number of theories, but some of the concepts they identified were not theories.	Better articulation of what a theory is and what is not provided in a form of a handout. Additional instruction on main theories.

Variations and Extensions

- Consider assigning a specific kind of graphic organizer that students could use to structure their information, such as a spider map, a fishbone map, a series of events chains, a network tree, or other. This allows you to see and assess a particular type of knowledge and information organization. The disadvantage is that it does not allow you to assess the ways in which individual students choose to organize information.

- Assign a Concept Map as a small-group project. Form teams, distribute paper and markers, and present the central concept that you want students to graph. In any reports, you will simply need to note that the information is a result of a group effort.
- Ask students to write explanatory essays based on their maps. Doing so will provide additional data that you can use to illustrate student learning. A thematic analysis of these data could be worthwhile.

Key References and Resources

Angelo, T. A., & Cross, K. P. (1993). CAT 16: Concept maps. In *Classroom assessment techniques* (2nd ed., pp. 197–202). San Francisco, CA: Jossey-Bass.

Barkley, E. F. (2010). SET 6: Team concept maps. In *Student engagement techniques: A handbook for college faculty* (pp. 219–225). San Francisco, CA: Jossey-Bass.

Barkley, E. F., Major, C. H., & Cross, K. P. (2014). CoLT 23: Word Webs. In *Collaborative learning techniques* (2nd ed., pp. 283–288). San Francisco, CA: Jossey-Bass.

Nilson, L. B. (2007). *The graphic syllabus and the outcomes map: Communicating your course.* San Francisco, CA: Jossey-Bass.

Novak, J. D., & Cañas, A. J. (2008). *The theory underlying concept maps and how to construct them.* Technical Report IHMC CmapTools 2006–01 Rev 01-2008, Florida Institute for Human and Machine Cognition, available at: http://cmap.ihmc.us/Publications/ResearchPapers/Theory UnderlyingConceptMaps.pdf.

Novak, J. D., & Gowin, D. B. (1984). *Learning how to learn.* New York, NY: Cambridge University Press.

LEARNING ASSESSMENT TECHNIQUE

Integration

24
Contemporary Issues Journal

Essential Characteristics	
Preparation	LOW
In-class implementation	LOW-MODERATE
Analysis	HIGH

Brief Description

Students look for recent events or developments in the real world that are related to their coursework readings and assignments, then analyze these current affairs to identify the connections to course material in entries that they write in a journal.

Purpose

This technique deepens student understanding of course-related ideas and concepts and guides them in applying them to "the real world." It helps students understand themselves in relation to that course content. It also can catalyze student curiosity. It makes material from coursework more relevant to them, which stimulates their motivation to learn it. It also provides an outlet for reflecting upon what they have learned, thus deepening the learning.

The journal entries and the completed journals are your Learning Artifacts. These artifacts provide a demonstrable record of what students think are important. They also demonstrate how well students can connect what they are learning in the classroom to their personal lives and the world around them. They are a clear documentation of students' ability to integrate information from various aspects of their lives. Contemporary Issues Journals typically are used for formative purposes, in which teachers assess how well they are understanding course concepts and their relevance. They may also serve a summative, in which teachers use them after a learning module to evaluate how well students have understood, applied, and integrated course content.

Key Learning Goals

- The ability to think holistically: to see the whole as well as the parts
- The ability to synthesize disparate but related information into a whole
- The ability to connect course concepts to concepts in other disciplines or fields
- The ability to connect course information to their daily lives

Implementation

Preparation

- Decide the journal parameters ahead of time. For example,
  - What will be the journal medium (a lined tablet, a computer-based word processing file, a formal bound booklet, an online blog)?
  - How frequently should students make entries, and will this technique be implemented for a course segment or the whole term?
  - What should a typical entry look like? Consider a three-part entry that includes (1) date of journal entry and news source, (2) summary (Who, What, Where, When, Why, How), and (3) the course principles, ideas, and concepts the event reflects.
- Construct a rubric to assess the journal. Consider the following as items for the rubric:
  - Clear statement about the relationship between text and events
  - Well-selected points of comparison and/or departure among the texts and events
  - Solid evidence (citation of sources) to prove the points of comparison
  - Logical ordering of information
- Create a handout that includes directions, clarifies your expectations, and provides examples.

Process

1. Discuss the purpose of the journal and allow time for questions.
2. Ask students to look for and record or post journal entries that connect course material to news events.
3. Collect the Learning Artifacts.

Online

This can be a simple, regular assignment in an LMS. If you have students blog within the LMS, you can set up preferences so that each student's blog is kept private from other students, but still allows you access as the instructor. Alternately you can ask students to set up their own blogs on which they can post their entries. Either way, students can enrich their text with images, links to web pages, media, and other blogs. To check their work, tell students you will be spot-checking blogs randomly throughout the term, or set up a formal evaluation schedule. As a variation, consider creating a single Threaded Discussion Forum for students to share insights from their Blogs, or set-up multiple Forums assigned to separate topics.

Analysis and Reporting

Check journals regularly or tell students that you will be evaluating them on a random basis to discourage them from waiting until the last minute to do all the entries. When you review the entries, use the rubric that you created during the planning stage to evaluate the journals. Provide a rating across categories, and consider adding comments about what is unique or interesting about each entry. Develop a written response to individuals that includes both rubric scoring and comments about any issues. Because students can see journaling as a "soft" activity, it can be a good idea to grade Contemporary Issues Journals in order to help students understand their importance. Consider making them worth sufficient points in the final grade for students to take them seriously (for example 10% of the final grade). Alternately, you can keep a simple tally and grade them for participation points.

To analyze and report aggregated information, first look across the rubric for item analysis. Develop mean scores across the different items. You might also consider a key word analysis, in which you look for certain concepts (in your instructions, you could ask students to highlight or bold key words so that they are easy for you to identify quickly). Alternately, consider a thematic analysis, in which you search for the key themes that students identified and compare them with your own list. Report rubric analysis results in a numeric table. If you do a qualitative analysis, consider a narrative table, a Concept Map (for key themes), or a word cloud (for a word count analysis).

Examples

Onsite: Music Business

In this course, students study the legal and business aspects of the music industry with an emphasis on publishing, licensing, and promotion. To help students understand the importance of the content to students' future professional lives, this instructor requires students to monitor the online site *Music Industry News Network* throughout the term, looking for current news stories that relate to course topics such as changing international copyright law in the multimedia industry and the Internet.

To complete their Contemporary Issues Journals, students write the date, source, a synopsis of the news story, and identify the laws or principles involved in a journal in preparation for the first class session of the week. The instructor uses the first 5 minutes or so of class for students to share their findings with partners as he walks around the room, making a +/– next to student names in the grade book based on a quick assessment of that week's entry. He then invites students to share their findings and interpretations with the whole class, using these reports as a basis for discussion and drawing connections to what will be studied during the upcoming week.

He keeps a running record of their journal entry completion, a sample of which is shown in Table 9.16.

Table 9.16 Journal Entry Completion

Name	1/6	1/13	1/20	1/27	2/3	2/10
Mandi	+	+	+	+	+	+
Yianni	+	–	+	–	–	+
Christina	+	+	+	+	+	+
Jingxian	+	–	–	–	–	+
Jasmine	+	–	–	+	–	+
Gagandeep	+	+	+	+	+	+
Roseanne	+	+	+	–	–	–

Online: Applied Ethics

The professor of this course wanted students to examine ethics by observing actual choices made by people in real situations. He asked students to monitor the news for stories of conflict related to controversial issues such as abortion, rationing of health care, animal rights, environmental concerns, gun control, same sex relationships, capital punishment, and so forth, record at least one item per week in a blog-based journal, and write and post a single-paragraph analysis using the terms and principles they were learning in class. Once per month, he assigned the topic so that all students would write about the same issue and could respond to each other's posts.

He reviewed the blogs two times a term, assigning grades based on the number of entries and the quality of the analyses determined by his rubric-based assessment of them. On the same-topic posts, he performed a word analysis using Wordle so he could see the key concepts students were highlighting, including the following data display on the question of whether the current economy is fair to workers (Figure 9.2).

Figure 9.2 Wordle

For the Final Exam, students selected an event in their journal and used the conceptual tools of meta-ethics and normative ethics they had learned throughout the term to write an extensive essay analyzing the main issue from multiple perspectives, and closing with the steps they believed could be taken to resolve the conflict in the specific news incident.

Variations and Extensions

- Ask students to expand their entries by including questions they have about the event, especially aspects that appear to be course-related but which have not yet been covered in class.

- Use the journal for reflective purposes, asking students to think about the event and relate it to their personal lives, answering questions such as, *Have you experienced anything similar in your own life? Given what you have learned about x in this course, what might you advise the participants to do now that would help them to move forward most productively?*

- Consider having students follow-up this activity with a formal essay in which they analyze, synthesize, or evaluate the information in their journal entries.

- If appropriate to course goals, ask students to monitor online news sites from other English-speaking countries and, for example, compare and contrast coverage of a single event from different international perspectives. Or ask students in foreign language courses to look for events or articles in the media of that country and translate and interpret their findings. "News and Newspapers Online" (http://library.uncg.edu/news/) provides links to news sites from all over the world and is a free service provided by the University Libraries of the University of North Carolina at Greensboro.

- Make this a collaborative learning activity by using CoLT 24: Dialogue Journals, in which students exchange journals with a peer who reads and responds to the entry with comments and questions. Journal writing can be particularly effective when writers know that someone who is interested in the topic will read and respond to their entries. Since reading and responding to students can be a time-consuming task, making this a collaborative activity helps ensure students receive timely and critical feedback (albeit from a peer) without adding to instructor workload (see Barkley et al., 2014).

- Consider creating a communal journal. Keep the journal on a desk or table in the classroom or your office or maintain an online forum or blog that is available for entries and responses by any class member.

Key References and Resources

Barkley, E. F. (2010). SET 29: Contemporary issues journal. In *Student engagement techniques: A handbook for college faculty* (pp. 276–279). San Francisco, CA: Jossey-Bass.

Barkley, E. F., Cross, P. K., & Major, C. H. (2014). CoLT 24: Dialogue journals. In *Collaborative learning techniques: A handbook for college faculty* (2nd ed.). San Francisco, CA: Jossey-Bass.

Bean, J. C. (2009). *Engaging ideas: The professor's guide to integrating writing, critical thinking, and active learning in the classroom* (2nd ed.). San Francisco, CA: Jossey-Bass.

LEARNING ASSESSMENT TECHNIQUE

Integration

25
Dyadic Essay

Complexity involved in	
Preparation	MODERATE
In-class implementation	MODERATE
Analysis	HIGH

Brief Description

Students individually write an essay question and model answer on a reading assignment, lecture, or other. Pairs exchange questions, write responses to each other's questions, and then compare the model with their own. The students next discuss their responses and in a final step, complete a peer evaluation of each other's performance.

Purpose

This LAT gives students practice identifying the most important feature of an assignment and formulating and answering questions about that assignment. It also gives students an opportunity to rehearse responding to essay questions, with the added advantage of having a sample response with which to compare their answers. This technique therefore can help students deepen their understanding as they write questions and then evaluate another's response to the question they design, while practicing their own skills at responding to a peer's question.

The Learning Artifacts for this technique include (1) the student developed essay question, (2) the student developed model response, (3) the partner's created essay response, and (4) the student's evaluation of the partner's essay response. These artifacts provide instructors with rich, in-depth insight into a students' ability to apply and evaluate, with the additional advantage of including a built-in layer of peer evaluation. This technique may be done during a learning unit or module to provide documentation of student progress that has been subjected to peer evaluation. It may also be used at the end of a learning unit or module to help you assess comprehension. As a substitute for the traditional essay exam, this LAT can help students strengthen their application of information and development of higher order thinking skills while providing instructors with rich information for summative assessment purposes, both at the individual and aggregate level.

Key Learning Goals

- The ability to think holistically: to see the whole as well as the parts
- The ability to synthesize disparate but related information into a whole
- The ability to connect a concept to other concepts within this course

Implementation

Preparation

- Provide guidance to students on how to write good essay questions and answers. It may be helpful to distribute a handout that includes a collection of question stems such as those in Table 9.18 "Essay Question Prompt Stems" at the end of this section. It can also be useful to share sample questions and responses with students that model the length and level of complexity and depth that you expect.
- Develop a system for assessing responses to the essay questions, both for you to use and for peers to use. You might consider the following, for example:
  - Accuracy
  - Completeness
  - Insightfulness

  You can use a scale for evaluation, such as 4 (excellent) to 1 (poor), to rate each of the attributes (Millis & Cottell, 1998, pp. 135–136). Consider sharing the guidelines and scale with students ahead of time, so that they understand your expectations.
- Prepare a handout with guidelines.
- Consider who will do the evaluations. Peer evaluation is a built-in component of the technique, but you may also include a self-evaluation component as well, which provides students with an opportunity to defend their own answers.

Process

1. Students reflect on a learning activity (such as reading an assignment, a lecture, or a film) and write an essay question related to it.
2. On a separate sheet of paper, students next prepare a model response to their own question.
3. Students form pairs, exchange essay questions, and write responses.
4. Students trade model answers and compare and contrast their answer with their partner's model answer.
5. Partners discuss their responses first for one essay question and then for the other, paying special attention to similar and dissimilar points.
6. Students assess their partner's responses to the questions they created, using the rubric you assign.
7. Students turn in their essay questions, their model responses, and peer reviews.

Online

Student pairs can exchange questions and answers through email attachments. This activity, however, is particularly well suited to blogging, whether students use their own blogs or you use the blog feature in your LMS.

Analysis and Reporting

For each Learning Artifact, consider the following ways to analyze the various components:

- Use a simple Likert system to evaluate the essay question, according to whatever criteria are most important to you (for example, 4 = highly relevant question to 1 = highly irrelevant question).
- Use the rubric you created while preparing for this LAT to score the model responses.
- Use the rubric you created while preparing for this LAT to score the partner's response to the original question.
- Score the peer assessment. Typically, you will want to consider accuracy (were they overly generous or were they candid and accurate in their assessments) as well as thoroughness (did they try to provide useful information or were they simply getting through the task).

Initial feedback on this activity is provided in the peer assessment phase, but students will likely want feedback from you as well, so share your rubric scoring with them. You may also want to share your scores of the peer assessment, as doing so can make them take this phase more seriously. Grading this LAT can cause students some anxiety, since someone who is not the teacher is creating the questions (which can cause them to doubt the validity of the question) and because their peers are making recommendations about their scoring/grades. Considerable effort can go into this technique, both by the students and by you, however, so it may be graded as well. If you wish to evaluate student work for a grade, consider assigning separate grades or points for the different components; participation points are also an option.

Because this technique involves multiple questions and multiple responses to these different questions, aggregated analysis of responses (including both the model responses or partner answers to the questions) is generally complicated and not advised. You could consider looking at the following information:

- Averaging rating of student questions.
- Identifying themes in students' questions (Are students asking questions about the same issues/topics? Are they asking the same types of questions, whether close ended or open ended? And so forth).
- Using the ratings of students question development over time, you may be able to spot trends.

To display the results of your analysis, consider a bar graph or a table to illustrate average scores. Compare individual performance over time by using a spreadsheet tracking scores at each test administration. If you have before and after implementation of this technique grades, consider a comparison. Also consider a visual display of the key words students use, such as creating a word cloud (for example through Wordle.com).

Examples

Onsite: African American Literature

The professor of this course had to report on student learning outcomes to her departmental assessment committee. One of her learning outcomes was that students would be able to formulate their own questions about African American literature. She also had a learning outcome that students would be able to summarize and explain key works in their own words. This professor used Dyadic Essays throughout the semester following each major assignment to assess these learning outcomes.

After watching a videotape of Maya Angelou reading from her work, *I Know Why the Caged Bird Sings*, for example, each student formulated an essay question about the work and wrote a model response that evening for homework. The next day, students exchanged questions and answered the question they received in class. Students then compared their responses, and each student submitted a question, model response, and response to the professor. They also submitted peer reviews of each other's responses to their questions.

The professor reviewed students' questions and assessed them for their basic understanding of the literature. She also assessed them for depth and originality. She kept a running scorecard of the students' performance on questions (Table 9.17) and was able to share with them how they were improving on question development and writing over time (Figure 9.3). In addition to scoring their questions, the professor reviewed each model response and each partner response for demonstration of understanding of the work.

Table 9.17 Running Scorecard (each area is rated on a 4-point scale: 1 = poor, 4 = excellent)

Students		Week 2	Week 4	Week 6	Week 8	Week 10
Craig	Addresses a salient issue	3	3	4	4	4
	Open ended, allowing for multiple responses	2	3	3	4	4
	Aligns with objectives for the course	2	2	3	3	4
	Wording indicates type of appropriate thinking for response	1	2	2	3	3
Ameen	Addresses a salient issue	2	2	3	3	4
	Open ended, allowing for multiple responses	3	3	3	4	3
	Aligns with objectives for the course	1	3	3	3	4
	Wording indicates type of appropriate thinking for response	1	2	2	3	3
Tanayah	Addresses a salient issue	1	2	2	3	3
	Open ended, allowing for multiple responses	1	2	3	4	4
	Aligns with objectives for the course	2	2	2	3	3
	Wording indicates type of appropriate thinking for response	1	1	2	2	3

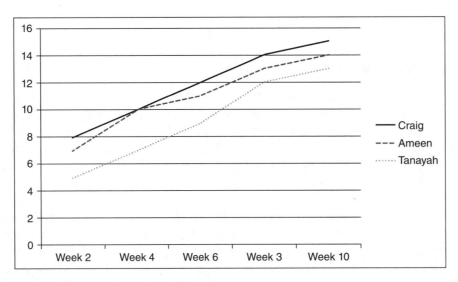

Figure 9.3 Analysis Over Time

 Online: Real Estate Principles

In this popular online class, the professor was worried that students were not doing their best work on essay exams. She decided to use Dyadic Essays to help students prepare for essay-based exams. She had a learning outcome that students would be able to examine a relevant topic from the perspective of different stakeholders.

She formed student pairs and posted a topic every two weeks that was coordinated with the assigned reading (for example, duties and responsibilities between broker, salesman, and client; enforceability of contractual rights; and so forth). For each topic, she asked students to formulate one good essay question and provide a model answer. Partners exchanged questions, wrote answers, shared model responses, and messaged each other on similarities and differences. They then sent their combined work along to her.

To grade, she simply spot-checked their work, assigned task completion points, and posted 1–2 exemplary questions and answers for all students to read. She believed Dyadic Essays helped her promote deeper learning among students and also fostered collaboration and community in the course. She also believed that the exercise helped students to write better essays on the exams, which was validated by her comparison of student grades prior to and after implementing the activity (Figure 9.4).

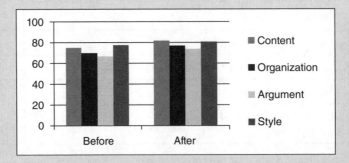

Figure 9.4 Students' Average Scores on Tests Before and After Implementing LAT

Table 9.18 Essay Question Prompt Stems

Question Type	Purpose	Example
Exploratory	Probe facts and basic knowledge	What research evidence supports ___?
Challenge	Examine assumptions, conclusions, and interpretations	How else might we account for ___?
Relational	Ask for comparison of themes, ideas, or issues	How does _compare to ___?
Diagnostic	Probe motives or causes	Why did ___?
Action	Call for a conclusion or action	In response to ___, what should ___ do?
Cause and Effect	Ask for causal relationships between ideas, actions, or events	If ___occurred, what would happen?
Extension	Expand the discussion	What are additional ways that ___?
Hypothetical	Pose a change in the facts or issues	Suppose ___ had been the case, would the outcome have been the same?
Priority	Seek to identify the most important issue	From all that we have discussed, what is the most important___?
Summary	Elicit syntheses	What themes or lessons have emerged from ___?
Problem	Challenge students to find solutions to real or hypothetical situations	What if? (To be motivating, students should be able to make some progress on finding a solution, and there should be more than one solution.)
Interpretation	Help students to uncover the underlying meaning of things	From whose viewpoint or perspective are we seeing, hearing, reading? What does this mean? or, What may have been intended by . . . ?
Application	Probe for relationships and ask students to connect theory to practice	How does this apply to that? or, Knowing this, how would you . . . ?
Evaluative	Require students to assess and make judgments	Which of these are better? Why does it matter? and, So what?
Critical	Require students to examine the validity of statements, arguments, and conclusions and to analyze their thinking and challenge their own assumptions	How do we know? and, What's the evidence and how reliable is the evidence?

Sources: Davis (2009), pp. 119–120; McKeachie (1994), pp. 51–52

Variations and Extensions

- This LAT is an adaptation of Dyadic Essay Confrontations (DEC) (Sherman, 1991). A primary purpose of the original DEC is to integrate current reading material with material previously covered. Sherman asks students to formulate questions that compare present and past reading assignments, thus providing students with a mechanism to connect differing text materials.

- Ask students to synthesize their practice response and the model response to create a new response.
- As an online variation, ask students to do abbreviated Dyadic Essays through a microblog, such as Twitter or Tumblr. If your field is a creative one, consider asking them to use a creative format, such as a haiku for their contributions.

Key References and Resources

Millis, B. J., & Cottell, P. G. (1998). *Cooperative learning for higher education faculty* (pp. 134–138). Phoenix, AZ: Oryx Press.

Millis, B. J., Sherman, L. W., & Cottell, P. G. (1993). Stacking the DEC to promote critical thinking: Applications in three disciplines. *Cooperative Learning and College Teaching, 3*(3), 12–14.

Sherman, L. W. (1991). *Cooperative learning in postsecondary education: Implications from social psychology for active learning experiences.* A presentation to the annual meetings of the American Educational Research Association, Chicago, IL, 3–7.

LEARNING ASSESSMENT TECHNIQUE

Integration

26
Synthesis Paper

Complexity involved in	
Preparation	MODERATE
In-class implementation	HIGH
Analysis	HIGH

Brief Description

Instead of responding to or reviewing a single reading assignment, students consider several readings together, work to draw commonalities from them, and then write about readings in a formal paper.

Purpose

The Synthesis Paper requires that students move beyond simple summary to a more complex representation of the complexity of issues and ideas from a variety of course readings. This LAT is particularly useful to help students think more critically about what they are reading, and it is useful when individual readings oversimplify a topic or issue. Synthesis requires students to understand connections between different things, such as ideas, experiences, different subject matter, what they learn in class and what they see in the real world. It challenges them to identify parts and then put them together to form a coherent or unique new whole.

The Learning Artifact is the final written paper, which provides a written record that demonstrates whether and how students are understanding content and pulling together ideas and information. It shows student ability to integrate information from multiple sources, identifying similarities and differences across them. This LAT may be done more informally during a learning module to determine how well students are understanding readings in the moment. It also can be done at the end of a learning module to make a judgment about how well they have understood.

Key Learning Goals

- The ability to differentiate closely related concepts in the subject area
- The ability to compare different aspects of a topic

- The ability to think holistically: to see the whole as well as the parts
- The ability to synthesize disparate but related information into a whole
- The ability to connect a concept to other concepts within this course

Implementation

Preparation

- Determine whether you will identify several related readings that highlight similar issues and themes related to a central concept, or whether you will allow students to select their own readings. Novice students will do better with the former, but if you have more advanced students, it can be useful for them to select their own works, as that is a skill that will serve them well in a number of different courses.
- Determine the parameters of the assignment, including length and how long students will have to complete it.
- Create a handout in which you define a Synthesis Paper and its purpose and in which you disclose the parameters of the assignment.
- Consider who will be involved in the assessment. Peer assessment can, for example, be a valuable addition to the learning process and can provide additional data for your report.

Process

1. Announce the activity and the parameters of the assignment; distribute your handout.
2. Provide students with time to complete the research and the writing.
3. Consider having students report out on the central themes they identified in the various readings.
4. Collect the Learning Artifacts, which are their final papers.

Online

Have students submit their assignments through the course learning management system if you are using one. Alternately, this assignment works well in a blog, particularly if implemented regularly, with students sharing their papers through blog postings.

Analysis and Reporting

For this LAT, a rubric assessment is particularly effective, but the trick is to highlight evaluation of the synthesis aspect in addition to the writing in general. Develop a rubric with a scale such as 4 (excellent), 3 (very good), 2 (poor), 1 (very poor) and include categories such as the following:

- Effectiveness of integration
- Accuracy of integrated information
- Use of evidence to document integration
- Communication of integrated information

You can also add space for comments about what was unusual or outstanding about the individual synthesis to the rubric assessment.

Alternately, you may wish to use a narrative form of analysis, particularly if you use the assignment regularly. To analyze papers in this way, determine what you are looking for (completeness or accuracy or efficiency or other). Read the individual's paper from start to finish, and assign a rating. Develop a narrative through which you explain your assessment of the work.

You will most likely want to grade this assignment, as it can require students to exert a significant amount of time in reading and writing. Simply assign the grade based upon your scoring system (e.g., such as the criteria you set in your rubric). If you do the assignment regularly, you may wish to use a simplified grading system, such as having students suggest their best effort paper for review, or alternately grading these papers at certain intervals (for example once a month).

To learn about the class performance as a whole, tally and then consider average scores for each item. If you used a more holistic approach to grading, review your own narrative for common themes, and consider how the themes varied. You can report your rubric analysis through a simple tally sheet or a bar graph or table. If you do a more holistic narrative and attempt to depict the themes you identified, consider a network or a Venn diagram.

Examples

Onsite: Introduction to Ethics

As a new faculty member in her college, the professor of this course was required annually to demonstrate evidence of creating outcomes, matching teaching methods to them, collecting data from the teaching, and identifying ways to make changes. In her introductory ethics course, she had a learning outcome that stated successful students would be able describe the central ethical issues confronting modern society. She wanted students to move beyond superficial descriptions, however, and engage in critical thinking about the readings they were using to help them understand the issues. Rather than viewing each article on its own, she wanted students to be able to think across them, drawing together ideas and key information.

As a mid-term project, she employed a Synthesis Paper, chose a topic, and then she created a reading list of 7–10 suggested articles. Students could elect to include others as well. Their assignment was to synthesize the articles, identifying common themes across them, and to develop a unifying thesis statement about them.

The professor implemented peer review of the papers, using a rubric for evaluating synthesis that she had developed. She provided students with additional time to make changes after receiving the peer reviews. She then assessed the papers by the same rubric, giving additional narrative of her own in response to their essays. She provided individuals with feedback on her assessment of the work.

To analyze the data, she looked across the categories of her rubric, and then tallied and averaged the scores (Figure 9.5). She found that students were good at summarizing the key themes but were not as proficient at providing evidence to support the themes that they identified.

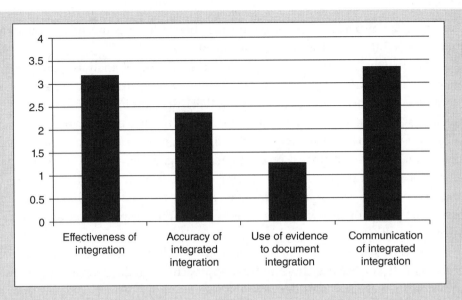

Figure 9.5 Rubric for Evaluating Synthesis

Online: English Composition

In this online course, the professor had a learning outcome that students would be able to synthesize key sources to support their own written thoughts. The professor was concerned that students could summarize information but could never get beyond simple summary to deeper thinking about the concepts that crossed multiple sources, a skill that she believed they needed for other classes as well. She decided to use a Synthesis Paper as one of the assignments. Students were to write about the topic of legalization of marijuana. She provided a list of readings about the topic, presenting both sides of the issue. She indicated that they should identify themes that crossed several of the articles and describe these and support their descriptions with evidence. They should ultimately take a stance and use the synthesis paper to present their opinion as well as the supporting and refuting positions.

When the deadline arrived, the professor collected the papers. She reviewed them for the effectiveness of their writing (e.g., assessing content, organization, diction, style, and mechanics), as she did for all of their written assignments. She then did a second assessment to determine the effectiveness of their syntheses.

She first summarized the key themes across papers so that she could report back to students, displaying her findings through a Venn diagram (Figure 9.6).

Next, she created a tally sheet for each paper, as shown in Table 9.19.

Figure 9.6 Venn Diagram of Key Themes

Table 9.19 Sample of Tally Sheet

Student	Themes	Effectiveness of Integration (Did they identify a reasonable theme?)	Accuracy of Synthesis (How right were they?)	Use of Evidence to Support Synthesis (How well did they prove they were right?)
Student 1	1	Very high	High	High
	2	High	High	High
	3	Very high	Very high	Very high
	4	High	High	High
	5	High	High	High
Student 2	1	Low	Low	Very low
	2	Low	Low	Very low
	3	Very low	Very low	Very low
Student 3	1	High	High	High
	2	Low	Low	Very low
	3	Low	Low	Low
Student 4	1	High	Low	Low
	2	High	Low	Low
	3	Low	Low	Very low
	4	Low	Low	Very low

(continued)

Table 9.19   *(Continued)*

Student	Themes	Effectiveness of Integration (Did they identify a reasonable theme?)	Accuracy of Synthesis (How right were they?)	Use of Evidence to Support Synthesis (How well did they prove they were right?)
Student 5	1	High	High	Low
	2	High	High	High
	3	Very high	Very high	High
	4	High	High	Low
	5	Very high	Very high	High
Student 6	1	Very high	High	High
	2	Very high	High	High
	3	High	High	High
	4	High	High	Low
	5	High	High	Low

On a quick scan, she could see that she needed to help students learn better how to support integrated ideas with evidence, and so she spent additional time on this topic during the next class session.

Variations and Extensions

- Instead of a Synthesis Paper, have students develop a matrix of common elements that the different readings share. This produces a different kind of data that is in some ways easier to analyze, as it can be done by a simple count of connections.
- Instead of multiple readings, consider assigning a shorter synthesis of ideas from a single larger, complex reading.

Key References and Resources

Anderson, L. W., & Krathwohl, D. R. (Eds.). (2001). *A taxonomy for learning, teaching, and assessing: A revision of Bloom's taxonomy of educational objectives.* New York, NY: Addison Wesley Longman.

Fink, D. (2013). *Creating significant learning experiences: An integrated approach to designing courses.* San Francisco, CA: Jossey-Bass.

Writing across the curriculum (WAC) clearinghouse. (2014). Event analysis. http://wac.colostate.edu /intro/pop5q.cfm.

LEARNING ASSESSMENT TECHNIQUE

Integration

27
Case Study

Complexity involved in	
Preparation	HIGH
In-class implementation	HIGH
Analysis	HIGH

Brief Description

Students receive a real-life scenario, or "case," related to course content. These cases usually present a brief history of how the situation developed and a dilemma that a key character within the scenario is facing, and students are charged with helping the character develop a solution to the problem.

Purpose

This activity guides students in the development of problem-solving capacities as they apply course concepts to identify and evaluate alternative approaches to responding to the case. It is inherently appealing to students because it has a "true-to-life" feel, and thus Case Study can help bridge the gap between theory and practice and between the academy and the workplace.

The Learning Artifacts are the written Case Study analyses. These artifacts provide teachers with useful information about student learning and their ability to make connections between what they have learned in the case to real-word practical scenarios. They provide information that teachers can use to incorporate into their lectures, discussion questions, or group activities. The analyses provide rich, thick data for teachers to analyze. Given sufficient time to respond, student responses can provide teachers with glimpses into errors in logic that they might not be able to identify through shorter assessments. It is also a useful way to check student understanding just after a learning unit or module. In this way, Case Study can help teachers determine how well students have developed appropriate content knowledge and how well they are able to apply it to new situations.

Key Learning Goals

- The ability to differentiate closely related concepts in the subject area
- The ability to compare different aspects of a topic

- The ability to think holistically: to see the whole as well as the parts
- The ability to synthesize disparate but related information into a whole
- The ability to connect a concept to other concepts within this course

Implementation

Preparation
- Craft a case based upon a real or hypothetical situation, keeping in mind that students are intrigued by situations that deal with current issues.
- Set the parameters of the assignment, including how long responses should be, how long students will have to write them, and what kinds of materials (if any) they can use to develop their responses.
- Prepare the case to distribute as a handout and consider including a series of questions to guide students in their analysis. These questions may ask students to sort out factual data, apply analytic tools, articulate issues, reflect on their relevant experience, draw conclusions, and recommend actions that resolve the dilemma or solve the problem in the case.
- Create a rubric for evaluating the case. You might consider the following categories:
  - Identification of main problem(s)
  - Analysis and evaluation of main problem(s)
  - Recommendations on effective solutions
  - Links to course readings
  - Writing mechanics and formatting guidelines
- Determine who will be involved in the evaluation. Peer evaluation of case reports can be particularly useful as students can learn from each other as they analyze each other's work.

Process
1. Present the handout that describes the case to the students.
2. Allow time for students to ask questions.
3. Ask students to study the case in depth to become familiar with the issues and decision options (this step typically takes anywhere from one class session to a few weeks, depending upon the complexity of the assignment).
4. Ask students to record their responses in writing.
5. Collect their responses.

Online

Present the case through whatever course platform you are using. Collect data as follows:

- Ask students to post their responses in the assignments sections of the LMS.
- If you are not using an LMS, consider setting up a way for students to share their assignments with you (for example Box or Dropbox).
- If the class is small, or you have created a manageable number of teams to work on the assignment, consider having students email their responses to you.
- Alternately, develop a different *wiki* for each team. Post the case study and ask students to collaboratively develop a solution.

Analysis and Reporting

The information that students develop may be analyzed in a couple of different ways:

- Read each response once through to get a general sense of them.
- Use a rubric to assess the case analyses you have collected.
- Develop a response to each individual, which can include your comments about what is unique to the Case Study response as well the scored rubric.

Whether to grade this activity or not depends on how you are using it. If you are using it as a spot check of student understanding of information, then it is best not to grade it. If you are using it to assess student knowledge at the end of a learning module, grading can be helpful. It signals the importance of the activity to students and encourages them to do their best work, in turn providing you with the best information about the level of their learning. Simply determine a percentage based upon the rubric scoring.

To record findings at the aggregate level, look across the individual items of the rubric and determine average scores; consider using mean, median, and mode as measures. Consider a thematic analysis of central ideas or of the differences between student papers on the different rubric elements. Data may be recorded in a quantitative table by providing aggregate scores for each category of the rubric. Data may also be presented in a narrative form, in which you provide a written description of the primary themes you have seen in the data, possibly augmenting it with a narrative table or boxed display. For example, you might consider whether everyone was equally successful at identifying the main problem. What were the differences in their approaches? How might you best illustrate those differences in your data display?

Examples

Onsite: Issues in Contemporary Art

An institution is preparing for an upcoming accreditation visit. The institutional assessment team has asked each college and school to collect data that document student learning outcomes. The College of Arts and Sciences has in turn asked each department to collect this evidence, and departments in turn have identified selected courses to provide such evidence. Instructors of these "showcase courses" must demonstrate that they have developed a learning outcome and collected information related to it. Instructors must also document their plans for improvement.

The art department has selected Issues in Contemporary Art as one of its showcase courses to document student learning outcomes. The professor has identified a learning objective of using appropriate knowledge to solve problems in the field. The professor has chosen to use Case Study as the assessment tool, as it has both teaching and assessment functions. That is, students learn while they are being assessed.

The case the professor has created introduces a graduate student who has been commissioned to create a monument to honor the contributions of the 18th century missionary

Father Serra to the city's heritage, but the commission is in danger of being cancelled due to Serra's controversial background. Students are charged with identifying what steps the graduate student might take to move the project forward while staying "true" to his own artistic vision. The professor asks students to write written responses to the case, which he uses as his Learning Artifact.

The professor scores the cases by a rubric he created. He returns the scores to the students. For the written report that documents student learning outcomes, he examines the rubrics together, developing a composite score for each section. He reports the average score for each cell. He also identifies the high scores (identification of the main problem) and low scores (links to course readings). He realizes that he has not assigned sufficient reading materials related to the case for students to make appropriate connections. He documents his plans to include such readings in future offerings of the course. He writes up his findings in a narrative format. He developed the following matrix (Table 9.20) to demonstrate his approach and included it in his narrative.

Table 9.20 Assessment Matrix

Objective	LAT	Subject/ Content Prompt	Intentional Active Learning Activity	Learning Artifact	Findings	Actions to Be Taken
Using appropriate knowledge to solve problems in the field	Case Study	Readings undertaken to answer the case	Completion of the case	Written case analysis	Students were able to identify findings but were not able to link course offerings.	Addition of reading materials to learning module

Online: Introduction to Teaching Online

This minicourse is part of an online training program for community college faculty who are preparing to teach online courses. The instructor frequently uses "scenarios" posted on a discussion forum to help faculty "students" discuss effective teaching strategies. The objective is to have each student be able to identify teaching problems and develop strategies for solving them.

For example, one scenario provides details about an actual case in which a student who had failed an online class complained to the dean that the grading procedure was unfair. The instructor asks students to look at the case from the perspective of the student, the instructor, or the administrator. Students make a recommendation for how to resolve the dilemma and how to prevent similar problems in future classes.

The instructor asks students to post their responses as formal written assignments. She grades according to rubrics. She also conducts a thematic analysis of student problem solving, looking for problem-solving strategies that cross multiple responses. She reports the results to the students in a solutions list, which she displays by way of a narrative table, a sample of which follows (Table 9.21).

Table 9.21 Narrative Table Displaying Case Study Problem-Solving Strategies

Proposed Solutions	Administrators	Instructors	Students
Talk to the instructor to find out his or her perspective on the problem	X	X	
Arrange a meeting with the dean, the instructor, and the student	X	X	X
Ask to see the syllabus and the work	X	X	
Begin a formal grade appeal procedure	X		X
Review the records of the online course to try to determine what is going on	X		

Variations and Extensions

- Case studies may be done as group assignments. Simply form groups and ask students to solve the problem presented in the case. This provides a different data set, one that is from the perspective of the group rather than the individual.

Key References and Resources

Barkley, E. F. (2010). SET 28: Case studies. In *Student engagement techniques: A handbook for college faculty* (2nd ed., pp. 272–274). San Francisco, CA: Jossey-Bass.

Barkley, E. F., Cross, K. P., & Major, C. H. (2014). CoLT 15: Case study. In *Collaborative learning techniques: A handbook for college faculty* (2nd ed., pp. 238–243). San Francisco, CA: Jossey-Bass.

McKeachie, W., & Svinicki, M. (2013). *McKeachie's teaching tips* (14th ed.). Independence, KY: Cengage Learning.

LEARNING ASSESSMENT TECHNIQUE

Integration

28
Class Book

Complexity involved in	
Preparation	LOW
In-class implementation	MODERATE
Analysis	HIGH

Brief Description

Individual students submit a scholarly essay or research paper that they believe represents their highest-quality work from the course, and then all students' best papers are published together in a Class Book.

Purpose

This LAT provides students with an opportunity to learn about a topic through intensive research and scholarly writing. This aspect of it requires students to think critically, synthesize information, and work through research within the course subject area. Because they choose their best work to contribute to the Class Book, it motivates them to strive for personal excellence, and it provides them with models of quality created by their peers.

Students produce two Learning Artifacts with this technique: an individual paper and a document that is a compilation of the class's work. In selecting their own work, they practice evaluation of their own work. When they compile the work, they integrate ideas and information across all students in the class. This LAT typically serves as a final product or a capstone assignment. Because of its cumulative nature, and the fact that it requires intensive research and writing on the part of the students, the technique typically is done post-instruction and thus provides faculty with an opportunity to assess performance and achievement over an academic term.

Key Learning Goals

- The ability to classify information in the subject area
- The ability to think holistically: to see the whole as well as the parts
- The ability to synthesize disparate but related information into a whole
- The ability to connect a concept to other concepts within this course

Implementation

Preparation

- Choose what kinds of assignments will be used in the Class Book and develop guidelines or rules for submission that specify topics, format, length, style guidelines, and quality expectations.
- Decide on the scope and quality of the final product (for example, simple stapled copies or a more elaborate, bound document using desktop publishing software) and whether or not you will be producing it yourself or assigning production to students.
- Determine a production schedule that is late enough in the term that students have time to complete their papers yet also provides sufficient time to produce the Class Book.
- Consider whether you want any intervening submissions, like a project proposal or a rough draft.
- Develop a rubric by which you will assess the individual contributions. You might consider categories like the following:
  - Topic/content
  - Organization
  - Logic/argumentation
  - Support of ideas/use of evidence
  - Written expression (style, diction, grammar)
- Consider developing a second rubric by which you will assess the full book. You might consider categories like the following:
  - Clarity of central theme
  - Coverage of central content and concepts
  - Links between ideas in papers
  - Quality of individual contributions
  - Appropriate formatting
- Consider having students develop a Class Memoir that is included as the preface or introduction to the book. This memoir can be an effective activity to encourage students to reflect on their learning experiences, build class community, and offer advice to subsequent students on how to learn the most and be successful in the course.
- Create a handout that provides assignment instructions, along with the rubric(s).
- Consider who will be involved in the review. Peer review, in which peers exchange papers and give each other feedback, is a very useful approach for this LAT. Students may self-assess as well, for example, by writing a few paragraphs that comment or explain the submission (for instance, the challenges they faced and overcame as they created the work, analysis and interpretation of the work, how much time and effort they put into the work, and so forth). Moreover, having an external reader/evaluator can provide additional insight and give the LAT a feeling of authenticity.

Process

1. Announce the assignment and distribute the handout. Emphasize that intellectual excellence is the criterion for inclusion in the book and that the goal is to produce a book containing high quality work, not just a "pretty book."

2. Allow time to answer student questions.

3. Provide students with time to brainstorm ideas.

4. Provide students with time to present their planned topics to each other, so that all students know what everyone is working on. This step allows students to avoid duplicating topics and to create unique contributions to the final book.

5. Provide students with sufficient time to complete their papers and any intervening assignments.

6. Collect the final papers and bind them yourself, or alternately have students bind them and submit the final manuscript.

Online

There are many ways to implement this LAT in an online course. One of the simplest ways is to have students submit their assignments as portable document files (PDFs) and create a list of links on a web page or forum. Students can also create a more sophisticated e-book publication, if they (or you) have sufficient knowledge about how to do so.

Analysis and Reporting

Analyze each individual contribution according to your predetermined criteria or rubric(s), and then analyze the Class Book according to your predetermined criteria or rubric(s). Consider a holistic analysis of the book as well as the rubric scoring. Report back to individuals about their own contributions and about the overarching book by sharing your rubric assessment with them. You may also wish to provide some written comments about the overall quality of both documents. This assignment is well suited for grading. Consider assigning a percentage to individual work as well as to the full group product, particularly if you have used peer review or other group assignments along the way. Doing so can promote individual achievement but also interdependence. Consider a larger portion to the individual grade (e.g., a 90/10% split or an 80/20% split, depending on student comfort level in working with each other as a group).

Use your rubric categories to examine student achievement. You may find for example that everyone selected important and relevant topics and that their ideas were well organized, or you may find that a significant number of students did not demonstrate the ability to support their ideas through details and examples or alternately that many suffered from problems with written expression. Consider also a thematic analysis of the documents, or pointing out what students demonstrated that they know and do well and where they might improve. Offer suggestions for how you might address weaknesses in the future.

Create a numeric or narrative table to convey overall strengths and weaknesses across individual papers. You can do this by sharing the average rubric scores for each item. Consider a qualitative data display to illustrate the key themes that cross student papers such as a network or a modified Venn diagram if the topics and themes are closely related.

Examples

Onsite: Composition, Critical Reading and Thinking

The professor of this course incorporates collaborative activities extensively in order to help students at this commuter college feel part of a community and because he believes it is the best pedagogical approach for his learning goals. The course has a learning outcome as follows: students will be able to demonstrate expository and argumentative writing based on critical reading and thinking about nonfiction texts. To motivate and challenge students to do their "personal best," the professor informs students on the first day of the term that two weeks before the semester ends, they will select what they consider to be their best essay for publication in a class compilation called *Showcase.* He explains that *Showcase* will provide them with a keepsake to remind them of their course experience, and it will give future students as well as the English Department assessment committee models of exemplary work. He asks for volunteers to serve on the production committee who, for extra credit, will be responsible for organizing, editing, and printing the compilation. He also has students complete a peer review assignment, in which each student reviews and rates two other students' submissions prior to the final paper.

Although the first time he implemented the assignment the students produced a simple, spiral-bound document, students in subsequent classes were motivated to outshine the previous classes and used desktop publishing software to produce high-quality, hard-cover editions that included a preface and photographs with short bios of the students. The cumulative *Showcase* editions are displayed in the English Department office.

The professor reviews each individual contribution each semester and assesses it based upon a rubric that he developed for the assignment and that he shares with students prior to their contributions (Table 9.22). He provides each student with a review of their contributions, which he scores by the rubric, along with handwritten notes on what they have done well and what they can do to improve their writing in the future. The professor also reviews the entire book, in a formal written book review, and he shares that document with the students (Table 9.23). Finally, he keeps track of what students have done well and poorly on in the aggregate so that he can use that information to improve his courses in the future (Table 9.24).

Table 9.22 Rubric for Individual Papers

	Excellent	Great	Average/ Acceptable	Needs Some Improvement	Needs Major Improvement
Topic/content	5	4	3	2	1
Organization	5	4	3	2	1
Logic/ argumentation	5	4	3	2	1
Support of ideas	5	4	3	2	1
Written expression	5	4	3	2	1

Table 9.23 Rubric for Complete Book

	Excellent	Great	Average/ Acceptable	Needs Some Improvement	Needs Major Improvement
Clarity of central theme	5	4	3	2	1
Coverage of central content and concepts	5	4	3	2	1
Links between ideas in papers	5	4	3	2	1
Quality of individual contributions	5	4	3	2	1
Appropriate formatting	5	4	3	2	1

Table 9.24 Aggregate scores for individual rubrics

Categories	Average Score
Topic/content	3.5
Organization	3
Logic/argumentation	2.5
Support of ideas	2.5
Written expression	3

 ### Online: History of American Higher Education

In this course, the professor has a learning goal stating that within the context of national history of higher education, students should understand the history of their own local institution. She is concerned that students in the online section of the course do not engage with each other sufficiently, and she therefore decides to assign a Class Book, believing that this assignment helps students connect to each other through research and writing.

In the articles and videos provided in the various learning modules, students learn about key time periods and key themes in the emergence and development of higher education in America. Each week, students blog about their own institutions' history during the specified time period, using archival information available in the historical collections library for additional evidence and correlating local and national key themes.

As a final product, students select their best blog post and revise it for inclusion in the Class Book. They also work together to make sure that the book has essays for each period and that the key themes are adequately represented in the final product. The class creates the book in Google Drive, by uploading their own papers. They are also responsible for reviewing two of their peers' papers. Finally, they are responsible for creating an introduction that documents connections across papers.

The professor reviews each individual paper with a rubric for content, writing, and effort. She makes note of trends in the information she sees across the papers. She also reviews the full work, assigning 25% of the final grade for the group product. She creates a network from the introduction that students develop, documenting the connections between their papers (Figure 9.7).

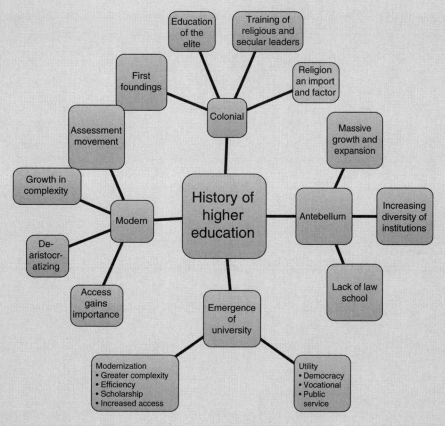

Figure 9.7 Network Displaying Student Connections in History of Education

Variations and Extensions

- This LAT is well-suited to courses in the visual and performing arts, with students submitting film clips, images, or music compositions that are compiled instead of or in addition to narrative.
- Students may work on their individual papers together, as co-authored works. The benefit of such an approach is that they learn to work and write collaboratively. This provides you with a picture of jointly held knowledge, rather than the knowledge of just an individual.
- Instead of a hard copy Class Book, create a magazine, with each class creating the next edition of the online publication. Students may do this online, in a form sometimes referred to as a zine, Ezine, Webzine, or Cyberzine. There are several software packages that

streamline the production process for online magazines that can be located by using a simple search with words such as "ezine publishing."

Key References and Resources

Barkley, E. F. (2010). SET 21: Class book. In *Student engagement techniques: A handbook for college faculty* (pp. 243–245). San Francisco, CA: Jossey-Bass.

LEARNING ASSESSMENT TECHNIQUE

Integration

29
E-Portfolios

Complexity involved in	
Preparation	MODERATE
In-class implementation	MODERATE
Analysis	HIGH

Brief Description

Students assemble examples of work that they have created throughout the semester during various assignments, and they supplement this digitized collection of examples with commentary about their significance.

Purpose

This LAT challenges students to synthesize their course work and to be creative as they generate ways to best represent and display their learning. In addition, the technique requires students to draft and carry out a workable plan while giving them a chance to take risks and judge their own work.

The Learning Artifacts, which are the E-Portfolios themselves, give teachers the opportunity to assess student knowledge and understanding as well as the degree to which a student can synthesize and communicate that information. E-Portfolios provide teachers and students with an alternative to conventional written reports. They provide not only evidence of student learning but also evidence of student ability to self-assess, to judge what is their best work. They can enhance critical thinking skills as well as technological literacy and multimedia communication skills. Finally, this technique provides an opportunity to see students' ability to reflect upon the learning process.

The technique requires selection of and reflection upon prior work. Because of this, it typically is done as a post-instruction summative assessment work to assess student performance over time. It may even be a capstone or final project to represent work done over an academic term.

Key Learning Goals

- The ability to think holistically: to see the whole as well as the parts
- The ability to synthesize disparate but related information into a whole
- The ability to connect a concept to other concepts within a course

Implementation

Preparation

- Determine the central purpose of the E-Portfolio. E-Portfolios may have several different goals, so it is important to you and to students to be clear about what you want to have them document. You might consider the following options:
  - To document growth. In these E-Portfolios, students demonstrate where they started the semester and where they ended up, showing change in learning over time.
  - To showcase best work. These E-Portfolios provide students with the opportunity to document their best work, which may have relevance to their future plans, for example, admission to graduate school or gaining employment.
  - To document learning achievement. These E-Portfolios require students to demonstrate that they have met certain benchmark criteria.
- Establish the parameters for the assignment, including
  - What materials/artifacts students should include in the E-Portfolio
  - How students should organize the information
  - What form the reflections should take
- Construct a rubric to evaluate the E-Portfolio. Keep the above goal in mind (such as documenting growth), use your course outcomes as the basis for the items, and create a scale (such as very high levels of growth to very low levels, very strong product to very weak product, or very high to very low achievement).
- Determine who will be involved in E-Portfolio assessment. You may want to involve faculty colleagues. Peer evaluation can be a useful addition. Moreover, you will likely include a self-evaluation as part of the process.
- Create a handout for the students explaining the guidelines and including the evaluation rubric.

Process

1. Announce the activity and the parameters, including the goal of the E-Portfolio. Respond to any questions students might have about the assignment.
2. Ask students to collect meaningful artifacts that represent their learning in the course.
3. Ask students to reflect upon their choices, whether through an annotation, a reflective essay, or other.
4. Allow time for students to share their E-Portfolios with the class.
5. Collect the Learning Artifacts: The finished E-Portfolios.

Online

Whether teaching onsite or online, many instructors today choose to have students create their E-Portfolios online. They typically do so through a blog or a website, but some institutions have their own software that can serve the purpose (such as Live Text). These E-Portfolios create a durable product that students can keep and share easily.

Analysis and Reporting

Because of the complexity of the assignment and the amount of time that students must typically expend in creating an E-Portfolio, these assignments typically are graded. They also typically are afforded a fair amount of the percentage of the final grade. Teachers range in how many percentage points they allocate, and the spread is anywhere from 20 to 100%. Use your rubric to evaluate the E-Portfolio and also look for anything unique in the individual responses. Report the results from your rubric assessment along with your narrative comments to individuals.

Use your rubric and aggregate results, tallying the number of responses for each item and determining a mean score. Look across the comments that you wrote to notice any patterns in the information. For your item analysis on individual, consider a bar graph or a table to illustrate percentages correct or incorrect. To report any outstanding features of E-Portfolios, best or worst cases, consider using a narrative table.

Examples

Onsite: Introduction to Biology

This biology course has been identified as one the department will use to collect evidence of student achievement of learning outcomes for an upcoming accreditation review. The professors of the various sections met to identify learning outcomes, describe methods of teaching those outcomes, illustrate student achievement of those outcomes, and describe plans for using data collected during the assessment to improve the course in the future.

The professors of the course identified several foundational knowledge learning goals, including understanding in the following areas: (1) scientific processes, (2) characteristics of life, (3) cell selection, (4) genetics selection, (5) evolution, and (6) ecology. They also identified the outcome that students would be able to integrate the information that they gained with information that they use in their daily lives. They decided to use E-Portfolios to help students achieve the goal of integration of information and to document that they had done so.

For their E-Portfolios, students had to demonstrate their learning achievement in each of the six key areas of foundational knowledge. They could include evidence from their previous assignments, including class work such as worksheets, lab reports, notes from lectures or discussions, graded quizzes, or other. They were also instructed to write a personal reflection on how the evidence demonstrated their knowledge (focusing on what they learned, how it can be applied in their everyday lives, why they chose the items they included, and what they represent). A final component was a letter to future biology students describing what they will learn about and what they should expect in the class, combined with advice on how to be successful in the course.

Table 9.25 Average Scores

Topic	Mean Score
Scientific processes	3.89
Characteristics of life	3.75
Cell selection	2.72
Genetics selection	2.82
Evolution	3.12
Ecology	3.53

The professors used a rubric to assess the E-Portfolios. They each scored all students across the different categories. They had a strong inter-rater reliability (they generally agreed upon their assessments, and when they disagreed, they discussed why and came to a resolution). They identified the averages shown in Table 9.25.

They noted that students seemed to perform at a higher level on three of the categories (scientific processes, characteristics of life, and ecology) than they did on three others (cell selection, genetics selection, and evolution) and believed it was possibly due to the more technical nature of the topics and determined that they should provide additional instruction in those areas.

They also reviewed student letters to determine how well they communicated what they had learned to other students. They focused on their synthesis of the key concepts they had learned. They rated the responses for insights and accuracy. They found that students did a better job of sharing their learning with others than they often demonstrated on factual tests of knowledge. These findings supported what they had learned from assessment of their foundational knowledge. They were heartened that students were getting the big ideas, but they knew that they had to focus more on the details so that students had sufficient knowledge in the following courses (Table 9.26).

Table 9.26 Assessment Matrix: E-Portfolios

Student Learning Outcomes	LAT	Findings and Interpretations	Actions to Be Taken
Describe (1) scientific processes, (2) characteristics of life, (3) cell selection, (4) genetics selection, (5) evolution, and (6) ecology. Integrate the scientific information into your daily lives.	E-Portfolios	Students demonstrated the lowest levels of understanding of cell selection and genetics selection, followed by evolution. They understood big picture themes and issues but need additional work on technical details.	Additional readings, lectures, and activities on cell selection, genetics, and to a lesser degree evolution. Add quizzes to assess knowledge immediately after lessons.

Online: Introduction to the History of Art II

The professor in this class is concerned that students simply memorize information in order to pass the course exams. She wants them to be able to integrate information about historical events that occurred during the same time, however, so that they can understand that art informs life and vice versa. In this class, the professor has three overarching learning goals: to help students to (1) understand a chronological account of the history of art for that era; (2) understand historic events associated with the period; and (3) communicate what they have learned through their historic studies to people in their everyday lives. She decided to implement E-Portfolios in order to help students achieve this goal and to help her assess their relative levels of achievement. She decided to have students create E-Portfolios to practice these skills and to provide her with an assessable artifact.

She uses several different assignments throughout the term to help students learn about the various periods and their representative artists. She uses for example "Hate It," an assignment in which students describe a work that they hate and why they hate it; "Love It," in which students describe a work they love and why they love it; and "In the Wild," where they report on a real-world encounter from a work of the period, all of which they post in a discussion forum and respond to each other's posts. She also has them write three historical events papers and complete an essay-format exam that links the events and the various art periods. They may use any of this information in the E-Portfolios.

She did a quick assessment of the different periods students related, scoring a simple +/− for whether they represented characteristics, artists, and historical events. She found that students were proficient in the different periods. They also did well on the more recent periods of Abstract Expressionism, Postmodernism, and Deconstructivism. In both the older and the newer periods, they documented knowledge of historical events better than they demonstrated their knowledge on tests. She created a simple table to show the results (Table 9.27).

Table 9.27 Table of Student References to Multiple Art History Periods in E-Portfolios

Period	Characteristics	Artists	Historical Events
Realism	19/20+	19/20+	18/20+
Impressionism	19/20+	19/20+	18/20+
Postimpressionism	19/20+	18/20+	19/20+
Expressionism	18/20+	19/20+	18/20+
Constructivism	17/20+	18/20+	17/20+
Surrealism	18/20+	19/20+	19/20+
Abstract Expressionism	19/20+	19/20+	18/20+
Postmodernism	18/20+	19/20+	18/20+
Deconstructivism	17/20+	18/20+	17/20+

Variations and Extensions

- If you are in a creative field, have students use creative work in their E-Portfolios, which you may want to call "exhibitions" in this instance. In art, they might use paintings as evidence of having achieved learning goals; in music, they might include recorded samples of their own work; in dance, they might include videos of themselves in action.
- Students in professional fields can include artifacts that demonstrate achievement of learning goals they will need to master in their professions. Education students might create teaching or course E-Portfolios, which sample their teaching whether in their own classes, as student teachers, or as teaching assistants. Computer science students might include samples of their coding or databases.

Key References and Resources

Lorenzo, G., & Ittelson, J. (2005). Overview of e-portfolios. Educause Learning Initiative. https://net.educause.edu/ir/library/pdf/eli3001.pdf.

Zubizarreta, J. (2004). *The learning portfolio: Reflective practice for improving student learning*. Boston, MA: Anker Publishing.

Zubizarreta, J. (2008). The learning portfolio: A powerful idea for significant learning. IDEA Paper # 44. http://ideaedu.org/sites/default/files/IDEA_Paper_44.pdf.

CHAPTER 10

Teaching and Assessing for the Human Dimension Domain

Know thyself" is an aphorism deeply embedded in our education tradition. When Plato, the founder of the first institution of higher learning in the Western world, had Socrates use the adage to stimulate his dialogues, he was already referencing long-established wisdom. Knowing who we are is an essential life skill. It helps us navigate through life consciously instead of wasting time reacting randomly to the situations in which we find ourselves, often repeating destructive patterns in a cycle that leaves us confused and frustrated. Self-knowledge leads to a more sharply focused sense of what we want, which in turn guides us in setting goals, determining the best course of action to achieve them, and then sustaining the motivation to be persistent even when there are setbacks. Students who know themselves and what they want are better poised to make decisions that result in a meaningful, satisfying, and successful education.

The quest for self-knowledge is counter-balanced by a basic human desire to understand and interact with others. Many educators recognize this goal as increasingly important in today's diverse but interconnected global society. Ignorance and stereotyping create mistrust, conflict, and the inability to gain consensus. Exposing students to multiple perspectives and helping them appreciate different viewpoints provides them with transferable skills requisite for success in the current collaborative international culture. Jacobs and Hyman (2009), for example, point to the power of education to liberate students from ethno- and egocentric tunnel vision and note that by guiding students to learn about others in the world, learners also gain a more complete view of their own place in it. Lao-Tzu, who probably preceded Plato by at least a century, combines both self-knowledge and the understanding of others in his saying, "He who knows others is wise; he who knows himself is enlightened." Attending to the human dimension of the Significant Learning Taxonomy means that we are accomplishing both of these objectives: we are helping students learn about themselves and others.

Clarifying Learning Goals Related to the Human Dimension Domain

Observing that college students frequently report that learning about themselves and others is among their most significant educational experiences, Fink added the "human dimension" of learning as the fourth level of his taxonomy. The "human dimension" component addresses the

Table 10.1 Goleman's Model of Emotional Intelligence

Personal Competence	Social Competence
Self-Awareness: The ability to recognize and understand one's own emotions, preferences, strengths and weaknesses, drives, values, and goals, as well as their impact on others.	Empathy: Recognizing, understanding, and considering the feelings, needs, and concerns of others.
Self-Regulation: Being able to manage or redirect one's emotions and impulses and adapt them to changing circumstances.	Social Skills: Adeptness at managing other's emotions and inducing them to move in the desired direction.
Motivation: The emotional tendencies that guide or facilitate our drives to achieve.	

Sources: Fink (2013), p. 53; Learning Theories.com (http://www.learning-theories.com/emotional-intelligence-goleman.html)

"important relationships and interactions we all have with ourselves and with others" (Fink, 2013, p. 50). He points out that the human dimension of learning is similar to Goleman's concept of emotional intelligence (1995, 1998). In Goleman's model, emotional intelligence is divided into five components organized under two broad categories: personal competence and social competence, as displayed in Table 10.1.

Attending to the human dimension in our teaching efforts involves designing activities that help learners learn about themselves or that enable them to better understand and interact with other people.

Two broad questions guide us in formulating learning objectives and outcomes related to the human dimension:

- What can or should students learn about themselves as individuals functioning within a social world?
- What can or should students learn about interacting with people they encounter now or in the future?

Once we have identified the answers to those questions, students can be guided toward those goals through a variety of learning activities.

Identifying Learning Outcomes for Human Dimension Learning

In Table 10.2, we offer examples of learning processes and outcomes for human dimension learning.

Aligning Course Level Human Dimension Learning Outcomes with Institutional Learning Goals

Institutional learning goals related to the human dimension of the Significant Learning Taxonomy are often reflected in core competency graduation requirements. Frequently these requirements address multiculturalism, civic responsibility, international cultural awareness and sensitivity, citizenship, and social justice. From another perspective, institutions address this

Table 10.2 Examples of Learning Processes and Outcomes for Human Dimension Learning

General Definition: The learner acquires increased self-knowledge and understanding of others.			
Learner Process	**Additional Terms**	**Definition**	**Sample Course Learning Outcome** **By the end of this course, successful learners will . . .**
Personal Dimension (Self)	Acts, discriminates, displays, influences	Self-awareness and self-regulation	. . . recognize their beliefs and values. . . . recognize ethical decisions embedded in what they do or face in a variety of settings. . . . develop confidence in their ability to _____ .
Social Dimension (Others)	Listens, modifies, revises, influences	Recognition of how and why others act the way they do or how the learner can interact more effectively with others	. . . be able to interact effectively with people different from themselves. . . . be able to identify ways in which one's personal life affects and is affected by interactions with other world religions. . . . be able to describe/identify the possible human motivations behind world events with insight and understanding.

Sources: Fink (2013); Krathwohl (1999)

dimension in stating the importance of ethics, students' learning to collaborate effectively, and developing leadership skills. Table 10.3 provides examples of institution level learning goals that address the human dimension of the Significant Learning Taxonomy.

Assessing Achievement of Learning Regarding the Human Dimension Domain

The human dimension offers its own challenges in relation to assessment. How do you assess students' beliefs and values? How do you assess their interactions with others? These questions

Table 10.3 Examples of Institution Level Learning Goals in the Human Dimension Domain

Learning Goals in the Human Dimension Domain	
Institution	A core mission of this institution is to ensure that graduates have acquired the civic capacity for global, cultural, and social justice. Students will recognize their role as local, national, and global citizens. They will participate in the democratic process, respect social and cultural diversity, appreciate the complexity of the world, and understand the significance of social justice.
Institution	All students graduating from this institution will demonstrate competency in mental wellness and personal responsibility. Students will recognize lifestyles that promote mental well-being and engage in self-reflection and ethical decision making.
General Education	All undergraduates are required to take and pass a course in American Cultures, which is a class that has been approved by the Senate as effectively introducing students to the diverse cultures of the United States through a comparative framework.

Sources: Multiple

are difficult, and point to the need to "assess" rather than "judge" or evaluate. In other words, you can sum up students' perspectives without rendering a judgment on them. That said, we also recognize that in some disciplines and fields, helping students develop certain values and dispositions is a critical component of the work.

We suggest that in assessing this dimension, teachers should look for students' commitment to values, empathy and respect, skills working with others, and so forth. Thus the LATs we have selected for inclusion in this section reflect those areas. They set forth conditions in which students demonstrate their abilities to understand themselves and others and to interact with others in real-world situations. Exhibits 10.1 and 10.2 offer two rubrics that assess different aspects of the human dimension domain.

Conclusion

Helping students learn about themselves is an important goal if we want to promote significant learning. Guiding students to examine their interior states in detail and in depth increases their insights into the way they think, feel, and behave. If students do not learn to know themselves— their values, their strengths and weaknesses, and what they want in their lives — their educational experiences will be superficial. Similarly important is helping students learn about others. As learners are exposed to different experiences, beliefs, and viewpoints, they are given the opportunity to acquire a more panoramic perspective of the world and enhance their repertoire of constructive responses. In short, attending to the human dimension of the Significant Learning Taxonomy enables the students in our classes to function and interact more effectively not only in learning, but in life.

Exhibit 10.1 Assessing Teamwork Using the AAC&U Teamwork VALUE Rubric

Definition

Teamwork is behaviors under the control of individual team members (effort they put into team tasks, their manner of interacting with others on team, and the quantity and quality of contributions they make to team discussions).

Framing Language

Students participate on many different teams, in many different settings. For example, a given student may work on separate teams to complete a lab assignment, give an oral presentation, or complete a community service project. Furthermore, the people the student works with are likely to be different in each of these different teams. As a result, it is assumed that a work sample or collection of work that demonstrates a student's teamwork skills could include a diverse range of inputs. This rubric is designed to function across all of these different settings.

Two characteristics define the ways in which this rubric is to be used. First, the rubric is meant to assess the teamwork of an individual student, not the team as a whole. Therefore, it is possible for a student to receive high ratings, even if the team as a whole is rather flawed. Similarly, a student could receive low ratings, even if the team as a whole works fairly well. Second, this rubric is designed to measure the quality of a process, rather than the quality of an end product. As a result, work samples or collections of work will need to include some evidence of the individual's interactions within the team. The final product of the team's work (e.g., a written lab report) is insufficient, as it does not provide insight into the functioning of the team.

It is recommended that work samples or collections of work for this outcome come from one (or more) of the following three sources: (1) students' own reflections about their contribution to a team's functioning; (2) evaluation or feedback from fellow team members about students' contribution to the team's functioning; or (3) the evaluation of an outside observer regarding students' contributions to a team's functioning. These three sources differ considerably in the resource demands they place on an institution. It is recommended that institutions using this rubric consider carefully the resources they are able to allocate to the assessment of teamwork and choose a means of compiling work samples or collections of work that best suit their priorities, needs, and abilities.

Table 10.4 Assessing Teamwork Rubric

	Capstone 4	Milestone 3, 2	Benchmark 1
Contributes to Team Meetings	Helps the team move forward by articulating the merits of alternative ideas or proposals.	Offers alternative solutions or courses of action that build on the ideas of others.	Offers new suggestions to advance the work of the group.	Shares ideas but does not advance the work of the group.
Facilitates the Contributions of Team Members	Engages team members in ways that facilitate their contributions to meetings by both constructively building upon or synthesizing the contributions of others as well as noticing when someone is not participating and inviting them to engage.	Engages team members in ways that facilitate their contributions to meetings by constructively building upon or synthesizing the contributions of others.	Engages team members in ways that facilitate their contributions to meetings by restating the views of other team members and/or asking questions for clarification.	Engages team members by taking turns and listening to others without interrupting.
Individual Contributions Outside of Team Meetings	Completes all assigned tasks by deadline; work accomplished is thorough, comprehensive, and advances the project. Proactively helps other team members complete their assigned tasks to a similar level of excellence.	Completes all assigned tasks by deadline; work accomplished is thorough, comprehensive, and advances the project.	Completes all assigned tasks by deadline; work accomplished advances the project.	Completes all assigned tasks by deadline.
Fosters Constructive Team Climate	Supports a constructive team climate by doing all of the following: • Treats team members respectfully by being polite and constructive in communication. • Uses positive vocal or written tone, facial expressions, and/or body language to convey a positive attitude about the team and its work. • Motivates teammates by expressing confidence about the importance of the task and the team's ability to accomplish it.	Supports a constructive team climate by doing any three of the following: • Treats team members respectfully by being polite and constructive in communication. • Uses positive vocal or written tone, facial expressions, and/or body language to convey a positive attitude about the team and its work. • Motivates teammates by expressing confidence about the importance of the task and	Supports a constructive team climate by doing any two of the following: • Treats team members respectfully by being polite and constructive in communication. • Uses positive vocal or written tone, facial expressions, and/or body language to convey a positive attitude about the team and its work. • Motivates teammates by expressing confidence about the importance of the task and the team's ability to accomplish it.	Supports a constructive team climate by doing any one of the following: • Treats team members respectfully by being polite and constructive in communication. • Uses positive vocal or written tone, facial expressions, and/or body language to convey a positive attitude about the team and its work.

• Motivates teammates by expressing confidence about the importance of the task and the team's ability to accomplish it. • Provides assistance and/or encouragement to team members.	• Provides assistance and/or encouragement to team members.	the team's ability to accomplish it. • Provides assistance and/or encouragement to team members.	• Provides assistance and/or encouragement to team members.
Passively accepts alternate viewpoints/ideas/opinions.	Redirects focus toward common ground, toward task at hand (away from conflict).	Identifies and acknowledges conflict and stays engaged with it.	Addresses destructive conflict directly and constructively, helping to manage/resolve it in a way that strengthens overall team cohesiveness and future effectiveness.

Responds to Conflict

Reprinted with permissions from VALUE: Valid Assessment of Learning in Undergraduate Education. Copyright 2015 by the Association of American Colleges and Universities. http://www.aacu.org/value/rubrics

Exhibit 10.2 Assessing Learning in the Human Dimension Domain Using the AAC&U Intercultural Knowledge and Competence VALUE Rubric

Definition

Intercultural Knowledge and Competence is "a set of cognitive, affective, and behavioral skills and characteristics that support effective and appropriate interaction in a variety of cultural contexts."

Framing Language

The call to integrate intercultural knowledge and competence into the heart of education is an imperative born of seeing ourselves as members of a world community, knowing that we share the future with others. Beyond mere exposure to culturally different others, the campus community requires the capacity to meaningfully engage those others, place social justice in historical and political context, and put culture at the core of transformative learning. The intercultural knowledge and competence rubric suggests a systematic way to measure our capacity to identify our own cultural patterns, compare and contrast them with others, and adapt empathically and flexibly to unfamiliar ways of being. The levels of this rubric are informed in part by M. Bennett's Developmental Model of Intercultural Sensitivity (Bennett, 1993). In addition, the criteria in this rubric are informed in part by D. K. Deardorff's intercultural framework, which is the first research-based consensus model of intercultural competence (Deardorff, 2006). It is also important to understand that intercultural knowledge and competence is more complex than what is reflected in this rubric. This rubric identifies six of the key components of intercultural knowledge and competence, but there are other components as identified in the Deardorff model and in other research.

Glossary

The definitions that follow were developed to clarify terms and concepts used in this rubric only.

* *Culture*: All knowledge and values shared by a group.
* *Cultural rules and biases*: Boundaries within which an individual operates in order to feel a sense of belonging to a society or group, based on the values shared by that society or group.
* *Empathy*: "Empathy is the imaginary participation in another person's experience, including emotional and intellectual dimensions, by imagining his or her perspective (not by assuming the person's position)" (Bennett, 1998).
* *Intercultural experience*: The experience of an interaction with an individual or groups of people whose culture is different from your own.
* *Intercultural/cultural differences*: The differences in rules, behaviors, communication, and biases, based on cultural values that are different from one's own culture.
* *Suspends judgment in valuing their interactions with culturally different others*: Postpones assessment or evaluation (positive or negative) of interactions with people culturally different from oneself. Disconnecting from the process of automatic judgment and taking time to reflect on possibly multiple meanings.
* *Worldview*: Worldview is the cognitive and affective lens through which people construe their experiences and make sense of the world around them.

Source: Bennett, J. M. (2008). Transformative training: Designing programs for culture learning. In *Contemporary leadership and intercultural competence: Understanding and utilizing cultural diversity to build successful organizations*, ed. M. A. Moodian, 95–110. Thousand Oaks, CA: Sage.

Table 10.5 Assessing Learning in the Human Dimension Domain Rubric

	Capstone 4	Milestone 3, 2	Benchmark 1
Knowledge Cultural self-awareness	Articulates insights into own cultural rules and biases (e.g., seeking complexity; aware of how her/his experiences have shaped these rules, and how to recognize and respond to cultural biases, resulting in a shift in self-description).	Recognizes new perspectives about own cultural rules and biases (e.g. not looking for sameness; comfortable with the complexities that new perspectives offer).	Identifies own cultural rules and biases (e.g. with a strong preference for those rules shared with own cultural group and seeks the same in others).	Shows minimal awareness of own cultural rules and biases (even those shared with own cultural group(s)) (e.g. uncomfortable with identifying possible cultural differences with others).
Knowledge Knowledge of cultural worldview frameworks	Demonstrates sophisticated understanding of the complexity of elements important to members of another culture in relation to its history, values, politics, communication styles, economy, or beliefs and practices.	Demonstrates adequate understanding of the complexity of elements important to members of another culture in relation to its history, values, politics, communication styles, economy, or beliefs and practices.	Demonstrates partial understanding of the complexity of elements important to members of another culture in relation to its history, values, politics, communication styles, economy, or beliefs and practices.	Demonstrates surface understanding of the complexity of elements important to members of another culture in relation to its history, values, politics, communication styles, economy, or beliefs and practices.
Skills Empathy	Interprets intercultural experience from the perspectives of own and more than one worldview and demonstrates ability to act in a supportive manner that recognizes the feelings of another cultural group.	Recognizes intellectual and emotional dimensions of more than one worldview and sometimes uses more than one worldview in interactions.	Identifies components of other cultural perspectives but responds in all situations with own worldview.	Views the experience of others but does so through own cultural worldview.
Skills Verbal and nonverbal communication	Articulates a complex understanding of cultural differences in verbal and nonverbal communication (e.g., demonstrates understanding of the degree to which people use physical contact while	Recognizes and participates in cultural differences in verbal and nonverbal communication and begins to negotiate a shared understanding based on those differences.	Identifies some cultural differences in verbal and nonverbal communication and is aware that misunderstandings can occur based on those differences but is still unable to negotiate a shared understanding.	Has a minimal level of understanding of cultural differences in verbal and nonverbal communication; is unable to negotiate a shared understanding.

(continued)

Table 10.5 (*Continued*)

	Capstone 4	Milestone 3, 2	Benchmark 1
	communicating in different cultures or use direct/indirect and explicit/implicit meanings) and is able to skillfully negotiate a shared understanding based on those differences.		
Attitudes Curiosity	Asks complex questions about other cultures, seeks out and articulates answers to these questions that reflect multiple cultural perspectives.	Asks deeper questions about other cultures and seeks out answers to these questions.	Asks simple or surface questions about other cultures.
Attitudes Openness	Initiates and develops interactions with culturally different others. Suspends judgment in valuing her/his interactions with culturally different others.	Begins to initiate and develop interactions with culturally different others. Begins to suspend judgment in valuing her/his interactions with culturally different others.	Expresses openness to most, if not all, interactions with culturally different others. Has difficulty suspending any judgment in her/his interactions with culturally different others, and is aware of own judgment and expresses a willingness to change.	Receptive to interacting with culturally different others. Has difficulty suspending any judgment in her/his interactions with culturally different others, but is unaware of own judgment.	States minimal interest in learning more about other cultures.

Reprinted with permissions from VALUE: Valid Assessment of Learning in Undergraduate Education. Copyright 2015 by the Association of American Colleges and Universities. http://www.aacu.org/value/rubrics

LEARNING ASSESSMENT TECHNIQUE

Human Dimension

30
Free Discussion

Complexity involved in	
Preparation	LOW
In-class implementation	MODERATE
Analysis	MODERATE

Brief Description

Small groups of students form quickly and extemporaneously to respond to course-related questions. Their discussion is an informal exchange of ideas, and students are assessed on their ability to participate effectively.

Purpose

Free Discussions are effective for generating information and ideas in a short time. By dividing the whole class into small groups, more students have the opportunity to express their thoughts. Because students have had a chance to practice their comments and to increase their repertoire of ideas in the Free Discussion, the whole class discussion that follows is often richer and more participatory.

The Learning Artifacts are your records of student interactions and may include rubric scoring or video recording. While "discussion" does not often appear on lists of assessment techniques, there is hardly one better for assessing competence and learning in the Human Dimension because of the importance of and focus on interpersonal and intrapersonal competence. Discussion is one of the best ways to promote development of these skills and for that to happen in a natural context that the instructor can observe. Finally, and critically for learning in the Human Dimension, Free Discussion provides teachers with an opportunity to assess how well students interact with each other and make meaning and construct knowledge together. Free Discussions may be done at the beginning of a learning module to gain a sense of what students know and do not know about a topic already, as well as to gauge their opinions of the issues surrounding it. This technique is also useful to be done "in the moment" of teaching to get a reading on how well students are understanding and are able to communicate course content.

Key Learning Goals

- Empathy for others
- Respect for others
- Interpersonal skills
- The ability to work productively with others
- Self-confidence
- Students' capacity to think for themselves

Implementation

Preparation

- Prior to class, decide what content or ideas the groups will discuss.
- Craft one or more engaging discussion prompts that tend toward the conceptual rather than factual and that will stimulate an open-ended examination of ideas. Try responding to the question(s) yourself so that you are confident that they will generate a variety of responses.
- Choose the manner in which you are going to present the prompt question(s), such as on a worksheet, presentation slide, or whiteboard.
- Choose the type of Learning Artifact you would like to retain. Some instructors ask groups to come up with a short summary of their interactions. Others have students report verbally and take their own notes.
- Create a rubric for your scoring, and potentially for self- and peer evaluations. We offer a sample self-evaluation rubric in Table 10.6 (adapted from Edutopia).

Table 10.6 Discussion Rubric Self-Evaluation

	Exceeds Expectations 4	Meets Expectations 3	Approaches Expectations 2	Needs Improvement 1
Preparation	I came *fully* prepared to the discussion. I completed the assigned readings *carefully* and crafted thoughtful questions.	I came prepared to the discussion. I completed all of the reading and developed questions.	I came *somewhat* prepared to our discussion. This means that I completed most of the reading and that I developed some questions.	I was not prepared for today's discussion because I did not focus on the reading or write questions in advance.
Listening	I listened carefully and respectfully to my classmates *all* of the time.	I listened carefully and respectfully to my classmates *most* of the time.	I listened carefully and respectfully to my classmates *some* of the time.	I spaced out a lot during our discussion and/or interrupted the speaker.
Speaking	I contributed *several* meaningful comments to the whole group discussion based on evidence from the text, without dominating the discussion.	I contributed *some* meaningful comments to the whole group discussion based on evidence from the text, without dominating the discussion.	I contributed *one* meaningful comment to the whole group discussion based on evidence from the text, without dominating the discussion.	I did not contribute to the group discussion *at all* or alternately I dominated the discussion.

Table 10.6 (*Continued*)

	Exceeds Expectations 4	Meets Expectations 3	Approaches Expectations 2	Needs Improvement 1
Depth of Thought	All of my questions and comments showed deep understanding and original, profound thought.	Some of my questions and comments showed deep understanding and original, profound thought.	A few questions and comments showed deep understanding and original, profound thought.	My questions and comments did not show very deep, original thinking.
MY TOTAL: _____				
WHAT WILL YOU REMEMBER FROM THIS DISCUSSION?				

Adapted from Edutopia. Discussion Rubric. http://bit.ly/1Q4u7PS

Process

1. Form groups, announce the discussion prompt(s) and time limit.
2. Ask group members to exchange ideas in response to the prompt(s).
3. Move from group to group to observe student interactions. Use your scoring template to record their processes.
4. Ask the students to return to whole class discussion, and then initiate it by restating the prompt.
5. Ask a member of each group to summarize and restate the most important ideas or information from their Free Discussion. Consider adding the instruction to imagine that the paraphrase should provide a succinct summary for a student who was not able to attend class that day. These paraphrases will illustrate how deeply students have understood and internalized the information generated in the discussions.

Online

Free Discussion can easily be done in a synchronous environment. To implement synchronously, create several chat rooms, divide students into groups, and assign each group to a room. Announce the time limit, post the prompt, and ask students to exchange ideas informally without trying to come to consensus. When the time limit is up, close the activity. The information you gather is about student online communication ability, an increasingly important skill. (*Note:* Just as in an onsite classroom, Free Discussion online can get out of control with students getting off task or contributing inappropriate responses. Therefore, make sure you are monitoring groups by moving among the different chat rooms and be prepared to intervene if necessary.)

Free Discussion can be adapted in an asynchronous class by way of discussion forums. Again, you are considering a different form of communication—online, asynchronous communication ability—and again this is an increasingly important skill for both future college classes and beyond.

Analysis and Reporting

Use a rubric to score the discussion itself. Use student summaries or your own on the key issues students raised during a discussion as well as your notes on the patterns of interactions.

To aggregate results, use your rubric and tally the number of responses for each item. Look across the comments that you wrote to notice any patterns in the information. Consider the discussion that students generate from a qualitative perspective. How do the key points they raise compare to those you hoped they would? What are they doing well while interacting with each other? Where might they improve? Use a simple table or chart to share aggregated information with stakeholders, whether students, department chairs, or assessment committees. In a narrative describe your interpretation of results.

Examples

Onsite: Leadership Issues in Community Colleges

A professor of a graduate-level seminar containing students who were primarily upper-level college administrators used Free Discussion to provide students with the opportunity to discuss the topic of mergers and consolidations in the community college sector. Students first read an article on the topic and were instructed to come prepared to class to discuss the following questions: *What is the difference between a consolidation and a merger? Have you had any experience with consolidations or mergers? What are some of the issues that would attend a consolidation or merger?* These were open-ended questions, and she hoped that students would be able to draw upon their own experiences in college administration to respond to them.

It soon became apparent that several students within each Free Discussion had experienced consolidations and mergers on their campuses, and that they had strong opinions about those experiences. When groups reported out, the professor used their comments as the basis for a whole class discussion. She was able to integrate the information that she had intended to cover in the lecture by offering comments such as, *"What Carol is describing is an example of what is called _____."*

In the whole class discussion, students explored the political issues, organizational problems, and personnel dilemmas associated with consolidations and mergers at a level that was deep and engaging. Free Discussion had provided a good introduction to the topic by allowing students to connect theoretical constructs to work-related situations that had occurred in their professional lives. Furthermore, by integrating what would have otherwise been her lecture on theory into the whole class discussion, the professor was able to offer her students a framework for understanding their personal experiences that illuminated the importance of connecting theory to practice.

Finally, by observing the Free Discussions, the teacher gained insight into how well they interacted with each other. She aggregated her rubric findings, identifying the percentage of students who fell into each category, to see what they revealed (Table 10.7).

Table 10.7 Discussion Rubric

	Exceeds Expectations 4	Meets Expectations 3	Approaches Expectations 2	Needs Improvement 1
Preparation	10%	50%	30%	10%
Listening	5%	40%	50%	5%
Speaking	15%	50%	30%	5%
Depth of Thought	10%	40%	40%	10%

She noted that not everyone had read the assigned article carefully. The biggest issues, however, were students who did not participate in discussion and then those who overparticipated in discussion. She shared the results with students and talked with the whole class about her expectations for discussion and determined to use self-evaluation in the next iteration so that they could become aware of their own strengths and weaknesses.

 ## *Online: Introduction to Organic Chemistry*

This professor decided to use Free Discussion in an online discussion forum. He wanted students to learn to interact with each other, which he knew meant a very different thing in an online environment than in an onsite one. While some students had taken online courses before, others were complete novices, so he knew that to be successful, they needed to learn the basics of interaction. In the discussion forum, he presented these prompts:

- Name some common chemical compounds in your household.
- Why is it important to know about these compounds?
- What are some of the potential health effects of exposure to these compounds?
- How can individuals limit exposure to these compounds?

Table 10.8 represents the rubric he employed for grading the threaded discussion entries.

Table 10.8 Rubric for Grading Threaded Discussion

Number of Points	Skills
9–10	Demonstrates excellence in grasping key concepts; critiques work of others; stimulates discussion; provides sample citations for support of opinions; readily offers new interpretations of discussion material. Ideas are expressed clearly, concisely; uses appropriate vocabulary.
7–8	Shows evidence of understanding most major concepts; will offer an occasional divergent viewpoint or challenge; shows some skill in support for opinions. Some signs of disorganization with expression; transition wording may be faulty.
5–6	Has mostly shallow grasp of the material; rarely takes a stand on issues; offers inadequate levels of support. Poor language use garbles much of the message; only an occasional idea surfaces clearly; expression seems disjointed; overuse of the simple sentence and a redundancy with words and commentary; paragraphs often appear unrelated to each other. This student requires constant prompting for contributions.
1–4	A minimal posting of material. Shows no significant understanding of material. Language is mostly incoherent. Does not respond readily to prompting.

Adapted from facultytraining.rutgers.edu

Students fell into categories as shown in Figure 10.1:

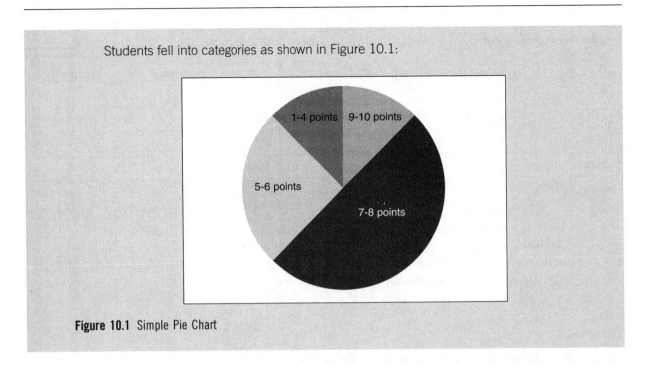

Figure 10.1 Simple Pie Chart

Variations and Extensions

- Assign the groups a task other than responding to questions. Instead, ask them to generate questions or ideas, share information, or solve problems.
- Hold the discussion without formal or structured questions, but rather as an opportunity to discuss the course texts in general or a specific assigned reading. This variation, called *Relaxed Free Discussion*, is simply a conversation. Students are required to keep the discussion focused on issues from the readings. They can question, highlight passages, look for the thesis, and identify flaws (Brookfield & Preskill, 2005).

Key References and Resources

Barkley, E., Major, C., & Cross, K. P. (2014). Buzz Groups. In *Collaborative learning techniques: A handbook for college faculty* (2nd ed.). San Francisco, CA: Jossey-Bass.

Bauer, J. F. (2002). Assessing student work from chat rooms and bulletin boards. New Directions for Teaching and Learning, No. 91, p. 35. San Francisco, CA: Jossey-Bass.

Brookfield, S. D., & Preskill, S. (2005). *Discussion as a way of teaching: Tools and techniques for democratic classrooms* (2nd. ed., pp. 104–105). San Francisco, CA: Jossey-Bass.

McKeachie, W. J. (1994). *Teaching tips: Strategies, research and theory for college and university teachers* (9th ed., p. 44). Lexington, MA: D. C. Heath.

LEARNING ASSESSMENT TECHNIQUE

Human Dimension

31
Nominations

Complexity involved in	
Preparation	LOW
In-class implementation	LOW-MODERATE
Analysis	HIGH

Brief Description

Students learn about an important award relevant to the field of study, for example someone in economics might learn about the Nobel Memorial Prize in Economic Sciences, including what makes someone qualified for nomination. They then research outstanding individuals in the field, select one for nomination, and write a short profile of the individual, indicating why he or she should be considered for the award.

Purpose

Nominations encourages students to learn about important and recent research done in a given field when they examine awards. Students must also consider what individual attributes are most valued in a given field as they weigh whom to nominate. They come to realize that well-deserving individuals with wonderful qualities may not be selected for the award. This realization helps them understand that issues related to the human dimension, for example interpersonal skills or social status, can manifest in disciplines and fields in different ways.

The Learning Artifacts are the biographic profiles that students submit. These Artifacts provide insight into student ability to conduct research as they learn about the award and evaluate individuals for nomination. It also provides insight into what students value from an intellectual perspective as well as from a humanistic perspective. This LAT may be used at the beginning of a course to promote and gauge student interest in the topic. It is most often used, however, toward the end of the course when students have learned more about the field; thus it has value as an indicator of student learning over time.

Key Learning Goals

- Empathy for others
- Respect for others
- A commitment to upholding their own values

Implementation

Preparation

- Identify the award for which students will nominate a candidate; if there is not a well-known award in your field, you may be creative and invent one yourself.
- Set the parameters for the award guidelines (including any parameters for individual nominations; e.g., must be living and working in the field) and for the nominations, including length of submission, qualities that should be addressed, style guidelines that should be used, and so forth.
- Create a handout announcing the activity and setting the parameters.
- Create a scoring rubric, such as shown in Table 10.9.
- Determine who will be involved in the assessment; you may wish to have colleagues select a "winner," for example, to give the activity an authentic feel.

Process

1. Present students with the handout, and allow time for questions.
2. Have students conduct research and write their nominations.
3. Collect the Learning Artifacts.
4. Provide the class with a list of the nominees, and consider informing them of the individuals' qualifications as well.

Table 10.9 Scoring Rubric

The nomination demonstrates the main achievements of the person's life based on the student's interpretation in light of the award specifications.	0 1 2 3 4
The nominator has clearly completed sufficient research on both the award and the individual he or she is nominating.	0 1 2 3 4
The individual's major accomplishments are evident.	0 1 2 3 4
The individual's significance is evident.	0 1 2 3 4
The nomination has a clear organization.	0 1 2 3 4
The writing is clear with no spelling or grammatical errors.	0 1 2 3 4

Scale: 0 = very poor; 1 = poor; 2 = adequate; 3 = good; 4 = excellent.

Online

Students submit their nominations as they would any other assignment in the class, whether through a blog post or an LMS system. You could also create a course wiki, on which students could post their nominations and create a course repository of information about key individuals in the field.

Analysis and Reporting

There are several ways to assess the learning artifact. Most typically you will want to score it with a rubric. Alternately or in addition, you may also choose to just keep a running list of qualities of the individuals that emerge in the nominations, conducting a key word or thematic analysis. Depending on the amount of writing that students do, you will probably want to assign a grade for this activity. If you use a rubric, you can return it to students, along with any written comments on their drafts.

To aggregate results, use your rubric scores. Tally the number of responses for each item. You may also choose to do a key word or thematic analysis across the different nominations to determine what characteristics or qualities individuals have identified. Use a simple table to report results from your rubric. Use a narrative table to report results from your thematic analysis.

Examples

Onsite: Introduction to Physics

In this class, the instructor had the following goals and objectives:

- Upon completion of this course, students will know/understand physics as a discipline, including key individuals who have made significant contributions to the field, and what it means to be a physicist.
- Upon successful completion of this course, students will be able to list individuals who have had a lasting impact on the field of physics.
- Student will be assessed on these learning outcomes by short, written assignments, including essays.

The professor wanted students to gain a broad understanding of the discipline early in the course to set the stage for more specific assignments later on in the term. He assigned Nominations as a way to introduce students to key individuals and their works as one of the first assignments in the class.

He had them research individuals who have received the Nobel Prize for Physics, and then review the list to nominate the individual they thought was *most* deserving of the award. He told students that each of them would write a one-page biography of the individual he or she chose to nominate.

He analyzed their responses for key words and came up with a list of features, a short version, as shown in Table 10.10.

Table 10.10 Key Word Analysis

Key word	Rank (Based on Frequency of Use)
Groundbreaking	1
Achievement	2
Quality	3
Theory	4
University	5

He led a class discussion about what it meant to be a physicist, discussing the affiliation with a university or research unit, the theoretical frameworks that individuals invented or drew upon, the tireless hours of work, and so forth. He felt that it was a good exercise that provided insights into the students' understanding of the field and set the stage for subsequent assignments.

 ## *Online: Broadcast Journalism*

In this class, the professor had the following learning goal: Upon completion of this course, students will know/understand what it takes to be a broadcast journalist.

The professor decided to use Nominations to help students understand what makes renowned journalists so great. She asked students to research the Peabody Award and to nominate an outstanding journalist for it. Each student had to write a two-page nomination of a current journalist to describe their qualification for the award. She conducted a thematic analysis of the responses (see Table 10.11). She organized the themes into two main categories: knowledge and skills. She talked with students about the responses and had a useful conversation about what it takes to be a broadcast journalist, including attributes and skills that students did not include in their nominations.

Table 10.11 Thematic Analysis of Student Responses

Attributes	Skills
Knowledgeable	Communication
Ethical	Language
Articulate	Investigation
Confident	Attention to detail
Dedication	Technical
Persistence	Collaboration
Creativity	Project management
Desire	Stress management
Likability	Timing
Versatility	
Resilient	

Variations and Extensions

- Have students work in small groups to nominate individuals for the award.
- Alternately have students work in small groups and share their individual nominations with each other. Then have them create a composite list of the characteristics the individuals have; this approach can help you to streamline the data analysis process.
- Bean (2009) recommends having students write bio-poems, in which students use a structure to provide information about a subject. In creative fields, it could be appropriate and fun to have students write bio-poems for their nominations and provide a different type of data. The formula is as follows (2009, p. 137):
  - Line 1: First name
  - Line 2: Four traits that describe the subject
  - Line 3: Relative of (list relatives)
  - Line 4: Lover of (list three things or people)
  - Line 5: Who feels (three items)
  - Line 8: Who needs (three items)
  - Line 7: Who fears (three items)
  - Line 8: Who gives (three items)
  - Line 9: Who would like to (three items)
  - Line 10: Resident of
  - Line 11: Last name

Key References and Resources

Angelo, T., & Cross, K. P. (1993). CAT 30: Profiles of admiral individuals. In *Classroom assessment techniques: A handbook for college teachers* (2nd ed., pp. 267–270). San Francisco, CA: Jossey-Bass.

Bean, J. C. (2009). *Engaging ideas: The professor's guide to integrating writing, critical thinking, and active learning in the classroom* (2nd ed.). San Francisco, CA: Jossey-Bass.

LEARNING ASSESSMENT TECHNIQUE

Human Dimension

32
Editorial Review

Complexity involved in	
Preparation	MODERATE
In-class implementation	MODERATE
Analysis	HIGH

Brief Description

Students assume roles as editors who must evaluate a set of works to select which ones to include in an upcoming publication, and then write to the authors with a decision and rationale about whether their work merits inclusion in the publication.

Purpose

This LAT gives students practice in evaluating works in the field and gaining an understanding of the field's standards of excellence. It also helps students to understand a specific type of publication and what kinds of works might be included in it. Because students have to assume the role of an editor who is communicating with an author, they begin to understand the human side of the publication process. They realize that people who write the articles or chapters have feelings, and that these authors must deal with acceptance and rejection of their work. It provides students with a different vantage point for reading journals or edited books as they gain understanding of the underlying human dimension.

There are three Learning Artifacts from this technique: the evaluations, the selection list, and the letters to the authors. They show students' knowledge of the standards of excellence in the field and their ability to evaluate works based on these standards. They provide evidence of students' ability to discriminate between works to identify which are better than others. They also show students' ability to communicate with understanding and integrity, as they recognize that their opinions will directly affect other human beings. This LAT requires time and effort and is particularly useful as a final course project.

Key Learning Goals

- Empathy for others
- Respect for others
- Interpersonal skills
- The capacity to make wise decisions
- The capacity to think for themselves
- A commitment to upholding their own values

Implementation

Preparation

- Identify a real or imaginary publication for which students will select the content, for example a journal issue or an edited book.
- Identify the guidelines for selecting works. For example, if you choose to have students serve as guest editors for an upcoming issue of a journal, you can let students know how many articles they can include, how long the pieces should be, what the style requirements are, and so forth.
- Select a set of works for students to review for potential inclusion in the publication, for example a set of articles. These can be previously published, from a previous semester, or even from a collection of current student work. You should select more works than will be accepted for inclusion so that students must discriminate between manuscripts and make difficult decisions about which ones will be accepted and which ones will be rejected.
- Create a scoring system for each of the three artifacts:
  - Artifact 1—Article ratings:
    - Compare them to your own and to other students' responses or evaluate them for level of thoughtfulness (e.g., excellent, very good, poor, very poor)
  - Artifact 2—Ranking and decisions:
    - Use a simple rating system for effort and rationale (e.g., excellent, very good, poor, very poor)
  - Artifact 3—Letters:
    - Consider creating a rubric based upon criteria such as the following:
      Communication of decision (from clear to unclear)
      Rationale for decision (from clear to unclear)
      Demonstration of empathy with accepted authors (high to low levels of integrity/compassion)
      Demonstration of empathy with rejected authors (high to low levels of integrity/compassion)
  - Create a handout of review guidelines that explains your plans for assessment.

Process

1. Announce the assignment, present students with the handout, and allow time for questions.
2. Have the students
   - Review the assigned works
   - Select works for inclusion in publication
   - Write letters to the authors of the accepted works and rejected works to explain your decisions
3. Collect the Learning Artifacts.

Online

Simply have students submit their three Learning Artifacts as assessments in whatever course tool you use; for example, a Learning Management System, blog, or file sharing system (e.g., Google Docs, Dropbox, Box).

Analysis and Reporting

To analyze individual artifacts, examine each student's review sheets and selections, using a simple scoring system such as +/– for completion and effort. Review students' letters using your rubric for evaluation and scoring elements such as clarity of communication and demonstration of compassion. Record any additional thoughts you might have. To report back to students, share your scoring and rubrics. If time and interest permit, write a memo or a brief letter to each student responding to their work.

To aggregate results, calculate how many +/– or other scores you have in the rubric categories for each of the assignments. Create a simple list or table to communicate your findings.

Examples

Onsite: English Literature

The professor of an English literature course wanted students to be able to critically read and evaluate short stories. He assigned students a collection of 15 readings. He gave them a template for reviewing the stories and asked them to give each a grade based on the rubric in Table 10.12, which allows him to see if their evaluations of the works are generally accurate.

Table 10.12 Editorial Review Evaluation Rubric

	A	B	C	D
Interest	Provides an interesting title and narrative	Provides a somewhat interesting title and narrative	Title and narrative are of little interest	Title and narrative are of no interest
Organization	Organizes beginning, middle, and end events	Presents a clear beginning, middle, and end	Presents a confusing beginning, middle, and end	Presents no clear order of events
Descriptive Writing	Contains rich details, uses effective adjectives, great word choice	Contains some details, uses adjectives, good word choice	Contains few details, uses at least a few adjectives	Contains hardly any details, uses no adjectives
Use of Language	Has a variety of sentences; contains no errors in grammar punctuation or spelling	Has some variety of sentences; contains few errors in grammar, punctuation, or spelling	Introduces some variety in sentences; contains some errors in grammar, punctuation, and spelling	Uses monotonous pattern of sentences; has many errors in grammar, punctuation, and spelling
Comments:				

He then tells the students that they are to assume the roles of editors of the next edition of the volume. However, to save publishing costs, they will only be able to choose 10 of the original 15 for inclusion. He asks students to rank order the articles and to choose the top 10. They turn in their rankings to him as well, which provides him with insights into what stories most interest students.

As the final phase of the activity, the professor asks students to write two letters, one that will go to the individuals whose works will appear in the next issue, and one to the individuals whose works will not be accepted. He reviews these letters to assess students' ability to communicate their thoughts as well as to effectively manage difficult decisions. He devised Table 10.13 to analyze his results.

He could see that students were much better at communicating with those authors whose works were accepted. He shared the results with the students and facilitated a discussion about how to face adversity and how to handle difficulty with integrity and compassion.

Table 10.13 Editorial Review Evaluation Results

	4	3	2	1
Reaching a decision	15%	40%	40%	5%
Rationale for decision	10%	40%	45%	5%
Clarity of the decision in the letter to the author	25%	50%	20%	5%
Demonstration of empathy with accepted authors	25%	55%	15%	5%
Demonstration of empathy with rejected authors	5%	30%	60%	5%

 Online: History of Art from Baroque to Post-Impressionism

In this online art history course, the professor asks students to review a set of master works of living artists. They then have to select art works for a special exhibit from the set. For example, during their review of modern artists, they have to choose whom to exhibit in their local Museum of Art from a loan from the Museum of Modern Art (MoMA). They have to rate a set of works, rank them and choose, and then write a letter to the individuals whose works were and were not selected. She reviews their ratings, rankings, and letters to assess their evaluative skills as well as their ability to communicate difficult decisions in a compassionate way to living artists.

Variations and Extensions

- Use this assignment in conjunction with LAT 45 Student Generated Rubric. Have students work together to develop a rubric by which they may evaluate the individual works.

- Assign student groups to review the articles or chapters as an editorial review board. Have each member do a separate rating and then have them decide together which works should be accepted for inclusion and which should be rejected. Then ask them to write the responses to the authors collaboratively (they can divide up the work and then exchange for revisions).

Key References and Resources

Slate Book Review. (2012). Kurt Vonnegut term paper assignment from the Iowa Writers Workshop. http://www.slate.com/articles/arts/books/2012/11/kurt_vonnegut_term_paper_assignment_from _the_iowa_ writers_workshop.html.

LEARNING ASSESSMENT TECHNIQUE

Human Dimension

33
Dramatic Dialogues

Complexity involved in	
Preparation	LOW
In-class implementation	LOW-MODERATE
Analysis	HIGH

Brief Description

Students create a dialogue based on an imagined discussion of a problem or issue between two different characters, imaginary or real, past or present.

Purpose

This LAT is especially useful for getting students to think deeply about course controversies and problems because it provides them with a structure to explore the range of perspectives inherent in complex topics. This process also contributes to their "owning" concepts that might otherwise be abstract and academic. It also requires learners to synthesize and draw upon their knowledge and understanding in order to generate the ideas and comments that result in a convincing dialogue. Finally, it has additional learning value in that it challenges students to explore both sides of an issue.

The Learning Artifacts are the written dialogues. These artifacts provide teachers with rich information on their students' depth of understanding as well as their creative ability in generating the content and delivery required to construct a credible conversation. It can be used at various points in the course. It is arguably most effective, however, as a post-instruction assessment, when students should have mastered core concepts, since they are now asked to apply and use this information to demonstrate what they have learned through the dialogues they create.

Key Learning Goals

- Empathy for others
- Respect for others

- Interpersonal skills
- A commitment to upholding their own values

Implementation

Preparation

- Identify one or more controversial topics that are important to your course content and that have two arguable and opposing sides.
- Decide how extensive an assignment you want this to be. Simple, straightforward topics can be discussed in 10–20 exchanges; more complex topics will require many exchanges to explore appropriately.
- Write your own dialogue so that you can uncover any potential problems with your selected problem or issue and so that you can determine how much time it takes to write an effective dialogue. Consider providing your practice run as a model for students.
- Create an evaluation rubric that includes elements such as number of ideas, originality, appropriateness, dramatic impact, and naturalness.
- Create a handout that includes instructions as well as the evaluation rubric. In the instructions, consider providing guidance on dialogue writing or links to Internet resources.
- Determine who will be involved in the assessment. Self- and peer assessments can be useful in helping students learn more about the concepts (since they not only have to create but also evaluate) and to provide you with additional information.

Process

1. Present students with the handout and allow time for questions.
2. The extent of the assignment will determine whether or not the dialogue can be constructed within an onsite class session or done as a homework assignment.
3. Consider asking for volunteers to read their dialogues to the whole class.
4. Collect the written assignment, which is your Learning Artifact.

Online

Have students create the dialogues and post them as an assignment in a learning management system or on a blog. If time and interest permit, they could create screencasts, which have audio-visual capabilities, of their dialogues and share the links through discussion forums or blogs.

Analysis and Reporting

In order to examine individual Learning Artifacts, use the rubric you created to evaluate dialogues. Look for problems in the individual responses that you might have anticipated given the topic, and also look for what is strong about each response. To provide individuals with feedback to improve their performance, develop a written response to each student that includes both rubric scoring and comments about any issues.

To examine the results in aggregate, use one of the rubrics and tally the number of responses for each item. Look across the comments that you wrote to notice any patterns in the information. You might, for example, notice areas in which students were consistently strong (for example, explaining the core problem), problems with the dialogue (such as unrealistic exchanges), or problems in the communication skills that students evidence (such as attacks on the part of the characters). Make note of these patterns.

Develop bar charts to demonstrate the rubric scoring. If you have used peer and self-evaluations, do comparison scoring. If the scores are largely in agreement, discuss inter-rater reliability. If they are not, discuss why you believe that to be the case (if you have no idea, consider interviewing a few of the students). Also describe the patterns you noted in the responses, most likely in a written narrative form.

Examples

Onsite: The Psychology, Biology, and Politics of Food

The College's assessment committee requires each department and program to demonstrate student learning outcomes in developing content knowledge in the field. As a result, each professor was required to write at least one objective to include in each syllabus related to this outcome. Students had to be able to either list, describe, explain, discuss, and so forth an area of content determined by the professor of the course. The professor also had to document that he or she had assessed that particular learning outcome to the committee and to document the results of the assessment.

The professor of this course decided she would have students demonstrate that they could discuss several key content areas in the course, including food aversions, regulation of hunger and satiety, organic versus traditional farming, genetically modified foods, the global obesity epidemic, the impact of food advertising on children, and so forth. She also wanted students to understand myriad opinions related to food so that when they worked in the field, they could negotiate the politics that surround food and argue for a better system. She created a sign-up sheet for students so that they could each select a different topic. Each student was responsible for creating two fictitious identities that reflected opposing viewpoints and crafting a 20–30 exchange dialogue between the two which laid out core perspectives in a persuasive and constructive manner. She informed the students of the assignment and provided them with the scoring rubric. She also told them to self-assess their own work. She assigned peer assessment as homework. Finally, she told them she would select the five top-rated dialogues for performance in class.

She used a rubric to assess student learning outcomes. And she had students self-assess their own dialogues and peer-assess five other students' papers. She scored each individual response, and developed a list of comments related to each student's paper. She gave both her comments and the student comments to the individuals.

The professor also aggregated the scores. She noted that most students scored highly (4 out of 5) on the number of ideas, originality, and dramatic impact, but there was much more variability in appropriateness and naturalness; the average score on these two categories being 2.5 out of 5, with some students on the extreme low end and some on the extreme high end. She believed that some students took the "creativity" aspect of the assignment further than others. She recorded the results in her preliminary report to the assessment committee, noting that she had a more traditional examination scheduled for later in the semester. Table 10.14 is the table she included.

Table 10.14 Assessment Results of Dramatic Dialogue Assignment

Category	Mean Rating
Number of ideas	4.5
Originality	4.75
Dramatic impact	4.3
Appropriateness	2.5
Naturalness	2.53

Online: A History of Philanthropy in the United States

In this online course, the professor had a learning goal that students would recognize the range of motivations underlying philanthropy. He chose to do a modified form of Dramatic Dialogues to not only help students reach this goal but also to provide evidence that it had been achieved.

He instructed students to choose a quote from the extensive collection of quotes on philanthropy provided on the National Philanthropic Trust's website. Each student then was responsible for constructing a brief, 10-exchange imaginary interview with that person that expanded upon the views expressed in the quote. Completed dialogues were submitted as an assignment and also posted in the discussion forum to share with the whole class.

The instructor scored the responses by a rubric (Table 10.15), which he returned to the students. He also averaged the scores for each item on the rubric, and he learned that students were stronger in some areas than others. The instructor examined student comments on each other's dialogues as a form of additional information. He examined their comments for key words, noting that they often congratulated each other, commenting that posts were "creative," "thought-provoking," "insightful," "original," and a host of other positive and supportive adjectives.

He wrote the assignment up as a part of his teaching dossier. He described the purpose of the assignment, included the actual assignment from his website, and used tables to report scores. He wrote a descriptive narrative about the assignment, noting that students had responded positively to the assignment, saying that they learned as much from each other's dialogues as from their own. He noted that the assignment not only helped him achieve his stated learning outcome, but it also helped him to establish and foster a collaborative community, which he noted can be difficult in completely online courses.

Table 10.15 Assessment Matrix

Student Learning Outcomes	LAT	Subject/ Content Prompt	Intentional Active Learning Activity	Learning Artifact	Findings and Interpretations	Actions to Be Taken
Students will recognize the range of motivations underlying philanthropy.	Dramatic Dialogues	Read the specified assignments prior to coming to class	Creating exchanges between two fictitious characters	The written dialogue	Achievement of learning outcomes: students could understand different perspectives on the subject of philanthropy; increased community in class	Continued use of the activity; adding step of peer review of dialogues

Variations and Extensions

- This assignment can also be done in pairs. It is especially helpful if each side of the topic has been, or could be, assigned an identifiable advocate.
- To implement this technique as a collaborative assignment online, it is best to work with dyads or base groups that have already been established with members who are comfortable working with each other. As members work together to construct their dialogues, they can send their contributions as email attachments and monitor individual contributions using the tracking features available in standard word processing programs. Alternately, have students use Documents/Wiki, which will automatically show who made contributions and edits.

Key References and Resources

Angelo, T. A., & Cross, P. K. (1993). CAT 17: Invented dialogues. In *Classroom assessment techniques* (2nd ed., pp. 203–207). San Francisco, CA: Jossey-Bass.

"Dramatic Dialogue Exercise" from Writing Really Good Dialogue. http://ywp.nanowrimo.org/files/ywp/ywp_10_hs_dialogue.pdf.

Gelb, M. J. (1998). Imaginary dialogues. In *How to think like Leonardo da Vinci: Seven steps to genius every day* (pp. 234–236). New York, NY: Delacorte Press.

LEARNING ASSESSMENT TECHNIQUE

Human Dimension

34
Role Play

Complexity involved in	
Preparation	MODERATE
In-class implementation	MODERATE-HIGH
Analysis	HIGH

Brief Description

A Role Play is a created situation in which students deliberately act out or assume characters or identities they would not normally assume in order to accomplish learning goals. Students often research their roles through independent study, but instructors may also provide specific assignments, such as readings, to serve as source material for the play.

Purpose

A Role Play provides an action environment for students to experience the emotional and intellectual responses of an assumed identity or imagined circumstance. At its essence, Role Play is an example of "learning by doing." The word "role" indicates that students must actively apply knowledge, skills, and understanding to successfully speak and act from a different, assigned perspective. The term "play" indicates that students use their imaginations and have fun, acting out their parts in a nonthreatening environment. Role Play thus engages students in a creative, participatory activity that requires them to apply course concepts as they assume fictional identities or envision themselves in unfamiliar situations.

The Learning Artifact for the Role Play is your record of it. You can choose to video the performance, or ask students to do it, or you can simply assess the performance in progress with a checklist or rubric. The data you gather during the play itself is a measure of student understanding of how humans can or should interact. Role Plays typically are used at the end of a module of content to check for understanding. It is possible, however, to do a Role Play as a pre-post assessment of student understanding.

Key Learning Goals

- Empathy for others
- Respect for others
- Interpersonal skills
- The ability to work productively with others
- Self-confidence
- Students' commitment to upholding their own values

Implementation

Preparation

- Spend thoughtful time designing the scenario for your Role Play. Appropriate scenarios require interaction from stakeholders with multiple perspectives. Therefore, identify the perspectives and define the type and number of characters and the framework for their actions.
- Consider assigning group process roles such as "moderator" (who can, for example, intervene if a person is falling out of character) or "observer(s)" (who interpret and comment on the action) in addition to roles for persons who are participating in the action.
- Craft the basic story line; begin by initiating the action through a critical event that the players must respond to, such as a comment by one of the actors or an incident that has just occurred.
- Identify resources (if any) for each of the playing roles.
- Decide how the activity will end. For example, will you set a time limit, or will you let the scenario end naturally?
- Consider what your Learning Artifact will be. Will you video the Role Play? If so, gather the appropriate equipment. Will you score it as it unfolds? If so, develop an appropriate rubric.
- Devise an appropriate rubric. You might consider the following criteria, with a range of points indicating Attempted/Acceptable/Good/Exceptional:
  - Quality of the content: Did the Role Play demonstrate clear understanding of the topic?
  - Degree of cooperation: Did all students contribute and accept ideas from each other?
  - Quality of the scenario: Were the dialogue and action natural and convincing?
  - Impact: Was the Role Play engaging, entertaining?
  - Presentation: Did students speak clearly, loudly, and use appropriate body language?
- Consider who will be involved in the assessment. Student self- and peer evaluation can be an effective addition. Groups can view the videotape and discuss the specific problems or general principles revealed in the tapes, perhaps summarizing and synthesizing their observations into an essay. Alternatively, the whole class can watch one or more of the films and discuss the critical issues or themes that emerge.
- Spend sufficient time prior to the activity to ensure that students understand the purpose of the Role Play. If they don't understand the learning goals, students may get off track or the Role Play may fall flat and seem artificial.

Process

1. Ask students to form groups with enough members in each group to assume each role.
2. Present the scenario and allow time for discussion of the problem situation. It is important to allow sufficient time for students to ask questions on any aspects of the scenario that are unclear.

3. Assign or ask students to each assume a role. Make sure students are clear on their tasks.

4. Inform students of the time limit or other parameters that will signify the end of the activity.

5. Instruct students to enact the Role Play. The Role Play should run only until the proposed behavior is clear, the targeted characteristic has been developed, or the skill has been practiced. They can do this in front of the class or in smaller clusters, depending upon the goals of the activity and the size of the class.

6. While students are enacting the Role Play, collect the Learning Artifact, whether it is a video, your notes, or a scored rubric.

7. Follow the Role Play with a discussion for closure. Take time to debrief on the lessons learned through the experience. Don't expect students to develop deep understanding of human situations after limited exposure in a single Role Play within the small groups and/or with the whole class. Discussion should focus on the students' interpretations of the roles and the motivations for and consequences of their actions.

Online

Role Play can be particularly effective online as students are provided with some anonymity, which can free them of some of their anxiety and self-consciousness with assuming different identities. This benefit is also a potential challenge, as students may feel so uninhibited by their assumption of a different role that they act inappropriately.

One of the best tools for implementing Role Play online is an *immersive environment*. Students can even create their own avatars as they interact with each other online. If this technique fits with your teaching, it is best if you are already using the immersive environment as part of regular class activities, as it can take a while for students to master the technology and learn to interact smoothly.

Role Plays may also be done online by way of microblogs. Ask students to assume an identity on Twitter (such as a past or current leader in your field), post a prompt, and then ask students to respond as if they were that assumed identity. Animation is another good tool for engaging in Role Play. Students can collaborate online to create animated Role Plays, developing them collaboratively through animation tools such as Animodo, Vokii, or Blabberize.

When implementing a Role Play in an online course, provide a set of ground rules for interaction to let students know what kinds of actions and communications are appropriate. Especially in Virtual Learning Environments, consider creating roles for students to manipulate the environment. For example, a "Manipulative Devil" sets up obstacles and creates challenges for the characters, or the "Improvising Storyteller" creates extensions to the scenario adapting to unforeseen twists in the action (No author cited; accessed 12/04/03: http://adulted.about.com/library/weekly/aa092502b.htm).

Analysis and Reporting

The "individual" in a Role Play is the group. That is, you assess an individual group rather than an individual student. This analysis can be challenging because of its collective nature. Score the Role Play using the rubric you prepared, and then also identify the key themes that the play emphasizes.

Use the same rubric to aggregate results. Tally the number of responses for each item, and determine an average score. Look across the plays to determine key themes and assess whether those themes are what you planned for students to take away. Use a numeric table or bar graph to illustrate class results by each item on the rubric. Consider a network to demonstrate themes across the plays.

Examples

Onsite: Oral Communication Skills I (ESL)

This professor knew that many of her students were extremely self-conscious about speaking up in her beginning ESL class. As non-native speakers, they came from countries around the world, and feared that they would make mistakes and that other students would not understand them. Yet it was essential that students practice extensively in order to develop vocabulary, grammatical accuracy, and clear pronunciation that they could use to communicate. Communication is an essential human relations skill, and thus was a key learning outcome for her course; she wanted students to demonstrate the oral communication skills necessary to negotiate typical social interactions, such as ordering dinner at a restaurant or asking for directions to the library on campus. She decided to use Role Plays to help students gain an understanding of these interactions and learn the skills necessary to negotiate them.

She created scenarios that emphasized everyday English. She then formed small groups so that students had more opportunities to practice speaking and so that the context would be less threatening than speaking up in the whole class. She asked them to develop scripts prior to the play and then to assume roles and act them out. In each cluster, she assigned a recorder to take notes on what they saw. She asked each group to perform their best play in front of the full class.

The data she collected were the written scripts, the student recording of the interactions, and the performance of one skit. She had created a rubric, which she used to assess the different aspects of the interaction. She assessed each group with a rubric score, such as shown in Table 10.16.

Table 10.16 Rubric Scores

Group 1	Written Skits	Performed Script
Quality of the content	3.5	3.5
Quality of the scenario	3.0	3.0
Quality of the organization	3.2	3.2
Impact	2.75	3.0
Presentation	3.0	2.5

She also took notes on their presentations.

She found that if she asked students to pretend they were someone else, it ameliorated some of their anxiety. Furthermore, if they assumed a role in a scenario that she created based on everyday situations, it motivated them because they immediately saw the usefulness of the exercises. She noted that their content was generally good, but she also found that they often omitted greetings and went straight to the request for information. She determined she needed to spend more time talking about this essential aspect of human relations and worked toward that end in future iterations of Role Plays.

 ### Online: Business Marketing Practices

A professor teaching an online course decided to use a Role Play to teach concepts and content. In particular, he wanted students to understand working dynamics of individuals working together to create a new company and product. He formed six groups with four students each, with each group representing a company and with each student assuming one of the following roles: CEO, Financial Officer, Operations Chief, or Marketing Executive.

Teams worked together to create a new business and model, new product, and a business plan. While they worked, they used discussion forums and each student had to stay in character, to the extent that he or she had to pose questions, raise points, etc., from the perspective of someone in that role would. Because they used chat rooms and discussion forums, he had documentation of their interactions with each other.

In addition to their understanding of content, the instructor assessed them on their interpersonal skills. He used the criteria shown in Table 10.17 and identified the mean scores across individual scores:

He realized that students needed additional development in collaborative skills and determined that he would add training for group work in the future.

Table 10.17 *Interpersonal Skills Assessment*

Leadership Skills	3.23
Teamwork	2.75
Diverse Perspectives Inclusion	2.5
Responsibility	3.33
Intrinsic Motivation	3.12

Variations and Extensions

- Combine this activity with a Fish Bowl (see Barkley et al., 2014, CoLT 9) by having one group perform the Role Play while another group watches, and then have the groups trade places. They can rate each other, which provides an additional data point.

Key References and Resources

Barkley, E. F., Major, C. H., & Cross, K. P. (2014). CoLT 9: Fish bowl. In *Collaborative learning techniques: A handbook for college faculty* (2nd ed., pp. 201–205). San Francisco, CA: Jossey-Bass.

Naidu, S., Ip, A., & Linser, R. (2000). Dynamic goal-based role-play simulation the Web: A case study. *Educational Technology & Society*, 3(3), 190–202.

Plous, S. (2000). Responding to overt displays of prejudice: A role-playing exercise. *Teaching of Psychology*, 27(3), 198–200.

LEARNING ASSESSMENT TECHNIQUE

Human Dimension

35
Ethical Dilemma

Complexity involved in	
Preparation	HIGH
In-class implementation	LOW-MODERATE
Analysis	HIGH

Brief Description

Students review an ethics-based, discipline-related scenario in which someone must choose a course of action between two or more difficult alternatives. Students write an essay response to the case in which they proceed through a sequence of prescribed steps that conclude with their choice of the most ethical decision.

Purpose

This LAT challenges students to think through their content-related values within the context of "real world" situations. It provides students with a forum to probe the motivations underlying and the consequences resulting from ethics-based choices in a safe environment. Because it gives them practice in evaluating situations they may confront in the real world, the technique prepares them to make better choices when they encounter similar situations in the future.

The Learning Artifacts are the students' essay responses to the scenario, in which they take a position and explain their stances. The Learning Artifacts provide teachers with a view of a most basic element of human interactions: ethical responses to real world situations involving people with different perspectives. This technique is typically done post instruction, after a unit of content, to document that students can use the information to make informed decisions that individuals face each day.

Key Learning Goals

- Empathy for others
- Respect for others
- The capacity to make wise decisions

- The capacity to think for themselves
- A commitment to upholding their own values

Implementation

Preparation

- Choose one specific ethical issue or question upon which to focus.
- Locate or create a short case that poses the essential dilemma realistically.
- Write a series of prompts that require students to take a position on the scenario and to explain or justify that position. Consider the following:
  1. Summarize the facts of this case.
  2. Define the ethical issue(s) involved.
  3. Identify the key stakeholders/actors.
  4. List the potential solutions and possible consequences for the stakeholders/actors depending upon their choices.
  5. Choose the most ethical decision and explain why you chose it (e.g. greatest good, moral rights, fairness/equity, virtuousness, or other).
- Create a rubric for scoring the different sections of the paper. Include qualities that help you determine to what extent the essay offers valid, persuasive reasons for accepting the position that the student-author advocates.
- Create a handout to distribute to students that includes the case and also provides students with assignment parameters and the assessment rubric.

Process

1. Announce the activity and the time frame students will have to work on the assignment.
2. Provide students with time to complete their research and writing.
3. At the assignment deadline, collect the student responses and sort them into categories. Consider using your sorting method as a basis for starting a discussion about the issues.

Online

Ask students to post their responses on a blog or as an assignment within an LMS. Alternately have them submit their assignments through file sharing (such as Dropbox, Box, or Google Docs).

Analysis and Reporting

Use your rubric for assessing individual papers, and code the student responses based on basic themes you see. For example, you might choose to code based upon why students made the decisions they did. Provide students with your rubric scoring, and describe anything outstanding about the paper that you identified in your thematic analysis. Finally, grade as you would a more traditional paper.

To examine aggregated information, look at your tallies, and determine an average score of individuals who answered a certain way. Examine your codes for patterns. For your rubric report, consider a numeric table. For your analysis of themes, use a descriptive table or a graph such as a pie chart to report results. You might also consider a concept map or a Venn diagram, depending upon the number of categories you identify.

Examples

Onsite: Freshman Seminar (Study Skills/Personal Development)

This interdisciplinary course serves several aims—among them, introducing first-year college students to the values and standards of the academic community. The professor hopes that students will be able to identify what academic integrity is and understand the importance of honoring and upholding it. To get a sense of her students' views on academic integrity, this psychology instructor decided to use Ethical Dilemma Essay.

She prepared a half-page case that she wrote and distributed to the class for an in-class essay response, an activity which she thought would help prepare students for essay examinations in the future. The case concerned a college student, Anne, and her roommate, Barbara. Barbara told Anne that she was planning to take her boyfriend's Final Exam for him in a required science class, a class that Anne was also taking. The activity asked the Freshmen Seminar students to respond anonymously, in less than half a page, to the following two questions: (1) What, if anything, should Anne do about the plans Barbara and her boyfriend have for cheating on the Final Exam? (2) Depending on your answer to question 1, why should or shouldn't Anne do something? The instructor allowed students 20 minutes of class time to respond to the dilemma; she then collected the essays.

When she read them after class, she was surprised to find that nearly 50 percent of the students thought that Anne should not do anything about the planned cheating. The reasons they gave were varied, but more centered on Anne's relationship to her roommate. Another quarter of the students thought that Anne should confront Barbara and try to talk her out of it, and a few favored informing some campus authority. The instructor shared these results with the class in pie chart shown in Figure 10.2.

The instructor formed the students into groups and asked them to uncover the values behind various answers. A lively discussion of academic integrity ensued (Angelo & Cross, 1993, p. 272).

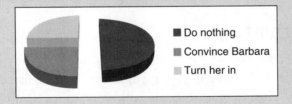

- Do nothing
- Convince Barbara
- Turn her in

Figure 10.2 Academic Integrity

She returned the scored essays in the following session. She graded them on five main components: content, organization, writing style, ethical understanding of the issue, and an ethical stance toward the situation that was in keeping with the honor code they had signed as university students. She returned the rubrics she used to grade them along with her own comments.

Online: Statistics

The professor of this online statistics course was concerned that students were learning the basic functions of statistics but were not understanding how human relations could in fact influence the math. The professor of this course then wanted students not only to understand the basics of statistics but also how statistics can be misused. This professor decided to use Ethical Dilemma Essay as a warm-up to a video presentation she had created on the role of ethics in statistics.

She posted an assignment, describing to her students a situation that she had encountered when she was still a graduate student: one of her peers was finishing his doctorate and working as a research assistant for the chair of his dissertation committee. The chair had a contract with a large pharmaceutical firm and was in charge of providing statistical analysis on one of the firm's products. The chair essentially told the student, "Here are the data; make them work."

After the instructor presented the dilemma, she asked students to think about what they would do in a similar situation. She asked students to discuss the questions (What should she have done? What are the challenges of responding ethically in that situation?) on a discussion forum. During the time students were discussing the issue, she tallied the responses. In a follow-up post, she shared the aggregated data of what she believed were the key themes they had identified (Figure 10.3).

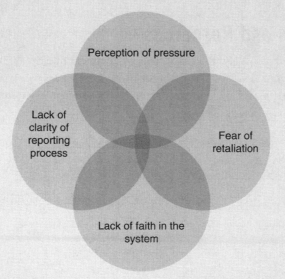

Figure 10.3 Key Ethical Themes

She also scored their discussion postings with a rubric, as follows.

Initial Post (6 points)
1. Mentions at least 3 specific points from the case that informs the decision. (2 points)
2. Discusses at a critical level, not just recitation of facts from the case. (2 points)
3. Makes a decision and justifies it with an appropriate ethical argument. (2 points)

Responses to Other's Postings (4 points)
1. Discuss one point you like/agree with, and one point you dislike/disagree with. (2 points)
2. Explain why you agree or disagree with the point. (2 points)

She provided students with ratings of their responses and then posted her video about the range of documented ethical violations of the national statistical system and closed with an assignment based on the American Statistical Association's "Ethical Guidelines for Statistical Practice" (http://www.amstat.org/profession/index.cfm?fuseaction=ethicalstatistics).

Variations and Extensions

- Consider using this activity as a formative technique. Have students submit their responses anonymously. When submitted anonymously, students are more likely to share their real opinions, and thus this technique gives teachers better insights into student attitudes and values than they might get if requiring students to submit work with their names.
- Consider adding a performance element to the task by having students role-play the situation or work in teams to argue each side of the dilemma.
- To make it a collaborative online activity, consider presenting the dilemma on a Forum, with students discussing hypothetical responses to the dilemma on a threaded discussion.

Key References and Resources

Angelo, T. A., & Cross, K. P. (1993). Everyday ethical dilemmas. In *Classroom assessment techniques* (2nd ed., pp. 271–274). San Francisco, CA: Jossey-Bass.

Barkley, E. (2010). SET 38: Ethical dilemmas. In *Student engagement techniques* (pp. 313–316). San Francisco, CA: Jossey-Bass.

LEARNING ASSESSMENT TECHNIQUE

Human Dimension

36
Digital Story

Complexity involved in	
Preparation	MODERATE
In-class implementation	LOW
Analysis	HIGH

Brief Description

Digital storytelling is the practice of using computer-based tools, such as video, audio, graphics, and Web publishing, to tell stories. The stories may be personal or academic, but for either focus, students share relevant life experiences as they attempt to connect to an audience about a given issue.

Purpose

This LAT also provides students with a creative outlet for self-authorship and for curating their lived experiences. Because students tell their own stories, they situate themselves within the context of the course subject area. They often tell about their lives through their interactions with others, thereby providing visible documentation of their learning in the Human Dimension. It also taps into their emotions, which can also improve their caring about a given topic.

The Learning Artifact is the digital story itself. This artifact provides teachers with rich data through multiple media from which to assess student learning and development. The stories provide evidence of student ability to reflect upon their learning and to connect it with their own lives and past experiences. The technique also provides evidence of student engagement and of multimedia literacy. Moreover, through sharing their own stories with an audience, and through intentionally connecting themselves and their stories to individuals in their lives, this technique provides strong evidence of student learning in the Human Dimension. This LAT is typically done at the end of a unit of content or even at the end of the course as a culminating experience to document student learning.

Key Learning Goals

- Interpersonal skills
- Self-confidence
- The capacity to make wise decisions
- The capacity to think for themselves

- A commitment to upholding their own values
- A commitment to their own emotional health and well-being

Implementation

Preparation

- Create a prompt for the assignment that establishes the content or topic area of the story (e.g., "Create a digital story that documents your journey as a student in higher education," or "Create a digital story that tells about your connection with a public health issue").
- Set the parameters of the assignment, such as length, time frame for completion of the work, and so forth.
- Ensure that students have adequate technical skills or alternately adequate technical support. Many students already know how to use technical tools such as iMovie, YouTube, and other technologies that can support this activity. Many institutions have student media centers that will support students working on technical projects. If your students do not have these skills and you don't have technical support available to them, you can either provide that support yourself or alternately allow students to do a "spoken word" real time presentation of their stories without technology.
- Determine who will be involved in the assessment and why. You will likely want to include self-assessment, and peer assessment can provide additional useful information as well.
- Create a rubric for assessing the digital stories. Sanders (2009, p. 18) identifies three main approaches for assessing digital stories that may be useful for rubric creation:
  - The storytelling approach focuses on particular elements of stories:
    - Story finding
    - Story telling
    - Story expanding
    - Story processing
    - Story reconstructing
  - The "levels of reflection" approach draws upon Moon's Model of Reflective Learning (Moon, 2004) and focuses on different levels of reflection:
    - Noticing
    - Making sense
    - Meaning making
    - Working with meaning
    - Transformative learning
  - The use of multimedia in reflective learning draws on student facility with the technological tools available for story telling:
    - Continuity editing
    - Audio editing
    - Lighting
    - Graphics
    - Animation

The University of Wisconsin Stout (nd) provides an example of a rubric for assessing student video projects, shown in Table 10.18.

Table 10.18 Video Project Rubric

Activity	Exemplary	Proficient	Partially Proficient	Unsatisfactory	POINTS
Use of Resources and Citations During Research and Note Taking	12 points Note cards indicate research questions, sources of information, and graphics and identify relevant pro and con arguments (if appropriate to the topic). Sources of information and graphics are properly cited using citations.	8 points Note cards show research questions, relevant information from multiple sources of information, and evaluate alternative points of view (if appropriate for the topic). All sources of information are clearly identified and credited using citations.	4 points Note cards show a few research questions from a few sources of information and fail to identify relevant counter-arguments (if appropriate for the topic). Most sources of information are identified using proper citation.	0 points Note cards do not include research questions or, sources of information and ignore alternative points of view. No citations are included.	___/12
Storyboard	6 points The storyboard illustrates the video presentation structure with thumbnail sketches of each scene. Notes of proposed transition, special effects, sound and title tracks include text, background color, placement and size of graphic, fonts—color, size, type for text and headings. Notes about proposed dialogue/narration text are included. All sketches are numbered, and there is a logical sequence to the presentation.	4 points The storyboard includes thumbnail sketches of each video scene and includes text for each segment of the presentation, descriptions of background audio for each scene, and notes about proposed shots and dialogue. All sketches are organized and numbered in a logical sequence.	2 points The thumbnail sketches on the storyboard are not in a logical sequence and do not provide complete descriptions of the video scenes, audio background, or notes about the dialogue.	0 points There is no evidence of a storyboard.	___/6
Content/ Organization	18 points The content includes a clear statement of purpose or theme and is creative, compelling, and clearly written. A rich variety of supporting information in the video contributes to understanding the project's main idea. The project includes motivating questions and advanced organizers that provide the audience with a sense of the	12 points Information is presented as a connected theme with accurate, current supporting information that contributes to understanding the project's main idea.	6 points The content does not present a clearly stated theme, is vague, and some of the supporting information does not seem to fit the main idea or appears as a disconnected series of scenes with no unifying main idea.	0 points The content lacks a central theme, clear point of view, and logical sequence of information. Much of the supporting information in the video is irrelevant to the overall message. The viewer is unsure what the message is because there is little persuasive information and only one or two	___/18

(continued)

305

Table 10.18   (Continued)

Activity	Exemplary	Proficient	Partially Proficient	Unsatisfactory	POINTS
	presentation's main idea. Events and messages are presented in a logical order.			facts about the topic. Information is incomplete, out of date, and/or incorrect.	
Introduction	6 points The introduction is compelling and provides motivating content that hooks the viewer from the beginning of the video and keeps the audience's attention.	4 points The introduction is clear and coherent and evokes interest in the topic.	2 points The introduction does not create a strong sense of what is to follow.	0 points The introduction does not orient the audience to what will follow.	__/6
Production Quality					
Video Continuity/ Editing	12 points The tape is edited with only high-quality shots remaining. Video moves smoothly from shot to shot. A variety of transitions are used to assist in communicating the main idea and smooth the flow from one scene to the next. Shots and scenes flow seamlessly. Digital effects are used appropriately for emphasis.	8 points The tape is edited throughout with only quality shots remaining. A variety of transitions are used. Good pacing and timing.	4 points The tape is edited in few spots. Several poor shots remain. Transitions from shot to shot are choppy, and the types of wipes and fades selected are not always appropriate for the scene. There are many unnatural breaks and/or early cuts.	0 points The tape is unedited and many poor shots remain. No transitions between clips are used. Raw clips run back to back in the final video.	__/12
Audio Editing	12 points The audio is clear and effectively assists in communicating the main idea. Background audio is kept in balance.	8 points The audio is clear and assists in communicating the main idea.	4 points The audio is inconsistent in clarity (too loud/too soft/garbled) at times and/or the background audio overpowers the primary audio.	0 points The audio is cut-off and inconsistent or overpowering.	__/12
Lighting	3 points Additional lighting is used to eliminate shadows and glares. All scenes have sufficient lighting for viewer to easily see action.	2 points Additional lighting is used. Few shadows or glares are apparent.	1 points Some scenes are too dark or too light to determine what is happening.	0 points Only ambient (available) light is used. Most scenes are too dark or too light to determine what is happening.	__/3

Criteria				Score
Camera Techniques (Exposure/Focus)	**12 points** All shots are clearly focused and well framed. The camera is held steady with few pans and zooms. Close-ups are used to focus attention.	**8 points** Most shots are clearly focused and well framed.	**4 points** Some shots are unfocused or poorly framed.	**0 points** Many shots are unfocused and poorly framed. Excessive panning and zooming distracts the viewer.	___/12
Graphics	**6 points** The graphics and/or animation assist in presenting an overall theme that appeals to the audience and enhances concepts with a high impact message. Graphics explain and reinforce key points during the presentation.	**4 points** The graphics or animation visually depict material and assist the audience in understanding the flow of information or content.	**2 points** Some of the graphics and/or animations seem unrelated to the topic/theme and do not enhance concepts.	**0 points** The graphics and/or animations are unrelated to the content. Graphics do not enhance understanding the content, or are distracting decorations that detract from the content.	___/6
Copyright	**6 points** Copyrighted information for photos, graphics, and music is clearly identified by source and nature of permission to reproduce.	**4 points** Every photo, graphic, or music is either original or permission for its use is documented.	**2 points** Some sources of photos, graphics, and music are not clearly identified with references, and permission to reproduce is missing.	**0 points** There is no reference to copyright information for photos, graphics, and music.	___/6
Moving Images	**3 points** Motion scenes are planned and purposeful, adding impact to the story line. "Talking heads" scenes are used when crucial to telling the story.	**2 points** The video includes some "talking heads," and backgrounds and video effects add interest. Most motion scenes make the story clearer or give it more impact.	**1 points** The video includes "talking heads" and a few motion scenes are added but do not improve understanding of the story line.	**0 points** The video features "talking heads" with little or no action to add interest or the video uses action excessively.	___/3
Timing	**3 points** Video clips show no slack time. "Three beat" timing (three actions per clip or three clips per event) is evident.	**2 points** Most video clips are edited to remove slack time and to emphasize action.	**1 points** Some video clips need to be edited to remove slack time and increase action.	**0 points** Video clips begin and end with slack time or no action.	___/3

TOTAL POINTS ___/99

A—Exemplary: 86–99 points
B—Proficient: 76–85 points
C—Partially Proficient or Unsatisfactory: Needs to be resubmitted—fewer than 75 points

Process

1. Announce the prompt.
2. Provide students with time to work as well as some guidance about how to proceed. The following suggestions are adapted from Lambert (2010):
   - Own your insights. Storytellers should find and clarify what their stories are about. We start with the question: "What's the story you want to tell?" and then as a follow-up, "What do you think your story means?"
   - Own your emotions. Consider the emotions in the story and determine how to convey these to an audience.
   - Find the moment in the story. Identify a single moment that can illustrate your insight. What was the moment things changed? When were you aware of the change?
   - See the story. How do visuals and sound bring things to life for the audience? How can you use them as part of the story?
   - Hear your story. The recorded voice of the storyteller is what makes a project a "digital story," but you can add music or other sounds. Both those other sounds are an excellent way to convey tone. Consider whether the story would be enhanced by additional layers of sound.
   - Assemble the story. What structure will you use? Chronological? Most important to least important? Vice versa? Consider what the necessary parts of the story are and how to order those pieces to engage the audience.
   - Share the story. Ask: "Who is your audience? What was your purpose in creating the story? Has the purpose shifted during the process of creating the piece? In what presentation format will the story be viewed? Will the story continue to have life after its presentation?"
3. Have students present their digital stories in class.
4. Collect the Learning Artifact by gathering together the URLs where students have their stories hosted.

Online

This LAT is easily completed in an online environment, particularly given its "digital" format. Simply have students share links to their videos, whether through an LMS discussion forum or alternately through posting replies to a course blog or wiki.

Analysis and Reporting

Use the rubric you created and look for anything unique in the individual responses. Because of the extensive amount of work that goes into preparing for, implementing, and assessing this LAT, teachers typically assign a significant grade to the activity, and indeed many students will want these projects to "count" given the amount of effort they take to create. However, Sanders (2009) found that some students are concerned about the use of Digital Stories for summative assessment, and while they valued the activity, they preferred them to be used for formative assessment purposes. Consider student characteristics and interests when making a determination of whether to assign a significant grade to this activity or not. To report to students, develop a written response to individuals that includes both rubric scoring and your comments about any issues.

Use one of the rubrics to aggregate results. Tally the number of responses for each item. Look across the comments that you wrote to notice any patterns in the information. Consider using a table to document results. In a narrative, describe your interpretation of results.

Examples

Onsite: Public Health

The professor of this course wanted students to engage in public health topics related to the lived experiences of those who have encountered issues. He wanted students to become aware of the "human" factor in health and health care, so he decided to ask students to create Digital Stories based on their own experiences with any issue related to public health issues.

He first announced the activity and asked students to work in groups to brainstorm topics. Each student then selected a topic. He was pleased to see a wide range of issues, including affordable care, autism, diabetes, pollution, women's reproductive health, water sanitation, and so forth. He provided students with time to work on their Digital Story in class, holding two class sessions in a computer lab, which allowed students to provide each other not only with advice and suggestions for their stories but also with technological support. He noted that students with more advanced technological skills were helping students who were not as advanced technologically.

The instructor invited other faculty to an "opening night" in which students introduced their stories, presented them live, and then reflected on the experience while doing them. He was thrilled with the results. Students had warmed to the activity and had obviously put great time and effort into their work. They had connected with the topics in real and meaningful ways, both their own stories and those of their peers. They said they had not previously thought about the real people involved in these issues and how they might experience them. To provide a formal assessment, he collected information from students on their own work, on the work of others, his colleagues, and his own work. He used the chart in Table 10.19 to guide his work, which he adapted from the University of Houston's guidelines for assessing Digital Stories.

Table 10.19 Guidelines for Assessing Digital Stories

	Assessment Tools			
Evaluator	*During the design process*	*During the development process*	*During the screening*	*After the project is completed*
The Creator(s)	Story specification Checklist of story artifacts	Graphics checklist Audio checklist Story draft Story board	The presentation	Reflective paper
Creator's Peers	Story ideas	Suggestion list	Notes on the presentation	Peer evaluation
The Teacher	Evidence of planning process	Interview with creator about development process Development rubric Checklist of story artifacts	Notes on the presentation	Rubric Narrative evaluation of story traits such as engagement, character, and development

Online: Introduction to Higher Education

The professor of this course was a new assistant professor who had to be reviewed annually for progress toward tenure. In addition to having high expectations for research, the department also had high expectations for teaching. They required individuals to demonstrate teaching excellence every year of the six-year process leading up to tenure.

The professor was assigned to teach an introduction to higher education course. While most of the courses in the program were offered at the graduate level, this course was an undergraduate course. The professor wanted students to come to understand their own journeys that led them to higher education and their own places in the institution. He decided to ask them to use Digital Stories to document their own experiences as learners and how this had led them to seek matriculation into that particular institution.

The students worked for weeks to develop their stories. While they had some time in class, a good bit of the work was done as a homework assignment or in the institution's media lab. The students shared their stories with each other in class. They all had interesting stories to share that brought up many important issues about higher education. Many students were first generation students who talked about their struggles and the "imposter syndrome." Many students were minority students who shared their experiences related to being enrolled in a predominantly white institution. Some students identified as gay or lesbian and shared the challenges they faced, whether as members of fraternities or sororities or simply their coming out experiences. Some talked about coming from a poor rural background and having had insufficient preparation for what they would experience in college. Some students talked about the financial challenges they faced, taking out student loans. Some had fewer challenges to share, but wanted to share what it was like being away from home for the first time, or gaining the freshman 15 pounds and not knowing what to do about it. All in all, through their shared experiences, the students brought to light many issues that they would investigate further in class. All expressed how moved they were to hear the stories of their peers.

The professor collected information from the students, not only through their stories, but also through self- and peer review of the experiences and their products. Through an analysis of all of the information sources, the professor created the matrix shown in Table 10.20 for inclusion in his promotion and tenure dossier.

Table 10.20 Assessment Matrix

Student Learning Outcomes	LAT	Findings and Interpretations	Actions to Be Taken
Students will understand their own journeys that led them to higher education and their own places in the institution.	Digital Story	Students used digital stories to make meaning of their educational journeys. They were best at research and resources used during story creation. They were excellent at story boarding and using technology. They were not as proficient at citing sources and getting clearance to use copyrighted images.	Because an important aspect for the course is learning to find and use sources appropriately, in the future, I will spend time discussing citation format and also copyright and intellectual property and how to respect ownership.

Variations and Extensions

- Instead of having students work on Digital Stories alone, have them work together to create a Digital Story about their shared or collective experiences.
- Instead of having students tell their own stories, have them interview others and tell the stories of their interviewees.

Key References and Resources

Lambert, J. (2010). Digital storytelling cookbook. http://static.squarespace.com/static/505a3ab2e4b0f1416 c7df69a/51684d91e4b0cbd5dcd536fd/51684d91e4b0cbd5dcd536ff/1332882649047/cookbook.pdf.

Sanders, J. (2009). Reflect 2.0: Using digital storytelling to develop reflective learning by the use of next generation technologies and practices. JISC.ac.uk. http://www.jisc.ac.uk/publications/documents /reflectfinalreport.aspx.

University of Houston. (2015). Assessment and evaluation. Educational uses of digital storytelling. http:// digitalstorytelling.coe.uh.edu/page.cfm?id=24&cid=24&sublinkid=43.

University of Wisconsin Stout. (nd). Video project rubric. https://www2.uwstout.edu/content/profdev /rubrics/videorubric.html.

CHAPTER 11

Teaching and Assessing for the Caring Domain

Most of us chose a career in academia because we care deeply about our academic discipline. As college professors, we typically find it immensely gratifying to share our scholarly specialty with others and often assume they will find it equally fascinating. It can be very discouraging, therefore, to deal with students' whose indifference to our course is palpable. Making little attempt to hide their apathy, these disengaged students distract themselves and others with their cellphones, keep glancing at the clock, and then bolt like freed prisoners the moment it seems safe to do so. It is also distressing to work with students who seem obsessed with their grades but appear to care little about the learning the grades are supposed to represent.

Professors around the country ask us, "What ever happened to students' curiosity and innate love of learning?" Teachers are sensing a decrease in student caring that is validated by statistics. In a special edition of the *Educational Leadership* journal titled "Do Students Care About Learning?" (2002b), Scherer draws on data from the National Center for Education Statistics (NCES) and reports a two-decade trend of steeply declining interest in school reported by high school seniors, many of whom have become our college students. In our own class surveys, most students respond that they are enrolled in our courses to meet an academic requirement, not because they are genuinely interested in learning the content.

Does it matter if learners care? Beyond the sheer annoyance and frustration we experience trying to teach indifferent students, there does seem to be a correlation between caring and the resultant quality of learning. Fink proposes, "When students care about something, they then have the energy they need for learning more about it and making it a part of their lives. Without the energy for learning, nothing significant happens" (2013, p. 360). Speculating on the relationship between caring about schoolwork and achievement, Scherer (2002a) cites a 2001 study that showed that success in math is highest in countries that foster a culture that cultivates *caring* about the acquisition of math skills. Certainly common sense and our own experience as teachers suggests that students who really care about what they are learning invest the time and effort to learn it well and remember it longer.

We want students to care about learning in general and our course in particular, but how do we achieve that? This chapter focuses on techniques and assessment related to the Significant Learning Taxonomy's dimension of caring.

Clarifying Learning Goals Related to the Caring Domain

What is "caring" within an educational context? When we care about something, we have acquired an affective disposition toward it that combines concern and perhaps even affection: we value it, appreciate it, and anticipate opportunities to encounter it. In terms of education, Fink describes the caring dimension as follows:

> When thinking about caring as an educational goal, it is important to remember that students can come to care about any of several possible foci for learning. As a result of their learning experiences, students might care more or differently about . . .
>
> - the phenomena studied: They may find a new interest in literature, history, birds, weather, rocks . . .
> - the ideas studied: They may become more curious about the perspectives through which geographers or historians study the world, the implications of the theory of relativity, the power of the theory of evolution to explain biological phenomena, the widespread insights offered by a feminist perspective on events . . .
> - their own self: "Maybe I have the potential for doing exciting things in life, more than I realized, or to become the kind of person I want to be."
> - the others they encounter in the class or the study: Students may find that people different from themselves—in terms of age, gender, ethnicity, religion, nationality, or whatever—are good people and that the process of understanding and interacting with them can be an exciting and enriching experience.
> - the process of learning itself: When students start to care about learning and want to learn, either in general or about particular things, then truly powerful things can happen educationally. Then students not only care about phenomena, ideas, and the like, but they also care about learning about them. (Fink, 2013, pp. 55–56)

Thus when our learning goal is that students will "care" about what they are learning in our course, we are aiming for a change in the degree to which students are interested in, or have feelings about, various aspects of their learning. Their caring can apply to an array of foci that include topic-specific phenomena and ideas, human beings, and the process of learning itself.

Promoting Caring in an Educational Context

Fink's observation that powerful things can happen educationally when students care about learning and want to learn resonates with Csikszentimihalyi's concept of *flow* (1993, 1997). When we are in a state of flow, we are so completely and enjoyably immersed in an activity that action and awareness merge. Absorbed in the task, the activity becomes autotelic and we are happy to do it for its own sake. In an interview with Csikszentimihalyi about how to help students care about their learning, he recommends strategies that are in precise alignment with the tenets of this book: clear, frequent, constructive assessment in conjunction with carefully designed learning activities that are collaborative, relevant, and authentic (Scherer, 2002b).

"Caring" resides in the affective domain and it is challenging to assess, but there are behaviors that can serve as *proxies* to demonstrate caring. For example, if students care about a course, they will be punctual and consistent in their attendance and will invest appropriate time

Table 11.1 Examples of Learning Processes and Outcomes for the Caring Domain

General Definition: The learner develops new feelings, interests, or values.			
Learner Process	Additional Terms	Definition	Sample Course Learning Outcome *By the end of this course, a successful learner will . . .*
Respond	Participate, answer, discuss, present, read, recite, report, select, tell, write	Ranges from acceptable participation in a learning situation to active interest and demonstrated enjoyment in a learning situation.	. . . listen actively to others in discussions of controversial issues. . . . report on the benefits of a specific social issue. . . . participate in a service learning project. . . . consider issues from multiple perspectives.
Value	Advocates, initiates, invites, joins, justifies, proposes, commits to, nominates, shares	The worth a student attaches to a particular object, phenomenon, or behavior that is based on the internalization of a set of specified values.	. . . demonstrate curiosity and enthusiasm about learning. . . . ask pertinent and thoughtful questions about social responsibility. . . . articulate an advocacy position on a social issue.

Sources: Composite

and energy into the learning activities. If students care about others, they will listen actively when others speak and demonstrate compassion and empathy as they develop deeper understanding of another's perspectives or experiences. If students care about the topic, they will ask pertinent questions and be sufficiently curious to go beyond the minimum class requirements. Fink suggests that to formulate learning goals related to this dimension we ask ourselves, "What changes would we like to see in students' interests, values, and feelings?" (2013, p. 84).

Identifying Learning Outcomes for the Caring Domain

Once we determine what it is that we want students to care about, we can formulate learning objectives and measurable outcomes. We offer Table 11.1 with examples of learning processes and outcomes for the Caring domain.

Aligning Learning Outcomes Related to Caring with Institutional Learning Goals

All institutions want students to care about learning. Most want them to care as well about contributing to the betterment of the world. These values are sometimes expressed in the mission statements of the institution, college, or program. Table 11.2 provides examples of learning goals at various levels of the institution that address the Caring domain of the Significant Learning Taxonomy.

Table 11.2 Examples of Institution Level Learning Goals that Address the Caring Domain of the Significant Learning Taxonomy

Institution/Mission Statement	One of our core missions is to enable students to rejoice in discovery and in critical thought and to assume responsibility for the consequences of personal actions.
Medical School/Mission Statement	Every graduate of the School of Medicine will display the personal attributes of compassion, honesty, and integrity in relationship with patients, families, and the medical community.
Business School	Our mission is to prepare innovative and ethical leaders who understand and care about the impact of business on society and create value for the world.

Sources: Composite

Assessing Achievement of Learning Outcomes in the Caring Domain

For some of us, even *thinking* about trying to assess student caring causes discomfort. To others of us, it is essential that we do so. To the former, we offer the reminder that assessment does not mean judgment, but rather, it means simply to size up or appraise the current state of something. We also offer the reminder that caring can and does relate to the level of mental effort a student is willing to expend on learning. Thus gathering information about the level of caring can help us better target our teaching to the group. For the latter, we suggest that caring can in fact be evaluated and even graded. Furthermore, there is nothing wrong in doing so. For both groups, we offer suggestions on how to assess caring. Because some of the components of caring are necessarily tied to the discipline, in our LATs, we have most often come at the issue from the perspective of caring about the course and caring about the subject matter. We offer Exhibit 11.1, the AAC&U rubric for assessing civic engagement, as an example of a rubric that addresses an aspect of "caring."

Conclusion

Helping students learn to care about course content as well as the world that surrounds them is an important element in significant learning. Whether it is a positive change in how students feel about topic-specific phenomena and ideas, human beings, or the process of learning itself, caring inspires students to invest energy in their learning. The techniques in this chapter help teachers foster and assess caring by providing a framework for guiding students in connecting with their own feelings about a targeted subject and then having them take action that is informed or influenced by these feelings.

Exhibit 11.1   Assessing Caring Using the AAC&U Civic Engagement VALUE Rubric

Definition
Civic engagement is "working to make a difference in the civic life of our communities and developing the combination of knowledge, skills, values and motivation to make that difference. It means promoting the quality of life in a community, through both political and non-political processes" (Ehrlich, 2000, p. vi). In addition, civic engagement encompasses actions wherein individuals participate in activities of personal and public concern that are both individually life enriching and socially beneficial to the community.

Framing Language
Preparing graduates for their public lives as citizens, members of communities, and professionals in society has historically been a responsibility of higher education. Yet the outcome of a civic-minded graduate is a complex concept. Civic learning outcomes are framed by personal identity and commitments, disciplinary frameworks and traditions, pre-professional norms and practice, and the mission and values of colleges and universities. This rubric is designed to make the civic learning outcomes more explicit. Civic engagement can take many forms, from individual volunteerism to organizational involvement to electoral participation. For students this could include community-based learning through service-learning classes, community-based research, or service within the community. Multiple types of work samples or collections of work may be utilized to assess this, such as

- The student creates and manages a service program that engages others (such as youth or members of a neighborhood) in learning about and taking action on an issue they care about. In the process, the student also teaches and models processes that engage others in deliberative democracy, in having a voice, participating in democratic processes, and taking specific actions to affect an issue.
- The student researches, organizes, and carries out a deliberative democracy forum on a particular issue, one that includes multiple perspectives on that issue and how best to make positive change through various courses of public action. As a result, other students, faculty, and community members are engaged to take action on an issue.
- The student works on and takes a leadership role in a complex campaign to bring about tangible changes in the public's awareness or education on a particular issue, or even a change in public policy. Through this process, the student demonstrates multiple types of civic action and skills.
- The student integrates their academic work with community engagement, producing a tangible product (piece of legislation or policy, a business, building or civic infrastructure, water quality or scientific assessment, needs survey, research paper, service program, or organization) that has engaged community constituents and responded to community needs and assets through the process.

In addition, the nature of this work lends itself to opening up the review process to include community constituents that may be a part of the work, such as teammates, colleagues, community/agency members, and those served or collaborating in the process.

Glossary
The definitions that follow were developed to clarify terms and concepts used in this rubric only.

- *Civic identity:* When one sees herself or himself as an active participant in society with a strong commitment and responsibility to work with others toward public purposes.
- *Service-learning class:* A course-based educational experience in which students participate in an organized service activity and reflect on the experience in such a way as to gain further understanding of course content, a broader appreciation of the discipline, and an enhanced sense of personal values and civic responsibility.
- *Communication skills:* Listening, deliberation, negotiation, consensus building, and productive use of conflict.
- *Civic life:* The public life of the citizen concerned with the affairs of the community and nation as contrasted with private or personal life, which is devoted to the pursuit of private and personal interests.
- *Politics:* A process by which a group of people, whose opinions or interests might be divergent, reach collective decisions that are generally regarded as binding on the group and enforced as common policy. Political life enables people to accomplish goals they could not realize as individuals. Politics necessarily arises whenever groups of people live together, since they must always reach collective decisions of one kind or another.
- *Government:* "The formal institutions of a society with the authority to make and implement binding decisions about such matters as the distribution of resources, allocation of benefits and burdens, and the management of conflicts."

- *Civic/community contexts:* Organizations, movements, campaigns, a place or locus where people and/or living creatures inhabit, which may be defined by a locality (school, national park, nonprofit organization, town, state, nation) or defined by shared identity (i.e., African Americans, North Carolinians, Americans, the Republican or Democratic Party, refugees, etc.). In addition, contexts for civic engagement may be defined by a variety of approaches intended to benefit a person, group, or community, including community service or volunteer work or academic work.
(Retrieved from the Center for Civic Engagement Website, May 5, 2009.)

Table 11.3 Assessing Caring Rubric

	Capstone 4	Milestone 3	2	Benchmark 1
Diversity	Demonstrates evidence of adjustment in own attitudes and beliefs because of working within and learning from diversity of communities and cultures. Promotes others' engagement with diversity.	Reflects on how own attitudes and beliefs are different from those of other cultures and communities. Exhibits curiosity about what can be learned from diversity of communities and cultures.	Has awareness that own attitudes and beliefs are different from those of other cultures and communities. Exhibits little curiosity about what can be learned from diversity of communities and cultures.	Expresses attitudes and beliefs as an individual, from a one-sided view. Is indifferent or resistant to what can be learned from diversity of communities and cultures.
Analysis of Knowledge	Connects and extends knowledge (facts, theories, etc.) from one's own academic study/field/ discipline to civic engagement and to one's own participation in civic life, politics, and government.	Analyzes knowledge (facts, theories, etc.) from one's own academic study/field/ discipline making relevant connections to civic engagement and to one's own participation in civic life, politics, and government.	Begins to connect knowledge (facts, theories, etc.) from one's own academic study/field/discipline to civic engagement and to tone's own participation in civic life, politics, and government.	Begins to identify knowledge (facts, theories, etc.) from one's own academic study/field/discipline that is relevant to civic engagement and to one's own participation in civic life, politics, and government.
Civic Identity and Commitment	Provides evidence of experience in civic engagement activities and describes what she/he has learned about her or himself as it relates to a reinforced and clarified sense of civic identity and continued commitment to public action.	Provides evidence of experience in civic engagement activities and describes what she/he has learned about her or himself as it relates to a growing sense of civic identity and commitment.	Evidence suggests involvement in civic engagement activities is generated from expectations or course requirements rather than from a sense of civic identity.	Provides little evidence of her/his experience in civic engagement activities and does not connect experiences to civic identity.
Civic Communication	Tailors communication strategies to effectively express, listen, and adapt to others to establish relationships to further civic action.	Effectively communicates in civic context, showing ability to do all of the following: express, listen, and adapt ideas and messages based on others' perspectives.	Communicates in civic context, showing ability to do more than one of the following: express, listen, and adapt ideas and messages based on others' perspectives.	Communicates in civic context, showing ability to do one of the following: express, listen, and adapt ideas and messages based on others' perspectives.

(continued)

Table 11.3 (*Continued*)

	Capstone 4	Milestone 3 2		Benchmark 1
Civic Action and Reflection	Demonstrates independent experience and shows initiative in team leadership of complex or multiple civic engagement activities, accompanied by reflective insights or analysis about the aims and accomplishments of one's actions.	Demonstrates independent experience and team leadership of civic action, with reflective insights or analysis about the aims and accomplishments of one's actions.	Has clearly participated in civically focused actions and begins to reflect or describe how these actions may benefit individual(s) or communities.	Has experimented with some civic activities but shows little internalized understanding of their aims or effects and little commitment to future action.
Civic Context/ Structures	Demonstrates ability and commitment to collaboratively work across and within community contexts and structures to achieve a civic aim.	Demonstrates ability and commitment to work actively within community contexts and structures to achieve a civic aim.	Demonstrates experience identifying intentional ways to participate in civic contexts and structures.	Experiments with civic contexts and structures, tries out a few to see what fits.

Reprinted with permission from "VALUE: Valid Assessment of Learning in Undergraduate Education." Copyright 2015 by the Association of American Colleges and Universities. http://www.aacu.org/value/rubrics

Caring

37
Stand Where You Stand

Complexity involved in	
Preparation	MODERATE
In-class implementation	MODERATE
Analysis	LOW

Brief Description

Students read assignments with opposing opinions on a controversial issue. Then, after the teacher presents a statement that reflects one of the sides, students individually decide whether and how much they agree or disagree. They then go stand in front of one of four room corner signs to signal their positions, take turns presenting their rationales, and move to another sign if the arguments they hear persuade them to change their minds.

Purpose

This activity encourages students to think critically as well as opportunities to practice developing and presenting arguments. Moreover, it provides an opportunity to listen carefully to others' points of view, especially to listen for strengths or weaknesses in opposing views. Additionally, by requiring all students to choose the position that represents their views and articulate their rationale for that position, it ensures all students make some level of personal commitment to the issue.

This LAT provides a visible indicator of students' positions on an issue. It is a quick way to gather data on "caring" about a specific issue in the field. It requires little investment in class time and generates quickly assessable data. This LAT is best used as an approach for assessing change in beliefs both before and after a class discussion, and it is typically done mid-learning module so that instructors can target instruction accordingly.

Key Learning Goals

- Motivation to learn in the subject area
- Openness to new ideas in the subject area

- An appreciation of diverse perspectives related to this subject
- A willingness to engage in class activities
- An acceptance of responsibility for their own behavior in the course
- Informed concern about current social issues relevant to the topic

Implementation

Preparation

- Identify a controversial topic important to your course and locate one or more essays that clearly support each side of the controversy.
- Reproduce sufficient copies to create one set for each student and distribute essays and assign reading.
- Create—and on the day of the class post—signs in the four corners of the room stating Strongly Agree, Agree, Disagree, or Strongly Disagree.

Process

1. Present students with a statement that reflects one of the two sides.
2. Ask students to individually decide whether they agree or disagree with the statement and to write down their rationales, using arguments, evidence, and quotes from the reading assignments to support their position.
3. When students have finished writing down their views, ask them to stand in front of the sign that most closely reflects their position on the statement.
4. Ask students at each station to take turns orally presenting their rationales for the position they have assumed so that the whole class may hear the rationale.
5. Invite students to move to another sign if they were persuaded to change their minds after hearing their peers' arguments.
6. Conclude the activity with a whole class discussion in which students share how their perspectives were or were not altered as a result of the activity.

Online

Due to the physical nature of this activity, it can be difficult to replicate online. Setting up a discussion forum with four separate threads to represent the different positions and having students post their opinions in the thread that most closely corresponds to their views can be a way to accomplish something similar. Alternately use an online survey, report the results on the course site, post a prompt for discussion in the forum, repeat the survey, and gauge any change.

Analysis and Reporting

The Learning Artifact is the physical model of the room and the students' statements about their positions. You can either take a photo to document and a video to record comments or alternately take your own notes to record student positions and comments. This technique is

Table 11.4 Tally of Students' Opinions

Strongly Agree	Agree	Disagree	Strongly Disagree
✓✓✓✓✓ ✓✓✓✓✓	✓✓✓✓✓ ✓✓✓✓✓ ✓✓✓✓✓ ✓✓✓✓✓	✓✓✓✓✓ ✓✓✓✓✓ ✓✓✓✓✓ ✓✓✓✓✓	✓✓✓✓✓ ✓✓✓✓✓

typically used as a formative assessment technique. Students have immediate feedback on their responses and those of their peers as they see the class lineup at the different areas of the room.

To examine the results in aggregate, look across the positions and make a quick tally on a grid with check marks representing a student standing in that area, as shown in Table 11.4.

When reporting to students, use a simple verbal summary of the positions (e.g., "we have 10 students who strongly agree, 20 who agree, 20 who disagree, and 10 who strongly disagree). Use a table to synthesize and summarize the data.

Examples

Onsite: Introduction to Sociology

To help students explore their ideas, values, and belief systems regarding the concept of "the nuclear family," the professor decided to use Stand Where You Stand to address the topic of adoption of children by same sex couples. The learning outcome was to understand diverse perspectives related to current social constructs. She collected two essays, one in favor and the other opposed. She had students read the essays prior to class. When students gathered in the classroom, she asked them to choose their position in response to the statement, *Gay couples should be given the same legal rights as heterosexuals in adopting children*, and go stand under the appropriate sign.

As students individually reported the rationales for their position, she made a list of the pros and the cons. When students had finished, she summarized the arguments for each side and invited students to move to a different sign if their opinion had changed. She realized that the discussion had strengthened the resolve of some of the students, and only a couple actually changed sides of the issue. The students who were firmly entrenched in their beliefs did not change their opinions either way. Still she felt some came to see the issue differently as a result of the discussion, and some had an even stronger stance toward social justice (Figure 11.1).

Students then were asked to return to their seats, and she closed with a whole class discussion of student reactions to the activity in general before moving into a presentation on the specific sociological concepts underlying their arguments.

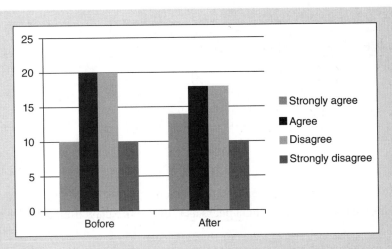

Figure 11.1 Student Positions Before and After Stand Where You Stand Activity

 ## Online: Drugs, Crime, and Public Policy

The professor of this online course in Public Affairs had to demonstrate the student learning outcome of developing a personal commitment and articulating a stance toward critical social issues, and decided to use Stand Where You Stand to document student progress toward the outcome. She assigned readings on the topic of legalization of marijuana, and then posed the question to the class: Should we legalize marijuana? She asked students to think for a moment and decide which position they most agreed with: I strongly agree we should legalize, I agree we should legalize, I disagree with legalization, I strongly disagree with legalization. Students were given 10 minutes to write down a rationale for their perspectives. She next asked students to line up at signs she had posted around the classroom indicating the different positions on the issue.

She had groups talk among themselves to develop the strongest rationale as possible for their position. She next asked a group leader to summarize the rationale for their groups, and then she allowed time for free discussion. The participants who were strongly opposed from the outset did not change their opinions as a result of the discussion, but those who were more moderate did make a positional change. She asked them to write for another 10 minutes about their positions. The teacher recorded the shifts and noted that all students were able to make a more informed case because of the activity (Table 11.5).

Table 11.5 Shifts in Position

	Strongly Agree	Agree	Disagree	Strongly Disagree
Before Discussion	10%	48%	37%	5%
After Discussion	12%	50%	23%	5%

Variations and Extensions

- Students may find having only four choices to be confining. Instead of the four corners, create a single line with the start marking one extreme and the end of the line the others. Have students talk to each other, and line up along the continuum. This variation, called Value Lines, allows for more nuance in choices and can have students engage in higher levels of thinking about the topic.

- Pair this activity with one of the other LATs. For example, have students individually or in small groups make a brief persuasive speech presentation (LAT 38: Three-Minute Message) or write a letter to the editor of the local newspaper (LAT 41: Editorial) about their stand. Students also work in pairs on these extensions.

Key References and Resources

Barkley, E. (2009). SET 40: Stand where you stand. In *Student engagement techniques: A handbook for college faculty* (pp. 321–322). San Francisco, CA: Jossey-Bass.

Brookfield, S. D., & Preskill, S. (2005). *Discussion as a way of teaching: Tools and techniques for democratic classrooms*. (2nd. ed., pp. 117–118). San Francisco, CA: Jossey-Bass.

LEARNING ASSESSMENT TECHNIQUE

Caring

38
Three-Minute Message

Complexity involved in	
Preparation	LOW
In-class implementation	HIGH
Analysis	MODERATE

Brief Description

Modeled on the Three-Minute Thesis (3MT) academic competition, students have three minutes to present a compelling argument and to support it with convincing details and examples.

Purpose

Oral communication is a critical skill that students will use beyond the limits of a single course. In this LAT, students learn the value of parsimonious oral presentation. The limited timeframe forces them to choose what is the most essential part of their message and then deliver their information in a clear and concise way using language that is accessible to a nonspecialist audience. Because students have to explain their work to others, they have to grapple with articulating their ideas and expose their thinking. In addition to helping students practice concise oral presentation, this technique allows students to learn from each other during the presentations.

The Learning Artifact is the presentation, which is captured on video or through the teacher's notes and rubric assessment. Oral presentations also present opportunities for probing questions in the moment. The Three-Minute Message is typically done after a unit of content and often in conjunction with another assessment. For example, students might write a LAT 27: Case Study or a LAT 43: Briefing Paper and then do a Three-Minute Message to share their results with the class. Alternately, a Three-Minute Message may be done as an impromptu activity at the end of a unit of content to demonstrate mastery. Either way, the Three-Minute Message is a type of performance assessment, with the performance being a demonstration of the learning that has occurred prior to the oral presentation.

Key Learning Goals

- A commitment to excellent work
- A willingness to engage in class activities
- The intention to make informed ethical choices

Implementation

Preparation

1. Oral presentations such as the Three-Minute Message may be used to assess a range of learning dimensions, and it is important to be clear at the outset what you want students to demonstrate. This might include concepts or theories or specific skills related to the subject of the course. In addition to these specific cognitive goals, this LAT can help you assess humanistic goals such as interpersonal competence, intrapersonal confidence (e.g., confidence, professionalism), and caring about the issue.
2. Select the focus of the message, whether student original research or course content that has been covered previously.
3. Create a rubric for assessing the Three-Minute Message. Table 11.5 is a sample rubric from University of Wisconsin Platteville (http://www.uwplatt.edu/system/files/UW-Mad%20Oral_presentation_rubric.pdf).
4. Set the parameters, such as the order of the presentations, the type of equipment they will have for displaying the slide (e.g., projector and slide, flipchart paper, or poster).
5. Determine how you will capture the Learning Artifact, whether through a video of each presentation, your rubric score of the presentation, your notes, student evaluations, or other.
6. Determine who will be involved in the assessment. In this technique, this means determining who will be able to ask questions of the student: an external assessor, a designated panel of peers, all peers, or other.

Process

1. Announce the activity, and discuss with students characteristics of an effective presentation.
2. Describe the parameters of the activity, noting that they will have exactly 3 minutes to make their presentations, they can use only one slide and there should be no animation or movement in the slide, and they should use spoken word (as opposed to music or poetry).
3. Share the presentation rubric with students so that they know how they will be assessed.
4. Give students time to prepare their messages.
5. Allow class time for the message presentations, and complete the rubric during the presentations.
6. Collect the Learning Artifacts, whether videos, rubric scores, peer evaluations, or other.

Online

Have students video record their message and post them in an agreed upon location (for example their blogs or in an LMS). They might also incorporate visuals, for example by creating a screencast (e.g. with Screencast-o-matic) or an animated presentation site (such as Powtoon). Students then watch each other's videos and comment on them.

Table 11.6 Sample Rubric for Evaluating Oral Presentation

	4 – Exceptional	3 – Admirable	2 – Acceptable	1 – Poor
Eye Contact	Holds attention of entire audience with the use of direct eye contact, seldom looking at notes or slides.	Consistent use of direct eye contact with audience, but still returns to notes.	Displayed minimal eye contact with audience, while reading mostly from notes.	No eye contact with audience, as entire report is read from note.
Body Language	Movements seem fluid and help the audience visualize.	Made movements or gestures that enhance articulation.	Very little movement or descriptive gestures.	No movement or descriptive gestures.
Poise	Displays relaxed, self-confident nature about self, with no mistakes.	Makes minor mistakes, but quickly recovers from them; displays little or no tension.	Displays mild tension; has trouble recovering from mistakes.	Tension and nervousness is obvious; has trouble recovering from mistakes.
Enthusiasm	Demonstrates a strong, positive feeling about topic during entire presentation.	Occasionally shows positive feelings about topic.	Shows some negativity toward topic presented.	Shows absolutely no interest in topic presented.
Speaking Skills	Uses a clear voice and speaks at a good pace so audience members can hear presentation. Does not read off slides.	Presenter's voice is clear. The pace is a little slow or fast at times. Most audience members can hear presentation.	Presenter's voice is low. The pace is much too rapid/slow. Audience members have difficulty hearing presentation.	Presenter mumbles, talks very fast, and speaks too quietly for a majority of students to hear and understand.
Length of Presentation	Within two minutes of allotted time +/–.	Within four minutes of allotted time +/–.	Within six minutes of allotted time +/–	Too long or too short; ten or more minutes above or below allotted time.
Subject Knowledge	An abundance of material clearly related to the research is presented. Points are clearly made and evidence is used to support claims.	Sufficient information with many good points made, uneven balance and little consistency.	There is a great deal of information that is not clearly integrated or connected to the research.	Goal of research unclear, information included that does not support research claims in any way.
Organization	Information is presented in a logical and interesting sequence which audience can follow. Flows well.	Information is presented in logical sequence which audience can follow.	Audience has difficulty following presentation because the presentation jumps around and lacks clear transitions.	Audience cannot understand presentation because there is no sequence of information.
Visuals	Excellent visuals that are tied into the overall story of the research.	Appropriate visuals are used and explained by the speaker.	Visuals are used but not explained or put in context.	Little or no visuals, too much text on slides.
Mechanics	Presentation has no misspellings or grammatical errors.	Presentation has no more than two misspellings and/or grammatical errors.	Presentation has three misspellings and/or grammatical errors.	Presentation has many spelling and/or grammatical errors.
Comments:				

Source: University of Wisconsin Platteville (http://www.uwplatt.edu/system/files/UW-Mad%20Oral_presentation_rubric.pdf)

Analysis and Reporting

Use the rubric you created to score and grade the Three-Minute Messages. Provide additional narrative comments about anything that stands out in a given presentation. Return scored rubrics to students along with any narrative comments. If you have had students also evaluate the presentations, create a composite of their evaluations to return to students.

Use one of the rubrics to aggregate results. Tally the number of responses for each item and then look across the comments that you wrote to notice any patterns in the information. Use a simple table or chart to present aggregated results from the rubric scoring.

Examples

Onsite: History of American Higher Education

In this onsite, graduate-level history course, the professor had a learning goal that students would be able to communicate the results of original research. As a part of the course, he had students researching the integration of the university in the university archives. Students read archival work, developed a thesis, and documented their argument through historical records. He decided to use the Three-Minute Message to have them present their work to the rest of the class because he wanted to keep the presentations tight, knowing that student presentations could be dull.

He announced the activity, and he shared his prepared rubric with the students. The class met for 3 hours and had 20 students enrolled. The first half of the class meeting, 10 students presented, they took a break, and then 10 more students presented. He scored the rubrics while students were presenting and also videotaped the presentations so that students could review their own performances and find ways to improve them in the future.

He created a bar graph of the results, which he shared with the students (Figure 11.2). He noticed and pointed out that nonverbal communication had the lowest ratings because students often read their speeches and that the content scores were the highest. He also asked them to review the taped sessions and to notice where they were struggling the most. Finally he asked them to write a reflection on what they would do differently next time, which he also used as data and presented a summary of suggestions at the next class session.

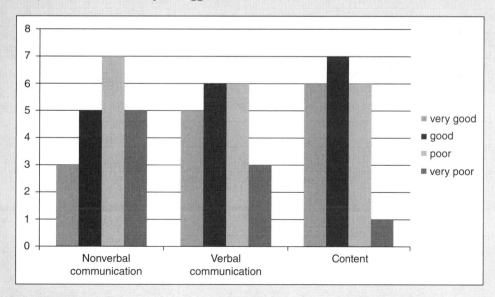

Figure 11.2 Sample Bar Graph Illustrating Number of Students Who Fell in Each Category of Response on the Rubric

Online: Social Media

This special topics communications course focused on the use of social media in contemporary society. A course goal was to demonstrate basic practical social media skills necessary to create and propagate content. The professor decided to use Three-Minute Messages so that students could teach each other about different social media and so that she could assess their basic level of familiarity with the various tools.

She assigned each student in the course a different tool such as Facebook, Tumblr, Twitter, and Diigo. Each student had to research the uses of the different tool and present a Three-Minute Message on why and how to use it. The students were responsible for creating their own videos and sharing them, and so she had a range of presentations from iMovie videos uploaded to YouTube to Prezi and Camtasia presentations. Students simply posted links to their presentations to the designated discussion forum.

Students were told to review each other's presentations and comment on them within the discussion forum. They had the specific task of identifying one thing the presenter did well and one thing upon which the presenter could improve. The professor made a composite of all of the comments (Table 11.7).

She found through her own analysis of the presentations via a rubric and through the students' comments on each other's presentations that students did have a good grasp of the tools and how to use them effectively. She noted, however, that they needed additional practice in the increasingly important skill of online presentation. She prepared materials for a module on using social media for online presentations and shared some examples with the class of effective online presentations. She introduced another Three-Minute Message later in the term to have students describe how to use the tool for scholarly communication.

Table 11.7 Social Media "How To" Presentations

What Were Students Praised For	What Were Students Criticized For
Knowing the tool/content inside out	Excessive pauses
Introducing the tool quickly and succinctly	Filler words ("um," "like")
Providing visual examples	Overfull slides
Keeping slides simple	Reading slides
Using humor	Fidgeting
Staying within the time frame	Not making eye contact with computer/audience

Variations and Extensions

- Place students in work groups to develop the content of the messages. Have them select a leader to present the results.
- Use a peer evaluation rubric in addition to the rubric you use to gather additional information from students.
- Consider having the students vote on "best Three-Minute Messages" as an additional data point.

- Instead of a Three-Minute Message, try a Three-Minute Elevator Pitch, in which students present an idea or product to a panel.
- For a longer version of this LAT, ask students to create a 15–20 minute classroom TED Talk.

Key References and Resources

Gordon, J. (nd). A short guide to oral assessment. https://www.leedsbeckett.ac.uk/publications/files/100317_36668_ShortGuideOralAssess1_WEB.pdf.

3MT. (nd). Three-minute thesis. http://threeminutethesis.org.

LEARNING ASSESSMENT TECHNIQUE

Caring

39
Issue Awareness Ad

Complexity involved in	
Preparation	LOW
In-class implementation	LOW-MODERATE
Analysis	HIGH

Brief Description

Students use research and persuasive skills to create an advertisement intended to raise awareness about a current course-related issue.

Purpose

Developing an advertisement requires students to use several important skills. They demonstrate creativity when they identify an issue, research skills as they investigate the issue, evaluating skills when they select the appropriate communication venues and tools for getting the message out about their cause, and persuasive skills when they create the advertisement to increase awareness. This LAT also requires students to make a commitment to an issue and then use research skills to investigate the issue and evaluation skills to select the appropriate communication venues and tools for getting the message out about their cause. It is an authentic task that can help increase their understanding of an issue as well as their level of caring about it.

The Learning Artifacts are the advertisements. These ads can take a variety of forms, depending on the goal of the campaign, but they all demonstrate student learning in a unique way that differs from traditional paper and pencil exams. Issue Awareness Ads reveal what students are concerned about through their selection of a topic, and they show the level of student commitment through the effort students expend toward learning about the issue and communicating their caring to others. This LAT is best used at the end of a learning module or course as a culminating experience.

Key Learning Goals

- Motivation to learn in the subject area
- Openness to new ideas in the subject area

- An appreciation of diverse perspectives related to this subject
- A willingness to engage in class activities
- Informed concern about current social issues relevant to the topic
- The intention to make informed ethical choices

Implementation

Preparation

- Determine whether you will provide students with a list of issues or whether you will allow them to decide what they would like to do. If you do the latter, consider whether you would like to add a step of "topic approval."
- Decide how specific you will be about the parameters of the assignment. You could for example ask students to create a newspaper ad, a poster, a short commercial, an online graphic, a promoted post for social media, or other. Or you could provide students with options and allow them to choose or come up with their own idea.
- Create a rubric for evaluating the ad, such as in Table 11.8.
- Create a handout to explain assignment parameters and evaluation criteria.
- Consider whom to involve in the assessment. Peer review can be particularly effective.

Process

1. Present students with the handout and allow time for questions.
2. Provide students with time to work on the assignment. This work could happen in class, out of class, or a combination of the two.
3. Collect the Learning Artifacts.

Online

Students can create the assignment and either post it on their blogs or YouTube and share link information or alternately they could add their contributions to a course wiki.

Table 11.8 Evaluation Rubric

Importance of the issue	5 4 3 2 1
Level of concern demonstrated	5 4 3 2 1
Creativity	5 4 3 2 1
Message	5 4 3 2 1
Composition	5 4 3 2 1
Overall Appeal	5 4 3 2 1

Table 11.9 Rubric

Category and Description	Exceeds Expectation 7–10 points	Meets Expectation 4–6 points	Below Expectation 0–3 points	Total
Message The ad has an important and compelling message.				
Audience The student has a clear target audience in mind.				
Design The layout has an appealing design and is neat. It includes a focal point, makes use of white space and color.				
Style There are no grammatical, punctuation, or spelling errors.				
Illustrations and Images Components are clearly related to and represent the product. They enhance the advertisement.				
TOTALS				

Analysis and Reporting

Use the rubric you created to score specific qualities and also look for anything unique in the individual responses (Table 11.9).

Develop a written response to individuals that includes both rubric scoring and comments about any issues.

Use your rubric to aggregate results. Tally the number of responses for each item, and then use a table to display information.

Examples

Onsite: Health Communication

The professor of this course had the following learning outcome: by the end of the course, students will engage in critical and creative thinking with regard to developing and evaluating public health communications campaigns. She also wanted students to effectively communicate understanding of and interrelationships among key concepts within the domain of public health communication. She decided to use the Issue Awareness Ad to help students develop these skills and understanding.

She announced the assignment in class, providing them with wide latitude about topics, intended audience, and what kind of ad to develop. She provided some in-class time for students to work so they could exchange ideas. At the deadline, students presented their ads to the class and she used a rubric to evaluate and also asked the class to vote for the top five ads presented (Table 11.10).

Table 11.10 Top Five Ads Evaluation

	5	4	3	2	1
Message	15%	40%	30%	10%	5%
Creativity	5%	30%	40%	20%	5%
Composition	5%	30%	30%	30%	5%
Overall	5%	30%	40%	20%	5%

She found that students were higher in the "message" category. That is, they had important things to say. They had more difficulty in the composition and creativity categories. She also noted that the ads in the top five were most highly correlated with her creativity ratings. When she presented the overarching scores to the class, this point led to an interesting discussion about the role of the medium in the message.

 Online: Instructional Technology

The professor of this Instructional Technology course had a goal that students would become more engaged online citizens. He decided to use Issue Awareness Ads and have students create an anti-cyber bullying campaign to help them achieve this goal and to provide him with evidence that they had achieved it.

He announced the assignment on the course blog. Students posted their ads to their own blogs, and because he had syndicated all of their blog feeds in the main course blog, all of their individual postings showed up on the main course blogs. He asked students to comment on each other's posts, saying one thing each student did well and one thing each student could improve. He evaluated the blogs with a rubric he had created, and then he shared the aggregated results of the assessment with the students.

Variations and Extensions

- Allow students to work in groups to create the ad. You will have a group product to assess rather than an individual one.
- Instead of a campaign ad, have students develop an advocacy petition. They identify the cause and write up the petition.

Key References and Resources

Silberman, M. (1996). TV Commercial. In *Active learning: 101 strategies to teach any subject* (p. 41). Des Moines, IA: Prentice Hall.

LEARNING ASSESSMENT TECHNIQUE

Caring

40
Proclamations

Complexity involved in	
Preparation	LOW
In-class implementation	HIGH
Analysis	HIGH

Brief Description

Students identify and analyze a problematic situation in the local community. They then write and deliver a speech that persuades others of the urgency of the problem and offers strategies for solving the problem.

Purpose

Encouraging students to work on problems that are authentic and relevant to them is refreshingly different from just assigning readings about problems and issues in a textbook. Thus this technique engages students in working for solutions that they find important and interesting. Researching and proposing solutions to problems helps students develop critical and creative thinking skills. Working on a "real" problem in the community can deepen understanding of theoretical concepts, demonstrate the relevance and importance of academic work, and help foster a greater sense of social and civic responsibility. Since students present their analysis and solution strategies in a persuasive speech, this LAT can also help students develop communication skills.

The Learning Artifacts for this LAT are the written speech and the presentation of the speech. These artifacts provides faculty with a unique way to gauge the level of time and effort students have put into creating a good case, which in turn is a demonstrator of how much they care about the assignment and topic. It also allows them to demonstrate their curiosity about and enthusiasm for learning, which is another indicator of caring.

Key Learning Goals

- Motivation to learn in the subject area
- A commitment to excellent work

- A willingness to engage in class activities
- Informed concern about current social issues relevant to the topic
- The intention to make informed ethical choices

Implementation

Preparation

- Spend time thinking through the parameters of this assignment. What kinds of community problems do you want students to identify? For example, can the problems be general (e.g., graffiti, reckless driving, noise, ethnic conflict, and so forth) or should they be discipline specific (e.g., art discipline–related community problems might include insufficient amateur artist exhibit opportunities, lack of information on how and where to dispose of art-related hazardous waste materials, artists' sense of social isolation, and so forth).
- Determine how you will select the final problems. You might ask students to use newspapers, media, the Internet, personal experience, and so forth to identify 2–3 local community problems that they would like to investigate. You might select from those to ensure good distribution of the topics, or you might have students select their own topics.
- Determine who the audience of the speech is. Is it a mayor, Chamber of Commerce, school district Board of Trustees, city planning? Consider involving students in this decision.
- If the skill level of your students is such that they require more scaffolding, consider identifying sample problems and writing a model speech yourself to help clarify your expectations. Also consider having students prepare a prospectus in which they state the problem, give specific examples of the problem, and identify possible reasons for the problem. Finally, consider providing them with guidance on writing speeches, such as suggesting that they create an outline, number points so audience members can follow, and after each point return to the main theme.

Process

1. Announce the activity and ask students to begin their work.
2. Allow time for students to analyze the problem, identify solutions, and decide on the central idea they are trying to convey.
3. Ask students to develop their speeches.
4. If desired, ask them to present the speeches, and collect the written documents.

Online

Have students write their speeches and create videos and then post them online on their blogs. They might also post their texts and videos to their course blogs.

Analysis and Reporting

Use a rubric to assess the written and spoken artifacts. To assess the outcome of "caring," these might, for example, focus on community or civic engagement. Consider the following options as rubric qualities:

- Knowledge relevant to civic engagement
- Skills in identifying activities that can address a community problem
- Articulated views that can support making a difference
- A well-defined plan for action

Share your assessment of their work with individuals. You may wish to assign a grade by determining a percentage of total scores that students receive on the rubric assessment. You may also choose to provide students with narrative comments responding to the different aspects of the rubric. These also can highlight issues of engagement such as how much time and effort students expended on creating and delivering their speeches.

To examine results in aggregate, use your rubric scores and determine mean scores for each item. Look across items to determine whether there are any obvious differences in the scores. Also look across the comments that you wrote to notice any patterns in the information. Use a numeric table or graph to describe the results of your analysis of the rubric. Use a narrative table to display the results of your analysis of key issues with the student work or key themes they related, depending on your goal.

Examples

Onsite: Race and Ethnic Relations

The professor of this course has to document student learning outcomes each year prior to his promotion and tenure review. In this particular course he focuses on the evolving meaning of race and ethnicity as it relates to intergroup relations in the United States. The professor has a learning outcome that students will develop knowledge necessary for civic engagement. The professor decided to use Proclamations to help students better bridge theory and practice and to help students recognize their potential power as change agents for improving relations in their community.

He asked students to write down on a piece of paper a list of five problems that they observed in their community that seemed to have some basis in the area's changed racial and ethnic demographics. He collected the papers, made a synthesized, composite list, and distributed the list to the class, asking students to choose a topic from the list. Their assignment included discussing the problem, coming to agreement on strategies to solve the problem, and then writing a speech to their classmates about a course of action to take.

He listened to their speeches and also examined the written records of them. He used the Learning Assessment Matrix to summarize his findings (Table 11.11).

Table 11.11 Learning Assessment Matrix: Proclamations

Student Learning Outcomes	LAT	Subject/ Content Prompt	Intentional Active Learning Activity	Learning Artifact	Findings and Interpretations	Actions to Be Taken
Students will describe their stances as social justice advocates.	Proclamations	Independent research	Writing a speech	The written or presented speech	Students identified a problem and took an engaged stance toward it. They need additional work in the area of civic communication, specifically in persuading an audience to action.	Additional instruction on writing an effective persuasive argument.

 ### Online: Urban Poverty

In this course, students critically examine the nature and perceptions of urban poverty in America. The professor was concerned that students were simply marking time in the course because they needed it for their major coursework, but that they were not really engaging with the content in significant ways. He wanted students to delve deeply into the topic in order to understand the structures that are in place that contribute to maintenance of poverty and to take a stance toward alleviating the problem. To help them learn about this issue and to help him assess their learning, he assigned Proclamations.

He formed small groups and asked students to brainstorm a list of structures (such as income inequality, land rights and ownership, wasteful or inefficient agriculture, health care costs, war) that they believed currently contribute to ongoing poverty in the United States. Each student had to choose a structure and research and develop a speech to articulate how it perpetuates poverty. He asked students to do their research and writing at home, but he informed them that they would deliver their speeches in class so that they all could learn from each other.

He assessed the written document on content and organization and the oral presentations based on delivery and expressiveness, as well as other criteria. To determine whether they understood the central concepts and had knowledge necessary for civic engagement, he did a key word analysis of their speeches, shown in Figure 11.3.

He was able to see that they had developed critical knowledge necessary for engagement through their work and determined that he would continue to use the activity in the future.

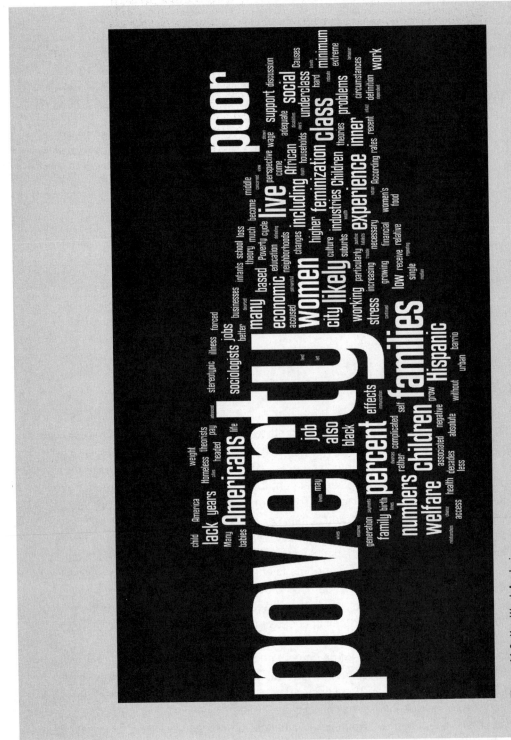

Figure 11.3 Key Word Analysis

Variations and Extensions

- Put students into groups so that they work on their speeches together.

Key References and Resources

Barkley, E. (2010). SET 26: Proclamations. In *Student engagement techniques: A handbook for college faculty* (pp. 264–266). San Francisco, CA: Jossey-Bass.

Berkowitz, B. (2007). "The community tool box: Bringing solutions to light." Work Group for Community Health and Development. University of Kansas. http://ctb.ku.edu/en.

Watts, M. M. (2007). *Service learning*. Upper Saddle River, NJ: Pearson/Prentice Hall.

LEARNING ASSESSMENT TECHNIQUE

Caring

41
Editorial

Complexity involved in	
Preparation	LOW
In-class implementation	MODERATE
Analysis	HIGH

Brief Description

In this adaptation of the classic newspaper editorial essay, the instructor guides students through the process of writing an editorial on a topic that interests them.

Purpose

Research-based persuasive writing can provide an authentic learning experience, since students can see many examples of this form of writing in their everyday lives. Although this LAT is based on an established, traditional writing format, it can be updated to reflect new forms of persuasive writing that appear in online forums. Students are motivated as they write for an authentic audience on a topic of personal interest. As students take a stance toward the issue, they also take ownership of it, and this creates opportunities to increase student caring about important issues in the field.

The Learning Artifacts of this LAT are the fully crafted editorials. These essays provide rich content for assessment. In particular, the level of expended effort and the student's ability to persuasively make a case for action serve as an indicator of caring about a topic or issue. This LAT is typically used as an assessment of student performance. It most often is used after students have had exposure to course content, occurring at the end of a learning module or unit.

Key Learning Goals

- Motivation to learn in the subject area
- A commitment to excellent work
- Informed concern about current social issues relevant to the topic
- A commitment to upholding their own values

Implementation

Preparation

- Set the parameters for the assignment, such as length of the editorial and time frame for completing it.
- Identify some examples of good editorials in your subject area, and make them available to students for review.
- Create a rubric for scoring, such as shown in Table 11.12.
- Determine who will be involved in the assessment. You may, for example, want to include student peer review as it can provide valuable data for you and the student writers.

Process

1. Ask students to brainstorm topics. They should select issues that they care about, that are related to course content, and that others would be interested enough to read about.
2. Ask students to gather background information about the topic, through reading newspaper articles, academic magazine articles, scholarly journal articles, seeking out experts, or other.

Table 11.12 Sample Rubric for Scoring Editorial

	Advanced (4)	Proficient (3)	Developing (2)	Beginning (1)
Viewpoint	The author states a clear opinion.	The author states an opinion.	The author implies an opinion.	The author states facts in a way that suggest opinion.
Call to Action	There is a clear request that readers take action.	There is a request that readers take action.	There is a hint to readers to take action.	The reader may be able to infer what action the author wants.
Evidence	There is clear and compelling evidence to support the opinion. The writer cites reliable sources.	There is clear evidence to support the opinion. The writer cites reliable sources.	There is evidence to support the opinion. The writer cites sources.	There is minimal evidence to support the opinion. The writer cites a minimum number of sources.
Persuasion	Author convincingly argues point of view by providing relevant background, using valid examples, acknowledging counter claims, and developing claims.	Author argues point of view by providing relevant examples and acknowledging counter claims.	Author argues point of view and acknowledges counter claims.	Author implies point of view.
Language	Editorial has a strong and engaging voice. The style and tone are appropriate to the purpose.	Editorial has a strong voice. The style and tone are appropriate to the purpose.	The style and tone are appropriate to the purpose.	The style and tone could be appropriate to the purpose given some revision.
Mechanics	The essay is written with correct grammar, spelling, and punctuation.	The essay is written with mostly correct grammar, spelling, and punctuation.	The essay is written with some correct grammar, spelling, and punctuation.	The essay has some sentence level errors that should be corrected.

3. Ask students to take notes on their articles, which they may do in a traditional way or through more recent technological tools such as Diigo or other bookmarking sites that allow for annotations and note-taking. They can consult the Online Writing Lab at Purdue University for additional guidelines including information about how to evaluate sources: (https://owl.english.purdue.edu/owl/section/2/8/).

4. Ask students to outline their arguments and then complete the final editorial. Again, the Online Writing Lab at Purdue University provides some useful guidelines, in this case on writing argumentative essays (https://owl.english.purdue.edu/owl/resource/724/1/).

5. Collect the Learning Artifacts.

6. If appropriate for your course and the topics, consider offering guidance on submitting the best editorials for publication.

Online

Post instructions and ask students to submit their editorials through whatever platform you are using, whether submitting through an LMS or posting to their own blogs.

Analysis and Reporting

Use your rubric to score the editorial essays. Because this activity requires a substantial amount of time and effort on the part of the students, most faculty assign a grade for it. To report their scores, develop a written response to individuals that includes both rubric scoring and comments about any issues that arise in the individual essays.

To aggregate results, use one of the rubrics. Tally the number of responses for each item. Look across the comments that you wrote to notice any patterns in the information. Use a simple table to provide aggregated information about the rubric scoring. In a narrative, describe any trends you see that are not captured in the rubric assessment.

Examples

Onsite: Writing About Global Science

This course is focused on providing students with experience in producing persuasive writing about global science topics. The instructor wants students to focus on learning how to translate global science into accessible true stories that reach wide audiences.

For one assignment, the professor has students develop a 1,500–2,000 word editorial on a global science/international sustainability issue. Students begin by outlining a plan of action—including sources to interview, events to cover, books to read, and information to uncover. She provides students with these instructions:

- Identify a current issue, and take a stance on it.
- Research information related to that position, both points that support your position and that suggest another side.

Table 11.13 Comparison of Student Editorial Self-Evaluation and Peer Evaluation Scores

Element	Average Writer's Evaluation	Average Reader's Evaluation
Writer clearly states position.	90%	75%
Writer includes facts to support that position.	85%	70%
Writer acknowledges opposing opinion.	90%	80%
Writer acknowledges facts from opposing side.	90%	60%
Writer makes effective challenges to opposing facts.	80%	60%
Writer makes appeal for support to the reader.	90%	85%

- Write an editorial promoting your specific point of view.
- When you have finished your editorial, consider whether you have included elements listed below. Mark with a checkmark if you think you have included the element and a zero if you think you have not.
- Exchange your editorial with a classmate and ask him or her do the same. Compare your answers. Discuss your writing with your classmate.

For the peer review, she also provides a handout. Next, she averaged self-evaluation scores as well as peer evaluation scores and made a direct comparison between the two (Table 11.13).

The professor found that the writers have higher opinions of their work than their readers. She used this information to hold a full class discussion about why this might be true and believed the conversation about how to be more aware of the audience was a productive one.

 Online: Editorial Column Writing (Journalism)

This course focuses on opinion writing for both print and online media. Major topics of the course include: strategies for finding editorial ideas, researching these ideas, and locating and evaluating sources. The course also focuses on the art of writing, including use of effective persuasion techniques, writing style and tone, and attention to diverse audiences. The course has several specific objectives including:

- Understanding the art of opinion writing
- Selecting and evaluating public issues for potential editorials
- Using a variety of styles, techniques, and organizational methods to produce effective editorials
- Employing logic to make arguments and to recognize fallacies
- Understanding the importance of opinion pages and online forums as means to serve a public purpose that serves a diverse audience

Table 11.14 Summary of Editorial Assignment Assessment Results

	Advanced (4)	Proficient (3)	Developing (2)	Beginning (1)
Viewpoint	10%	50%	30%	10%
Call to Action	25%	35%	25%	15%
Evidence	10%	25%	40%	25%
Persuasion	25%	35%	35%	5%
Language	60%	20%	15%	5%
Mechanics	75%	15%	5%	5%

Over the course of the academic term, students write four editorials, which comprise 60% of their course grade. From previous courses, the professor knows that having an opinion is easy, but supporting that opinion with credible information is harder. She decides to use data to examine whether her intuition about students' weaker areas is accurate. To begin the activity, the professor provided students with these process guidelines:

- Identify an issue that has at least two potential sides.
- Identify your position on the issue.
- Write down three facts that support your position.
- Identify the opposing position.
- Write down at least three facts that support the opposing position.
- Describe your response or challenge to the opposing arguments.
- Develop an outline that will allow you to support your position and refute the opposing arguments.
- Draft your editorial.
- Revise your editorial.

She collected the final editorials and assessed them using a rubric. Table 11.14 represents her results:

She noted that most of the students were fairly good writers, but, as she suspected, they were not proficient at providing their opinions and supporting them with evidence. She determined to target her teaching to these particular skills.

Variations and Extensions

- Provide students with opportunities to collaborate on their editorials. They may do so for only one aspect, such as the research, or collaborate from beginning to end.
- Ask students to complete a peer review of each other's editorials.
- Have students read their editorials to the class or in small groups.
- Consider adding a competitive aspect of this assignment and have students "vote" on best editorial.

Key References and Resources

Gonchar, M. (2014). For the sake of argument: Writing persuasively to craft short, evidence-based editorials. http://learning.blogs.nytimes.com//2014/02/07/for-the-sake-of-argument-writing-persuasively-to-craft-short-evidence-based-editorials/.

LEARNING ASSESSMENT TECHNIQUE

Caring

42
Debate

Complexity involved in	
Preparation	LOW
In-class implementation	HIGH
Analysis	MODERATE

Description

In a debate, students research and analyze a controversial topic and then engage in a series of oral presentations of their arguments against an opposing team.

Purpose

Preparing for, participating in, and listening to debates offers many benefits to students. Debates can increase motivation, enhance research skills, promote critical thinking, and develop communication proficiency. Debates expose the class to a focused, in-depth, multiple-perspective analysis of issues. This LAT can move students beyond simple dualistic thinking, deepen their understanding of an issue, and help them to recognize the range of perspectives inherent in complex topics. In this way, a debate may also build appreciation for diversity and develop tolerance for other viewpoints. Moreover, the competitive aspect of the technique is motivating for many students.

The debate itself is the Learning Artifact, and this may be recorded and kept for viewing and reviewing. The advantage of this kind of assessment activity is that it is a form of "authentic assessment." That is, students realize that they have to be effective at arguing from an informed position, and this technique provides a low-threat situation in which that can happen. It provides teachers with an in-the-moment view of how well students can communicate their ideas clearly and succinctly and how well they can argue their cases. Finally, the effort that students put into the debate stands as a potential measure of caring about a topic or issue. The technique then can not only increase caring about a topic but also provide an assessable indicator of that caring.

This technique works best if students have a reasonably deep knowledge or understanding of the topic so that they can make better arguments and rebuttals. Debate is therefore best used after students have had time to investigate a topic beforehand either through lecture, discussion, or reading assignments. It is possible to use a scaled down version of the debate, more of a structured argument, as a formative assessment during a lesson of how well students are learning what they should be.

Key Learning Goals

- Motivation to learn in the subject area
- Openness to new ideas in the subject area
- An appreciation of diverse perspectives related to this subject
- A willingness to engage in class activities
- Informed concern about current social issues relevant to the topic
- The intention to make informed ethical choices

Implementation

Preparation

- Spend sufficient time selecting a controversial topic in the field with two identifiable, arguable, and opposing sides that are appropriate to debate. The topic must be one that is engaging. It is especially effective when topics address issues that are contemporary and connected to students' lives.
- Carefully craft the debate proposition into a one-sentence statement, such as "Universities should use affirmative action policies to determine student admission." Proposition statements should avoid ambiguity, yet be general enough to offer students flexibility in building arguments.
- Determine whether students need any background information to address the proposition. Prepare students for the debate through lecture, assigned reading, discussion, or student research on the topic.
- Identify ground rules. For example, allow students to use as many arguments as they wish, or have students spend 5–10 minutes brainstorming all possible arguments supporting their position and then select their five best arguments. Consider whether each team should select one person as spokesperson, or whether each member of the team will be responsible for presenting at least one of the arguments. Thinking about ground rules ahead of time will also provide the opportunity to decide whether to assign team members specific roles, such as team leader or timekeeper.
- Determine who will be involved in the assessment and why. You may, for example, want students to self-assess or peer assess or you may want to bring in external stakeholders to serve as a judging panel.
- Create a rubric. Chan (2009) offers Table 11.15 as an example.

Process

1. Divide students into 4–6 member teams, with half the teams assigned to one side of the argument and the other half assigned to the opposing argument.
2. Explain ground rules and give students time to assign roles and organize how they will prepare for and conduct the debate.

Table 11.15 Sample Rubric for Evaluating Debate

	Excellent	Proficient	Average	Poor
Preparation	Prepared a very broad scope of information and deep, critical analysis of the given topic; information is collected from a wide range of sources and perspectives which effectively contribute to development of arguments	Satisfactory preparation of information and analysis for the given topic; major issues about the topic was well covered	Demonstrated preparation for the basic information of the given topic, but no evidence of analysis coming from the student was shown	Failed to prepare even the basic and essential information of the given topic
Organization and Presentation	Logical flow in the presentation of arguments; information organized in a coherent manner; powerful and persuasive presentation	Generally clear flow of arguments; presentation is persuasive but with minor problems	Able to give the basic framework of the presented ideas, but lack of persuasive power	Information not appropriately digested; presented without any focus; chaotic flow
Use of Arguments	Plenty of very strong and persuasive arguments	Many fairly strong arguments but a few are not persuasive	Arguments are generally on the right track but not convincing and strong enough	Arguments are not significant and even irrelevant to the debate topic
Rebuttal	Excellent defense and attack against the opposite side; able to identify the weakness of the opposite side	Satisfactory defense and attack against the opposite side; attempted to find out weakness of the opposite side	Fail to defend for some issues; a few successful attacks against the opposite side	Fail to defend against the opposite side; unable to attack the opposite side in most of the issues

3. Give students time to prepare their arguments (such as 15 to 30 minutes).

4. Pair teams representing opposing sides.

5. Announce and allow time for the debate to proceed (Chan, 2009, recommends the following sequence):

   • The affirmative team captain begins by introducing the debate, and defines the motion by stating what his/her team understands by the motion. The student will then introduce the team members and outline the perspectives they plan to approach the issue in question. Next, the student raises the first argument for the motion.

   • There should be no interruption from the opposing team during the speeches, and each person is given a strict time limit to speak.

   • The captain of the team arguing against the motion then completes the same process as the other captain, except that he/she would be raising the argument against the motion.

   • The debate then proceeds by having the team members presenting their arguments and rebuttals: Affirmative Member 1, Negative Member 1, Affirmative Member 2, Negative Member 2, Affirmative Member 3, Negative Member 3, and so forth.

   • After the team members finished their presentations, the captain of the Negative team gives a summary, in which no new material is added. The captain of the Affirmative team will then give the summary for his/her team.

- The host may allow some time for the two teams to challenge each other's perspectives.
- As part of the scoring system, the host can ask the audiences for a show of hands to see if they have changed their viewpoints after the debate.

6. Hold a whole class discussion to summarize the important issues and to allow students to discuss their opinions freely.

Online

Debates are typically held in real-time and in a shared space, characteristics that contribute to the sense of immediacy that is so important to the process. To maintain the sense of spontaneity, use synchronous tools such as Web conferencing or immersive environments and use a combination of group chat and full group discussion. Alternately, consider implementing this in an asynchronous environment by using Discussion Forums. (See "Sociology: Contemporary Issues example.)

Although an asynchronous debate may lack the sense of immediacy achieved in an onsite debate, the essential characteristics of requiring students to assume, investigate, and debate a contrary perspective are preserved. Additionally, student responses may be more reflective. Consider posting a follow-up Threaded Discussion in which students can share how it felt to assume a position contrary to their beliefs and inviting them to say whether participating in the debate changed their viewpoints.

Analysis and Reporting

Use the rubric you created to score the debate. Because it can be a significant amount of work, teachers often assign a grade to this activity. If you do a scaled back version which requires less preparation, you may not want to grade it or alternately to assign a low stakes grade. Return your rubrics to the students. You may also take a vote on the "winner" of the debate (either from external stakeholders or alternately by students assigned to the role of audience) which provides additional feedback to the two teams.

To examine Learning Artifacts in aggregate, look across rubric categories to note areas in which most teams performed well and where most need improvement. Use a simple tally of rubric results, and consider adding a narrative review.

Examples

Onsite: Philosophy of Law

Due to an increase in illegal immigration, terrorist attacks, and Internet sabotage, the professor was starting the semester amid heightened publicity on the need to improve national security. One solution that received significant media attention was a proposal to implement an expanded, federally maintained and integrated individual-identification system. The professor believed that it was important for his law students to understand the complexity of the issues regarding individual versus national rights underlying proposals such as this. He therefore decided to add to his course a unit on privacy rights.

Table 11.16 Summary Assessment Results of Debate Activity

	Excellent	Proficient	Acceptable	Poor
Preparation	10%	40%	40%	10%
Organization and Presentation	90%	10%	0%	0%
Use of Arguments	10%	40%	40%	10%
Rebuttal	10%	40%	40%	10%

To introduce the unit, he had students complete a survey in which they rated from 1–5 their level of agreement with a series of statements on the national collection, maintenance, and disposal of personal records. During the weeks that followed, he took care to cover a wide range of examples of the basic conflict from several perspectives, including real life scenarios concerning everything from financial and medical records to confidentiality of opinions expressed in email and on the Internet. By the completion of the unit, students had at least a basic knowledge of the challenges from both the individual's and the government's perspectives.

To help students synthesize the information presented in the unit and to help them clarify their personal views, he closed the unit with a debate. Using the initial survey as a guide, he organized students into two groups based on their overall tendency to support individual or national rights. The professor then assigned individual students to a team charged with arguing for or against the proposal: *The government is justified in collecting and maintaining personal information on private citizens.* Wherever possible, he assigned students to a team asked to argue the side contrary to their general beliefs. He rated their arguments as shown in Table 11.16.

He noted that students prepared at different rates, but that most fell somewhere in the middle of preparation, not great but not poor. He noted that most observed the structure and rules of the debate. Some were better at arguments and rebuttals than others, and these not surprisingly seemed directly related to their preparation.

After the debate, he had students re-take the original survey. He then had students compare their individual pre- and post-responses to the survey, noting any areas of change. As a final activity, he had students write an essay responding to the prompt by summarizing the issues using concrete examples and concluding with their personal viewpoints.

Online: Sociology: Contemporary Issues

This instructor decided to use Debate to explore issues related to gun control. He first asked students to rank their opinions from *strongly in favor of changes to gun control laws* to *strongly opposed.* Next, he posted a paragraph that explained the rationale behind Debate, provided the discussion proposal, and gave assignment directions.

He organized the students into "Pro" or "Con" teams of eight students each and created a forum for each team. He made the forums "protected access" so that only team members could access their forum.

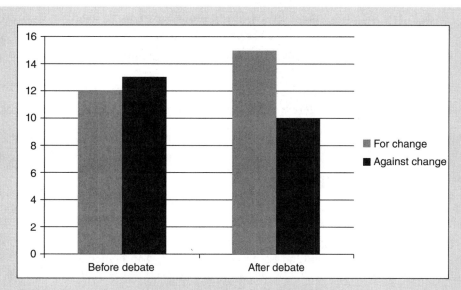

Figure 11.4 Bar Graph Illustrating Student Positions Before and After Debate

On the whole-class discussion board, he informed students of their team assignments and gave team members one or two weeks to research and post their arguments on the appropriate forum. After the deadline, he opened forums to all students, required students to read through the arguments on a forum from the side opposed to their own, and allowed an additional week for students to formulate and post rebuttals.

He then summarized and synthesized the debate (see Figure 11.4). He developed a follow-up threaded discussion, in which students could share whether participating in the debate changed their viewpoints.

Variations and Extensions

- Instead of forming teams, ask students to work in pairs to present opposing sides to each other.
- Identify a topic that has three clear sides, and set up a three-way debate.
- Use a within-team debate in which a team researches the topic. One student presents an argument for one side, and then another student presents an argument from the opposing side. The debate continues as various members within the team alternate between additional arguments and rebuttals.
- In a variation called Structured Academic Controversy (Millis & Cottell, 1998, pp. 140–143), student partners review material on an issue and then synthesize the information to support their position. Two pairs with opposing positions form a quad, and each pair presents the arguments supporting their position to the other pair. Pairs then reverse their positions and argue for the opposing position. The pairs work together to synthesize their findings and to prepare a group report. All four students must agree with the summary. To close the activity, teams make a presentation to the whole class.

- Add a writing component by requiring students to work together to draft the four best arguments for their side. After the groups have had time to write out their arguments, ask groups to share their arguments supporting or opposing the proposition. This creates additional data for assessment.
- Ask students to write a follow-up paper describing issues that they clarified or confirmed, surprises they encountered, new information they gained, or the sources they used to validate new information. This creates additional data for assessment.

Key References and Resources

Barkey, E. F., Major, C. H., & Cross, K. P. (2014). CoLT 6: Critical debate. In *Collaborative learning techniques: A handbook for college faculty* (2nd ed., pp. 180–186). San Francisco, CA: Jossey-Bass.

Bean, J. C. (2009). *Engaging ideas: A professor's guide to integrating writing, critical thinking, and active learning in the classroom* (2nd ed., pp. 6–7, 176–177). San Francisco, CA: Jossey-Bass.

Brookfield, S. D., & Preskill, S. (2005). *Discussion as a way of teaching: Tools and techniques for democratic classrooms* (2nd. ed., pp. 114–115). San Francisco, CA: Jossey-Bass.

Chan C. (2009). Assessment: Debate. *Assessment Resources @HKU*, University of Hong Kong. http://ar.cetl.hku.hk.

McKeachie, W. J. (1994). *Teaching tips: Strategies, research and theory for college and university teachers* (9th ed., p. 44). Lexington, MA: D. C. Heath.

Caring

43
Briefing Paper

Complexity involved in	
Preparation	LOW
In-class implementation	LOW
Analysis	HIGH

Brief Description

Students select a current problem, and they research it through independent or group study. They next prepare a summary of the main issues involved and outline proposed solutions, which they then evaluate for strengths and weaknesses. In their papers, students often make a call to action.

Purpose

Briefing Papers allow students to explore problems that are interesting and relevant to them, rather than receiving one pre-selected by the teacher. In this technique, students tend to write for a specific audience, such as a government agency, which needs information about the problem and that can potentially help to achieve resolution to it.

Since they write to a specific audience, one who holds authority to do something about the problem, the activity feels authentic. Because of this, students often are motivated to participate and learn.

A Briefing Paper has the advantages common to most written assessments, including a fairly in-depth and comprehensive Learning Artifact (the final paper). These artifacts provide rich information that allow teachers to see students' logic as well as their ability to communicate their logical processes. Given the time-consuming nature of this technique for both students and instructors, and the likelihood that both would become bored with having to write or read the same paper twice, this technique is not typically used as a pre-post assessment in its truest sense. However, it is possible to collect the initial papers as above and to ask students to improve them after instruction, so that both of these Learning Artifacts may be assessed. Most often, this activity is used as a post-instruction assessment of student performance on a given topic area. In particular, it can be used to determine their level of engagement in the content when applied to a real-world situation. While many Briefing Papers are extended activities that suggest their use for grading and reporting purposes, abbreviated versions can be used within a single class session to gather information that can be used solely for the purpose of determining where students are and meeting them there with instruction.

Key Learning Goals

- Understanding of perspectives and values of this subject
- Ability to appreciate important contributions to this subject
- Level of openness to new ideas
- Level of informed concern about contemporary social issues
- The commitment to exercise the rights and responsibilities of citizenship
- Level of informed historical perspective
- Informed appreciation of other cultures

Implementation

Preparation

- Determine the learning outcome you will assess when you examine the Briefing Paper.
- Determine what content students will use in researching their papers, specifically whether you will provide reading materials or whether students will engage in independent study.
- Develop a set of guidelines for the paper. Students typically will want to know how long the paper should be, how many solutions they should develop, whether they are required to cite sources and if so how many, and how they should evaluate solutions (e.g., rank order or a more qualitative assessment of worth).
- Determine a set of deadlines. Consider whether you will want the following: a topic submitted to you for approval, drafts due along the way, or only the final paper.
- Determine who will be involved in assessing the paper: you, external assessors (e.g., colleagues), the student (e.g., self-assessment), the student's peers (e.g., peer assessment of the paper), or other.

Process

1. Announce the assignment and the timeframe for completing it. Provide students with time to ask questions about it.
2. Ask students to write their papers, identifying an important problem, creating potential solutions to it, and evaluating their suggested solutions.
3. Consider having students report out their best solutions.
4. Collect the Learning Artifacts: the completed Briefing Papers.

Online

Students submit their papers as an assignment in a learning management system. Alternately, they can post them on their own websites or blogs.

Analysis and Reporting

Use a rubric to assess each student's briefing paper, and consider a narrative assessment in which you provide students with additional comments. This technique is well suited to grading. Teachers can use a rubric for assessing problem solving and/or for writing ability. Simply assign a percentage score based upon your rubric scoring and determine a grade based upon those.

To examine data in the aggregate, determine the mean or median scores of the problems students identified. Consider a qualitative analysis of student papers based upon the outcomes you hope to see (see the rubric), analyzing key themes that emerged. For example, you could report that nearly all students were able to identify important problems, and you could provide examples of the various problems that they identified. You could report variation among ability to provide relevant information, perhaps describing the quality of sources used (for example, some of them may have used Wikipedia, while others may have gone to top-tier peer-reviewed journals in your field). Use a numeric table to report rubric scoring by item. For narrative reports, consider a narrative table or a network to document any themes you have identified.

Examples

Onsite: Issues in Education

The professor of this special topics class decided to use a Briefing Paper to learn about student ability to identify a critical problem in education, to develop potential solutions, and to identify potential issues in implementation. She asked the students to assume the position of briefing a policy maker, in this case a ranking official in the Department of Education, about a problem that they believed needed to be solved. She assigned the template in Exhibit 11.2 for the paper.

Exhibit 11.2 Issues in Education Briefing Paper

Date:
Prepared by:
Email:
Telephone:

1. Problem
   a. The problem to be addressed in the briefing paper.
2. Background
   a. Provide a summary of past and/or current events that provide a context for the topic or issue, including any policies or past practices.
   b. Provide information about existing literature that addresses this problem.
3. Analysis
   a. Identify significant aspects of the problem.
   b. Identify the options or courses of action that should be considered, including details about the advantages and disadvantages of each.
   c. Identify actions currently taken or recommended to address the issue.

4. Cautionary Notes
   a. Identify potentially sensitive aspects of problem that could affect potential solutions.
5. Recommended Action
   a. Provide your recommended action that you wish the Department of Education would take.

The instructor analyzed the data on the following criteria (rating each item on a scale of 4–0, with four being the highest and zero being the lowest):

- Importance of the issue
- Connections made between the discipline and the problem at hand
- Relevance of the sources used
- Viability of the proposed action
- Effective communication of the problem to external constituents

She calculated grades based on scores on these items (20 points per item = assessed score). She averaged the scores to determine mean across items, as shown in Table 11.17. She then reported overall scores to the class.

Table 11.17 Mean Scores on Rubric Criteria for Briefing Paper Assignment

Topic	Mean Score
Importance of the issue	3.75
Connections made between the discipline and the problem at hand	2.95
Relevance of the sources used	3.66
Viability of the proposed action	3.3
Effective communication of the problem to external constituents	3.5

 Online: Public Health

The professor in this course needed to see how well students were meeting the following learning outcome: Successful students will be able to identify central public health issues related to recent events and communicate the issues with important stakeholders. He assigned a Briefing Paper in order to help him make this assessment.

For the activity, he wrote a brief case, identifying a hypothetical event: a sudden and severe outbreak of the flu at a nearby rural community. He also assigned an audience for the students: area health providers. The case asked the students to identify the problem at hand as they saw it, making additional assumptions as necessary to complete the assignment, and to prepare a briefing paper on how to solve the problem.

Table 11.18 Assessment Matrix: Briefing Paper

Student Learning Outcomes	LAT	Subject/ Content Prompt	Intentional Active Learning Activity	Learning Artifact	Findings and Interpretations	Actions to Be Taken
Identify central public health issues related to recent events and communicate the issues with important stakeholders.	Briefing Paper	Class reading assignments and independent research	Identifying a problem and writing a report to brief stakeholders	The paper	Students had no difficulty identifying the key issues in the case. They were not as successful in writing for an external audience, and used a heavy academic writing style.	Additional instruction in writing for the public, providing specific examples of effective written communications, including a model "briefing report" students can refer to.

He presented the case as an assignment in his LMS. He gave them one week to post their responses, and then he evaluated them according to the rubric he had developed (Table 11.18). He then aggregated individual scores to come up with a composite score. In a synchronous session using VoIP, he debriefed the students after the assessment, letting them know what they had done well on and what they would be working on in the future. Additionally, he included the activity and the scores in his teaching dossier as evidence of teaching effectiveness, noting that he planned to demonstrate connections between the field and critical problems more in the future.

Variations and Extensions

- This technique can be paired with a Case Study, as in the example from public health above. Making this pairing will provide data on how well students are analyzing the overall situation as well as how they communicate the problem and attending issues to others.

Key References and Resources

Angelo, T. A., & Cross, K. P. (1993). Analytic memos. In *Classroom assessment techniques: A handbook for college teachers* (2nd ed.). San Francisco, CA: Jossey-Bass.

Davis, J. (2012). Briefing paper. http://www.cs.grinnell.edu/~davisjan/tut/100/2012F/assignments/briefing-paper.html.

CHAPTER 12

Teaching and Assessing for the Learning How to Learn Domain

While students come into any given class equipped with prior knowledge and skills, they do not always come in knowing much about the learning process itself or how to become a more self-directing learner. Yet the ability to not only manage their own learning in their courses but also to continue learning effectively after the courses end are often goals we teachers have for students. In this chapter, we describe how to clarify goals and assess learning related to the learning how to learn dimension of the Significant Learning Taxonomy, and then present a set of techniques aimed at helping students learn how to learn.

Clarifying Learning Goals Related to the Learning How to Learn Domain

In his description of the various domains of his Taxonomy of Significant Learning, Fink suggests that Learning How to Learn occurs when students learn about the process of learning itself. This form of learning may involve learning how to engage in a particular kind of inquiry that is specific to a discipline or field (e.g., the scientific method). It also may involve becoming self-directing learners. Fink suggests that these activities are important because they enable students to continue learning in their future endeavors and it allows them to do this with greater efficiency and effectiveness.

Part of what Fink is referring to is a process that psychologists refer to as metacognition, an important meta-level set of cognitive strategies that enables learners to perform better. Flavell (1976, 1979) distinguished two characteristics of metacognition: knowledge of cognition (what Fink refers to as learning about learning) and self-regulation of cognition (what Fink refers to as self-directed learning). Since the term *metacognition* can be interpreted to mean "thinking about thinking," it is not the same as thinking about learning, Fink prefers the term *meta-learning*. Nilson (2013) argues that metacognition is an important component of self-regulation, but the latter is the larger concept:

Self-regulation encompasses the monitoring and managing of one's cognitive processes as well as the awareness of and control over one's emotions, motivations, behavior, and environment as related to learning. (p. 5)

Activities such as planning how to approach a given learning task, monitoring comprehension, and evaluating progress toward the completion of a task play a critical role in successful learning in college and university courses.

Fink, extending his view of Learning How to Learn beyond traditional conceptions of metacognition and self-regulation, adds his conception of the ability to engage in a particular kind of inquiry that is specific to a discipline or field. In short, he believes that for significant learning, students need to be able to conduct scholarly inquiry appropriate to the discipline. The ultimate results of such an inquiry, as Fink suggests, can be the development of new knowledge. This could occur through natural or social science research, literary analysis, historical investigation, or a host of other discipline-specific modes of inquiry. For Fink, helping students to ask and answer questions that are important in a discipline or field is an essential aspect of Learning How to Learn.

Identifying Learning Outcomes for the Learning How to Learn Domain

Table 12.1 provides examples of learning processes and outcomes related to Learning How to Learn.

Aligning Learning Outcomes Related to Learning How to Learn with Institutional Learning Goals

Learning goals related to the learning how to learn dimension of the Significant Learning Taxonomy are sometimes reflected in an institution's general mission statement. More often, they are stated explicitly in the mission statements of Academic Skills Centers. These statements typically include a description of purpose that focuses on assisting students to develop the skills they need to achieve academic success. Institutional goals associated with the learning how to learn dimension are also often embedded within programs that focus on providing additional academic support to targeted groups, such as freshmen or ethnic minorities (Table 12.2). Indicating how studying for college is often quite different from studying in high school, they might articulate the ways in which they help students improve their academic skills and thus their academic performance.

Assessing Achievement of Learning Outcomes in the Learning How to Learn Domain

Helping students learn to function as self-regulating and autonomous learners can be challenging for teachers. Another challenge is how to gather direct evidence of student achievement

Table 12.1 Examples of Learning Processes and Outcomes for Learning How to Learn

			Sample Course Learning Objectives/ Outcomes *By the end of this course, a successful learner will be able to . . .*
Learner Process	**Additional Terms**	**Definition**	
General Definition: The learner knows about learning, can describe his or her learning skills and abilities, and can monitor and evaluate his or her learning.			
Describe	Explain, contrast, list	Describe various strategies for learning new material.	. . . articulate a personal plan for learning new content.
Appraise	Consider, conclude	Articulate a preference for a learning activity.	. . . describe his or her preferred method of learning.
Plan	Question, recall, identify	Determine what they need to learn, what they already know, what they need to find out.	. . . develop a process for learning new material.
Implement	Conduct, do, act	Engage with the scientific method during an investigation.	. . . carry out an original investigation in the field.
Monitor	Appraise, judge, assess	Determine how well they are doing and whether they need to adjust.	. . . write a report evaluating progress in completing a project.
Evaluate	Judge, criticize, predict, extend	Describe the level of success in the process and the product.	. . . conduct a self-evaluation of work and learning during a given project.
Focus	Define, identify, isolate, pinpoint	The ability to adjust and sharpen scope such that a central theme is identified and clarified as most important.	. . . define the scope of a project that consists of either a basic science experiment, a clinical trial, or a population-based study appropriate for research in the cardiovascular sciences. . . . identify a creative, focused, and manageable topic that addresses potentially significant yet previously less-explored aspects of the topic.
Investigate	Examine, explore, study, probe, scrutinize	The ability to seek, identify, and use relevant sources of information and extract key information and ideas to support a point of view or conclusion.	. . . select and use information to investigate a point of view or conclusion. . . . carry out a systematic or formal inquiry to discover and examine appropriate facts.
Organize	Systematize, arrange, coordinate	The ability to identify the elements of a communication or situation and recognize how they fit together into a coherent structure and then build systematic and coherent connections among elements.	. . . arrange and plan an activity appropriate for the capstone project.

Sources: Composite

Table 12.2 Examples of Institution Level Learning Goals in the Learning How to Learn Domain

Institution/Mission	This university aims to provide students with a foundation upon which self-reliance and habits of lifelong learning are built. We expect that students will graduate and lead lives that advance knowledge, promote understanding, and serve society.
Institution/Medical School	Every graduate of this medical school will understand the limits of personal knowledge and experience and will demonstrate the intellectual curiosity to actively pursue the acquisition of new knowledge and skills necessary to refine and improve his/her medical practice or to contribute to the scientific body of medical knowledge.
Institution/First Year Programs	The First Year Program is intended to introduce first year students to key learning strategies and resources that will help them to succeed in their four years on campus.
Institution/Academic Skills Center	The core mission of the Academic Skills Center is to help all students be more effective and efficient learners through the offering of a variety of retention and support services.
Institution/Mentoring Program	The purpose of this program is to facilitate teams consisting of members from a wide variety of economic, ethnic, and cultural backgrounds to work together to strive for the highest possible achievement for each individual member. Our primary goal is to see that every student in our program has the opportunity of success regardless of his or her past educational experiences.

Sources: Composite

in this domain. Indeed, many of the research studies involve gathering student opinions and self-assessments of whether they have achieved in this area, but assessment committees and accreditors generally want direct, rather than indirect, assessments of such learning. The techniques we provide in this chapter are an effort to address these challenges. They each have one or more of the following characteristics:

- They ask students to develop plans for current and future learning.
- They take a snapshot of student effort while engaged in learning.
- They ask students to describe the processes they take as they are engaged in learning.

We also include at the end of this chapter the AAC&U Value Rubric for Foundations and Skills for Lifelong Learning as Exhibit 12.1 to offer additional ideas for assessing learning in this domain.

Conclusion

Self-regulating students who know how to learn are poised for success in almost any type of learning activity. Unfortunately few students, particularly those new to the college environment, have given any serious consideration to how they learn. Yet encouraging students to think about thinking and learn about learning gives them the opportunity to engage in their own endeavors as students in more meaningful and substantive ways. Being more aware of themselves as learners can help students understand what it is they are doing, how they prefer to do it, and how they learn in relation to others. This, in turn, helps them to be more effective and efficient learners in our courses, in college in general, and in their personal and professional lives long after they have left our institution.

Exhibit 12.1 Assessing Learning How to Learn Using the AAC&U Foundations and Skills for Lifelong Learning VALUE Rubric

Definition

Lifelong learning is "all purposeful learning activity, undertaken on an ongoing basis with the aim of improving knowledge, skills and competence." An endeavor of higher education is to prepare students to be this type of learner by developing specific dispositions and skills described in this rubric while in school. (From The European Commission. 2000. Commission staff working paper: A memorandum on lifelong learning. www.see-educoop.net/education_in/pdf/ lifelong-oth-enl-t02.pdf.)

Framing Language

This rubric is designed to assess the skills and dispositions involved in lifelong learning, which are curiosity, transfer, independence, initiative, and reflection. Assignments that encourage students to reflect on how they incorporated their lifelong learning skills into their work samples or collections of work by applying the following skills and dispositions will provide the means for assessing those criteria. Work samples or collections of work tell what is known or can be done by students, while reflections tell what students think or feel or perceive. Reflection provides the evaluator with a much better understanding of who students are because through reflection students share how they feel about or make sense of their learning experiences. Reflection allows analysis and interpretation of the work samples or collections of work for the reader. Reflection also allows exploration of alternatives, the consideration of future plans, and provides evidence related to students' growth and development. Perhaps the best fit for this rubric are those assignments that prompt the integration of experience beyond the classroom.

Table 12.3 Assessing Learning How to Learn Rubric

	Capstone 4	Milestone 3 2	Benchmark 1
Curiosity	Explores a topic in depth, yielding a rich awareness and/or little-known information indicating intense interest in the subject.	Explores a topic in depth, yielding insight and/or information indicating interest in the subject.	Explores a topic with some evidence of depth, providing occasional insight and/or information indicating mild interest in the subject.	Explores a topic at a surface level, providing little insight and/or information beyond the very basic facts indicating low interest in the subject.
Initiative	Completes required work, generates and pursues opportunities to expand knowledge, skills, and abilities.	Completes required work, identifies and pursues opportunities to expand knowledge, skills, and abilities.	Completes required work and identifies opportunities to expand knowledge, skills, and abilities.	Completes required work.
Independence	Educational interests and pursuits exist and flourish outside classroom requirements. Knowledge and/or experiences are pursued independently.	Beyond classroom requirements, pursues substantial, additional knowledge and/or actively pursues independent educational experiences.	Beyond classroom requirements, pursues additional knowledge and/or shows interest in pursuing independent educational experiences.	Begins to look beyond classroom requirements, showing interest in pursuing knowledge independently.

Transfer	Makes explicit references to previous learning and applies in an innovative (new and creative) way that knowledge and those skills to demonstrate comprehension and performance in novel situations.	Makes references to previous learning and shows evidence of applying that knowledge and those skills to demonstrate comprehension and performance in novel situations.	Makes references to previous learning and attempts to apply that knowledge and those skills to demonstrate comprehension and performance in novel situations.	Makes vague references to previous learning but does not apply knowledge and skills to demonstrate comprehension and performance in novel situations.
Reflection	Reviews prior learning (past experiences inside and outside of the classroom) in depth to reveal significantly changed perspectives about educational and life experiences, which provide foundation for expanded knowledge, growth, and maturity over time.	Reviews prior learning (past experiences inside and outside of the classroom) in depth, revealing fully clarified meanings or indicating broader perspectives about educational or life events.	Reviews prior learning (past experiences inside and outside of the classroom) with some depth, revealing slightly clarified meanings or indicating somewhat broader perspectives about educational or life events.	Reviews prior learning (past experiences inside and outside of the classroom) at a surface level, without revealing clarified meaning or indicating a broader perspective about educational or life events.

Reprinted with permission from "VALUE: Valid Assessment of Learning in Undergraduate Education." Copyright 2015 by the Association of American Colleges and Universities. http://www.aacu.org/value/rubrics

LEARNING ASSESSMENT TECHNIQUE

Learning How to Learn

44
Study Outlines

Complexity involved in	
Preparation	LOW
In-class implementation	MODERATE
Analysis	MODERATE

Brief Description

Study Outlines are a scaffolded structure that guide students through synthesizing and organizing course information to help them prepare for an important course activity, such as a test.

Purpose

Some students come to college without having developed effective methods of preparing for tests. This LAT guides students through reviewing and summarizing material from a given learning module, which can aid their study processes.

The resulting Learning Artifact, the Study Outline itself, provides information about what students see as the most essential aspects of the content, which also offers insight into how well students have learned that content. Additionally, the Study Outline provides evidence of students' ability to organize information in an efficient and effective way. Study Outlines are a good way to review a completed learning module before an upcoming test and are typically used toward the end of a learning module.

Key Learning Goals

- The ability to set goals
- The ability to follow directions/instructions
- Study skills and strategies
- The capacity for lifelong learning in the subject area

Implementation

Preparation

- Make a list of the main concepts students should know as a result of their study.
- Determine what type of outline students should create, for example whether they should develop a key word outline, a topic outline, or a full sentence outline. Also decide whether students should create a bare outline or use a prefix system; if the latter, decide whether they should use alphanumeric (perhaps the most common type of outline, e.g., I, A, 1, 2), decimals (1.1., 1.2), or other system.
- Set the parameters for the Study Outline, for example what the length or the extent of the study guide should be (e.g., 1-page outline or 10-point outline) and how long students will have to complete the Study Outline.
- Determine whether you will allow students to use the outlines when taking the upcoming test.
- Determine who will be involved in the assessment. Peer assessment for example could provide students with additional exposure to the content and new organizational ideas that could allow them to improve their own outlines.
- Create a rubric for scoring outlines, or develop another scoring system. The rubric shown in Table 12.4, which we adapted from Instructional Computing at University of California, Santa Cruz, is an example of one used for scoring an outline.

Process

1. Announce the activity, telling students that they will create a Study Outline for an upcoming test, and that you will assess the outline. Allow time for questions.
2. Provide time for students to work on the Study Outlines.
3. Collect the Learning Artifacts, which are the completed Study Outlines.

Online

Students simply create their outlines in a word processing document, as they would most likely do even in an onsite class, and upload them to the course wiki, Google Docs, their blogs, or as an assignment in an LMS.

Analysis and Reporting

Use your rubric for scoring the Study Outline. You may also wish to mark the outlines themselves, with a simple +/– for accurate or inaccurate information, which can assist you when completing the rubric. While this assignment can take considerable time and effort, it is probably best to treat it as a formative assessment. A low stakes grade is appropriate. You can return student outlines along with your scoring marks and rubric so that they know whether they were on target or not along with written comments about how they might improve their outlines.

To aggregate data, use your rubrics. You can also do an average number of accurate and inaccurate points as well as keep a running list of problem areas. Work across your rubrics to create average scores in each cell. Use a numeric table to record the average number of points or accuracies and inaccuracies. Use a narrative table to provide a list of where students are having difficulties.

Table 12.4 Outline Grading Rubric. Total possible = 40 pts.

	Excellent (10 points)	Very Good (8 points)	Satisfactory (4 points)	Unsatisfactory (0 points)
Length, format	Required length, typed and double spaced.	Close to required length, typed and double spaced.	Shorter than expected, typed and double spaced.	Much less than required length, much more than required length, or not typed.
Organization and development	Logical development of ideas, and presentation elements are thorough and clear. Presentation elements follow logically, clearly belong as organized.	Generally logical organization, but idea progression and presentation elements not perfected.	Poor presentation; elements seem out of place or poorly thought out.	No evidence of structure or organization for presentation.
Focus and quality of presentation content	Outline is on topic, and the content is appropriate.	Almost all of the outline is on topic; some content seems tangential and does not address main focus.	The outline is largely off topic; most content does not address main focus.	Presentation is off topic; content does not address main focus.
Feasibility of outline for accomplishing intended purpose (e.g., study for the exam)	The outline will clearly be a benefit to studying for the exam.	The outline will likely be a benefit to studying for the exam.	The outline will be a small benefit to studying for the exam.	The outline could actually harm the exam-studying process.

Adapted from Instructional Computing at University of California, Santa Cruz

Examples

Onsite: Masterpieces in Western Literature and Philosophy

In this course, students read a number of works that would classically fall into the "cannon." The professor has the following learning goal: Upon completion of this course, students will be able to describe key structural elements of Dante's *Inferno*.

At the end of completing a learning module on Dante's *Inferno*, he asks the students to create Study Outlines to describe the nine circles of Hell through which the poet Virgil led Dante in the epic poem. He suggests that they use the nine circles as their primary organizers and list 2–3 sub points for each circle and create a topic outline. He handed out this structure for scaffolding:

1. Limbo
   a. _____
   b. _____
   c. _____

2. Lust
   a. _____
   b. _____
   c. _____
3. Gluttony
   a. _____
   b. _____
   c. _____
4. Greed
   a. _____
   b. _____
   c. _____
5. Anger
   a. _____
   b. _____
   c. _____
6. Heresy
   a. _____
   b. _____
   c. _____
7. Violence
   a. _____
   b. _____
   c. _____
8. Fraud
   a. _____
   b. _____
   c. _____
9. Treachery
   a. _____
   b. _____
   c. _____

The professor provided students time to work on the outlines, open book, in class. He collected them at the end of the class and told students he would return them at the next class session.

When he scored them, he simply marked an "x" by any responses that were inaccurate. To aggregate, he looked back across the sheets for the categories that had primarily correct and complete responses versus those that had primarily incorrect or incomplete responses (Table 12.5).

He noticed the sharp drop-off at the end. He reviewed the responses again and noticed that violence had complete but incorrect responses, and fraud and treachery had incomplete responses. He concluded that while students did not seem to fully understand the violence circle (indicated by the high percentage of incorrect responses), students simply ran out of time finishing the outline (indicated by large number of incomplete responses for the fraud and treachery circles), so he could not accurately gauge their level of understanding of these two circles.

Table 12.5 Assessment Summary of Accurate Responses

Circle	Percentage of Accurate Responses
1. Limbo	90%
2. Lust	95%
3. Gluttony	90%
4. Greed	85%
5. Anger	85%
6. Heresy	90%
7. Violence	55%
8. Fraud	70%
9. Treachery	75%

He handed the outlines back at the next session. He reviewed the violence section and then gave students additional time to complete fraud and treachery. When he walked around the room, he noted that students seemed to have a good handle on them. At the end of class, he suggested that students review their outlines for an upcoming essay test on the poem.

 ## Online: Fundamentals of Physics

In this open online course, the professor had these goals: Upon successful completion of this course, students will be able to describe Newton's Laws of Motion. He gave students the following structure to use as they completed their outlines:

Newton's Laws of Motion
1. Newton's First Law:
   a. Summary:
   b. Key terms:
   c. Example:
2. Newton's Second Law:
   a. Summary:
   b. Key terms:
   c. Example:
3. Newton's Third Law:
   a. Summary:
   b. Key terms:
   c. Example:

He then had them post their outlines as an assignment within the course platform. He scored them with a + for accurate responses and a − for inaccurate ones. He did a quick tally of responses (Table 12.6) across students and quickly noted that the students could summarize the law and state key terms but that they had much more difficulty providing concrete examples.

Table 12.6 Response Tally

	Law 1	Law 2	Law 3
Summary	90%	90%	90%
Key terms	95%	90%	95%
Example	75%	65%	70%

He noted that he needed to provide them with more concrete examples and posted some demonstrations in the learning module.

Variations and Extensions

- Arrange students in groups of 4–5 to work on the assignment. Try to strive for mixed ability/preparation within each group. Assign one question to each group. Have groups work to complete a Study Outline on their assigned questions.

Key References and Resources

Chicago Manual of Style. (2010). "Lists and Outlines (6.121–126)." (16th ed.). Chicago: University of Chicago Press.

Purdue Online Writing Lab. (nd). Developing an outline. https://owl.english.purdue.edu/owl/resource/544/1/.

LEARNING ASSESSMENT TECHNIQUE

Learning How to Learn

45
Student Generated Rubrics

Complexity involved in	
Preparation	MODERATE
In-class implementation	MODERATE
Analysis	MODERATE

Brief Description

Teachers provide students with examples of outstanding disciplinary-based products such as an essay, research paper, musical composition, mathematical proof, or scientific lab report, which students analyze to determine the common characteristics and develop assessment rubrics. They then apply the rubric to test rubric viability.

Purpose

Teachers often have students examine models of exemplary work so that they learn the standards of the field, have a pattern for their own work, and can understand the "bar" by which they might evaluate the work of others. This LAT helps teach students how to identify the features of excellent work and allows them to internalize the meaning of high standards. It also results in a set of grading rubrics that contain explicit criteria and standards that guide students as they complete their assignments and allow them to self-assess their own work. Finally, involving students in the process of developing the rubrics can be motivating to them.

The Learning Artifact, the Student Generated Rubric, helps teachers understand whether or not students understand the standards of excellence in the field and of a given assignment. This in turn is evidence of student ability to evaluate a work in the field, as is their actual evaluation using the rubric. This LAT typically is used prior to a formal speaking or writing assignment. It is thus a formative assessment that helps students understand and buy into the standards by which they will be evaluated as well as potentially improving student performance on the formal assignment.

Key Learning Goals

- Study skills and strategies
- The ability to monitor their own progress
- The ability to self-assess their performance
- The capacity for lifelong learning in the subject area

Implementation

Preparation

- Take time to think about your overall course objectives so that you can identify an assignment (or assignment type) that is important to the class and requires students to work at sophisticated levels of thinking.
- Locate three exemplary models done by professionals, prior students, more advanced students, or students of colleagues. Note for yourself why each work exemplifies excellence.
- Go through the steps using the models to create a simple evaluation rubric yourself, noting the characteristics that come to mind. This process will help you to ensure the assignment is feasible and also provide you with guidance when reviewing the Student Generated Rubrics so that you can point out any adjustments or changes that need to be made.
- Using your own experience as a guide, create a handout that directs students through the steps to develop a simple rubric. For example:
  - Look at these three model examples and
    - Identify and list the criteria, dimensions, or traits that stand out to you in each model (e.g., "the essay has a clear thesis statement" or "the portfolio is visually attractive and well organized").
    - From your three lists, select five traits that seem to be essential and that all three of the models share.
    - Describe the qualities that make that dimension or trait excellent (the thesis is clear to the reader, seems to be appropriately limited in scope, shows synthesis and original thought, and so forth).
  - Depending upon the type of assignment, duplicate the models so that you have a set of three for each group of 4–6 students (if the assignment is extensive, such as a portfolio) or one for each student in the group (if the assignment is short, such as a poem or brief essay).

Process

1. Explain to students that you are providing them with examples of work that meet your expectations of quality work. Tell them that you want them to analyze the works to identify the specific characteristics that make the examples so good.
2. Distribute the handout and talk through the steps, answering any questions.
3. Form groups of 4–6 students, ask them to identify roles such as recorder, reporter, and facilitator, and provide each group with a set of the exemplary models.
4. Ask each group to create a simple grading rubric.
5. Collect the Learning Artifacts, which are the rubrics.
6. Consider using students' rubrics as the basis for a single, consolidated rubric that you inform students you will be using to evaluate their future work.

Online

This LAT is most effective when students can look at the models and interact "in the moment" to discuss the attributes that make it excellent. If having students generate grading rubrics seems as though it would be particularly valuable in your course, consider presenting students with 1–3 models, and either establish a synchronous session or set up a threaded discussion forum in which students post their observations, and then use these to create an evaluation rubric.

Analysis and Reporting

Since it is a formative assessment, you will not likely assign a high-stakes grade to this assignment. To score individual rubrics, compare them to your own. Alternately, use a simple +/− system to note relevant or irrelevant categories.

To aggregate information, look across rubrics to determine what similarities they share and where they are different. Consider whether they have included all relevant categories or whether they have excluded important ones. Create a table of your findings.

Examples

Onsite: Principles of Marketing

As the final project in this class, the professor formed groups of students and assigned them to identify a product and then develop a marketing strategy for the product. To increase the sense of "real world" applicability of the assignment, she had students make a presentation on their strategy to the class as though they were talking to a group of business managers. She decided to use Student Generated Rubrics to help students see what was required for a high quality presentation.

She showed three videos of past student presentations, asking students to take careful notes on what made the presentations effective. Students noted qualities such as "had a clear introduction that set out the plan for the presentation," "spoke loudly, slowly, and with modulated voice quality," and so forth.

She formed students into groups of 5. She asked the groups to organize their ideas into 4–6 main categories. She then asked groups to come to consensus on their categories. They came up with this list:

- Subject knowledge
- Organization
- Speaker voice
- Enthusiasm

She could see that students had not noticed speaker nonverbal skills (e.g., body language and poise, such as having some movement but not fidgeting) and also had not noted some of the more technical aspects (such as timing, visual aids, impressive graphics, and so forth). She talked with the class about these and they agreed that they were important, so they added them to the rubric.

She informed them that she would use their ideas as the basis of a rubric with which they would assess their peers' presentations (Table 12.7).

Table 12.7 Rubric

Subject Knowledge Completed appropriate research Demonstrated knowledge by sharing it Answered questions from other students	5 4 3 2 1
Organization Presented an overview Stayed with the outline presented originally Used effective transitions	5 4 3 2 1
Speaker Voice Had a clear voice Used precise pronunciation Was audible	5 4 3 2 1
Speaker Nonverbal Presence Made eye contact Use gestures to enhance articulation and emphasize key points Seemed relaxed	5 4 3 2 1
Enthusiasm Seemed to have a positive feeling about the topic Seemed happy to present	5 4 3 2 1
Technical Used effective graphics Had no observable errors in visuals	5 4 3 2 1

Online: Reading Educational Research

The professor of this online course had goals and objectives as described in Table 12.8.

Table 12.8 Student Learning Goals and Objectives in Reading Educational Research Course

Upon completion of this course, students will know/understand:	Upon successful completion of this course, students will be able to:	Student will be assessed on these learning outcomes by:
Educational research	Recognize the basic features of a social science research article and evaluate articles for quality	In-class activities, homework assignments, and the final paper, a research synthesis

The professor assigned three quantitative and three qualitative educational research articles, and told students to read the articles carefully. She put students into groups and asked them to communicate with each other in the way that they chose. Some used Google Hangouts, while others used Note.ly. Each group was to create a list of the characteristics of an effective quantitative article and the characteristics of an effective qualitative article.

She asked a representative of each group to merge their lists in the course wiki. She then asked the leaders to group the ideas together and to insert a 4–1 rating scale for each primary category. She reviewed the rubrics (one for qualitative articles and one for quantitative) and noticed that while they had given attention to the methods, they had not focused on the introduction and literature nor the conclusions. She was able to talk with the class through a discussion board about these important parts of a research paper. They agreed and suggested new categories for connection to other works and results, which she added (Table 12.9).

Table 12.9 Student Generated Rubric for Analyzing a Quantitative Study (4 = best, 1 = worst)

Background	4 3 2 1
Is the research connected to prior research?	
Is there a theoretical or conceptual framework?	
Is the theory clear, insightful, and appropriate?	
Is there an alternate theory that would be a better choice?	
Research Question	4 3 2 1
Is the question clear?	
Is the question important?	
Research Design	4 3 2 1
Is it descriptive or causal?	
Does the design match the research question?	
If you were to ask yourself the best way to answer the question, would you have selected this design?	
Site and Sample	4 3 2 1
Was the site of the study described?	
Were the participants a reasonable group to select?	
Were they selected in a reasonable way?	

(continued)

Table 12.9 (*Continued*)

Data	4 3 2 1
What data were used? Were they clearly described? Were there samples size issues? Could the data sources be biased? Are there better sources? How were data collected? Were the instruments valid and reliable?	
Data Analysis	4 3 2 1
How were data analyzed? Were the methods clearly described? Were the methods selected the best ones?	
Results	4 3 2 1
Do they answer the research questions? Are the conclusions convincing? Are there other possible explanations for the results?	

To complete the assignment, she asked students to use the rubric that they created when they reviewed the next article.

Variations and Extensions

- Instead of three examples of excellent work, give students examples that represent a range of quality (such as excellent, average, poor) and ask them to identify how the examples differ.

Key References and Resources

Barkley, E. F. (2010). SET 49: Student-generated rubrics. In *Student engagement techniques: A handbook for college faculty* (pp. 354–356). San Francisco, CA: Jossey-Bass.

Stevens, D. D., & Levi, A. (2005). *Introduction to rubrics: An assessment tool to save grading time, convey effective feedback, and promote student learning.* Sterling, VA: Stylus.

LEARNING ASSESSMENT TECHNIQUE

Learning How to Learn

46
Invent the Quiz

Complexity involved in	
Preparation	LOW
In-class implementation	MODERATE
Analysis	MODERATE

Brief Description

Students write a limited number of test questions related to a recent learning module and then create an answer sheet, or alternately a model answer and scoring sheet, to accompany the test questions.

Purpose

Students often come to college unprepared to take examinations and have little practice at anticipating what questions might be on an exam. Teachers often attempt to help students by giving them practice tests, but this technique takes the guidance further by having students practice creating tests. This technique thus provides students with a structured opportunity to gain practice on anticipating and preparing for tests and to have important feedback from the instructor about whether their preparations are on target.

This LAT allows faculty to determine whether students have been able to understand and summarize important content. The activity also allows instructors to gather written documentation of what students think are the most important concepts in the learning module. It provides information about what students see as useful questions. It also provides teachers with an opportunity to see whether students have misunderstood any information, since students create answers for their own questions. Moreover, it provides teachers with information about students' expectations for an upcoming quiz. Finally, writing questions and responses simply helps students to review and thus learn the content more deeply, and it provides a structure that allows them to see gaps or insufficiencies in their own learning, which you can reinforce by your comments on their quizzes and answer sheets so that they can adjust accordingly. Because it requires an adequate exposure to content to be able to complete the activity, this LAT is typically done toward the end of a learning module but prior to taking an examination. It is best used then as a formative assessment for the intent of helping students to improve their knowledge prior to a summative assessment.

Key Learning Goals

- Knowledge about themselves as learners
- Study skills and strategies
- The ability to monitor their own progress
- The capacity for lifelong learning in the subject area

Implementation

Preparation

- Determine what type of question students should write: multiple choice, fill in the blank, short answer, short essay, or other.
- Determine the length of the quiz students will create. Depending on the type of question, you might choose 5–10 items.
- Create a couple of questions yourself as models and share them with the class so that students have some idea of what effective quiz questions look like.
- Provide students with advice on how to write good questions. There are several useful sites online that provide guidance, for example the following from the University of Waterloo: https://uwaterloo.ca/centre-for-teaching-excellence/teaching-resources/teaching-tips /developing-assignments/exams/questions-types-characteristics-suggestions.
- Create a checklist that helps you track question relevance, difficulty, and clarity. You might score them, for example, on a scale of 4–0, with four being the highest score and zero the lowest, such as in Table 12.10, where you would simply circle the most accurate number for each rating.
- Create a similar scoring system for the answers that students supply, using criteria for the type of test question. For example, if you chose short essay, you might include categories like those in Table 12.11.
- Create a handout for students in which you explain the activity.

Table 12.10 Sample Score Sheet

Question	Relevance	Difficulty	Clarity
1.	4 3 2 1 0	4 3 2 1 0	4 3 2 1 0
2.	4 3 2 1 0	4 3 2 1 0	4 3 2 1 0
3.	4 3 2 1 0	4 3 2 1 0	4 3 2 1 0
4.	4 3 2 1 0	4 3 2 1 0	4 3 2 1 0
5.	4 3 2 1 0	4 3 2 1 0	4 3 2 1 0

Table 12.11 Sample Score Sheet

Answer	Accuracy	Originality	Thoroughness
1.	4 3 2 1 0	4 3 2 1 0	4 3 2 1 0
2.	4 3 2 1 0	4 3 2 1 0	4 3 2 1 0
3.	4 3 2 1 0	4 3 2 1 0	4 3 2 1 0
4.	4 3 2 1 0	4 3 2 1 0	4 3 2 1 0
5.	4 3 2 1 0	4 3 2 1 0	4 3 2 1 0

Process

1. Present students with the handout and explain the purpose of the activity. Allow time for questions.
2. Provide students with time to write the questions and answer sheets.
3. Collect the Learning Artifacts, which are the test questions and answers.

Online

Have students submit the test and answer sheet as an assignment.

Analysis and Reporting

To examine individual artifacts, and to report back to students, use your checklist to score each test and answer sheet. Also comment on anything outstanding or unusual about the questions or the answer sheets. Provide a small stakes grade for completing the assignment, whether participation or homework, so that students have additional information about how well they did.

To aggregate findings across student responses, review the topics of the students' questions. Did they include all of the important topics? Are some important topics under-represented? Are some overrepresented? Examine the check-sheets and average scores. Look for patterns in the data (for example, a pattern of students writing questions that are too easy). Present your findings in a table.

Examples

Onsite: Introduction to Marketing

This marketing professor identified the following goals and objectives in her syllabus (Table 12.12).

Table 12.12 Marketing Course Goals and Objectives

Upon completion of this course, students will know/understand:	Upon successful completion of this course, students will be able to:	Student will be assessed on these learning outcomes by:
Supply and demand	Recognize the relationship between supply and demand	In-class quizzes and activities, homework problems, and in-class exams

She decided to use Invent the Quiz prior to a test to help students learn the material more deeply as well as to help their test performance. She announced the activity and shared a handout that asked students to develop five short answer questions and to create the answer sheets as a homework assignment. The handout also provided guidance on writing short answer questions.

She collected the students' quizzes and answer sheets in the next class session. She scored each quiz and answer sheet and then averaged the scores of all of the questions from the students' quizzes and answers sheets to get a composite score. She created tables so that she could more clearly see the patterns (Tables 12.13 and 12.14).

Table 12.13 Average Question Scores

Relevance	Difficulty	Clarity
3.9	2.1	3.3

Table 12.14 Average answer scores

Accuracy	Originality	Thoroughness
3.75	3.3	2.5

From the tables she could see that the students were expecting easier questions and that they were not being as thorough in their answers as she would expect. She addressed these issues in the next class session, and in her discussion of them, she shared a sample question and answer of her own.

Online: Psychology

The professor of this online psychology course had the following goals and objectives (Table 12.15).

He decided to use Invent the Quiz to help students prepare for an upcoming exam. He asked students to create ten multiple-choice questions that represented the personality disorders that they had been discussing. He indicated that the questions should have the

Table 12.15 Psychology Course Goals and Objectives

Upon completion of this course, students will know/ understand:	Upon successful completion of this course, students will be able to:	Student will be assessed on these learning outcomes by:
Personality disorders	List symptoms associated with different personality disorders	Quizzes and examinations

disorder followed by a list of symptoms, asking the respondent to check any symptoms that apply to the disorder. For example:

Antisocial personality disorder. Indicate all the symptoms that apply:

- Breaks the law
- Disregards safety of self and others
- Has problems with substance abuse
- Lies
- Has no guilt
- Seeks attention

He asked students to post their quizzes in the course wiki, which he had set up to allow for the quiz questions (he told them they would later post their answer sheets). He thought this would allow students to see all the potential questions and answers to study for the exam.

When they had posted, he reviewed the question for topic coverage. He created a table (Table 12.16), which he also posted to the course wiki, with the suggestion that students give particular attention to areas they had neglected in creating their own quizzes.

Table 12.16 Table Illustrating Topics of Student Questions

Good Coverage (appeared at least once in each quiz)	Fair Coverage (most students included)	Underrepresented (only a few students included)	Absent (no students included)
Antisocial Avoidant Borderline Dependent Obsessive compulsive Schizoid	Narcissistic Paranoid	Histrionic	Schizotypal

Variations and Extensions

- Ask students to work in groups to create their tests and answer sheets. This approach generates a group product rather than an individual one.
- Put students into groups and then have them quiz each other.
- Consider including some of the quiz questions on your next quiz or examination or alternately in your Team Tests (LAT 9) or Team Games Tournament (LAT 10).

Key References and Resources

Angelo, T. A., & Cross, K. P. (1993). CAT 25: Student generated test questions. In *Classroom assessment techniques: A handbook for college teachers* (2nd ed., pp. 240–243). San Francisco, CA: Jossey-Bass.

Finley, T. (2014). Dipsticks: Efficient ways to check for understanding. *Edutopia: What Works in Education, 72*(5), 1–9.

LEARNING ASSESSMENT TECHNIQUE

Learning How to Learn

47
Learning Goal Listing

Complexity involved in	
Preparation	LOW
In-class implementation	LOW
Analysis	LOW

Brief Description

Students generate and prioritize a list of their learning goals at the beginning of the academic term, a unit of study, or a specific learning activity. If time permits, students can estimate the relative difficulty of achieving these learning goals.

Purpose

Goal identification can be a powerful focusing activity for helping students to become conscious of what they hope to accomplish and encouraging them to accept responsibility for their learning. Identifying what they want to learn can help students better recognize and resist distractions and better organize their time and resources to be more successful. If teachers concur with and support students' goals, it can improve student motivation, as students can see how their own personal goals dovetail with course goals. Goal identification also provides students with a framework against which to measure progress, giving them guidance on how to get back on track if they have strayed. Moreover, working with students on their goals allows us to help them develop appropriate and learning oriented, rather than performance, goals. Thus goal identification is an important part of learning how to learn, which can benefit students beyond the boundaries of a specific course.

The Learning Artifact for this activity is the student's list of goals. It provides teachers with a quick glimpse into what students understand about the learning they are about to undertake. It allows teachers to assess student ability to distinguish important from unimportant, to determine what is the main focus from what are distracting details, and to share with the class the goals that are common to many students. This LAT is used most often as a diagnostic assessment of what students want to learn as well as students' ability to prioritize. It is thus best used at the start of a course or learning module. It may be done once more or even several times over the course of an academic term to gauge change over time.

Key Learning Goals

- Knowledge about themselves as learners
- The ability to set goals
- Study skills and strategies
- The capacity for lifelong learning in the subject area

Implementation

Preparation

- Take time to identify and write out your goals for student learning so that you have a reference point for comparing what you want students to learn with what students say they want to learn. If your learning goals differ from students' learning goals, decide to what extent you would be willing to substitute or alter your goals to accommodate their interests on either a class or individual basis.
- Decide whether to use this LAT at the course, unit, or activity level; whether it will be a one-time activity (such as at the beginning of the course or before a major project) or used multiple times throughout the term; and how you or your students will monitor progress.
- Consider creating a handout that provides students with guidance on identifying appropriate learning goals, such as shown in Table 12.17.
- To help them get started, you may wish to provide them with a list of course or module goals and then have students use this as the basis from which to craft personal learning goals. Consider adapting the Learning Goals Inventory for student use.
- Consider giving students advice on writing goals. For example, effective goal statements focus on:
  - The learning resulting from an activity rather than on the activity itself
  - Important, nontrivial aspects of learning

Table 12.17 Learning Goals

Your learning goals for the course (please list five learning goals in rank order):	Do your goals match current course objectives?
1.	Yes No
2.	Yes No
3.	Yes No
4.	Yes No
5.	Yes No

- Skills and abilities central to the discipline
- Goals that are general enough to capture important learning but clear and specific enough to be measurable
- Aspects of learning that will develop and endure (Adapted from Huba & Freed, 2000, p. 98)

Process
1. Announce the activity, and explain to students what you mean by goals.
2. Announce the timeframe in which students will have to generate goals.
3. Distribute the handout, and ask students to create a ranked list of learning goals.
4. Collect the Learning Artifacts.
5. Consider holding a discussion about the learning goals.
6. Remind students how you will use the data, and let them know when you will discuss the results.

Online

This LAT is easily implemented online, but how you do so will depend on what you are trying to accomplish. If, for example, you are using the activity to guide students in clarifying their class goals at the beginning of the term, have students generate and prioritize their lists individually and then ask students to post 1–2 of their highest priority goals on a Threaded Discussion, but adding only ones that have not already been posted by other students. Consider responding to the students' list with a list of your own goals as well as comments regarding how teacher/learner goals compare or contrast and any accommodations, if any, you intend to make. On the other hand, if you are using the activity to help students monitor their personal progress, you may want students to generate their lists and then include a follow-up assignment such as periodic So What? Journal reflections (What? So What? Now What? Journal, LAT 48) throughout the term reflecting on how well they are or are not meeting their goals.

Analysis and Reporting

Collect the Learning Artifacts and score them. Consider a simple "completed" or "incomplete" rating system. Note any that are particularly interesting. You can acknowledge students' goals by handing back their scored sheets and including any additional comments you have.

The easiest way to analyze the data in aggregate is to look for common themes or patterns in the different student goals. Consider how many students identify the same goals. When you identify the ones that are common across many students, you next identify those that are different and treat them separately. You may then want to compare them with course goals; how are they similar, and how are they different? Use a simple narrative table to list the different goals and the number of students who voted for each.

Examples

Onsite: Multicultural Literature

The professor of this upper-level course included the following learning objectives in the syllabus:

1. Examine poetry and drama written by a diverse group of writers.
2. Describe the stylistic characteristics of multicultural works.
3. Link representative works of multicultural literature to human values in various contexts.
4. Demonstrate knowledge of multiculturalism.
5. Analyze critical texts.
6. Interpret and critique selected works of multicultural literature.

She had taught the course multiple times and knew that some students take it to fulfill major requirements; others, to prepare for graduate work in African American or Women's studies or English; and a third group, to prepare themselves for careers as professional writers.

She used this information to create three working groups within the class, and she asked each group to rank the course goals according to which they thought were most important to them. The professor took up their ranked lists and created a table, depicted in Table 12.18, which she shared with the class to start a discussion about how the course could be important to them in their future careers. She believed that it helped with student buy-in to the course and found the students particularly motivated that term.

Table 12.18 Summary of Students' Reasons for Taking Multicultural Literature Course

	Ranking of primary reasons for taking the course		
	Major required	**Graduate school bound**	**Professional development**
Examine poetry and drama written by a diverse group of writers.	5	5	2
Describe the stylistic characteristics of multicultural works.	6	4	3
Link representative works of multicultural literature to human values in various contexts.	1	6	1
Demonstrate knowledge of multiculturalism.	2	1	6
Analyze critical texts.	3	3	5
Interpret and critique selected works of multicultural literature.	4	2	4

Online: Introduction to Business Statistics

The professor knew that many students were afraid to take his course and were focused only on trying to earn a passing grade rather than to learn statistics in a way that could help them in their future careers in business. To help students develop a more positive view of course content, he decided to use Learning Goal Listing to help them develop their own learning goals for the course. Before handing out a syllabus, he formed small groups and asked students to brainstorm ideas of what they might need to know about statistics in business and what statistical skills they might need. He asked them to create lists, and he created a composite list on the board. He noted which of their outcomes corresponded with course objectives (Table 12.19).

Table 12.19 Goals and Objectives Comparison Table

Top 5 ranked student learning goals	Course objective?
1. Read statistics to make business decisions.	Yes
2. Use statistics in business presentations.	Yes
3. Evaluate business claims by using statistics.	Yes
4. Use statistics to identify potential outcomes of changes made.	Yes
5. Conduct analysis of data to identify mean, median, and modes.	Yes

He found the activity to be a constructive one as students had to generate their own ideas about why the course is important to their futures, and he then handed out the syllabus to show them the overlap between their ranked lists and the course objectives.

Variations and Extensions

- Use this LAT throughout the academic term to help students see goals not as terminal destinations but rather as guideposts to measure progress, to reassure them that they are headed in the right direction, and to provide them with feedback to make adjustments if necessary to get back on course.
- Ask students to prioritize their goals by relative importance, then to prioritize the goals based on other criteria such as "difficulty to achieve" or "amount of time needed to accomplish the goal."
- Have students elaborate by writing next to each goal answers to questions such as why do I want to accomplish this goal? or what kinds of support structures (e.g., people, place, things) do I need to accomplish this goal?
- Consider having students break down large goals into incremental, small, concrete steps that they can take to achieve the goal.
- Use this LAT in conjunction with a strategy such as "Choice Boards" in order to promote student autonomy. To implement a Choice Board, the teacher creates a menu of options for

learning or assessment usually displayed on a grid. The choices can be designed around any aspect of the course from developing skills and processing information to synthesizing and reflecting upon key understandings. For example, a 9-cell Choice Board might allow students to choose (1) a subject to research from three topical areas, (2) to do this research individually, with a partner, or in a group of 3–5, and (3) to communicate their understanding by either writing a traditional research paper, constructing a web page with hyperlinks, or giving a formal presentation to the class. Choice Boards can also be tiered in terms of complexity or effort required and weighted accordingly (Dodge, 2005, pp. 64–71). Combining this with goal setting encourages students to accept responsibility for their choices.

- Break the class into small groups and direct the students in each group to come up with mutually acceptable goals.

Key References and Resources

Angelo, T. A., & Cross, K. P. (1993). CAT 35: Goal ranking and matching. In *Classroom assessment techniques: A handbook for college teachers* (2nd ed., pp. 290–294). San Francisco, CA: Jossey-Bass.

Barkley, E. F. (2010). SET 43: Go for the goal. In *Student engagement techniques: A handbook for college faculty* (pp. 332–335). San Francisco, CA: Jossey-Bass.

LEARNING ASSESSMENT TECHNIQUE

Learning How to Learn

48
What? So What? Now What? Journal

Complexity involved in	
Preparation	LOW
In-class implementation	LOW
Analysis	MODERATE-HIGH

Brief Description

Students write journal entries to reflect on their recent course-related activities or experiences. The questions that comprise the name of this LAT provide students with a structure for critical analysis during these reflections, prompting students to respond to the main questions and relevant subquestions.

Purpose

In this technique, students reflect by linking a current experience to previous learning and future plans, which helps them to connect what they know and what they are learning. This encourages students to process information and to synthesize and evaluate their experiences, which can improve their retention of ideas and information. It also encourages students to apply what they have learned to contexts beyond the original situations in which they learned it, which can deepen their learning. When students have an opportunity to reflect on their work, it enhances the meaning of the work. Thus this LAT provides structure, time, and opportunity for deep insights and complex learning.

The Learning Artifacts for this activity are the students' journals. They provide evidence of a student's ability to take in an experience or activity and describe it. They also provide insight into a student's ability to connect this experience to past learning or to texts in the course. In addition, they provide evidence of a student's ability to make a plan for the future, which is an indicator of a student's capacity for lifelong learning. Thus the artifacts yield many different types of information that provide a more holistic view of student learning. This LAT is often used with service learning so that students can reflect upon their service in the field and connect it course readings, but it also has application to many other kinds of course activities as well, from reflecting upon class experiments to processing group work to reflecting upon readings. This LAT is typically done at the conclusion of a learning unit or module.

Key Learning Goals

- The ability to set goals
- The ability to follow directions/instructions
- The capacity for lifelong learning in the subject area
- The ability to create a concrete plan to learn more about the subject in the near future

Implementation

Preparation

- Clarify the content students should write. Consider these questions and subquestions:
  - **What?** What happened? Was there a difference between what you expected and what happened? What did you do?
  - **So What?** What have you learned? Why does that matter? To you? To your peers? To other stakeholders? Is the experience in alignment, informed by, in conflict with class texts or other activities?
  - **Now what?** How can you apply your learning? What information can you share with others? What would you like to learn more about?
- Determine assignment parameters, such as how often students should write, how long journal entries should be, and how often you will review journals and then create a handout with instructions.
- Consider who will be involved in the assessment. It is important for you to review the journal and respond to the entries or students may feel that the assignment is busy work. Peer assessment can also be beneficial so that students have the chance to see each other's work.

Process

1. Distribute the handout, discuss the purpose of the journal, and allow time for questions.
2. Ask students to record entries in their journals for the predetermined amount of time.
3. Collect the Learning Artifacts.

Online

This LAT can be adapted to an online course through use of a blog for students to write their entries. If you use an LMS, you can set up preferences so that each student's blog is kept private from other students, but still allows you access as the instructor. If you have them use their own blogs, their responses are in the open. The nature of the assignment influences the learning (Weimer, 2015).

Analysis and Reporting

To assess the individual artifact, score them with a simple +1 system. For example, you might score as follows:

- What? = 1 point
- So what? = 1 point + 1 point for each connection to a lecture or reading
- Now what? = 1 point + 1 point for a concrete action plan or evidence of action taken.

Alternately take notes on key themes that you see in the data. You may want to assign a grade for this task, but it will likely not be one for a large portion of the grade. Some teachers assign around 10%, as this is a sufficient number to influence a student's grade, but not typically as high as major class projects or exams. To share information with students, return the scored journals along with any comments you might have.

To aggregate results, tally the scores you assessed and develop an average score. Create a simple table that displays the information.

Examples

Onsite: Algebra 1

This math professor had a learning outcome that students would learn to solve linear and quadratic equations using analytic, graphical, and numerical methods. She also had an outcome that students would learn how to be lifelong learners in the area of mathematics. She believed that writing about math was an important way to learn about it and for students to internalize what they have learned, so she assigned What? So What? Now What? Journals. She also believed this was a technique they could continue to use in their other mathematics courses.

After each class, students were to complete a journal entry that responded to the specific day's lesson with these questions as prompts:

- Ask yourself "What?" and record your basic observations of the mathematical concept or situation we covered in class today. For example:
  - What are you learning about in Algebra 1?
  - What did you do or observe during the lesson?
  - What are some specific examples of a concept, problem, or task related to this topic?
- Ask yourself "So what?" and add insights and connections. For example:
  - What connections can you make with previous math learning?
  - How confident do you feel about your understanding of this topic?
  - What parts of the topic are still unclear?
- Ask yourself "Now what?" and consider what this means for your future learning in mathematics. For example:
  - What have you learned?
  - What do you wonder about now?
  - What will you do next?

They were to post their journal entries online so that she could review them prior to class and base the next day's lesson on them. On the first day of reviewing the quadratic equation, a concept she knew was challenging for many students, she scanned their entries and made the summary notes to herself, as shown in Table 12.20.

Table 12.20 My Summary Notes on What? So What? Now What? Learning Activity

What?	So What?	Now What?
Almost all students who attended class understood we were covering quadratic equations. Two students seem to have this concept confused with linear equations. Three students were absent and seem lost.	A few students seem to have advanced knowledge in this area; they seem to distinguish between standard form and hidden form. (Use these as group leaders in tomorrow's group work session.) Most students are fairly *un*comfortable with this concept (we are going to have to spend more time on it, and I'll give a few quizzes to give practice and improve confidence.)	A few students know how to study this. Most students are struggling with where to go next. The textbook does not seem to help them (provide additional readings) them to.

Because she used the journaling, she was able to assess how students were feeling toward the class quickly, and discovered that while she had a few students who knew what they were doing, the majority of students were really struggling. She made changes in her teaching to provide these students with more support.

 ### Online: Paralegal

In this paralegal class, the instructor had a learning goal that students would describe the paralegal profession within in the context of the U.S. legal system as well as current ethical, regulatory, educational, and workplace issues. She also wanted them to be able develop beginning legal analysis skills. She decided students would be assessed through several assignments in which the students were required to complete tasks in the "real world," including visiting a courthouse, interviewing a currently working paralegal, and interviewing a lawyer who works with paralegals, in addition to quizzes, tests, and the final paper. To help students reflect on their "real world" experiences, the professor decided to use What? So What? Now What? Journals. She asked them to complete journal entries after each experience and post their entries in their course blogs, which were contained within the course LMS.

- What? What did you do?
- So what? What did you learn? How did it connect to course readings?
- Now what? What will you do to learn more?

She assigned each entry a +1 for completion and a +1 for any additional information or connections they supplied. The maximum number of points was 9 (1 point per question, 2 additional responses per question counted).

Question	Average Score
What?	3
So what?	2
Now what?	1.5

She could see that students were more proficient at explaining what they did. They were least proficient for determining where they could go to learn more. Since that was a key course goal for her, she knew that she had to provide additional information and instruction in this area.

Variations and Extensions

- What? So What? Now What? can take many forms other than a journal entry. For example, you could ask students to submit a written assignment, art project, poster presentation, oral presentation, discussion, or a combination.

Key References and Resources

Lubins, J. (2009). What? So what? Now what? *Library Leadership and Management, 23*(3), 140–149.

Eyler, J., & Giles, D. E. (1996). *A practitioner's guide to reflection in service-learning*. Nashville, TN: Vanderbilt University.

Weimer, M. (2015). How assignment design shapes student learning. Faculty Focus. http://www .facultyfocus.com/articles/teaching-professor-blog/how-assignment-design-shapes-student-learning/.

LEARNING ASSESSMENT TECHNIQUE

Learning How to Learn

49
Multiple-Task Mastery Checklist

Complexity involved in	
Preparation	HIGH
In-class implementation	HIGH
Analysis	HIGH

Brief Description

Multiple-Task Mastery Checklist provides a structured format for carrying out a multistage formative assessment of a formal project. It involves identifying the sequence of project activities and ensuring that students master each one in the series prior to moving forward to the next one.

Purpose

Teachers who use extensive projects as a part of their instructional processes often have students approach these in multiple small, sequenced steps that build upon each other. Each of these steps provides teachers with a unique opportunity for assessment. Multiple-Task Mastery Checklist is a multiphase formative assessment that provides students with ongoing and regular progress checks as they move toward a goal. This approach can ensure that students are advancing towards their goals and that they receive feedback on their progress so that they can make corrections as needed.

The Learning Artifact of this LAT is the checklist, which documents the activity sequence and allows for each link to be deemed "completed" prior to a student moving to the next level. While the work that students produce may be rich and varied, the Multiple-Task Mastery Checklist provides an efficient and effective way to manage the information in a single document. This LAT is a formative assessment that has application in many disciplines and fields. The teacher creates the checklist, uses one checklist for each student, and builds the artifact as each student passes each level.

Key Learning Goals

- Study skills and strategies
- The ability to monitor their own progress
- The ability to self-assess their performance
- The capacity for lifelong learning in the subject area
- The ability to create a concrete plan to learn more about the subject in the near future

Table 12.21 Project Checklist

Student Name_____	Date of Completion	Level of Quality
1.		
2.		
3.		
4.		

Implementation

Preparation

- Identify a significant project for students to take on. The project could be anything, from an exhibit of student creative work to a research paper to a project that demonstrates student skills.
- Break the project up into smaller steps in which students will submit a portion of the project that you may assess for completeness, quality, and so forth.
- Determine how you will score the product that students turn in for each level. Because this assessment has multiple steps, you will want to keep scoring simple, for example: complete/incomplete or high quality/average quality/low quality.
- From the smaller steps, create a checklist that you can use to track student work (Table 12.21).
- Create a handout that explains the project and expectations to students.

Process

1. Explain the project and the steps, share your handout with students, and allow time for questions.
2. Provide students with time to work to reach the first step for completion.
3. Check their products.
4. Repeat steps 2 and 3 until students have completed the final projects.
5. Review the Learning Artifacts.

Online

A useful way to keep track of a Multiple-Task Master Checklist is through a course LMS grading function. Alternately, you can set up folders for each student in a file sharing system (e.g., Dropbox, Box, or Google Docs) and keep track that way.

Analysis and Reporting

To assess the individual artifact, use your scoring system. Return the scored learning products to students with your score. Be available for questions, and if time permits and it makes sense to do so, schedule meetings with students to discuss their progress. For most of the levels on the checklist, you will not assign a grade, as the goal is to provide students with formative assessment.

To aggregate information, look at each item on the checklist and determine an average for each student, such as average level of quality. You can also look at the relationship between quality of the different levels and quality of the final product. Present your results in a simple table.

Examples

Onsite: Preparing for College-Level Teaching

This professor had a goal that students would be able to develop a plan to learn more about college teaching in the next one to three years after the course. He decided to use Multiple-Task Mastery Checklist and developed the following sequence chain In Figure 12.1 to outline the activities.

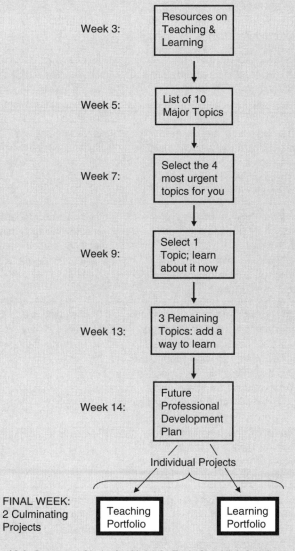

Figure 12.1 Sequence Chain for Multiple-Task Checklist Activity

Adapted with permission from L. D. Fink (personal correspondence).

He then devised a list of tasks and evidence that students would supply to demonstrate mastery (Table 12.22).

Table 12.22 Multiple-Task Mastery Checklist Assignment for Preparing for College-Level Teaching

Student Name:			
Week Assigned	**Student Task**	**Evidence of Mastery and Teacher Response**	**Date Mastered**
3	Find *5 resources* on the subject of the course: college-level teaching. These might be bibliographies, websites, references from major books on teaching, and so forth.	At the deadline, students bring their lists to class, share them within their groups, and give them to me. I will put all the different resources students found into a master resource list that I will distribute to all students.	
5	Review the master list of resources and find *10 topics* on college teaching that go beyond what we will be studying in the course. The question is: What topics are "out there" in addition to what we will be studying in this course?	At the deadline, students bring their lists to class, share them within their group, and give them to me. I will make a master topic list and distribute to all students.	
7	Using this master list of topics, *identify 4 topics* that you consider to be the most urgent to learn about in the "near future," meaning the next 1 to 3 years. You will then write a short essay in which you (a) identify the 4 topics and (b) explain in one paragraph for each topic why you consider that topic to be important to learn about in the near future.	At the deadline, students bring their short essays identifying the 4 topics along with rationale to class, share with the group, and submit to me. I will create a forum that links these essays as PDFs so that all students can read them.	
9	Take *1 of those 4 topics* and *learn about it* over the next 4 weeks. You can read a book, talk to a professor who is using some new idea, find some information on a website, or if you are teaching you can try the idea out and see how it works.	At the deadline, students bring to class a brief essay in which they (a) explain *what they did to learn* about the new topic and (b) *what they learned* about it.	
13	Now take the other 3 topics on your "short list" of important topics and, for each one, write a brief (1–2 paragraphs) statement indicating how you could learn about those topics if you had more time, i.e., 1 to 3 years. After you have completed this activity, you have a PLAN for directing your own learning on college teaching in the future. You have the 2 essentials of this plan: a learning agenda (*what* you want to learn) and a learning strategy (*how* you will learn that agenda).	At the deadline, students bring to class an essay in which they explain *what they can do to learn* about the new topic.	
14	You will then put this statement (your plan for future learning) into Part IV of both your Learning Portfolio (for this course) and your Teaching Portfolio (your description of yourself as a teacher at this early point in your career).	At the deadline, students submit both the Teaching and the Learning Portfolios to me as Culminating Projects for the course.	

Adapted with permission from L. D. Fink (personal correspondence)

He used the checklist to ensure that all students were making good progress and found that the activity did a good job of supporting students and also allowing him to assess how well students were "learning how to learn."

Blended: Qualitative Research in Sociology

The professor of this course had a goal that students will learn to conduct qualitative research in the field. The professor wanted them to demonstrate that they accomplish this goal by completing a focused case study (bounded case, 5–7 participants) and writing a research paper. She assigned readings about each of the phases, and she talked about it in class. She had group activities and also provided students with in-class work time so that she would be available for questions. Students submitted their work through the course LMS. She developed the checklist shown in Table 12.23 to assess their progress.

Table 12.23 Progress Checklist

Student Name_____	Due Date	Date of Completion	Level of Quality
Identify a topic in sociology that would be appropriate for a qualitative bibliography.	Week 2		
Develop an initial bibliography.	Week 3		
Develop a research question.	Week 4		
Develop a plan for the research methods, including sample selection, data collection process, plans for analysis.	Week 5		
Develop interview protocol.	Week 6		
Conduct interviews.	Weeks 7–8		
Analyze data.	Week 10		
Submit paper draft.	Week 12		
Submit final paper.	Week 16		

She noticed that several students did not submit their work in week 5 and asked them to meet with her individually. She was able to determine that they were having difficulties conceptualizing their methods, and she talked with them and helped them through it. Students were back on track and submitted their remaining assignments on time. She also had a second small group of students who submitted very weak paper drafts in week 12. Again, she asked the students to meet with her individually and was able to discuss her concerns with them. In most instances the students understood that she had higher expectations than they had anticipated and were able to bring up their papers.

Variations and Extensions

- Have students work in groups to complete group projects and use the Multiple-Task Mastery Checklist to gauge their progress.

50
Personal Learning Environment

Complexity involved in	
Preparation	LOW
In-class implementation	LOW-MODERATE
Analysis	MODERATE

Brief Description

A Personal Learning Environment (PLE) is a set of people and digital resources an individual can access for the specific intent of learning. Students illustrate these potential connections through the creation of visible network of the set. Nodes represent the resources, and ties suggest the relationship between the sources. A PLE then is a visual representation of a learner's informal learning processes and a concrete demonstration of an individual's capacity for future learning.

Purpose

This LAT helps students identify information sources, whether tools or individuals, that may help their professional development and growth in the future. Students may use their PLEs to learn from content area specialists, to learn about new technology, to find interesting news, and so forth. A PLE provides students with a way to map their future connections and to let them understand that their environments can and should grow. A PLE also supports multiple pathways to learning, by illustrating learning in emerging learning contexts, specifically social media spaces.

Being intentional about the process of information gathering and curation can help learners to recognize and realize the process of lifelong and social learning. It can help them to understand that no matter where they are, there is always some source available from which they may seek the answers to questions or even to come up with new questions, which they document in an ever-expandable network. It can be an empowering and transformational experience through prompting students to create a lifelong learning infrastructure.

The Learning Artifact is the network itself. It provides an illustration of a student's ability to obtain information from others in the future. It documents the current and future process of learning, rather than simply capturing evidence that learning has happened in a single snapshot in time. An illustrated PLE is essentially a mind map of how an individual believes that he or she can learn in the future.

This LAT should involve the creation of a network that realizes extended study that goes on during a term. That is, students need exposure to course-related content and concepts to be familiar enough with the subject area to create a PLE. For that reason, a PLE is typically done toward the end of an academic term, and it has been used by some as a final course experience.

Key Learning Goals

- Knowledge about themselves as learners
- The capacity for lifelong learning in the subject area
- The ability to create a concrete plan to learn more about the subject in the near future

Implementation

Preparation

- Collect sample PLEs to share with students so that they have an idea of what one might look like. There are many posted on the Internet, and a simple Google search can help you identify some samples, or you can create your own. Figure 12.2 offers a rudimentary example.
- Create a rubric that you can use to assess the Learning Artifacts. We offer the rubric shown in Table 12.24, which you can expand and tailor to your own needs.
- Determine who will be involved in the assessment. Having students peer review each other's work can provide an opportunity to learn from other students.

Figure 12.2 Sample Basic PLE

Table 12.24 Learning Artifacts Assessment Rubric

Content
 	
   Breadth of Resources
   Depth of Resources
   Number of nodes and ties
	4 3 2 1

Organization
 	
   Clarity of ties
   Betweenness (connection clusters)
	4 3 2 1

Tools
 	
   Content gathering (e.g., digital notebook; RSS readers)
   Social bookmarks
   Blogs
   Internet search tools
	4 3 2 1

Purposiveness
 	
   Focus of resources
   Likelihood of resources serving the stated purpose
	4 3 2 1

Aesthetics
 	
   Professional appearance
   Clean appearance
	4 3 2 1

Mechanics
 	
   Standard spelling
   Accuracy of names of tools
	4 3 2 1

Process
1. Announce the activity, and share an example of a PLE.
2. Explain to students that they make the decisions when setting up a PLE, including:
   - What tools will you use?
   - Who will be in the network?
   - What do you want to learn?

However, make it clear to them that the focus should be learning how to learn in the subject area.
3. Provide students with time to work.
4. Collect the Learning Artifacts.

Online

This activity is easily adaptable to an online environment. There are many online tools such as Popplet and Bubbl.us that allow for creating networks.

Analysis and Reporting

Personal Learning Environments are just that: Personal. However, using technological tools and networking are key skills in many professional careers that support the individual's growth and learning. As a skill, it should be possible to assess, without being judgmental, the degree to which an individual is successful. Because students have different needs and different goals for a PLE, it is best not to assign a high stakes grade to this activity. Instead, consider assigning points for participation in or completion of the activity. Develop a written response to individuals that includes summarizing what you see that they did well and where you feel they might improve.

When aggregating information, tally the number of responses for each item in your rubric. Alternately keep a running list of sources students use and look for what they did well and where there might be gaps.

Example

Blended: College and University Teaching

This class was designed to help graduate students in a range of disciplines and fields learn about college teaching and how to do it better. One of the professor's goals was to provide students with sufficient knowledge of the field to help them continue to learn about college teaching in the future. She decided to use PLE.

She announced the activity on the first day of class, during the syllabus review. Over the course of the term, students read about various topics related to college teaching, and they used several different technologies, such as blogs and Twitter to support their in class work. She talked to the students periodically about how their PLEs were progressing. Students submitted their PLEs for review by posting them to their blogs three weeks before the last class session. Figure 12.3 is an example; the number of nodes and ties is reduced so that it would fit the printed page.

She scored the PLEs using the rubrics and returned those to students. She also kept a running list of the technologies that students used, as shown in Table 12.25.

She could see that students were heavily relying on the tools that she had incorporated into the class. She realized that she had modeled these and given students experience in using them. She decided she would consider implementing additional tools in future classes, particularly those that students would likely rely on most in future learning about college teaching.

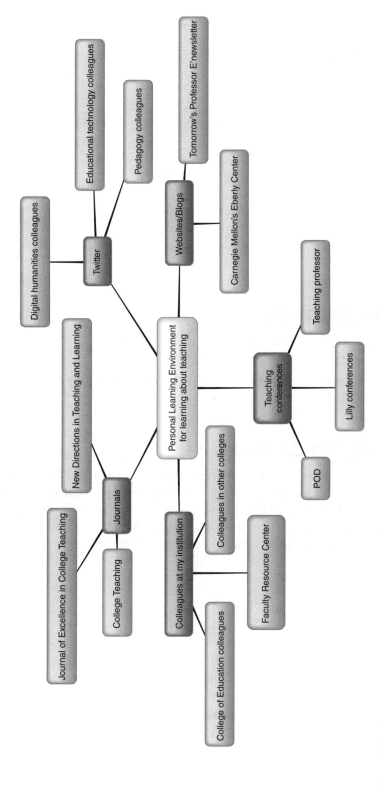

Figure 12.3 Sample PLE for College and University Teaching Course

Nodes in the diagram:

- Personal Learning Environment for learning about teaching (center)
- Twitter
  - Digital humanities colleagues
  - Educational technology colleagues
  - Pedagogy colleagues
- Websites/Blogs
  - Tomorrow's Professor E'newsletter
  - Carnegie Mellon's Eberly Center
- Journals
  - New Directions in Teaching and Learning
  - Journal of Excellence in College Teaching
  - College Teaching
- Colleagues at my institution
  - College of Education colleagues
  - Faculty Resource Center
  - Colleagues in other colleges
- Teaching conferences
  - Teaching professor
  - Lilly conferences
  - POD

Table 12.25 [need caption]

Tool	Number of Students
Personal blog (RSS)	25
Microblog (Twitter, Tumblr)	25
Social networking site (e.g., Facebook)	25
News and blog reader (RSS)	20
Social bookmarking (e.g., Diigo)	10
Video conferencing (contacts and synchronous communication tools, e.g., Google Hangouts)	10
Podcasts (RSS)	5
Online courses and presentations (e.g., MOOCs; Webinars)	0
Online journals	0

Variations and Extensions

- Put students into working groups and allow them to create a collaborative learning environment.
- If you have interest, ability, and resources consider a more formal social network analysis of the students' PLEs.

Key References and Resources

Martindale, T., & Dowdy, M. (2010). Personal learning environments. In G. Veletsianos (Ed.), *Emerging technologies in distance education* (pp. 177–193). Edmonton, Canada: Athabasca University Press.

Drexler, W. (2010). The networked student model for construction of personal learning environments: Balancing teacher control and student autonomy. *Australasian Journal of Educational Technology* 26(3), 369–385. http://www.ascilite.org.au/ajet/ajet26/drexler.pdf.

BIBLIOGRAPHY

[3MT] (nd). Three-minute thesis. http://threeminutethesis.org (Accessed 5.1.15).

Alexander, P. A., Kulikowich, J. M., & Schulze, S. K. (1994). The influence of topic knowledge, domain knowledge, and interest on the comprehension of scientific exposition. *Learning and Individual Differences, 6*(4), 379–397.

Allen, I. E., & Seaman, J. (2013). *Changing course: Ten years of tracking online education in the United States.* Wellesley, MA: Babson College.

Amabile, T. M. (1996). *Creativity in context.* Boulder, CO: Westview Press.

Ambrose, S. A., Bridges, M. W., Di Pietro, M., Lovett, M. C., & Norman, M. K. (2010). *How learning works: Seven research-based principles for smart teaching.* San Francisco, CA: Jossey-Bass.

Anderson, J. R. (2004). *Cognitive psychology and its implications* (6th ed.). New York, NY: Worth Publishers.

Anderson, L. W., & Krathwohl, D. R. (Eds.). (2001). *A taxonomy for learning, teaching, and assessing.* New York: Addison Wesley Longman.

Angelo, T. A. (1995, Nov.). Reassessing (and defining) assessment. *AAHE Bulletin, 48*(3), 7.

Angelo, T. A., & Cross, K. P. (1993). *Classroom assessment techniques: A handbook for college teachers* (2nd ed.). San Francisco, CA: Jossey-Bass.

Association of American Colleges and Universities. (nd). VALUE Rubrics. http://www.aacu.org/value/rubrics (Accessed 7.20.15).

Association of American Colleges and Universities. (2007a). College learning for the new global century. http://www.aacu.org/leap/documents/GlobalCentury_final.pdf (Accessed 5.1.15).

Association of American Colleges and Universities. (2007b). Liberal education and America's promise (LEAP). http://www.aacu.org/leap/index.cfm (Accessed 8.20.14).

Bain, K. (2004). *What the best college teachers do.* Cambridge, MA: Harvard University Press.

Banta, T. W., & Blaich, C. (2011). Closing the "assessment loop." *Change: The Magazine of Higher Learning, 43*(1), 22–27.

Barkley, E. F. (2010). *Student engagement techniques: A handbook for college faculty.* San Francisco, CA: Jossey-Bass.

Barkley, E. F., Major, C. H., & Cross, P. K. (2014). *Collaborative learning techniques: A handbook for college faculty* (2nd ed.). San Francisco, CA: Jossey-Bass.

Barr, R. B., & Tagg, J. (1995). From teaching to learning: A new paradigm for undergraduate education. *Change: The Magazine of Higher Learning, 27*(6), 13–25.

Bauer, J. F. (2002). Assessing student work from chat rooms and bulletin boards. New Directions for Teaching and Learning, No. 91, p. 35. San Francisco, CA: Jossey-Bass.

Bean, J. C. (2009). *Engaging ideas: The professor's guide to integrating writing, critical thinking, and active learning in the classroom* (2nd ed.). San Francisco, CA: Jossey-Bass.

Belenky, M. F., Clinchy, B. M., Goldberger, N. R., & Tarule, J. M. (1986). *Women's ways of knowing: The development of self, voice, and mind.* New York: Basic Books.

Bennett, M. J. (1993). Towards ethnorelativism: A developmental model of intercultural sensitivity. In R. M. Paige (Ed.), *Education for the intercultural experience* (pp. 22–71). Yarmouth, ME: Intercultural Press.

Bennett, J. (1998). Transition shock: Putting culture shock in perspective. In M. Bennett (Ed.), *Basic concepts of intercultural communication* (pp. 215–224). Yarmouth, ME: Intercultural Press.

Berkowitz, B. (2007). The community tool box: Bringing solutions to light. Work group for community health and development. University of Kansas. http://ctb.ku.edu/en (Accessed 5.1.14).

Bernard, H. R., & Ryan, G. W. (2010). *Analyzing qualitative data: Systematic approaches.* Thousand Oaks, CA: Sage.

Biemans, H. J., & Simons, P. R. J. (1996). Contact-2: A computer-assisted instructional strategy for promoting conceptual change. *Instructional Science, 24*(2), 157–176.

Biemiller, A., & Meichenbaum, D. (1992). The nature and nurture of the self-directed learner. *Educational Leadership, 50,* 75–80.

Blaich, C. F., & Wise, K. S. (2011, January) From *Gathering to using assessment results: lessons from the Wabash National Study.* NILOA Occasional Paper No. I. Urbana, IL: University of Illinois and Indiana University, National Institute for Learning Outcomes Assessment.

Bloom, B. (1980). The new direction in educational research: Alterable variables. *Phi Delta Kappan* (Feb.) 382–385.

Bloom, B. S. (1976). *Human characteristics and school learning.* New York, NY: McGraw-Hill.

Boettcher, J. V., & Conrad, R. (2010). *The online teaching survival guide: Simple and practical pedagogical tips.* San Francisco, CA: Jossey-Bass.

Bonwell, C. C., & Eison, J. A. (1991). *Active learning: Creating excitement in the classroom. 1991 ASHE-ERIC Higher Education Reports.* ERIC Clearinghouse on Higher Education, The George Washington University.

Borkowski, J., Carr, M., & Pressely, M. (1987). "Spontaneous" strategy use: Perspectives from metacognitive theory. *Intelligence, 11,* 61–75.

Boulanger, F. D. (1981). Instruction and science learning: A quantitative synthesis. *Journal of Research in Science Teaching, 18,* 311–327.

Bowen, G. A. (2005). Preparing a qualitative research-based dissertation: Lessons learned. *Qualitative Report, 10*(2), 208–222.

Boyer, E. L. (1990). *Scholarship reconsidered: Priorities of the professoriate.* Princeton, NJ: Carnegie Foundation for the Advancement of Teaching.

Bransford, J. D., Brown, A. L., Cocking, R. R., Donovan, S., & Pellegrino, J. W. (2000). *How people learn: Brain, mind, experience, and school.* Washington, DC: National Academy Press.

Braun, V., & Clarke, V. (2006). Using thematic analysis in psychology. *Qualitative Research in Psychology,* *3*(2), 77–101.

Brookfield, S. D., & Preskill, S. (2005). *Discussion as a way of teaching: Tools and techniques for democratic classrooms.* (2nd ed.). San Francisco, CA: Jossey-Bass.

Brookhart, S. (2013a). Assessing creativity. *Educational Leadership, 70*(5), 23–34 http://www.ascd .org/publications/educational-leadership/feb13/vol70/num05/Assessing-Creativity.aspx (Accessed 7.28.14).

Brookhart, S. M. (2013b). *Grading and group work: How do I assess individual learning when students work together?* Alexandria, VA: Association for Supervision and Curriculum Development (ASCD).

Brookhart, S. M. (2013c). *How to create and use rubrics for formative assessment and grading.* Alexandria, VA: Association for Supervision and Curriculum Development (ASCD).

Brophy, J. (2004). *Motivating students to learn* (2nd ed.). Mahwah, NJ: Lawrence Erlbaum.

Bruer, J. T. (1997). Education and the brain: A bridge too far. *Educational Researcher, 26,* 4–16.

Bruffee, K. A. (1995). *Collaborative learning: Higher education, interdependence, and the authority of knowledge.* Baltimore, MD: The Johns Hopkins University Press.

Cameron, J. (1996). *The vein of gold: A journey to your creative heart.* New York: Putnam.

Carnegie Mellon Eberly Center for Teaching Excellence and Educational Innovation. (nd). Teaching principles. http://www.cmu.edu/teaching/principles/teaching.html (Accessed: 7.18.15).

Carnegie Mellon Eberly Center for Teaching Excellence and Educational Innovation. (nd). Using concept tests. http://www.cmu.edu/teaching/assessment/assesslearning/concepTests.html (Accessed 8.21.14).

Chan C. (2009). Assessment: Debate. *Assessment Resources @HKU,* University of Hong Kong. http://ar .cetl.hku.hk. (Accessed: 3.26.15).

Chicago Manual of Style. (2010). Lists and Outlines (6.121–126). (16th ed.). Chicago, IL: University of Chicago Press.

Chickering, A. W., & Gamson, Z. F. (1987). Seven principles for good practice in undergraduate education. *The Wingspread Journal, 9*(2).

Cleland, J., Rillero, P., & Zambo, R. (nd). Effective prompts for quick writes in science and mathematics. http://ejlts.ucdavis.edu/sites/ejlts.ucdavis.edu/files/articles/Jocleland.pdf (Accessed 5.1.14).

Clinchy, B. (1990). Issues of gender in teaching and learning. *Journal on Excellence in College Teaching.* Reprinted in K. A. Feldman and M. B Paulsen (Eds.) (1994). Teaching and Learning in the College Classroom. ASHE Reader Series. Needham Heights, MA: Ginn.

College Learning for the New Global Century. (2007). Association of American Colleges and Universities. http://www.aacu.org/leap/documents/GlobalCentury_final.pdf (Accessed 5.1.15).

College Standards and Accreditation Committee. (1994). *Guidelines to the development of standards of achievement through learning outcomes.* Ontario Ministry of Colleges and Universities.

Conrad, R., & Donaldson, J. A. (2011). *Engaging the online learner.* San Francisco, CA: Jossey-Bass.

Cottell, P. G., & Millis, B., (2010). Cooperative learning in accounting. In B. Millis, (Ed.), *Cooperative learning in higher education: Across the disciplines, across the academy* (pp. 11–33). Sterling, VA: Stylus Publishing.

Council of Graduate Schools. (2015). Preparing Future Faculty to Assess Student Learning. http:// www.cgsnet.org/preparing-future-facultypreparing-future-faculty-assess-student-learning (Accessed 5.1.15).

Craft, A. (2005). *Creativity in schools: Tensions and dilemmas.* Abingdon: Routledge.

Cross, K. P. (1986). A proposal to improve teaching or what "taking teaching seriously" should mean. http://files.eric.ed.gov/fulltext/ED274257.pdf (Accessed 12.4.14).

Cross, K. P., & Angelo, T. A. (1988). *Classroom assessment techniques. A handbook for faculty.* Ann Arbor, MI: National Center for the Improvement of Postsecondary Teaching and Learning.

Cross, K. P., & Fideler, E. F. (1988). Assessment in the classroom. *Community/Junior College Quarterly of Research and Practice, 12*(4), 275–285.

Cross, K. P., & Steadman, M. H. (1996). *Classroom research: Implementing the scholarship of teaching.* San Francisco, CA: Jossey-Bass.

Csikszentmihalyi, M. (1993). *The evolving self: A psychology for the third millennium.* New York, NY: HarperCollins.

Csikszentmihalyi, M. (1997). Intrinsic motivation and effective teaching: A flow analysis. In J. Bess (Ed.), *Teaching well and liking it: Motivating faculty to teach effectively* (pp. 72–89). Baltimore, MD: The Johns Hopkins Press.

Darling-Hammond, L. (Ed.). (2014). *Next generation assessment: Moving beyond the bubble test to support 21st century learning.* San Francisco, CA: Wiley/Jossey-Bass.

Davis, B. H. (2009). *Tools for teaching* (2nd ed.). San Francisco, CA: Wiley/Jossey-Bass.

Davis, J. (2012). Briefing paper. http://www.cs.grinnell.edu/~davisjan/tut/100/2012F/assignments/briefing-paper.html (Accessed 5.1.15).

Deardorff, D. K. (2006). The identification and assessment of intercultural competence as a student outcome of internationalization. *Journal of Studies in International Education, 10,* 241–266.

Diamond, R. (1998). *Designing and assessing courses and curricula.* San Francisco, CA: Jossey-Bass.

Dochy, F. J., & Alexander, P. A. (1995). Mapping prior knowledge: A framework for discussion among researchers. *European Journal of Psychology of Education, 10*(3), 225–242.

Dochy, F., Segers, M., & Buehl, M. M. (1999). The relation between assessment practices and outcomes of studies: The case of research on prior knowledge. *Review of Educational Research, 69*(2), 145–186.

Dodge, J. (2005). *Differentiation in action.* New York, NY: Scholastic Inc.

Dramatic Dialogue Exercise from Writing Really Good Dialogue. http://ywp.nanowrimo.org/files/ywp/ywp_10_hs_dialogue.pdf (Accessed 8.5.14).

Dreon, O. (2013). Applying the seven principles for good practice to the online classroom. *Faculty Focus: Higher Ed Teaching Strategies from Magna Publications* (February 25, 2013). http://www.facultyfocus.com/articles/online-education/applying-the-seven-principles-for-good-practice-to-the-online-classroom/ (Accessed 5.29.14).

Dressel, P. (1983). Grades: One more tilt at the windmill. In A. W. Chickering (Ed.), *Bulletin.* Memphis, TN: Memphis State University, Center for Study for Higher Education.

Driscoll, M. (2000). *Psychology of learning for instruction.* Needham Heights, MA: Allyn & Bacon.

Duffelmeyer, F. (1994). Effective anticipation guide statements for learning from expository prose. *Journal of Reading, 37,* 452–455.

Education Commission of the States. (1996, Apr.). What research says about improving undergraduate education. *AAHE Bulletin, 48,* 5–8.

Ehrlich, T. (2000). *Civic responsibility and higher education.* Phoenix, AZ: Oryx Press.

Ellison, M. (2012). *Chucking college: Achieving success without corruption.* Durango, CO: Devoted Maidenhood.

ERIC Retrospective. (nd). 50 years of ERIC: 1964–2014. http://eric.ed.gov/pdf/ERIC_Retrospective.pdf?v=2 (Accessed 5.21.14).

Erwin, T. D. (1991). *Assessing student learning and development.* San Francisco, CA: Jossey-Bass.

Ewell, P. T. (1997). Organizing for learning. *AAHE Bulletin, 50*(4), 3–6.

Ewell, P. T. (2007). Defining the quality-driven institution. *Assessment Update*, 4(5), 1–5.

Ewell, P. T. (2013, Jan.). The Lumina Degree Qualifications Profile (DQP): Implications for Assessment. (Occasional Paper No. 16). Urbana, IL: University for Illinois and Indiana University, National institute for Learning Outcomes Assessment.

Eyler, J., & Giles, D. E. (1996). *A practitioner's guide to reflection in service-learning*. Nashville, TN: Vanderbilt University.

Eynon, B., Gambino, L. M., & Torok, J. (2014). What difference can eportfolio make? A field report from the connect to learning project. *International Journal of ePortfolio*, 4(1), 95–114.

Feldman, D. H. (1999). The development of creativity. In R. J Sternberg (Ed.), *Handbook of creativity*. Cambridge, England: Cambridge University Press.

Feldman, K. A., & Newcomb, T. M. (1969). *The impact of college on students*. San Francisco, CA: Jossey-Bass.

Feleti, G., & Ryan, G. (1994). The triple jump exercise in inquiry-based learning: A case study. *Assessment & Evaluation in Higher Education*, 19(3), 225–234.

Fink, L. D. (2013). *Creating significant learning experiences: An integrated approach to designing college courses*. San Francisco, CA: Jossey-Bass.

Finley, T. (2014). Dipsticks: Efficient ways to check for understanding. *Edutopia: What Works in Education*, 72(5), 1–9.

Flavell, J. H. (1976). Metacognitive aspects of problem solving. In L. B. Resnick (Ed.), *The nature of intelligence* (pp. 231–236). Hillsdale, NJ: Lawrence Erlbaum.

Flavell, J. H. (1979). Metacognition and cognitive monitoring: A new area of cognitive-developmental inquiry. *American Psychologist*, 34, 906–911.

Flavell, J. H. (1987). Speculations about the nature and development of metacognition. In F. E. Weinert & R. H. Kluwe (Eds.), *Metacognition, motivation, and understanding* (pp. 21–29). Hillside, NJ: Lawrence Erlbaum.

Fulks, J. (2006). Student learning outcomes assessment. http://www2.bakersfieldcollege.edu/courseassessment/Section_1_Introduction/Introduction1.htm (Accessed 5.1.15).

Gantz, J., & Reinsel, D. (2011). Extracting value from chaos. Sponsored by EMC Corporation. http://www.emc.com/collateral/analyst-reports/idc-extracting-value-from-chaos-ar.pdf.

Gelb, M. J. (1998). *How to think like Leonardo da Vinci: Seven steps to genius every day*. New York, NY: Delacorte Press.

Gladwell, M. (2008). *Outliers: The story of success*. Boston, MA: Little, Brown.

Glasersfeld, E. V. (1984). An introduction to radical constructivism. In P. Watzlawick (Ed.), *The invented reality* (pp. 17–40). New York, NY: Norton.

Glassick, C., Huber, M., & Maeroff, G. (1997). *Scholarship assessed: Evaluation of the professoriate*. San Francisco, CA: Jossey-Bass.

Glassick, C. E. (2000). Boyer's expanded definitions of scholarship, the standards for assessing scholarship, and the elusiveness of the scholarship of teaching. *American Medicine*, 75(9). https://www.academicpeds.org/events/assets/Glassick%20article.pdf (Accessed 5.1.15).

Goleman, D. (1995). *Emotional intelligence*. New York, NY: Bantam.

Goleman, D. (1998). *Working with emotional intelligence*. New York, NY: Bantam.

Gonchar, M. (2014). For the sake of argument: Writing persuasively to craft short, evidence-based editorials. http://learning.blogs.nytimes.com//2014/02/07/for-the-sake-of-argument-writing-persuasively-to-craft-short-evidence-based-editorials/ (Accessed 5.1.15).

Gooblar, D. (2014). Want to take group work to the next level? Give team tests. *ChronicleVitae*. https://chroniclevitae.com/news/656-want-to-take-group-work-to-the-next-level-give-teamtests?cid=at&utm_source=at&utm_medium=en#sthash.VGFdlvMm.dpuf (Accessed 8.26.14).

Gordon, J. (nd). A short guide to oral assessment. https://www.leedsbeckett.ac.uk/publications/files /100317_36668_ShortGuideOralAssess1_WEB.pdf (Accessed 5.1.15).

Groom, J. (nd). How to write up assignments like a blogging champ. http://ds106.us/handbook/success -the-ds106-way/writing-up-assignments/ (Accessed 5.1.15).

Hacker, D. J., Dunlosky J., & Graesser A. C. (Eds.). *Handbook of metacognition in education.* New York, NY: Routledge.

Hailikari, T., Katajavuori, N., & Lindblom-Ylänne, S. (2008). The relevance of prior knowledge in learning and instructional design. *American Journal of Pharmaceutical Education, 72*(5), 1–9.

Hall, T., & Strangman, N. (1999–2004). Graphic organizers. http://www.cast.org/ncac/Graphic Organizers3015.cfm (Accessed 3.22.04).

Hanna, G. S., & Cashin, W. C. (1988). *IDEA paper no. 19: Improving college grading.* Center for Faculty Evaluation and Development, Division of Continuing Education, Kansas State University. http:// ideaedu.org/sites/default/files/Idea_Paper_19.pdf (Accessed 5.1.15).

Heward, W. L. (1996). Three low-tech strategies for increasing the frequency of active student response during group instruction. In R. Gardner III, D. M. Sainato, J. O. Cooper, T. E. Heron, W. L. Heward, J. W. Eshleman, & T. A. Grossi (Eds.), *Behavior analysis in education: Focus on measurably superior instruction* (pp. 283–320). Pacific Grove, CA: Brooks/Cole.

Heward, W. L. (2001). *Guided notes: Improving the effectiveness of your lectures.* Columbus, OH: The Ohio State University Partnership Grant for Improving the Quality of Education for Students with Disabilities. http://ada.osu.edu/resources/fastfacts/ (Accessed 5.1.15).

House, J. (1977). The three faces of social psychology. *Sociometry, 40,* 161–177.

Huba, M. E., & Freed, J. E. (2001). *Learner-centered assessment on college campuses: Shifting the focus from teaching to learning.* Needham Heights, MA: Allyn and Bacon.

Huber, M. T., & Hutchings, P. (2005). *The advancement of learning: Building the teaching commons.* San Francisco, CA: Jossey-Bass.

Hutchings, P., Jankowski, N., & Ewell, P. (2014). Catalyzing assignment design activity on your campus: Lessons from NILOA's Assignment Library Initiative. http://learningoutcomesassessment.org /niloaassignmentlibrary.htm.

Jacobs, L. F., & Hyman, J. S. (2009, Aug. 12). Professors' guide: Why does diversity matter at college anyway? *U.S. News & World Report.* http://www.usnews.com/education/blogs/professors-guide /2009/08/12/why-does-diversity-matter-at-college-anyway (Accessed 1.22.15).

James, A., & Brookfield, S. D. (2014). *Engaging imagination: Helping students become creative and reflective thinkers.* San Francisco, CA: Jossey-Bass.

Jankowski, N. (2014, Sept. 12). Mapping learning outcomes: What you map is what you see. *Myths and Movements: Reimagining Higher Education Assessment.* Retrieved on October 21, 2015 from http:// www.learningoutcomesassessment.org/Presentations/Mapping.pdf

Jankowski, N., Kinzie, J., & Kuh, G. (2014). What provosts say about student learning outcomes assessment. Presentation at AAC&U, January 24, 2014. http://www.learningoutcomeassessment.org /Presentations/AACU%20NJ%20JK%20GK.pdf.

Johnson, D. W., & Johnson, R. T. (1984). *Circles of learning.* Washington, DC: Association Supervision and Curriculum Development.

Johnson, D. W., Johnson, R., & Smith, K. (1998). *Active learning: Cooperation in the college classroom.* Edina, MN: Interaction Book Co.

Johnson, D. W., Johnson, R., & Smith, K. (2014). Cooperative learning: Improving university instruction by basing practice on validated theory. *Journal on Excellence in College Teaching, 25*(3–4), 85–118.

Kagan, S. (1990). The structural approach to cooperative learning. *Educational Leadership, 47*(4), 12–15.

Kagan, S. (1992). *Cooperative learning* (2nd ed.). San Juan Capistrano, CA: Resources for Teachers.

Kagan, S. (1996). *Cooperative learning.* San Clemente, CA: Kagan Cooperative Learning.

Kearns, K. D., & Sullivan, C. S. (2011). Resources and practices to help graduate students and postdoctoral fellows write statements of teaching philosophy. *Advances in Physiology Education, 35*(1), 136–145. http://www.facultyfocus.com/articles/philosophy-of-teaching/strategies-for-writing-better -teaching-philosophy-statements/#sthash.QNJnw8Kt.dpuf (Accessed 5.1.15).

Kegley, K., & Robbins, T. (2009). Teaching creativity for 21st century students. Clemson Computer and Information Technology http://www.clemson.edu/ccit/about/publications/facultydirections/Fall09 /creative_thinking.html (Accessed 8.4.14).

Kraft, U. (2005, Apr.). Unleashing creativity. *Scientific American Mind,* 16–23.

Krathwohl, L. W., & Anderson, D. R. (Eds.). (2001). *A taxonomy for learning, teaching, and assessing: A revision of Bloom's taxonomy of educational objectives.* New York, NY: Longman.

Krathwohl, L. W., Bloom, B. J., & Masia, B. B. (1999). *Taxonomy of educational objectives, Book 2: Affective domain* (2nd ed.). New York, NY: Longman.

Krosnick, J. A., & Fabrigar, L. R. (1997). Designing rating scales for effective measurement in surveys. In L. Lyberg, P. Biemer, M. Collins, L. Decker, E. DeLeeuw, C. Dippo, N. Schwarz, & D. Trewin (Eds.), *Survey measurement and process quality.* New York, NY: Wiley-Interscience.

Kuh, G. D., Ikenberry, S. O., Jankowski, N. A., Cain, T. R., Ewell, P. T., Hutchings, P., & Kinzie, J. (2015). *Using evidence of student learning to improve higher education.* San Francisco, CA: Wiley/Jossey-Bass.

Lambert, J. (2010). Digital storytelling cookbook. http://static.squarespace.com/static/505a3ab2e4b 0f1416c7df69a/51684d91e4b0cbd5dcd536fd/51684d91e4b0cbd5dcd536ff/1332882649047 /cookbook.pdf (Accessed 5.1.15).

Larsy, N. (nd). Peer instruction: Comparing clickers to flashcards. http://arxiv.org/pdf/physics/0702186 .pdf (Accessed 5.1.15).

Learning Theories.Com. (2015). Knowledge base and webliography. http://www.learning-theories.com (Accessed 1.21.15).

Lehrer, J. (2012). *Imagine: How creativity works.* Boston. MA: Houghton Mifflin Harcourt.

Lemov, D. (2010). *Teach like a champion: 49 strategies that put students on the path to success.* San Francisco, CA: Jossey-Bass.

Lent, R. C. (2012). Overcoming textbook fatigue: 21st century tools to revitalize teaching and learning. http://www.ascd.org/publications/books/113005/chapters/Background-Knowledge@-The-Glue -That-Makes-Learning-Stick.aspx (Accessed 5.1.15).

Linn, R. L., & Gronlund, N. E. (2000). *Measurement and assessment in teaching* (8th ed.). Upper Saddle River, NJ: Prentice Hall.

Livingston, J. A. (1997). Metacognition: An overview. http://gse.buffalo.edu/fas/shuell/CEP564/Metacog .htm (Accessed 5.1.15).

Lochhead, J., & Whimby, A. (1987). Teaching analytical reasoning through thinking-aloud pair problem solving. In J. E. Stice (Ed.), *Developing critical thinking and problem solving abilities* (pp. 72–93). New Directions for Teaching and Learning. No. 30. San Francisco, CA: Jossey-Bass.

Lorenzo, G., & Ittelson, J. (2005). Overview of e-portfolios. Educause Learning Initiative. https://net .educause.edu/ir/library/pdf/eli3001.pdf (Accessed 5.1.15).

Lubins, J. (2009). What? So what? Now what? *Library Leadership and Management, 23*(3), 140–149.

MacGregor, J. (1990). Collaborative learning: Shared inquiry as a process of reform. In M. D. Svinicki (Ed.), *The changing face of college teaching* (pp. 19–30). New Directions for Teaching and Learning, No. 42. San Francisco, CA: Jossey-Bass.

Major, C. H. (2015). *Teaching online: A guide to theory, research, and practice*. Baltimore, MD: Johns-Hopkins University Press.

Maki, P. (2004) *Assessing for learning*. Sterling, VA: American Association for Higher Education.

Marzano, R. J. (2006) *Classroom assessment and grading that work*. Alexandria, VA: Association for Supervision and Curriculum Development (ASCD).

Marzano, R. J. (2012). Art and science of teaching: The many uses of exit slips. *Students Who Challenge Us, 70*(2), 80–81.

Mason, L. (2009). Bridging neuroscience and education: A two-way path is possible. *Cortex, 45*(4), 548–549.

Mastascusa, E. J., Snyder, W. J., & Hoyt, B. S. (2011) *Effective instruction for STEM disciplines: From learning theory to college teaching*. San Francisco, CA: Jossey-Bass.

Matthews, R. S., Cooper, J. L., Davidson, N., & Hawkes, P. (1995, July/Aug.). Building bridges between cooperative and collaborative learning. *Change, 27*, 34–40.

Mayer, R. E. (2001). *Multimedia learning*. New York, NY: Cambridge University Press.

Mazur, E. (1997). *Peer instruction: A user's manual*. Upper Saddle River, NJ: Prentice Hall.

McClary, L. M., & Bretz, S. L. Diagnostic tool to identify organic chemistry students' alternative conceptions relative to acid strength. *International Journal of Science Education, 34*(5), 2317–2341.

McCombs, B. L. (1992, Aug.). *Learner-centered psychological principles: Guidelines for school redesign and reform* (rev. ed.). Washington, DC: American Psychological Association, APA Task Force on Psychology in Education.

McConnell, D. A., Steer, D. N., Owens, K. D., Knott, J. R., Van Horn, S., Borowski, W., . . . Heaney, P. J. (2006). Using concept tests to assess and improve student conceptual understanding in introductory geoscience courses. *Journal of Geoscience Education, 54*(1), 61.

McKeachie, W. J. (1994). *Teaching tips: Strategies, research and theory for college and university teachers* (9th ed.). Lexington, MA: D. C. Heath.

McKeachie, W. J., & Svinicki, M. (2013). *McKeachie's teaching tips* (14th ed.). Independence, KY: Cengage Learning.

McKinney, M. (2011, Spring). Know thyself. But why? *Vision: Insights and New Horizons*. http://www.vision.org/visionmedia/personal-development/self-knowledge/44343.aspx (Accessed 1.23.15).

Michaelsen, L. K., & Black, R. H. (1994). Building learning teams: The key to harnessing the power of small groups in higher education. In S. Kadel & J. Keehner (Eds.), *Collaborative learning: A sourcebook for higher education, 2* (pp. 65–81). State College, PA: National Center for Teaching, Learning and Assessment.

Michaelsen, L. K., Fink, L. D., & Knight, A. (1997). Designing effective group activities: Lessons for classroom teaching and faculty development. In D. DeZure (Ed.), *To improve the academy: Resources for faculty. Instructional and organizational development, 16* (pp. 373–397). Stillwater, OK: New Forums Press Co.

Michalko, M. (1998). *Cracking creativity: The secrets of creative genius*. Berkeley, CA: Ten Speed Press.

Miller, J. (2009). Evidence-based instruction: A classroom experience comparing nominal and focused listing groups. *Organizational Management Journal, 6*(4), 229–238.

Millis, B. J., & Cottell, P. G. (1998). *Cooperative learning for higher education faculty*. Phoenix, AZ: Oryx Press.

Millis, B. J., Sherman, L. W., & Cottell, P. G. (1993). Stacking the DEC to promote critical thinking: Applications in three disciplines. *Cooperative Learning and College Teaching, 3*(3), 12–14.

Mirsky, A. F., Anthony, B. F., Duncan, C. C., Ahearn, M. B., & Kellam, S. G. (1991). Analysis of the elements of attention: A neuropsychological approach. *Neuropsychology Review, 2*, 109–145.

Moon, J. A. (2004). *A handbook of reflective and experiential learning: Theory and practice.* New York, NY: Routledge.

Moore, D. W., & Readence, J. E. (1984). A quantitative and qualitative review of graphic organizer research. *Journal of Educational Research, 78*(1), 11–17.

Mumford, M. D. (2003). Where have we been, where are we going? Taking stock in creativity research. *Creativity Research Journal, 15,* 107–120.

Nagy, W. E., Anderson, R. C., & Herman, P. A. (1987). Learning word meanings from context during normal reading. *American Educational Research Journal, 24*(2), 237–270.

Naidu, S., Ip, A., & Linser, R. (2000). Dynamic goal-based role-play simulation the Web: A case study. *Educational Technology & Society, 3*(3), 190–202.

Naisbitt, J. (1982). *Megatrends.* New York, NY: Warner Books.

Nietfeld, J. L., & Shraw, G. (2002). The effect of knowledge and strategy explanation on monitoring accuracy. *Journal of Educational Research, 95,* 131–142.

Nilsen, C., Odahlen, B., Geller, L., Hintz, K., & Borden-King, L. (2011). *Fifty ways to teach your students.* Presented at 30th Annual Conference on the First Year Experience. http://www.minotstateu.edu/cetl /pdf/50waystoteachyourstudents.pdf (Accessed 5.1.15).

Nilson, L. B. (2007). *The graphic syllabus and the outcomes map: Communicating your course.* San Francisco, CA: Jossey-Bass.

Nilson, L. (2013). *Creating self-regulated learners: Strategies to strengthen self-awareness and learning skills.* Sterling, VA: Stylus.

Novak, J. D., & Cañas A. J. (2008). *The theory underlying concept maps and how to construct them.* Technical Report IHMC CmapTools 2006–01 Rev 01–2008, Florida Institute for Human and Machine Cognition. http://cmap.ihmc.us/Publications/ResearchPapers/TheoryUnderlyingConcept Maps.pdf (Accessed 5.1.15).

Novak, J. D., & Gowin, D. B. (1984). *Learning how to learn.* New York, NY: Cambridge University Press.

Nuhfer, E., & Knipp, D. (2003). The knowledge survey: A tool for all reasons. *To Improve the academy,* v. *21,* pp. 59–78. https://www.vcu.edu/cte/workshops/teaching_learning/2007_resources/knowledge _survey.pdf (Accessed 8.16.14).

On Course E-Newsletter. (nd). Six ways to use quick writes to promote learning. http:// oncourseworkshop.com/life-long-learning/six-ways-use-quick-writes-promote-learning/ (Accessed 5.1.15).

Oxford Centre for Staff Development. (1992). Improving student learning. Oxford, England: Oxford Brookes University. Reprinted in Deep learning, surface learning, *AAHE Bulletin,* April 1993, pp. 10–11.

Palloff, R. M., & Pratt, K., (2009). *Assessing the online learner: Resources and strategies for faculty.* San Francisco, CA: Jossey-Bass.

Pascarella, E. T., & Terenzini, P. T. (1991). *How college affects students.* San Francisco, CA: Jossey-Bass.

Pascarella, E. T., & Terenzini, P.T. (2005). *How college affects students: A third decade of research.* San Francisco, CA: Jossey-Bass.

Patton, M. Q. (1990). *Qualitative evaluation and research methods.* Newbury Park, CA: Sage Publications.

Pennsylvania State University. (nd). Instructor's guide to media activities. http://mediacommons.psu .edu/faculty/ (Accessed 5.1.15).

Perkins, D. N. (1992). Transfer of learning. *International Encyclopedia of Education* (2nd ed.). Oxford, England: Pergamon Press. https://learnweb.harvard.edu/alps/thinking/docs/traencyn.htm (Accessed 9.2.14).

Pink, D. H. (2005). *A whole new mind: Moving from the information age into the conceptual age.* London: Allen & Unwin.

Pink, D. H. (2009). *Drive: The surprising truth about what motivates us.* New York, NY: Riverhead Books.

Plous, S. (2000). Responding to overt displays of prejudice: A role-playing exercise. *Teaching of Psychology, 27*(3), 198–200.

Pressley, M., Borkowski, J. G., & Schneider, W. (1987). Cognitive strategies: Good strategy users coordinate metacognition and knowledge. In R. Vasta & G. Whitehurst (Eds.), *Annals of child development, 4,* 80–129. Greenwich, CT: JAI Press.

Prince, M. (2004). Does active learning work? A review of the research. *Journal of Engineering Education, 93*(3), 223–231.

Purdue Online Writing Lab. (nd). Developing an outline. https://owl.english.purdue.edu/owl/resource/544/1/ (Accessed 5.1.15).

Ratey, J. J. (2002). *A user's guide to the brain.* New York: Vintage Books.

Resnick, L. B. (1983). Mathematics and science learning: A new conception. *Science, 220*(4596), 477–478.

Richman, W. A., & Ariovich, L. (2013, Oct.). *All-in-one: Combining grading, course, program, and general education outcomes assessment.* (Occasional Paper No.19). Urbana, IL: University of Illinois and Indiana University, National Institute for Learning Outcomes Assessment.

Roediger, H. L., & Butler, A. C. (2011). The critical role of retrieval practice in long-term retention. *Trends in cognitive sciences, 15*(1), 20–27. http://people.duke.edu/~ab259/pubs/Roediger&Butler%282010%29.pdf (Accessed 5.1.15).

Roediger, H. L., & Karpicke, J. D. (2006). The power of testing memory: Basic research and implications for educational practice. *Psychological Science, 1,* 181–210.

Sanders, J. (2009). Reflect 2.0: Using digital storytelling to develop reflective learning by the use of next generation technologies and practices. http://www.jisc.ac.uk/publications/documents/reflectfinalreport.aspx (Accessed 5.1.15).

Savin-Baden, M., & Major, C. H. (2013). *Qualitative research: The essential guide to theory and practice.* New York, NY: Routledge.

Scherer, M. (2002a). Perspectives/who cares? And who wants to know? *Educational Leadership, 60*(1), 5–5. http://www.ascd.org/publications/educational-leadership/sept02/vol60/num01/Who-Cares%C2%A2-And-Who-Wants-to-Know%C2%A2.aspx (Accessed 1.17.15).

Scherer, M. (2002b). Do students care about learning? A conversation with Mihaly Csikszentmihalyi. *Educational Leadership, 60*(1), 12–17. http://www.ascd.org/publications/educational-leadership/sept02/vol60/num01/Do-Students-Care-About-Learning%C2%A2-A-Conversation-with-Mihaly-Csikszentmihalyi.aspx (Accessed 1.17.15).

Schiefele, U., & Krapp, A. (1996). Topic interest and free recall of expository text. *Learning and Individual Differences, 8*(2), 141–160.

Schön, D. A. (1983). *The reflective practitioner.* New York, NY: Basic Books.

Schraw, G., & Dennison, R. S. (1994). Assessing metacognitive awareness. *Contemporary Educational Psychology, 19,* 460–475.

Shank, J. D. (2014). *Interactive open educational resources: A guide to finding, choosing, and using what's out there to transform college teaching.* San Francisco, CA: Jossey-Bass.

Shavelson, R. J. (2007). *A brief history of student learning assessment: How we got where we are and a proposal for where to go next.* Association of American Colleges and Universities, The Academy in Transition. http://cae.org/images/uploads/pdf/19_A_Brief_History_of_Student_Learning_How_we_Got_Where_We_Are_and_a_Proposal_for_Where_to_Go_Next.PDF (Accessed 5.1.15).

Sherman, L.W. (1991). *Cooperative learning in postsecondary education: Implications from social psychology for active learning experiences.* A presentation to the annual meetings of the American Educational Research Association, Chicago, IL, 3–7.

Shulman, L. S. (1987). Knowledge and teaching: Foundations of the new reform. *Harvard Educational Review, 57,* 1–22.

Siemens, G. (2004). Connectivism: A learning theory for the digital age. *International Journal of Instructional Technology and Distance Learning.*

Silberman, M. (1996). *Active learning: 101 strategies to teach any subject.* Des Moines, IA: Prentice Hall.

Slate Book Review. (2012). Kurt Vonnegut term paper assignment from the Iowa Writers Workshop. http://www.slate.com/articles/arts/books/2012/11/kurt_vonnegut_term_paper_assignment_from_the_iowa_writers_workshop.html (Accessed 5.1.15).

Slavin, R. E. (1990). *Cooperative learning: Theory research and practice.* Boston, MA: Allyn and Bacon.

Snyder, A., Mitchell, J., Bossomaier, T., & G. Pallier. (2004). The creativity quotient: An objective scoring of ideational fluency. *Creativity Research Journal, 16*(4), 415–520. http://www.centreforthemind.com/publications/CQPaper.pdf (Accessed 7.30.14).

Sousa, D. A. (2006). *How the brain learns.* Thousand Oaks, CA: Corwin Press.

Sperling, R. A., Howard, B. C., Staley, R., & DuBois, N. (2004). Metacognition and self-regulated learning constructs. *Educational Research and Evaluation, 10*(2), 117–139.

Stanley, C. A. (2002). Involved in the classroom. C. A. Stanley & Porter, M. E. (Eds.), *Engaging large classes: Strategies and techniques for college faculty.* In Bolton, MA: Anker.

Stanley, C. A., & Porter, M. E. (2002). *Engaging large classes: Strategies and techniques for college faculty.* Bolton, MA: Anker.

Sternberg, R. J. (1989). *The triarchic mind: A new theory of human intelligence.* New York, NY: Penguin.

Stevens, D. D., & Levi, A. (2005). *Introduction to rubrics: An assessment tool to save grading time, convey effective feedback, and promote student learning.* Sterling, VA: Stylus.

Study Group on the Conditions of Excellence in American Higher Education. (1984). *Involvement in learning: Realizing the potential of American higher education.* Washington, D.C.: National Institute of Education.

Suskie, L. (2009). *Assessing student learning: A common sense guide* (2nd ed.) San Francisco, CA: Jossey-Bass.

Svinicki, M. D. (2004). *Learning and motivation in the postsecondary classroom.* Bolton, MA: Anker.

Tague, N. R. (2004). Decision matrix. In *The quality toolbox* (2nd ed., pp. 219–223). Milwaukee, WI: ASQ Quality Press.

Ten assessments you can perform in 90 seconds. TeachThought.com. http://www.teachthought.com/teaching/10-assessments-you-can-perform-in-90-seconds/ (Accessed 8.1.14).

Thiede, K. W., Anderson, M. C., & Therriault, D. (2003). Accuracy of metacognitive monitoring affects learning of texts. *Journal of Educational Psychology, 95,* 66–73.

Tobias, S. (1994). Interest, prior knowledge, and learning. *Review of Educational Research, 64*(1), 37–54.

Torrance Tests of Creative Thinking. (1974, 1984). The TTCT: Scholastic Testing Service, Inc. Gifted Education. (http://ststesting.com/) (Accessed 7.31.14).

University of Houston. (2015). Assessment and evaluation. Educational uses of digital storytelling. http://digitalstorytelling.coe.uh.edu/page.cfm?id=24&cid=24&sublinkid=43 (Accessed 5.1.15).

University of Waterloo, Centre for Teaching Excellence. (nd). Group decision making. https://uwaterloo.ca/centre-for-teaching-excellence/teaching-resources/teaching-tips/developing-assignments/group-work/group-decision-making (Accessed 7.18.15).

University of Wisconsin Madison. (2012). Teaching with digital media assignments. http://www.engage
.wisc.edu/dma/.

University of Wisconsin Stout. (nd). Video project rubric. https://www2.uwstout.edu/content/profdev
/rubrics/videorubric.html (Accessed 5.1.15).

Van Manen, M. (1990). *Researching lived experience: Human science for an action sensitive pedagogy.*
Albany, NY: State University of New York Press.

Walvoord, B. E., & Anderson, W. J. (2010). *Effective grading* (2nd ed.). San Francisco, CA: Jossey-Bass.

Watts, M. M. (2007). *Service learning.* Upper Saddle River, NJ: Pearson/Prentice Hall.

Weimer, M. (2002). *Learner-centered teaching: Five key changes to practice.* Hoboken, NJ: Wiley.

Weimer, M. (2015). How assignment design shapes student learning. Faculty Focus. http://www
.facultyfocus.com/articles/teaching-professor-blog/how-assignment-design-shapes-student
-learning/ (Accessed 5.1.15).

Whipple, W. R. (1987). Collaborative learning. *AAHE Bulletin, 40* (2, Oct.), 3–7.

Wiggins, G. P. (1998). *Educative assessment: Designing assessments to inform and improve student
performance* (Vol. 1). San Francisco, CA: Jossey-Bass.

Wiggins, G. P., & McTighe, J. (2005). *Understanding by design* (2nd ed.). Upper Saddle River, NJ: Merrill
Prentice Hall.

Zimmerman, B. J. (2002). Becoming a self-regulated learner: An overview. *Theory Into Practice, 41*(2),
64–72.

Zimmerman, B. J., & Moylan, A. R. (2009). Where metacognition and motivation intersect. In D. J.
Hacker, J. Dunlosky, & A. C. Graesser (Eds.), *Handbook of metacognition* (pp. 299–316). New York,
NY: Routledge.

Zubizarreta, J. (2004). *The learning portfolio: Reflective practice for improving student learning.* Boston,
MA: Anker Publishing.

Zubizarreta, J. (2008). The learning portfolio: A powerful idea for significant learning. IDEA Paper # 44.
http://ideaedu.org/sites/default/files/IDEA_Paper_44.pdf (Accessed 5.1.15).

Zull, J. (2002). *The art of changing the brain.* Sterling, VA: Stylus.

APPENDICES

APPENDIX A
About the Learning Goals Inventory (LGI)

To create the Learning Goals Inventory, we followed several steps. In this section, we describe the instrument and provide an overview of the steps we took in its development and validation.

The Instrument

The Learning Goals Inventory (LGI) is an instrument designed to help faculty begin the important process of learning assessment. It does so by providing prompts for them to consider and rate and then determine a score.

The LGI is comprised of four parts: course information, the learning goals rating scale, the learning goals self-assessment, and responder characteristics. The LGI classifies the 54-question learning goals rating scale into six domains, which are based upon Fink's (2013) Taxonomy of Significant Learning: foundational knowledge, application of knowledge, integration of knowledge, the human dimension, the caring dimension, and the learning how to learn dimension.

The six domains are grouped into two dimensions. The first, the cognitive dimension, is comprised of foundational knowledge, application of knowledge, and integration of knowledge. The second, the humanistic dimension, is comprised of the human dimension, the caring dimension, and the learning how to learn dimension. Each of the domains is comprised of nine questions for a total LGI containing 54 questions. Item response scales are based upon a Likert-type scale with response options of high (5), moderately high (4), moderately low (3), low (2), and not applicable (1). Participants are asked to respond according to item importance only for the course they self-reported. Subscores for the domains range from 0–9 for not applicable, 10–18 for low importance, 19–27 for moderately low importance, 28–36 for moderately high importance, and 37–45 for high importance.

The instrument, which can be found in Appendix B in this text, is also housed online at the University of Alabama at: https://universityofalabama.az1.qualtrics.com/jfe/form/SV _a3owNYXnmi9yS0J.

Development of the Instrument

To develop the LGI, we began by modeling it, with publisher permission, after the Teaching Goals Inventory (TGI) developed by Angelo and Cross (1993), Cross and Angelo (1988), and Cross and Fideler (1988). We note that other researchers have created inventories based on the TGI as well, for example Walter (2002) and Shin (2006). Our version is a more extensive adaptation of the TGI than previous instruments, however.

As we worked through the creation of our own instrument, we moved away from TGI in several important ways. We made the following revisions:

- Changed the focus of the instrument to *learning goals* rather than teaching goals
- Simplified the question stems
- Split compound items into two or more items
- Deleted items that were self-limiting (those that seemed restricted to only a few disciplines or fields)
- Aligned items with Fink's Taxonomy of Significant Learning
- Added items as necessary to fill out domains from Fink's Taxonomy of Significant Learning that were not completely addressed in the original inventory

Validation of the Instrument

After we developed the instrument, Dee Fink and a psychometrician reviewed it. We also administered it to a small group of approximately 15 faculty members to consider item clarity. We next conducted a pilot study with 50 faculty members prior to proceeding to a larger sample.

We administered the LGI using 2015 Qualtrics, LLC.

The survey had a completion rate of 64%. A total of 336 surveys were attempted; 217 surveys were completed giving a confidence interval of 6.65 with a 95% confidence level. We judged surveys for exclusion based upon nonresponse or lack of completion. We excluded surveys that demonstrated a failure of completion for more than 18% of LGI questions, or one domain. We included all surveys with other missing data patterns and coded them with 0 for no score based upon the rubric. We also included surveys that lacked demographic information, since we made providing that information optional.

Respondents were majority female, white, and full-time instructors at four-year institutions who taught undergraduate students (see Tables A.1 and A.2). The majority of respondents indicated that they were working in a professional field, like business or education, or in the arts and humanities (see Table A.3).

Learning Goals Rating Scale

None of the six domains were classified as not applicable, of low importance, or of moderately low importance in this sample. Domains classified as being of moderately high importance overall included foundational knowledge, application of knowledge, the human dimension, and the learning how to learn dimension. Domains classified as being of high importance overall included integration of knowledge and the caring dimension (see Table A.4). On average for this

Table A.1 Demographic Information

Variable	n	%
Gender Identity	197	
Woman	118	59.9
Man	79	40.1
Ethnicity	196	
White	168	85.7
Black/African American	8	4.1
Hispanic/Latino	9	4.6
Asian/Pacific Islander	6	3.1
American Indian/Native American	1	0.5
Two or More Races	4	2
Age	197	
25–34	14	7.1
35–44	33	16.8
45–54	67	34
55–64	57	28.9
65–74	25	12.7
75 or older	1	0.5

Table A.2 Responder Characteristics

Variable	n	%
Employment Status	196	
Full-time	163	83.2
Part-time	33	16.8
Rank	197	
Teaching Assistant	2	1
Instructor or Lecturer	56	28.4
Assistant Professor	31	15.7
Associate Professor	47	23.9
Emeritus	37	18.8

(*continued*)

Table A.2 (*Continued*)

Variable	n	%
Another Rank	4	2
	20	10.2
Highest Degree	197	
Associate's	1	0.5
Bachelor's	4	2
Master's	49	24.9
Professional	8	4.1
Doctoral	135	68.5
Years Teaching College	197	
1–5 yrs	25	12.7
6–10 yrs	45	22.8
11–15 yrs	34	17.3
16–20 yrs	32	16.2
21–25 yrs	24	12.2
26 yrs or Longer	37	18.8

Table A.3 Course Information

Variable	n	%
Type of Institution	215	
4 yr	175	81.4
2 yr	25	11.6
Other	15	7
Course Level	215	
Undergraduate	163	75.8
Graduate	47	21.9
Another Course Level	5	2.3
Teaching Environment	217	
Onsite	148	68.2
Online	36	16.6
Blended or Hybrid	33	15.2

Table A.3 (*Continued*)

Variable	n	%
Discipline Taught	217	
Arts or Humanities	45	20.9
Kinesiology/P.E.	2	0.9
Natural Science, Computer Science, or Math	29	13.5
Professional Field	89	41.4
Vocational/Technical	2	0.9
Social Science	26	12.1
Another Discipline	22	10.2

sample, the foundational knowledge domain was seen as the least important, and the caring dimension and integration of knowledge domains were seen as the most important.

Reliability analyses of the LGI subscales indicate all domains have good to excellent internal consistency (see Table A.4).

Learning Goals Self-Assessment

The learning goal self-assessment revealed the majority of respondents, 65.1%, to rate "using foundational knowledge for purposes such as problem solving, developing skills, or thinking critically, creatively, or practically" as the most important cognitive aspect.

Table A.4 Reliability Indices for Scales Measuring Learning Goals

Dimension[a]	Domain[b]	M	SD	Range min	max	a*
Cognitive Dimension		102.58	13.93	30	125	0.85
	Foundational Knowledge	28.50	4.67	3	37	0.72
	Application of Knowledge	35.13	6.00	8	45	0.77
	Integration of Knowledge	36.81	5.52	5	45	0.77
Humanistic Dimension		104.83	19.73	24	135	0.93
	Human Dimension	32.72	8.40	2	45	0.90
	Caring Dimension	37.55	6.47	4	45	0.81
	Learning How to Learn Dimension	34.56	7.40	0	45	0.87
Total Scale[c]		205.82	30.06	54	255	0.94

Note: n = 217; * a = Cronbach alpha value; all values are deemed acceptable (Nunnaly, 1978)
[a] Dimensions have a total of 27 questions.
[b] Domains have a total of 9 questions.
[c] Total scale is 54 questions.

The most important humanistic aspect was "acquiring knowledge about the process of learning and developing the ability to become mores self-directing learners" at 49.8%.

Note

Our thanks go to Lauren Holmes and Stacy Hughey-Surman for their support in the development of this instrument, the validation of it, and the write-up of this appendix.

References

Angelo, T. A., & Cross, K. P. (1993). *Classroom assessment techniques: A handbook for college teachers.* (2nd ed.). San Francisco, CA: Jossey-Bass.

Ary, D., Jacobs, L. C., Razavieh, A., & Sorensen, C. (2006). *Introduction to Research in Education.* Florence, KY: Thomson/Wadsworth.

Cross, K. P., & Angelo, T. A. (1988). *Classroom assessment techniques. A handbook for faculty.* Ann Arbor, MI: National Center for the Improvement of Postsecondary Teaching and Learning.

Cross, K. P., & Fideler, E. F. (1988). Assessment in the classroom. *Community/Junior College Quarterly of Research and Practice, 12*(4), 275–285.

Dillman, D. A. (2000). *Mail and internet surveys: The tailored design method* (Vol. 2). New York: Wiley.

Fink, A., & Kosecoff, J. (1998). *How to conduct surveys: A step-by-step guide.* Thousand Oaks, CA: Sage.

Fink, D. L. (2013). *Creating significant learning experiences: An integrated approach to designing college courses.* San Francisco, CA: Jossey-Bass.

Fowler, F. J. (2002). *Survey research methods.* Thousand Oaks, CA: Sage.

Gall, M. D., Gall, J. P., & Borg, W. R. (2007). Collecting research data with questionnaires and interviews. In *Educational research: An introduction* (pp. 227–261). Upper Saddle River, NJ: Pearson.

Krosnick, J. A. (1999). Survey research. *Annual Review of Psychology, 50*(1), 537–567.

Krosnick, J. A., & Fabrigar, L. R. (1997). Designing rating scales for effective measurement in surveys. In L. E. Lyberg, et al. (Eds.), *Survey measurement and process quality* (pp. 141–164). Hoboken, NJ: Wiley.

Nunnaly, J. (1978). *Psychometric theory.* New York, NY: McGraw-Hill.

Schonlau, M., Fricker, R., & Elliott, M. (2002). *Conducting research surveys via e-mail and the web.* Santa Monica, CA: RAND.

Shin, L. B. (2006). Improving the learning approach of college freshmen and future teachers through curricular intervention. All Theses and Dissertations. Paper 513. http://scholarsarchive.byu.edu/cgi/viewcontent.cgi?article=1512&context=etd.

Visser, P. S., Krosnick, J. A., & Lavrakas, P. J. (2000). Survey research. In H. T. Reis & C. M. Judd (Eds.), *Handbook of research methods in social and personality psychology* (pp. 223–252). New York, NY: Cambridge University Press.

Walter, M. (2002). A window into students' learning goals: The learning goals inventory, Presented at AAHE National Meeting, Chicago.

APPENDIX B
The Learning Goals Inventory with Scoring Sheet

Part 1: Purpose

The Learning Goals Inventory (LGI) is a self-assessment of learning goals. Its purpose is threefold:

1. To help college teachers focus and articulate their goals for student learning in their individual courses
2. To help college teachers locate appropriate Learning Assessment Techniques that they can use to help teach and assess how well students have achieved the learning goals
3. To provide a starting point for discussion of teaching and learning goals among colleagues

Please select ONE course in which you are interested in assessing student learning:

_____

(Title of course)

Part 2: Learning Goals Rating Scale

Please rate the following 54 items based upon their importance in the course you listed. Use the following 5-to-1 rating scale, recording your choice by marking an X in the most appropriate space.

(5) High
(4) Moderately High
(3) Moderately Low
(2) Low
(1) Not Applicable

At the end of each section, add the numbers to determine a subtotal.

Items	5	4	3	2	1	Write in the # you rated this item
Examples:						
As a result of their participation in the course, students should <u>develop</u>:						
1. Knowledge of central facts in this subject area			X			3
2. Knowledge of key terms of this subject area			X			3
3. Knowledge of important theories in the subject area		X				4
4. Historical knowledge relevant to this subject area		X				4
5. Knowledge of key individuals who have contributed to the field		X				4
6. Recognition of the difference between fact and opinion related to this subject area	X					5
7. The ability to translate key ideas from this subject area into own words		X				4
8. Clarity about common misconceptions in this subject area	X					5
9. Knowledge of current issues related to the subject area	X					5
Subtotal for Foundational Knowledge:						37
Your Ratings *As a result of their participation in the course, students should <u>develop</u>:*						
1. Knowledge of central facts in this subject area						
2. Knowledge of key terms of this subject area						
3. Knowledge of important theories in the subject area						
4. Historical knowledge relevant to this subject area						
5. Knowledge of key individuals who have contributed to the field						
6. Recognition of the difference between fact and opinion related to this subject area						

Items	5	4	3	2	1	Write in the # you rated this item
7. The ability to translate key ideas from this subject area into own words						
8. Clarity about common misconceptions in this subject area						
9. Knowledge of current issues related to the subject area						
Subtotal for Foundational Knowledge						
10. Reading skills						
11. Writing skills						
12. Technological skills						
13. Analytical skills						
14. Creative Thinking skills						
15. Critical Thinking skills						
16. Decision-making skills						
17. Problem-solving skills						
18. Research skills						
Subtotal for Application of Knowledge						
19. The ability to differentiate closely related concepts in the subject area						
20. The ability to compare different aspects of a topic						
21. The ability to classify information in the subject area						
22. The ability to think holistically: to see the whole as well as the parts						
23. The ability to synthesize disparate but related information into a whole						
24. The ability to connect a concept to other concepts within this course						
25. The ability to connect a course concept to concepts in other relevant courses within the discipline or field						
26. The ability to connect course concepts to concepts in other disciplines or fields						
27. The ability to connect course information to their daily lives						
Subtotal for Integration of Knowledge						
28. Empathy for others						

(*continued*)

Items	5	4	3	2	1	Write in the # you rated this item
29. Respect for others						
30. Interpersonal skills						
31. The ability to work productively with others						
32. Self-confidence						
33. The capacity to make wise decisions						
34. The capacity to think for themselves						
35. A commitment to upholding their own values						
36. A commitment to their own emotional health and well-being						
Subtotal for Human Dimension						
37. Motivation to learn in the subject area						
38. Openness to new ideas in the subject area						
39. An appreciation of diverse perspectives related to this subject						
40. A commitment to excellent work						
41. A commitment to success in learning						
42. A willingness to engage in class activities						
43. An acceptance of responsibility for their own behavior in the course						
44. Informed concern about current social issues relevant to the topic						
45. The intention to make informed ethical choices						
Subtotal for Caring						
46. Knowledge about themselves as learners						
47. The ability to set goals						
48. The ability to follow directions/instructions						
49. Study skills and strategies						
50. The ability to organize and use time effectively						
51. The ability to monitor their own progress						
52. The ability to self-assess their performance						
53. The capacity for lifelong learning in the subject area						
54. The ability to create a concrete plan to learn more about the subject in the near future						
Subtotal for Learning How to Learn						

Learning Goals Rating Summary

Subtotal for Foundational Knowledge	
Subtotal for Application of Knowledge	
Subtotal for Integration of Knowledge	
Subtotal for Human Dimension	
Subtotal for Caring	
Subtotal for Learning How to Learn	

Part 3: Learning Goal Self-Assessment

1. In general, what do you think is the *most important cognitive aspect* of learning for students to develop by the end of the academic term. Choose *one* item from the list below:
   a. Understanding and recalling key facts, principles, ideas, and concepts.
   b. Understanding foundational knowledge for purposes such as problem solving, developing skills, or thinking critically, creatively, or practically.
   c. Connecting different ideas within the course, among courses, and extending beyond courses into students' daily lives.
2. In general, what do you think is the *most important humanistic aspect* of learning for students to develop by the end of the academic term. Choose *one* item from the list below:
   a. Learning about themselves and how to better understand and interact with other people.
   b. Developing new interests, feelings, and values associated with the course material.
   c. Acquiring knowledge about the process of learning and developing the ability to become more self-directing learners.

Scoring

Use the following rubric to determine whether you rated items in each category as high, moderately high, moderately low, or not applicable.

Part 2 Scoring:

Categorical Interpretation Rubric					
	45–36 5-High	35–26 4-Moderately High	25–16 3-Moderately Low	15–10 2-Low	9 or below 1-Not Applicable
Foundational Knowledge	Your ratings suggest that you place a high value on students	Your ratings suggest that you place a moderately high	Your ratings suggest that you place a moderately low	Your ratings suggest that you place a low value on students	Your ratings suggest that this learning

(*continued*)

(Continued)

Categorical Interpretation Rubric					
	45–36 5-High	35–26 4-Moderately High	25–16 3-Moderately Low	15–10 2-Low	9 or below 1-Not Applicable
	developing the ability to remember and understand important facts and concepts.	value on students developing the ability to remember and understand important facts and concepts.	value on students developing the ability to remember and understand important facts and concepts.	developing the ability to remember and understand important facts and concepts.	domain is not applicable to the course.
Application	Your ratings suggest that you place a high value on students developing the ability to apply what they have learned in new situations and to demonstrate critical, creative, or practical thinking.	Your ratings suggest that you place a moderately high value on students developing the ability to apply what they have learned in new situations and to demonstrate critical, creative, or practical thinking.	Your ratings suggest that you place a moderately low value on students developing the ability to apply what they have learned in new situations and to demonstrate critical, creative, or practical thinking.	Your ratings suggest that you place a moderately low value on students developing the ability to apply what they have learned in new situations and to demonstrate critical, creative, or practical thinking.	Your ratings suggest that this learning domain is not applicable to the course.
Integration	Your ratings suggest that you place a high value on students developing the ability to integrate information and demonstrate connections between concepts, people, and different realms of life.	Your ratings suggest that you place a moderately high value on students developing the ability to integrate information and demonstrate connections between concepts, people, and different realms of life.	Your ratings suggest that you place a moderately low value on students developing the ability to integrate information and demonstrate connections between concepts, people, and different realms of life.	Your ratings suggest that you place a moderately low value on students developing the ability to integrate information and demonstrate connections between concepts, people, and different realms of life.	Your ratings suggest that this learning domain is not applicable to the course.
Human Dimension	Your ratings suggest that you place a high value on students learning about themselves and others and how humans interact.	Your ratings suggest that you place a moderately high value on students learning about themselves and others and how humans interact.	Your ratings suggest that you place a moderately low value on students learning about themselves and others and how humans interact.	Your ratings suggest that you place a low value on students learning about themselves and others and how humans interact.	Your ratings suggest that this learning domain is not applicable to the course.

(Continued)

Categorical Interpretation Rubric					
	45–36 5-High	35–26 4-Moderately High	25–16 3-Moderately Low	15–10 2-Low	9 or below 1-Not Applicable
Caring	Your ratings suggest that you place a high value on students learning to care about the learning goals, the course, or the subject matter.	Your ratings suggest that you place a moderately high value on students learning to care about the learning goals, the course, or the subject matter.	Your ratings suggest that you place a moderately low value on students learning to care about the learning goals, the course, or the subject matter.	Your ratings suggest that you place a low value on students learning to care about the learning goals, the course, or the subject matter.	Your ratings suggest that this learning domain is not applicable to the course.
Learning How to Learn	Your ratings suggest that you place a high value on students learning how to learn.	Your ratings suggest that you place a moderately high value on students learning how to learn.	Your ratings suggest that you place a moderately low value on students learning how to learn.	Your ratings suggest that you place a low value on students learning how to learn.	Your ratings suggest that this learning domain is not applicable to the course.

Part 3 Scoring:

Use the following information to determine which domain you rated as the highest based on the description of the domain.

Question 1: Cognitive Aspect

(a) Foundational Knowledge
(b) Application of Knowledge
(c) Integration of Knowledge

Question 2: Humanistic Aspect

(a) Human Dimension
(b) Caring
(c) Learning How to Learn

APPENDIX C
Key to Classroom Environment and Discipline in LAT Examples

Dimension	LAT #	LAT Name	Course Title	Discipline	Classroom Environment
FK	1	First Day Final	Introduction to Business Information Systems	Professional and Vocational	Onsite
FK	1	First Day Final	English for Second Language Learners: Composition and Reading	English	Online
FK	2	Background Knowledge Probe	Introduction to Statistics	Math and Statistics	Onsite
FK	2	Background Knowledge Probe	Technology and Higher Education	Professional and Vocational	Online
FK	3	Entry and Exit Tickets	History of Western Civilization to 800 AD	Arts	Onsite
FK	3	Entry and Exit Tickets	Calculus	Math and Statistics	Online
FK	4	Guided Reading Notes	Evolution, Systematics, and Ecology	Biological and Physical Sciences	Onsite
FK	4	Guided Reading Notes	Introduction to Social Psychology	Social Sciences	Online
FK	5	Comprehensive Factors List	Form and Function in Plants and Animals	Biological and Physical Sciences	Onsite

(Continued)

(*Continued*)

Dimension	LAT #	LAT Name	Course Title	Discipline	Classroom Environment
FK	5	Comprehensive Factors List	Social Work in the Schools	Professional and Vocational	Online
FK	6	Quick Write	Introduction to Scientific Methods	Natural and Physical Sciences	Onsite
FK	6	Quick Write	Contemporary Mathematics	Math and Statistics	Online
FK	7	Best Summary	Introduction to Astronomy	Biological and Physical Sciences	Onsite
FK	7	Best Summary	Business Law I	Professional and Vocational	Online
FK	8	Snap Shots	Introduction to Geoscience	Biological and Physical Sciences	Onsite
FK	8	Snap Shots	General Physics	Biological and Physical Sciences	Online
FK	9	Team Tests	Music Theory and Composition	Arts	Onsite
FK	9	Team Tests	English Poetry of the Romantic Period	English and Languages	Online
FK	10	Team Games Tournament	Introduction to Genetics	Biological and Physical Sciences	Onsite
FK	10	Team Games Tournament	English Composition and Reading	English and Languages	Online
App	11	Prediction Guide	Physics	Biological and Physical Sciences	Onsite
App	11	Prediction Guide	Business Statistics	Professional and Vocational	Online
App	12	Fact or Opinion	General Biology	Biological and Physical Sciences	Onsite
App	12	Fact or Opinion	Reading Educational Research	Professional and Vocational	Online
App	13	Quotation Summaries	Introduction to Shakespeare	English and Languages	Onsite
App	13	Quotation Summaries	Principles of Advertising	Professional and Vocational	Online
App	14	Insights-Resources-Applications (IRAs)	Public Health Nursing	Professional and Vocational	Onsite
App	14	Insights-Resources-Applications (IRAs)	Survey of International Business	Professional and Vocational	Online

(*Continued*)

Dimension	LAT #	LAT Name	Course Title	Discipline	Classroom Environment
App	15	Consider This	Geography and Globalization	Social Sciences	Onsite
App	15	Consider This	Music History: 18th Century Classicism	Arts	Online
App	16	What's the Problem?	Critical Reading	English and Languages	Onsite
App	16	What's the Problem?	Music Theory and Composition	Arts	Online
App	17	Think-Aloud Problem-Solving Protocols	Programming in BIOPERL	Computers and Technology	Onsite
App	17	Think-Aloud Problem-Solving Protocols	Elementary Algebra	Math and Statistics	Online
App	18	Peer Problem Review	Urban Planning	Professional and Vocational	Onsite
App	18	Peer Problem Review	Advanced Pathophysiology and Patient Management	Professional and Vocational	Online
App	19	Triple Jump	Psychology: Psychometrics	Social Sciences	Onsite
App	19	Triple Jump	Nursing Care for Older Adults	Professional and Vocational	Online
App	20	Digital Projects	Recording Studio Production	Arts	Onsite
App	20	Digital Projects	History of the United States from 1914 to the Present	Humanities	Online
Int	21	Knowledge Grid	Romantic Poetry	English and Languages	Onsite
Int	21	Knowledge Grid	Music of Multicultural America	Arts	Online
Int	22	Sequence Chains	History of Western Civilization: Ancient Through the Middle Ages	Humanities	Onsite
Int	22	Sequence Chains	Human Physiology	Natural and Physical Sciences	Online
Int	23	Concept Maps	Physics	Natural and Physical Sciences	Onsite
Int	23	Concept Maps	Application of Learning Theories to Instruction	Professional and Vocational	Online
Int	24	Contemporary Issues Journal	Music Business	Arts	Online

(*Continued*)

(*Continued*)

Dimension	LAT #	LAT Name	Course Title	Discipline	Classroom Environment
Int	24	Contemporary Issues Journal	Applied Ethics	Humanities	Onsite
Int	25	Dyadic Essay	African American Literature	English and Languages	Onsite
Int	25	Dyadic Essay	Real Estate Principles	Professional and Vocational	Online
Int	26	Synthesis Paper	Introduction to Ethics	English and Languages	Onsite
Int	26	Synthesis Paper	English Composition	English and Languages	Online
Int	27	Case Study	Issues in Contemporary Art	Arts	Onsite
Int	27	Case Study	Introduction to Teaching Online	Professional and Vocational	Online
Int	28	Class Book	English: Composition, Critical Reading, and Thinking	English and Languages	Onsite
Int	28	Class Book	History of American Higher Education	Professional and Vocational	Online
Int	29	E-Portfolios	Introduction to the History of Art II	Arts	Online
Int	29	E-Portfolios	Introduction to Biology	Biological and Physical Sciences	Onsite
HD	30	Free Discussion	Leadership Issues in Community Colleges	Professional and Vocational	Onsite
HD	30	Free Discussion	Introduction to Organic Chemistry	Biological and Physical Sciences	Online
HD	31	Nominations	Introduction to Physics	Natural and Physical Sciences	Onsite
HD	31	Nominations	Broadcast Journalism	Professional and Vocational	Online
HD	32	Editorial Review	English Literature	English and Languages	Onsite
HD	32	Editorial Review	History of Art from Baroque to Post-Impressionism	Humanities	Online
HD	33	Dramatic Dialogues	The Psychology, Biology, and Politics of Food	Social Sciences	Onsite
HD	33	Dramatic Dialogues	A History of Philanthropy in the United States	Humanities	Online

(Continued)

Dimension	LAT #	LAT Name	Course Title	Discipline	Classroom Environment
HD	34	Role Play	Oral Communication Skills (ESL)	English and Languages	Onsite
HD	34	Role Play	Business Marketing Practices	Professional and Vocational	Online
HD	35	Ethical Dilemma	Freshman Seminar (Study Skills/Personal Development)	Freshman Seminar	Onsite
HD	35	Ethical Dilemma	Statistics	Math and Statistics	Online
HD	36	Digital Story	Public Health	Professional and Vocational	Onsite
HD	36	Digital Story	Introduction to Higher Education	Professional and Vocational	Online
Caring	37	Stand Where You Stand	Introduction to Sociology	Social Sciences	Onsite
Caring	37	Stand Where You Stand	Drugs, Crime, and Public Policy	Professional and Vocational	Online
Caring	38	Three-Minute Message	History of American Higher Education	Professional and Vocational	Onsite
Caring	38	Three-Minute Message	Social Media	Social Sciences	Online
Caring	39	Issue Awareness Ad	Health Communication	Professional and Vocational	Onsite
Caring	39	Issue Awareness Ad	Instructional Technology	Computers and Technology	Online
Caring	40	Proclamations	Race and Ethnic Relations	Social Sciences	Onsite
Caring	40	Proclamations	Urban Poverty	Social Sciences	Online
Caring	41	Editorial	Writing About Global Science	Natural and Physical Sciences	Onsite
Caring	41	Editorial	Editorial Column Writing	Professional and Vocational	Online
Caring	42	Debate	Philosophy of Law	Professional and Vocational	Onsite
Caring	42	Debate	Sociology—Contemporary Issues	Social Sciences	Online
Caring	43	Briefing Paper	Issues in Education	Professional and Vocational	Onsite
Caring	43	Briefing Paper	Public Health	Professional and Vocational	Online

(Continued)

(Continued)

Dimension	LAT #	LAT Name	Course Title	Discipline	Classroom Environment
L2L	44	Study Outlines	Masterpieces of Western Literature and Philosophy	English and Languages	Onsite
L2L	44	Study Outlines	Fundamentals of Physics	Natural and Physical Sciences	Online
L2L	45	Student Generated Rubric	Principles of Marketing	Professional and Vocational	Onsite
L2L	45	Student Generated Rubric	Reading Educational Research	Professional and Vocational	Online
L2L	46	Invent the Quiz	Introduction to Marketing	Professional and Vocational	Onsite
L2L	46	Invent the Quiz	Psychology	Social Sciences	Online
L2L	47	Learning Goal Listing	Multicultural Literature	English and Languages	Onsite
L2L	47	Learning Goal Listing	Introduction to Business Statistics	Professional and Vocational	Online
L2L	48	What? So What? Now What? Journal	Algebra 1	Math and Statistics	Onsite
L2L	48	What? So What? Now What? Journal	Paralegal	Professional and Vocational	Online
L2L	49	Multiple-Task Mastery Checklist	Preparing for College-Level Teaching	Professional and Vocational	Onsite
L2L	49	Multiple-Task Mastery Checklist	Qualitative Research in Sociology	Social Sciences	Blended
L2L	50	Personal Learning Environment	College and University Teaching	Professional and Vocational	Blended

INDEX